Understanding Directory Services

New Riders

Other Books by New Riders Publishing

Inside Windows 2000 Server
William Boswell
ISBN: 1-56205-929-7

Planing for Windows 2000
Eric Cone, Jon Boggs, and Sergio Perez
ISBN: 0-7357-0048-6

Windows NT DNS
Michael Masterson, Herman Knief,
Scott Vinick, and Eric Roul
ISBN: 1-56205-943-2

Windows NT Network Management:
Reducing Total Cost of Ownership
Anil Desai
ISBN: 1-56205-946-7

Windows NT Performance:
Monitoring, Benchmarking, and Tuning
Mark Edmead and Paul Hinsberg
ISBN: 1-56205-942-4

Windows NT Registry:
A Settings Reference
Sandra Osborne
ISBN: 1-56205-941-6

Windows NT TCP/IP
Karanjit Siyan
ISBN: 1-56205-887-8

Windows NT Terminal Server and
Citrix MetaFrame
Ted Harwood
ISBN: 1-56205-944-0

Windows NT Power Toolkit
Stu Sjouwerman and Ed Tittel
ISBN: 0-7357-0922-X

Cisco Router Configuration and
Troubleshooting
Mark Tripod
ISBN: 0-7357-0024-9

Exchange System Administration
Janice Rice Howd
ISBN: 0-7357-0081-8

Implementing Exchange Server
Doug Hauger, Marywynne Leon, and
William C. Wade III
ISBN: 1-56205-931-9

Network Intrusion Detection:
An Analyst's Handbook
Stephen Northcutt
ISBN: 0-7357-0868-1

Understanding Data Communications,
Sixth Edition
Gilbert Held
ISBN: 0-7357-0036-2

Understanding Directory Services

New Riders

201 West 103rd Street,
Indianapolis, Indiana 46290

Beth Sheresh
Doug Sheresh
Systems Research Corporation

Understanding Directory Services

Beth Sheresh and Doug Sheresh

International Standard Book Number: 0-7357-0910-6

Library of Congress Catalog Card Number: 99-067429

Printed in the United States of America

First Edition

03 02 01 00   7 6 5 4 3 2 1

Interpretation of the printing code: The rightmost double-digit number is the year of the book's printing; the rightmost single-digit number is the number of the book's printing. For example, the printing code 00-1 shows that the first printing of the book occurred in 2000.

Trademarks

Warning and Disclaimer

Publisher
David Dwyer

Executive Editor
Al Valvano

Managing Editor
Gina Brown

Product Marketing Manager
Stephanie Layton

Development Editors
Lisa M. Thibault
Ami Frank Sullivan

Project Editor
Alissa Cayton

Copy Editor
Keith Cline

Indexers
Cheryl Lenser
Craig Small

Technical Reviewers
Marcus Williamson
Marc Charney

Book Designer
Louisa Klucznik

Cover Designer
Aren Howell

Compositor
Amy Parker

About the Authors

Beth Sheresh is a Certified Netware Engineer (CNE) with a decade of information technology experience, performing systems and network consulting, systems administration, technical course design, and Web development. She has also supported a wide range of products, from mainframe–PC connectivity products on Fortune 500 enterprise networks to children's software (and she really misses talking to 9 year olds about their computers).

Beth recently co-authored the *Microsoft Windows NT Server Administrators Bible — Option Pack Edition* (IDG Books). In addition to her writing, she is currently focusing on projects designed to encourage girls to become involved in the information technology fields.

Beth is a principal of Systems Research Corporation, a technology consulting and research firm. She can be reached at `beth@src.nu`.

Doug Sheresh has worked in the computer industry for the last two decades gaining a range of experience encompassing network and Internet consulting, software development, and all aspects of technical course development from design to delivery.

In 1994, while working for Microsoft, Doug was one of the first 500 people to earn Microsoft Certified Professional status and has since achieved MCP+Internet, and Microsoft Certified Systems Engineer certifications.

One of Doug's recent projects was the *Microsoft Windows NT Server Administrators Bible — Option Pack Edition* (IDG Books). Doug was previously the lead technical writer of the *Microsoft Windows 95 Resource Kit* (Microsoft Corporation).

Doug is a principal of Systems Research Corporation. He can be reached at `doug@src.nu`.

About the Technical Reviewers

Marcus Williamson is Managing Director of Connectotel Limited, a Novell-specialist consultancy based in London, UK. Until July 1996 he was Team Leader of Novell Consulting (Europe), based in Duesseldorf, Germany and responsible for consulting activities in Eastern Europe, Germany, Austria, and Switzerland. He worked with Novell for six and a half years and has worked with NetWare for the last twelve years. Marcus has contributed many times to the Novell Research *AppNotes* and other technical publications, is a regular speaker at Novell's Brainshare events in the US and Europe, and is a Sysop on the Novell Support Connection forums on the Internet. Marcus's home page can be found at `www.connectotel.com/marcus`.

Marc Charney has twelve years of experience in the computer industry. After receiving his degree from the University of California, Berkeley in 1987, Marc worked for the Federal Reserve Bank of San Francisco, where he helped design computer models of the United States economy. Marc then moved on to Sybase, where he helped develop its sales-office integration, automation, and networking strategy. In his next position at Delta Life & Annuity, Marc managed a complete overhaul of its network and systems infrastructure. Marc is currently working as a Technical Project Manager for Symbol Technologies. His current efforts are focused on wireless networking and systems integration related to automated data capture and Internet technologies.

...for all who teach,
and all who seek to learn...

Contents

Acknowledgments

"Poof, it's a book!"
—Al Valvano, 1999

If it were only that easy ... yet any book project requires the effort of a great many people in addition to the authors. A number of people have been integral to the success of this project and we would like to express our appreciation for all their work.

First, we'd like to commend the staff of New Riders for their professionalism, flexibility, and responsiveness. This team has been a pleasure to work with. We have been grateful to have their experience, perspectives, and sense of humor with us on this project.

- Al Valvano, our acquisitions editor at New Riders, has supported this project from the beginning. Al's ability to see the big picture has helped maintain the focus of the book. When we started this project, Al described his vision for "author-driven books" to us—amazingly enough, he *meant* it! His belief in our vision for this book has allowed us to focus on writing it.

- Our development editors Lisa Thibault and Ami Frank Sullivan deserve special credit for helping turn the words on our computer screens into the book you are holding in your hand. They were particularly adept at managing the development process, as well as running interference for us when it came to dealing with the publishing side of creating a book.

- Keith Cline, our copy editor, is one of the most meticulous wordsmiths with whom we have had the pleasure of working. His attention to detail (and willingness to thrash out existential questions of grammar) contributed a great deal to this book.

- Gina Brown deserves a round of applause for pulling a few strategic rabbits out of hats—on deadline and under pressure.

- Our project editor Alissa Cayton was especially helpful in getting a handle on the flurry of last-minute details.

- The graphics artist for this book, Mike LaBonne, aka "The Art Guy" we thank for particularly careful attention to detail.

We'd particularly like to thank Marcus Williamson (CNI, CNE) for lending his many years of technical expertise to this project. His painstaking technical review of our manuscript was invaluable.

We'd also like to express our appreciation to Marc Charney for providing detailed and thoughtful feedback.

A special thanks is due David Stanley, MCSE, who technically reviewed our rough drafts (and we *do* mean rough), frequently under entirely unrealistic deadlines.

We would also like to express our gratitude to the folks who reviewed specific chapters. Your collective contributions have helped polish this material in ways that would never have happened without each of your unique perspectives.

- Thomas Willingham, CNI, CNE, MCT, MCSE

- Cory Hendrix, MCSE

- Andrew Mason, MCSE+I

- Brian Boston, MCSE

Our ongoing appreciation to Melinda Wynn Klein for questioning.

We want to thank Christopher Stone of Novell for his assistance in locating needed technical information.

Amy Michaels and Dave Kearns each provided assistance at key points in the process—sometimes a little help goes a long way, thanks!

Thanks are also due to the Seattle Webgirls for their ongoing technical support, commentary, and insights.

We'd also like to acknowledge the debt we owe to the many teachers who have helped us along the way. In the course of writing this book, we invoked the names of a couple of our early English teachers repeatedly: Barbara Carlson and Pamela (Ashwood) O'Keefe, wherever you are … we thank you!

We are grateful that our friends and family are still talking to us after our year-long seclusion … you *are* still talking to us, right?

…and finally, a special thanks to our friend in Australia who shall remain nameless, but who provided us with valuable feedback and perspective.

Your Feedback Is Valuable

As the reader of this book, *you* are our most important critic and commentator. We value your opinion and want to know what we're doing right, what we could do better, what areas you'd like to see us publish in, and any other words of wisdom you're willing to pass our way.

As the Executive Editor for the Networking team at New Riders Publishing, I welcome your comments. You can fax, email, or write me directly to let me know what you did or didn't like about this book—as well as what we can do to make our books stronger.

Please note that I cannot help you with technical problems related to the topic of this book, and that due to the high volume of mail I receive, I might not be able to reply to every message.

When you write, please be sure to include this book's title and author, as well as your name and phone or fax number. I will carefully review your comments and share them with the author and editors who worked on the book.

Fax: 317-581-4663

Email: newriders@mcp.com

Mail: Al Valvano
            Executive Editor
            New Riders Publishing
            201 West 103rd Street
            Indianapolis, IN 46290 USA

Introduction

Understanding Directory Services presents directory services from a networking perspective, starting with basic theory and archetypes, working its way up to the current Novell Directory Service and Active Directory implementations.

In our discussion of directory services, we have focused on explaining the technologies and operations as objectively as possible. Although many books promote specific directory service products, this book provides something a little different: It aims to help you understand how directory services work.

Who This Book is For

Understanding Directory Services is designed for networking professionals and anyone studying network technologies. If you want to *understand* the subject of directory services, especially as it pertains to networking, this is the right book for you.

Readers of this book will want to be familiar with the fundamentals of networking theory and operations, as an understanding of networking terminology and concepts is assumed.

How This Book Is Organized

The book starts with an overview of directory services and their core characteristics, highlighting the key information, distribution, and storage factors. It next explores the X.500 standards to help you understand the foundations of directory services, then reviews LDAP, the emerging standard for directory access, and then examines DNS. The book next discusses how to evaluate a directory service for your network, and concludes by examining the design and operations of Novell Directory Services and Active Directory.

Directory services are a dense topic, filled with as many acronyms and models as any other networking technology. By presenting information in small pieces, starting with the big picture and then focusing on details, we hope to make the topic easier to grasp. Accordingly, this book is designed to be read in a linear fashion, where material in later chapters builds on information presented in earlier chapters.

The following list gives a brief overview of what you can expect to learn from each chapter.

Chapter 1: Introduction to Directory Services (the big picture)—Explains directory services in an overview.

Chapter 2: Evolution of Directory Structures—Explores the evolving nature of the information the directory contains, and the factors involved in organizing and managing it.

Chapter 3: Storing Directory Information—Methods of information distribution and storage are discussed, focusing on distributed directory services.

Chapter 4: X.500: A Model for Directory Services—Reviews the X.500 standards—the archetype for directory services.

Chapter 5: Lightweight Directory Access Protocol—Describes the LDAP protocol, its emerging role in directory access and more.

Chapter 6: Domain Name System—Examines DNS from a directory service perspective, noting parallels in structures and operations.

Chapter 7: Evaluating Directory Services—Discusses how to evaluate a directory service for use in your network environment, including business considerations.

Chapter 8: Novell Directory Services—Explains Novell Directory Services based on the latest version (NDS 8), describing the underlying directory architecture and its foundations in X.500.

Chapter 9: Active Directory—Explores how Microsoft has integrated the technologies of NT 4, LDAP, and DNS into an exciting new entry into the directory services arena.

Feedback about this book is encouraged and can be sent to `uds@src.nu`. There is a companion site to this book available at `www.src.nu/uds`.

Conventions Used

In this book, certain typographical conventions have been applied. Command-line entries, directory names, domain names, and directory objects are all highlighted in `monospaced font`.

Pay special attention to the terms that appear in italic. These terms are followed by their acronym or abbreviation in parentheses—*Active Directory* (AD), for example. Those acronyms and abbreviations will subsequently be used throughout the book without spelling out the term again, both for the sake of brevity and also to get you used to thinking in directory services terminology.

...to climb an oak tree,
one must first plant an acorn...

1

Introduction to Directory Services

DIRECTORY SERVICES ARE A SIGNIFICANT EMERGING technology with a wide range of applications, from general information systems management to administration of distributed networks. Directory services are employed to manage complex systems of interrelated information, and to support the distribution and retrieval of information contained within the directory.

The explanations of directory services throughout this book revolve around networking-focused directory services from both a technological and administrative perspective. Cumulatively, throughout these chapters, we describe the current state of the integration of directory service technologies with leading networking environments.

Although our focus is directory services from a networking perspective, clearly the scope of directory service technologies and implementations goes well beyond networking. General-purpose directory services are being used to fill a wide range of business needs with implementations providing key informational support for security, messaging, and e-commerce aspects of the enterprise.

When looking at the integration of directory services in networking, it is clearly a significant shift in network information management, and one of the most significant emerging network technologies today. Many networking vendors are releasing them, many corporations are deploying them, and increasing numbers of network administrators are managing their networks with them. Directory services in networking can provide a powerful technology, supplying logically centralized management of a physically distributed computing environment. Yet directory services can also be complicated, requiring understanding of both the day-to-day operations and the underlying conceptual models of directory service technologies.

Much as the widespread introduction of networking changed the way that computers can interoperate with each other, directory services are changing the way that people interact with those networked systems. When networking emerged as a critical new technology, many people were forced to choose and implement a network with little real understanding of how it all worked. Likewise, many people are now being asked to select, implement, and integrate directory services with equally little background as to how they operate.

This book describes the theory behind directory services, explaining the range and characteristics of directory services, as well as the directory service models of X.500. This book also describes the functionality and significance of the LDAP protocol, as well as the integration of the DNS location services and their use in directory services.

To help you apply this theory to real networking environments, later chapters also cover directory service evaluation dimensions and criteria. There is also a review of the two most significant directory service implementations for networks, *Novell Directory Services* (NDS) and *Active Directory* (AD).

First, it's important to take a look at what directory services actually are: what they do; how they work; how they have evolved; and what this means to you as an IT professional.

Why Networks Need Directory Services

For the first time in human history, we have the capacity for global information sharing, and direct interactive multimedia communications with hundreds of millions (eventually billions) of people. This global interactive network provides an unparalleled context for new forms of commerce, which brings with it new (and somewhat conflicting) requirements for both public access to corporate information, and security for that same corporate information.

The internal corporate use of networked computers has increased substantially in both quantity and diversity, and is undergoing constant and rapid change. While advancements in internetworking and communication capabilities increase connectivity and enhance content delivery, with these advancements come concomitant increases in complexity, interdependencies, and technical problems.

Simply put, as networks increase in size and complexity, so does the difficulty of locating network resources and managing users and services within the distributed computing environment.

Increased complexity in a corporate network commonly results in decreased productivity for many network users, as they struggle with the underlying difficulties of esoteric resource location schemes, changing resource names, and the lack of effective integration between the network and applications.

Clearly some mechanism is needed to effectively mask the intricacies of the underlying network and application namespaces while optimizing the distributed computing environment for both user and administrator.

What Is a Directory Service?

To begin with, when someone says "directory service," they might literally mean anything that provides a way to associate two or more pieces of information concerning a specific person or resource. The term may be used to describe different capabilities—from a simple text file containing a list of resources (and the means to locate them), to a sophisticated system of servers providing interrelated services that supply network-wide support for information and resource management.

In its most general definition, a directory service provides the means to hierarchically organize and manage information, and to retrieve the information by name association.

Directories have been used for many years in the simple form of telephone white pages. More recently, networking environments have evolved into using limited directory services for name resolution and network resource management. Over the past decade, a general-purpose directory service architecture, X.500, has emerged as the industry standard for large-scale distributed directory systems.

To reiterate this point for clarification—and because there is a range of meanings of the term "directory"—in common parlance, "directory" may refer to an integrated network-wide service that provides a powerful tool used to simplify management and use of complex information systems and networks. Or it may just refer to an email address book.

It is likely that the computer network you use daily has numerous "directories" on it, providing a variety of services to users, applications, and so on. Some of these directories may actually be called "directories," although others probably are not. Most likely, you directly access at least one directory as a consumer of the information it contains (such as your email). Assuredly, many more work behind the scenes, managing applications, resources, and network security.

Many software products, especially applications and network services, utilize directories and provide access for network users and applications to this stored information. Yet what is considered a "directory service" is an evolving set of criteria.

Defining Directory Services

Directory services provide an information management technology that can be applied to a wide range of internal and external business operations. General-purpose directory services excel in the complex information system management required by large enterprise operations. A general-purpose directory service may be employed in a variety of ways—from a parts classification catalog in support of purchasing operations, to the more complicated real-time information management of the military and its secure messaging needs.

The focus of this discussion, however, is distributed networks, and in contrast to the general-purpose directory previously mentioned, the networking-focused directory is oriented toward the management of network information.

A directory service operates within a network to facilitate access to network resources and to ease network administration and usage by providing a unified organization of network resources. The directory contains a set of information about network resources and services, including users, workstations, servers, and the services they provide.

A directory *object*—a data structure with a specified set of attributes and syntax—represents each network entity (user, server, and so forth). Every object definition has a specific set of *attributes* (also referred to as *properties*), either mandatory or optional. Each property is constrained to a particular type of syntactical representation—for instance, the phone number attribute is a numeric string, and so on.

The *schema*—the core data structure that defines all objects that can exist in the directory—internally defines the directory contents. The schema also defines the properties that can be assigned to the object classes, and the syntax for the values of those properties. In addition to defining the directory objects, the schema determines how the directory is structured.

The directory schema can be thought of as the "definition" of the directory, because it defines the essential structure of all directory objects, as well as their possible relationships. The schema information provides rules used to enforce the specified definitions of an object. These definitions are used to specify the directory hierarchy and structure the relationships and interactions between directory objects. The schema effectively defines the directory *namespace*.

In its most generic sense, a namespace can be described as a collection of objects that reside within a common container (an object that can contain other objects) and follow the same naming convention. From a technical perspective, a namespace is a logical and programmatic construct used to define a discrete area containing objects named in compliance with a specified naming model. A namespace is defined by the set of logical rules that determine structural characteristics of the directory (hierarchical or flat), and determines how objects are named. Objects that conform to the naming convention can be said to exist within that namespace.

The logical structure of the information in a directory is represented as a directory tree, or as defined in X.500, as the *Directory Information Tree* (DIT). A directory tree is a hierarchical arrangement of defined directory objects contained within a contiguous (logically connected) namespace. The directory tree is used to represent a logical hierarchy, as well as to visually display the arrangement of objects within the tree.

The information in the directory is stored in a distributed form that X.500 defines as the *Directory Information Base* (DIB). For network centric directories, the DIB contains the information about the computers, devices, resources, groups, and users on your network. In contrast, a general-purpose directory may contain virtually any set of information (from application data and distributed project management information to multimedia content).

The DIB can be subdivided into *partitions* to support large or geographically distributed information systems or networks. Directory services may directly support some form of *replication* (that is, copying) of the DIB to multiple directory servers (usually close to clients who need the information). Common network directory services do this sort of direct managing of partitioning and replication. However, a directory service may also be designed to operate separately from the data storage subsystem, and may not be involved in data storage at all. General-purpose directory services commonly will not directly manage the data storage, but rather use commercial scalable databases (such as Oracle) for back-end data management.

A *directory service* also includes the services provided to network clients and administrators, and information from directory-enabled applications and network services. A typical directory provides services that support resource location, user and group management, network security, and distributed application requirements.

Simple, huh?

A look at a familiar directory will show how this all comes together. A simple directory used in an email application is used in this example.

Most corporations publish an internal directory that lists employees along with their email addresses and perhaps additional information such as job title, phone number, and office location. In this example, the email address book could be considered a namespace that contains objects (employees) and properties (name, email address, job title, and so on) that describe those objects. The address book namespace follows a specific naming convention (last name, first name) that facilitates identification and location of objects residing within it.

The needs of the messaging application define the schema of the email directory. Because the purpose of this directory is to support email, email addresses are a mandatory property of each user, but job title is probably optional. There is likely to be a copy of the directory information on each mail server, and there may well be cached copies of portions of the directory information on client machines acting as local address books.

Similar to other directory services, email applications use a client/server model that employs server-side and client-side software components to supply the directory functionality. The email directory provides services such as email address lookups and searches to clients, as well as supplying the data needed to support internal operations such as interserver communication.

Qualities of a Directory Service

Historically many forms of information directories have been called "directory services." At this point in the development of the networking industry, however, general-purpose and network directory services commonly share some fundamental design concepts and a core set of functionality.

To help differentiate between applications or services that use some kind of directory, and what is at this point (in the evolution of networking technologies) referred to as a *directory service*, consider the following characteristics:

- **A defined namespace**—Directory services operate in and utilize a *namespace*, essentially a data structure arranged according to a specified naming model. The X.500 standards specify a hierarchical namespace logically arranged in an inverse tree.

- **An extended search capability**—Directory services provide robust search capabilities, allowing searches on individual attributes of objects. This provides a powerful tool for finding network information based on relevant attributes. If you want to find a color printer close to your office, you can search for one, provided the necessary information (printer type, location, and so on) has been entered in the directory.

- **Scales from small to large networks**—A key factor in scalability is the effective distribution of the directory data to multiple servers on the network. A directory service is designed to work as well on an enterprise network connected via WAN and Internet links, as it does on a small LAN.

- **A distributed information system**—A directory service provides the mechanism to distribute the directory across multiple computers within the network. Partitioning of the directory provides for the logical subdivision of the DIB to allow delegation of control and to speed access to directory information.

- **Replicated data**—Directories support replication to make your information system or network more resistant to failure (should a directory server go down) and more accessible to users.

- **A datastore optimized for reads**—The storage mechanism used for a directory service is usually designed to support an extremely high ratio of read to write operations. It is common for directory product designs to assume that 99% of the operations accessing the DIB will be reads (lookups and searches), with relatively few writes (changes and additions).

- **An extensible schema**—Most directory services support the extension of the directory schema, enabling developers and administrators to extend the native directory object set and implement new and customized directory objects as needed (such as adding a user's photograph to the directory).

How Does a Directory Service Work?

At the core of directory service architecture lies the design for a general-purpose hierarchical information management system, which can be applied to managing complex networking and information systems.

Directory services for networks may use a somewhat narrower focus, and are centered around an information repository of all network resources, which is distributed throughout logically and physically diverse server components of the network. Effective directory service integration into the *network operating system* (NOS) can enable the kind of distributed networking capability needed in modern enterprise networks.

Directory services implement some sort of location or naming service and central repository for information on all network resources, and provides the means to locate and manage network resources within a distributed environment. The directory provides for authentication and access control over all objects represented within this distributed directory information.

A directory service design also defines software agents that provide directory access by performing the needed lookup and object manipulation tasks. Directory services operate by using a client/server exchange between an agent that accesses the directory and an agent that provides services to the network client. The server agent also provides a means for communication among server software components to allow multiple physical servers to act as one logical directory. Chapter 4, "X.500: A Model for Directory Services, " discusses these software agents in more detail.

Common Directory Service Implementations

A number of different kinds of directory service products are in use today.

Directory service products are commonly categorized by the types of objects they contain (*scope of content*) and the types of client and management functionality (*range of services*) they support. The directory for an email application typically contains a set of registered users, for example, and provides services such as mail transfer and address books to clients in addition to the management capabilities provided to the administrator.

We can subdivide directory service implementations currently in use in the WAN/LAN network environment into five major types, by scope of content and services:

- **Networking-focused directories** are designed to support NOS functionality such as user accounts, security, and management of network resources. Early NOS implementations had simple directories, yet as networking platforms evolved they have integrated (to varying degrees) aspects of the directory service technology defined in the X.500 standards.

- **Application directories** store information about users of a specific application, the types of operations they can perform, and possibly some configuration information as well. The most common use of application directories is for messaging and groupware products. Software agents (programs) are employed to integrate user and application information, and to synchronize directory information across the application platform.

- **Limited-use directories** are designed to store information used for a single purpose, although that purpose can be nearly anything. One example of such a directory is the *Domain Name System* (DNS), which is used to associate the easy-to-remember domain names with the difficult-to-remember IP addresses. Another type of limited-use directory is the publicly accessible information directories available on the Internet (such as InfoSpace, Four11, and so on). These directories allow user access from a Web browser or similar client application. The Internet directories are used for a diverse set of functions, ranging from providing large public directories of email addresses and phone numbers to locating other users for chat.

- **General-purpose directories** commonly provide the widest range of directory services and functionality, and thus support the diverse requirements of an enterprise business as well as the networking environment. The current general-purpose directory products are usually based on the widely accepted X.500 standards, and support standard protocols and services such as LDAP and DNS.

- **Meta-directories** provide a means of managing and integrating information stored in multiple directories. Meta-directories use software agents to collect the data from diverse network and application directories, which are then integrated to varying degrees. Meta-directory operations are characterized by their capability to communicate with diverse directory implementations, providing functional interoperability with divergent NOS or application namespaces.

Although each of these directory implementations supports different applications and has different requirements, you will find (as you review the overall structure of directory services and components) that these diverse directory implementations have much in common. Chapter 2, "Evolution of Directory Structures," examines each of these directory types in greater detail.

What Benefits Does a Directory Service Provide?

The nature of the benefits that might be provided by a directory service depends on the sort of directory service products you are implementing and on the business need you are addressing with these products. You might implement a general-purpose directory service to perform e-commerce customer management, for example, with some expected benefits including streamlined administration and ease of customer access.

Likewise, you might install a network centric directory service, with the expected benefits including simplified management of the distributed network, delegation of administrative authority, and ease of network resource location.

Benefits of Directory Services

This section describes benefits derived from networking-focused directories, while ignoring the many informational and business benefits derived from general-purpose directory service products. Such directory service implementations are being applied to all operational and informational aspects of large businesses and organizations, and as such, the range of application and potential benefits of general-purpose directory services exceeds the scope of this material. Yet many of the factors and benefits described here also apply to general-purpose directory service implementations as well.

For most network administrators, the decision to implement comprehensive directory services on a network requires a significant change in how the network is organized, managed, and dealt with by network users. Implementation of such a directory service may require new software and hardware, as well as training of users and administrators alike.

To justify the cost of the disruption, training, and additional hardware and software, a directory service has to provide substantial benefits. Although cost and risk factors are involved, comprehensive directory services can enhance your enterprise network by providing the following benefits:

- Facilitates distributed networking
- Eases network administration
- Enhances network reliability and performance
- Unifies access to distributed resources
- Improves security

Facilitates Distributed Networking

Directory services can provide substantial benefits to network administrators, network users, and the enterprise employing them. Directory services are designed to be scalable from LANs to enterprise-wide networks, speed lookup of network resources, simplify user access, and improve network interoperability and reliability.

When directory services are integrated with the NOS, it provides for centralized network organization and administration. Because enterprise networks rarely use a single NOS, however, most users and administrators must access resources within a heterogeneous network environment. Directory services are being used in these complex network environments to provide a unified index and datastore for all the components of that distributed network.

In addition, directory services support the integration of diverse namespaces provided by different NOS and application vendors, and provide the critical support for distributed applications development.

Scales from LAN to Enterprise Networks

As LANs are increasingly linked via WANs and use the Internet as a connectivity backbone, the capability of the network directory to scale to the needs of the enterprise is becoming critical. To address and remedy limitations of earlier NOS-based directories, a directory service implementation is structured to be highly scalable.

The distributed services and database management provided by directory services allows your network to scale from small business LANs to WAN-linked global enterprise networks. A truly robust directory service can scale from a single directory server managing a few hundred network objects to a system using hundreds of directory servers that collectively manage a million or more directory objects.

Enhances Network Interoperability

As most enterprise networks are not limited to a specific NOS, a well designed directory service can expand interoperability among the diverse network components commonly in use in the corporate environment.

- **Integrate heterogeneous networks**—Directory services can provide the interoperability needed in the administration of heterogeneous network environments. By integrating open standards for directory services with cross-platform namespace support, a directory service can support connectivity to external directory namespaces via standard interfaces.

- **Support Internet standards**—Because of the integration of the Internet with corporate network computing, and the widespread implementation of intranet and extranet operations, most current directory services are designed with support for critical Internet standards. Many of the technological advances within directory services are rooted in industry standards, protocols, and naming services, most notably X.500, LDAP, and DNS.

Eases Network Administration

One of the issues facing network administrators is the lack of ability to organize enterprise subdivisions and network resources in a unified and hierarchical fashion. The integration of network resource data provided by directory services consolidates the tasks involved in administration of the network and minimizes task complexity with regard to managing services, systems, and user accounts. Directory services provide a greater degree of administrative flexibility and control, including the following:

- **Single point of administration**—Directory services enable comprehensive network administration from any point within the network. With a unified directory tree and a single point of logon, it's possible to administer the entire network and its resources from any point within the network, instead of having to be at a specific computer.

- **Finer degree of control**—Directory services provide the network administrator with far greater control over exactly what information an individual has access to, as well as providing the means to control the user's ability to change the information. Access rights can be set on individual properties of a directory object, providing enhanced control of information. The increased granularity of access control available in directory services greatly improves the ability to assign discrete administrative tasks.

- **Delegation of administration**—The hierarchical modeling of your organizational structure facilitates easy delegation of administrative control and administrative tasks. Directory services allow the administration of the network to be delegated as needed, allowing organizational subdivisions to be locally administered by granting network administrators the rights to manage local user and group accounts. Especially with larger enterprise networks, this is an important capability because it enables the administrator to subdivide and delegate network responsibilities and administration tasks along the same organizational subdivisions that exist within the corporation.

- **Directory tree hierarchy can reflect business structure**—The directory service hierarchy is implemented as a logical tree that can model the structure of your enterprise, providing operational and administrative boundaries. When designing a directory tree, you can use the hierarchical properties of directory objects to reflect your organizational structure, network topology, and operational needs. You can use the inherent properties of the object hierarchy and flow of access rights to help structure and delineate the organization of your directory tree.

Enhances Network Performance and Reliability

When examining network technologies, a key consideration for most network administrators is the impact on network performance and reliability. Two important, although perhaps less obvious, aspects of directory services are improved network performance and a more robust and fault-tolerant network.

Storing the directory information in a distributed DIB allows for directory services and operations to be supported across physically distributed network servers. Directory services provide for replication and partitioning of the directory to these distributed servers as a means of improving network performance and stability. A replicated and partitioned directory can increase performance and reliability for basic network operations as well as for other components of the enterprise computing environment.

- Replication of a directory enhances both the network reliability and performance by providing backup directory servers for redundancy and load balancing.

- Partitioning of a directory can help control network traffic and enhance the responsiveness of directory servers to client requests.

Improves Reliability

A critical aspect of any network is its capability to function even if one or more servers become unavailable. Directory services improve network reliability by enabling you to place multiple directory servers on your network to support network operations in case of server failure. By replicating the directory to multiple servers, you can guarantee that even if one server becomes unavailable, the entire network will not become inaccessible. If a single directory server stops functioning, directory service queries will be routed to the next available replica (copy) of the directory partition.

Directories can also provide a degree of fault tolerance for applications and services whose configuration and operational data they contain. This support for fault tolerance of network services and functionality can, for instance, redirect network clients to a backup application server in the event of a primary system failure.

Enhances Performance

Network performance can be improved by placing multiple replicas of the directory on servers distributed throughout the network. Authentication to the network and directory queries should take place at the server closest to the user, resulting in minimal network traffic.

In a large network, or a network using WAN links, the directory can also be subdivided into *partitions*, or subsets of directory information. By using partitions and locating replicas of the appropriate partitions physically close to the people who will be using that portion of the directory, network traffic can be minimized. Partitions also provide a mechanism for load balancing, by subdividing the DIB into smaller pieces to be managed by individual directory servers. Using replicas of these partitions enables you to direct access to an array of servers to distribute a large workload.

To further speed user access to resources, many directory services use a fast lookup index to network resources called a *catalog*. Directory catalogs use a subset of the directory contents to provide a fast way to locate network resources. Catalogs can be distributed around the network, improving response time to directory queries. Proper design and placement of directory catalogs allows for a minimum of network traffic, because most lookup requests can be resolved locally, without referrals to other directory servers for resource location.

Unifies Access to Distributed Resources

For users and administrators to identify and access network resources, they first must locate those resources. Directory services provide an essential lookup functionality for network clients, operating as a fast-search index to network resources.

Initially, NOS directories were server based and contained information pertaining to local resources only. These earlier, and simpler, directory implementations frequently supply limited support for browsing or searching the network for resources. While this provides a method for resource location on small networks, it falls short of the more sophisticated directory service required in today's distributed networking environments.

Distributed networks require both a centralized means of locating a resource (or range of resources) existing on the network, as well as logical and easy-to-use naming semantics. The unified access to directory content allows for a single point of user logon to the network, and access to diverse resources is eased by support for standardized naming conventions. A well-designed directory using intuitive naming and a logical directory structure can speed resource location.

Simplifies Location of Network Resources

Directory services provide the software mechanism to simplify location of, and access to, required network resources. By integrating information about all network services, systems, and accounts, directory services can minimize complexity for users trying to get to needed resources on the network.

Directory services provide fundamental methods of querying or accessing the directory, including browsing of the directory, and searches based on a variety of criteria (such as object name, type, and so on).

In a network directory service, servers and users on the network are logically presented as objects in a hierarchical tree, easing user location of required network resources via a top-down organizational structure.

Integration of the information about all network objects into a centralized directory provides the directory service user with an easily searchable reference to the contents of the network, simplifying user access to network information and resources.

Provides for Single Network Logon

Directory services provides for a single user logon to access diverse resources in a distributed network. With a single logon, users can commonly access the content of disparate directories for NOS, messaging, and applications. The distributed access to network resources is transparent to the directory user. The client just logs on to any directory server and is granted access to the resources on the network. The physical location of the resources is not relevant because it is masked by the directory services.

This integration of access to directory information can result in simplified administration and operation of the network, and can also reduce the security and usability issues associated with multiple passwords.

Supports a Standard Naming Convention

Within the directory, a single naming format can be used to access resources that may have previously required several naming styles, simplifying use of the network. In addition, many directory services use multiple familiar naming conventions, easing user location of network resources. More directory service vendors are beginning to leverage the well-established naming conventions used on the Internet and within the X.500 community, providing support for RFC 822 email naming, DNS domain names, and X.500 style names.

Improves Security

Security in a non-distributed directory, where each server controls security for its own resources, is both a very simple and a very complicated task. If network clients access resources attached to only a single server (perhaps assigned by a physical location or workgroup), the security provided by a non-distributed directory may be adequate. If so, it will certainly be much faster to configure such a network for a small group of people than to deploy a full-scale distributed directory.

Because a large network with this localized style of security management requires significant configuration of interdirectory exchange of security information, however, it is a very complex security model to implement for a large or distributed network. Integration of network security services with directory services effectively provides controlled access to all network resources and the information they contain.

Many proprietary security models and implementations exist in various network operating systems and distributed applications, complicating network security management. Directory services commonly enhance network security by integrating multiple security standards and technologies, which provide the scalable security and access control required in an enterprise network. Current directory products also commonly provide support for industry security and encryption standards such as public key certificates and the Kerberos protocol, in addition to the NOS-specific security models.

Network Security

All network administrators face the fundamental issues of controlling which users can log on to the network and who can access which data and network resources. The security functionality in a directory service commonly supports the NOS operations employed in user authentication and access control. *Authentication* is the mechanism that verifies the identity of the individual user. *Access control* provides differential levels of access to system services and operations.

Early directory implementations use server-based or domain-based access rights, requiring a separate user account for each server or domain and making network operations cumbersome for administrators and users alike. Some of these directories, such as that supplied with NT 4, have mechanisms for interdomain authentication and access control support. However, they can require a rather complicated configuration of *domain trusts* (the NT method of exchange of security information between domains) to support interdomain operations.

As you can imagine, such centralized security models require substantial administrative overhead when used in large-scale or diverse heterogeneous networks. By comparison, a distributed, hierarchical directory (which encompasses all network resources) provides access to the entire network with a single logon and simplifies security configuration for the administrator.

Directory Object Security

Because the directory contains sensitive and confidential information about individual users as well as network resources, security must be provided for the directory itself. Directory services define containers (objects that can contain other objects), as well as user and group accounts as objects within the directory namespace, and assign access rights to the objects. Each object in the directory can contain a full set of security descriptors, controlling actions taken on the object, in addition to the security settings for the underlying network resource represented by the directory object.

Access control can generally be set on a per-property basis, providing a high degree of granularity on directory object security settings. This enables a network administrator to delegate management tasks while ensuring unauthorized administrative actions are blocked and guaranteeing confidentiality of sensitive data.

Because security controls can be assigned on an object level, an object can be moved and all its access rights will move with it. When a distributed directory is used as the storage location for users and network objects, the associated access rights are stored with the object, allowing for distributed security control. As a directory is partitioned and distributed among network servers, both security privileges and administration can be logically subdivided within the directory.

Permissions Flow

In contrast to a flat directory, a hierarchical directory can provide structure for the assignment of security information. A hierarchical directory tree provides a framework for the flow of assigned security rights downward through the directory (known as *inheritance*). Rather than requiring the assignment of access rights for individual users or groups, permissions assigned to a directory container object apply to all objects in the container.

Permissions assigned anywhere in the tree are implicitly assigned to the entire subtree below that point, unless explicitly blocked. Filters can be established to block this inheritance at the container level, providing the means to create a security boundary around a specific portion of the directory.

By taking advantage of this security design, network administrators can simplify the management of an enterprise network. Permissions that apply to the entire company, such as the ability to browse network resources, can be granted close to the root (top) of the directory tree and thus *implicitly* applied to everyone via inheritance. More specific rights, such as the ability to write to a file share, can then be assigned to the container holding the objects representing the people or groups who need to write to the share. Departments that need to be isolated, such as Sales or Development, can have the rights inheritance blocked and specific permissions granted only to those users and groups who need to access the information.

Supports Multiple Security Providers

Although leading NOS and directory service vendors commonly use proprietary algorithms for encryption and authentication, a number of new technologies and standards are being integrated into network and directory products. Many directory services are providing support for open standards for security protocols, including Kerberos as well as public key certificate channels such as *Secure Sockets Layer* (SSL) and *Private Communications Technology* (PCT). Implementing SSL and PCT protocols in directory services provides additional support for strong authentication.

Because Kerberos and SSL/PCT are two significant emerging security standards, and are being increasingly supported by directory services, it's important to take a brief look at each of these security protocols.

- **Kerberos**— The Kerberos protocol is essentially a shared secret authentication methodology in which both the user and the security services share the user's secret password. Kerberos security utilizes an encrypted form of the user's password, upon which a security token called a *ticket* is based. This ticket is then used to authenticate user access to network resources. Utilizing the Kerberos authentication protocol provides a directory service with faster server authentication, delegation of user authentication, and transitive security relationships.

- **SSL/PCT**—Directory services may also implement public key certificates to establish secure communications channels via SSL or PCT that are employed for user authentication and access control. Certificates are a form of security token detailed in the X.509 specification. The SSL and PCT security protocols use these X.509 certificates to support strong authentication for network clients. Directory services support this by storing a user's public key certificates as an attribute of the user object in the directory.

An Example: Managing PK Certificates

One clear advantage to using a directory service is that you can let the directory manage complicated sets of processes and information for you. Take a look now at an example of a complex area of security management—public key certificates—to see how this might work.

`<story>`

Not so long ago, a person had to remember only one or two passwords to use the resources needed to get a job done. All the requisite resources were available on the local network and, in most cases, people seldom communicated with anyone outside of that environment.

Then the Internet came along and everyone started using public channels to communicate, a clear step forward in terms of linking people and companies. However, it's seldom so straight forward....

`</story>`

If you are sending data across public data channels, as opposed to a private LAN, you need to think about security from a different perspective. One popular method of handling security over the Internet is by using public key certificates. This is a great way to ensure that your data can't be easily compromised, but it requires certificates for each person, maybe more than one—and each certificate may have to be obtained and installed individually on each computer.

It is important to note that certificates are *not* like passwords—you can't memorize them, and they require specific information to be stored in a file somewhere. Those certificates have to be available to the user and other network entities from a number of different physical locations. Clearly, storing certificates somewhere other than the client machine's hard drive is desirable.

Certificate storage and management is one of those places where a directory can help substantially. If you have implemented a directory service on your network, you can store security certificates, either as an attribute of the user they belong to or as a linked object. The person who needs the certificates no longer has to supply a certificate, it's just there.

This also simplifies management of the certificates because if they need to be renewed, changed, or revoked, they are easily accessible to any directory administrator.

This is only one example of a management task that can be offloaded to the directory. As you begin to assess the usage of a directory in your particular environment, you will likely come up with many more.

How Are Directory Services Used?

Not surprisingly, the answer to this question depends on whom you ask.

For instance, a general-purpose directory service might be employed for virtually anything—from managing a distributed e-commerce application, a parts distribution tracking system, or the deployment of military resources.

Use of network centric directory services is more oriented toward the enterprise networking environment and the people who use the network to conduct the operations of the business.

Network administrators, applications, and the people who have to use your distributed enterprise network all use the directory for different purposes (and they use different interfaces).

- People use directory services to find and access network resources and the enterprise information stored there. People commonly interact with the directory via client-side applications, web browsers, and extensions to the NOS user interface.

- Network administrators use directory services to help manage the complex requirements of a distributed network environment. In addition to the client-side interfaces described previously, administrators also use server-side directory management and schema management tools to manage the enterprise network.

- Distributed applications use directory services to identify and connect to network resources and to store application-specific data. Applications commonly use available *Application Programming Interfaces* (APIs) and protocols to use the directory service operations and to store application-specific configuration data.

Consider a directory from the consumer side for a minute. Understanding what users, administrators, and applications expect of the directory is important if the directory is to provide the expected functionality. You could ask:

"It's a directory *service*, so what services should it be providing?"

The following section examines how directory services are used by people, administrators, and applications.

How People Use Directory Services

How people use a directory service relates directly to what it is designed to do. With an email directory service, for example, it may only be used to send and receive email. In contrast, a general-purpose directory service can be implemented in a wide range of applications, and therefore people may use it in a wide variety of ways.

For networking-focused directory services, however, the range and nature of directory usage tends to be somewhat more constrained.

To put it concisely, people in enterprise networking environments use directory services to obtain information and complete tasks related to their jobs. People primarily use directories to browse or search for network resources they need access to (such as databases, printers, file shares, and so on), and to manage their network information sources (such as email address books).

This is a good start, because finding and accessing network resources is baseline functionality for any network directory service; however, a well-implemented directory service can provide additional benefits to the people who use them proficiently. In addition to helping them find needed network resources, people can use the directory to provide access to (and control of) information associated with their network account (such as certificates), which are otherwise problematic to manage.

Finding Network Resources

For a network client to access a network service or resource, the client has to have some way of locating it. Those who use Windows-based computer networks, for example, generally identify resources by server and share name (\\server\share). When two computers communicate, however, they use numeric network addresses. Name resolution is required for a network to correlate a server's logical name (which the user provides) to its numeric address (which the computer requires).

The operation that maps the name of a network computer to its network address is referred to as a *naming service* (also called *location* or *lookup* services). Naming services are a client/server operation in which the client requests the location of the host on the network by name, and a name server responds by locating the requested server name in a database and providing the corresponding network address back to the client.

The most familiar naming service is probably DNS, widely used for name resolution on TCP/IP networks. When a network client attempts to connect to a Web server by submitting the domain name (such as www.mythical.org), the provided host and domain name must be translated to its corresponding IP address to enable communication between machines. DNS resolves such *name queries* by looking up the host.domain name and providing the corresponding IP address to the client. DNS also provides support for reverse lookups of a host.domain name by its IP address.

Motivation...

The amount of effort a person is willing to put into learning a new technology usually relates to the benefit to be derived from the technology. Understanding the benefits of using a directory can motivate people to use it well, which will simplify the task of administering the network.

As you can tell from the past few paragraphs, multiple naming services are almost always in operation on any network, which increases usage complexity. If everyone has to master several naming schemes to just locate and get to the required resources daily, it can slow down work, increase user frustration, and likely require more technical support.

A directory service can perform the task of handling resource lookup requests by network clients through a unified interface to all resources on the enterprise network. Integrated directory services is a fundamental shift in network location services and in management of network resource information.

The hierarchical directory tree provides a network client with more intuitive access to distributed network resources. The directory tree unifies the objects representing network entities into a single namespace, and the directory service provides integrated user access to all of these network resources. Using a hierarchical directory tree simplifies the user's understanding of the relative location of entities within the network and eases location and usage of network resources.

Directory Searches

Even with the enhanced modeling capabilities of a directory service, resources may still be difficult to locate. A distributed directory supplies a comprehensive directory-wide search of operations for directory objects, with filters to select from a range of object properties. A directory service commonly provides for user-friendly search methods along with query syntax that is robust yet simple to use. Because most directory services support the *Lightweight Directory Access Protocol* (LDAP), Chapter 5, "Lightweight Directory Access Protocol," discusses how these LDAP queries are formed and processed.

Control of Data Display

Directory vendors may also provide the capability to set directory security at a very granular level, down to the individual property of a directory object. This can be a powerful addition to management capability because it allows selective display of object information, based on the security assigned to the information and the access control rights of the person attempting to view the data. This provides a means to display an object (such as a user) with a subset of its attributes (name, email address, phone) while hiding other properties (salary or other sensitive data) from unauthorized access.

Administrative rights can also be set with this sort of granularity, providing a means to distribute subsets of administrative tasks while protecting confidential information from unauthorized access. This means that individuals can be allowed to access and change personal information, while that data is still protected from unauthorized access by others. Yet with this increase in granularity and control comes an increased complexity in management of all these assignable rights.

How Administrators Use Directory Services

Like usage, administration can vary with the type of directory service implemented. While the demands of various directory service implementations could be unique, the underlying principles of directory management are consistent. Directory service administration uses the properties of a hierarchical tree structure, naming, and inheritance to organize information, control access, and provide a framework for delegation of administration and information management.

Network administrators use directory services to manage distributed networks and the users, resources, applications, services, and information that they contain. In most organizations, management of the enterprise networks requires substantial administrative resources.

To manage any set of resources effectively, you must first have the information available in a unified and manageable form. Directory services can provide the key functionality of integrating information on network users and resources into a manageable and accessible information system. A directory service can provide an interface that simplifies network management by logically unifying network resources and providing a single point of administration.

Distributed directory services can provide a framework for secure delegation of administrative responsibilities within an enterprise by supplying a highly granular resource management and security capability. This enables network administrators to delegate a subset of tasks, such as password management, while protecting other data from unauthorized access.

Managing Network Resources

Many early network implementations required the administrator to be physically present at the server containing the information on the network resources to be managed. It was frequently literally true that this was *the only server* containing this set of resource information, a situation that clearly presented management as well as reliability and performance issues. On any network with multiple servers, server-based network management presents numerous administrative problems, not the least of which is the required administration time.

Although remote administration tools have been developed which allow management of network resources from a secondary (remote) system, they may only provide a subset of the capability needed. Many implementations of remote management tools do not provide access to all network server functionality, but rather are limited to the most commonly used subset of administrative tasks.

Directory services supply an important administrative capability in networking, that can ease the management of network resources distributed in logically or geographically diverse locations. The implementation of directory services within the context of the NOS provides administrators with a more detailed information base about network resources, systems, users, and groups. All network resources are accessible through the directory services, providing quicker access to far more information about your network resources than was possible to obtain from earlier NOS directories.

A directory service can provide the network administrator with the ability to "manage the network from any point in the tree." This refers to the ability of a network administrator to access all network resources and management functionality via the directory services; whether the administrator is logged on at their normal workstation, at a satellite office, even using a dial-up connection from another country.

Another limitation of early directory implementations was the scope of network resources that could be managed via the directory. When a directory references only those resources that have a corresponding physical object, administrators can only manage objects such as servers, printers, and users.

By comparison, current directory service implementations allow the creation of objects solely as a means of creating a logical entity that represents an application, process, service, and so on. This directory object can then be assigned security controls and an administrator can manage it using normal directory operations. This approach provides a methodology whereby a single enterprise-wide directory can integrate the management of physical entities (such as users and hardware), and logical processes (such as applications and network services) with network-wide security and access control.

Additionally, vendors of configurable network hardware that currently require separate and complex management tools are working to integrate their products fully into major directory services. One notable example is Cisco, which plans to integrate their router configuration into leading networking-focused directory service products such as NDS and AD.

Delegating Management Tasks

The overall flexibility of network administration when using integrated directory services makes it feasible for an individual to administer any aspect of an enterprise network, or to delegate management tasks. Network management can be divided among a number of local administrators in areas isolated by security boundaries or geographic regions. Administration can also be delegated based on the type of directory data being managed.

The scope of the delegation can take on several forms:

- An entire subtree can be delegated—typically a geographic or organizational subdivision.
- Control of a particular type of object(s)—such as the set of objects used to manage printers and print servers.
- A subset of specific object attributes—this could be used to enable people to manage *only* their own telephone numbers.

Directory service implementations commonly include tools that provide the means to assign control of an object or subtree in a distributed directory, allowing effective delegation of administration for discrete subsections of the directory. Predefined groups, with rights designed for particular subsets of administrative functionality (such as user account management), are also commonly provided.

Another important way that a directory supports delegation of directory data management is by providing a way for the source to update information directly. For example, in an enterprise network, the person who cares most about an employee's home address being correct is probably the employee. By allowing people to update their addresses themselves, two things happen:

- The administration workload decreases (update is self-administered).

- The source most likely to have and provide accurate, up-to-date information controls the information.

Directory Management Tools

A directory service managed network requires powerful, flexible management tools that allow the creation and manipulation of directory objects and the assignment of properties. These tools provide for the editing of network objects, attribute values, and the full operational control of the network.

Directory management tools also provide the functionality for fundamental directory operations including basic directory administration, tree operations (*prune, graft*, and *tree merge*), object operations (assignment of values and rights), as well as *schema management*.

Schema management tools are used to customize the directory schema to allow for new objects, attributes, or attribute syntax. These tools are commonly standalone programs allowing access to modify or add to the directory schema. Clearly, administrators will find it easier to work with a directory that allows efficient methods for accessing and managing the schema.

The advantages of a directory-centered management approach should be clear: Fewer tools are needed to manage the network (or other information system), resource data is logically centralized, and the tools may even be customizable. Some directory management tools provide a framework for easily extensible and customizable management views.

Store Client Profiles

The client configuration information used by the NOS can also be stored in the directory, providing support for roaming users and a way to recover from client machine failure. In addition, application configuration data for each user can be stored in the directory, further reducing the need to individually configure client machines and applications.

New Network Functionality

New functionality such as *Quality of Service* (QoS), which provides bandwidth control, is being built into directory services to enhance network performance for measured network services used by applications such as video on demand. The level of service allowed, or guaranteed, for a specific person can be set according to certain factors such as group membership (for instance, the people who use video conferencing are guaranteed enough bandwidth for a regular weekly meeting). As these and other new services are implemented, the directory can easily be extended to accommodate the additional functionality, and the administration of complicated operations becomes simpler.

How Applications Use Directory Services

An important aspect of the utility of a network directory service is the extent to which it supports the integration of application-specific information. To avoid redundant databases of user information, developers increasingly design applications to use the directory to store application data. A well-designed directory service can provide robust application and programming support for software developers.

Applications that use a directory service can provide users with a more personalized application environment, as well as the benefits that accrue from the integration of directory, network, and application security (eliminating the need for multiple logons and passwords, for example).

Application Interfaces to the Directory

To be widely adopted, a directory service must provide APIs to facilitate interaction between the directory and applications that require directory information or services. Applications can then be developed around the exposed APIs, and this provides the means to access the data stored in the directory and to use the underlying directory operations. Most current directory service products provide support for proprietary interfaces to their directory data and services. Because LDAP is being widely used, many vendors are adding support for the LDAP C API as well, providing an open API for programmatic directory access.

Directory service implementations commonly enable developers to extend the directory schema to implement new objects or properties that contain application-specific values. This approach also has clear advantages for network administrators, who reap an important benefit from developer use of directory APIs—the elimination of separate application-specific directories. This helps to reduce unnecessary administrative tasks and cuts down on redundant network management information.

Information about Resources

In addition to the requirements of network users, the directory supports applications and network services that require directory information. When directory service functionality is integrated into the network operating systems, developers can write network applications to leverage existing directory information and operations. Application developers can use the existing directory information on network resources, users, and security instead of having to implement a method to track this data on a per-application basis.

Distributed applications can access information contained in the directory to locate necessary resources or to control access to application resources. Email services must access user authentication information and mailbox locations, for example, and must provide lookup services for addressing outbound mail. A directory service can provide all of these services on a network-wide basis.

User Configuration

Applications currently store information about the people who use them in a variety of ways. There may be application directories or configuration files on the application server, and configuration data is also likely to be stored on the client computer. Essentially, you have a single copy each of several incomplete subsets of configuration information distributed across several computers. This is not a very efficient means of providing access to the information needed for proper application functionality.

When a directory is deployed, user configuration data can be centralized, eliminating the problems associated with the earlier, more scattered approach. Rather than the previously described design, with a directory service you have all the configuration information stored in a common logical location, and different directory servers around the network can have several *complete* copies of this information. This is clearly a better way to deal with such configuration data, and is being employed by many applications (such as email) as well as desktop management initiatives such as Novell's ZENworks.

How Are Directories Integrated?

Directory integration can take on many forms—from sharing little (or no) information to exchanging security credentials and all directory information. An email directory may (or may not) share its email directory information with other applications, for example. In contrast, a meta-directory program is likely to exchange information with many (or most) commercial directories, and unify that information for administrative purposes. A general-purpose directory service might be used to integrate the information of many diverse sources (including other directories), and provide top-down management of distributed information systems.

To control resources in a network environment, many components of the network information structure (services, applications, and so on) maintain discrete directory services and databases, identifying the users of each specific service or resource, as well as other administrative information. A typical corporate network environment includes multiple NOS and application directories that authenticate users and provide access to network resources. Many networks have a discrete directory for each NOS as well as for email and other messaging services, for example, as well as other directories for groupware and applications.

Each of these directories is likely to have a different naming convention, proprietary datastore, and set of administrative tools. Each directory implementation has a different schema, further complicating directory interoperability. As there is not as yet a broadly accepted standard for directory replication and synchronization, there is no easy way for information to be dynamically shared and updated.

Although these discrete directories frequently have little in common, what many of these directories do share is the information contained within them. A single network user will commonly have an entry in each of the multiple directories, often with the same information duplicated.

As you might guess, much of the information stored in any given directory is likely to be duplicated within another directory. As more network services rely on directories, the level of redundancy in the stored information is increasing significantly.

Security concerns arise with redundant directory information because each user on your network must have an account within the NOS directory and another account for email (at a minimum), each requiring a unique logon name and password. This duplication of information, and the necessity to remember multiple passwords, leads to one of the more common security concerns in corporate networks today: unsecured passwords (usually written down and left stuck to a monitor, in a desk drawer, or elsewhere).

Another part of the problem with disparate directory structures is the issue of data synchronization between directories. If information about a user is changed in a specific directory in one location, and this data must then be propagated to other directories that use different storage and synchronization methods, compatibility issues arise. For corporations attempting to track their user and resource information across a distributed network with different directory databases and different storage and update mechanisms, the synchronization of directory content is a key issue in integrated directory operations.

Directory integration can take multiple forms: The controlling directory can update the external directory while allowing the external directory's native tools to also manage it, or one directory can subsume the other directory totally, and so on.

Clearly the resolution for disparate directory management lies in the development of a unified architecture, management interface, and set of APIs to integrate application, messaging, and NOS-specific directory namespaces.

An enterprise-wide directory service can be used to integrate discrete physical and logical namespaces into a unified administrative environment. Although migration of a heterogeneous network to a unified directory namespace does involve substantive namespace interoperability factors, they can be addressed at programmatic levels and thus remain transparent to the network client.

Integrating Network Directories

Using a single network operating system directory in your enterprise network provides some distinct advantages. A single operating system and platform simplifies user access to resources and allows directory service operations to be used across the entire enterprise. Standardized network directories simplify maintenance and administration by obviating directory interoperability issues and providing consistent operations across enterprise subdivisions.

In current enterprise environments, networks are frequently comprised of multiple NOSs, each with a different degree of directory service functionality. Additionally, every network provides its own proprietary naming model, directory protocols, and security scheme, each of which has little, if any, interoperability with foreign NOS directories.

Clearly what is needed is a directory-enabled NOS that can connect to and integrate foreign NOS namespaces and provide the functionality of fully implemented directory services while effectively interoperating with common networking platforms.

Some of the existing NOS directory services can work with foreign directories, such as directory service products from IBM and Novell. IBM's Directory Security Server provides some access to X.500-compliant directories, for example, as well as to the Windows NT directory. Other NOS vendors are addressing this by developing their proprietary directory service to run on multiple platforms; Novell, for example, has ported NDS to run on Windows NT and Solaris, as well as its native NetWare. Others, such as Microsoft with Active Directory, are opting to build their directory services around widely supported open standards (LDAP and DNS) to provide support for directory operations across multiple namespaces.

Application Directory Interoperability

Most companies have invested a significant amount of money and administrative effort in multiple directory namespaces operating within application-specific and network-specific frameworks. Although the underlying information is frequently overlapping, these directory namespaces generally do not interoperate or use a common information storage mechanism.

The integration of existing application-specific directory namespaces into a single unified namespace would reduce administrative overhead. To accomplish this, many vendors are writing their applications to leverage the existing directory services.

Although this is a step in the right direction, such an approach has difficulties of its own. Although an application may be capable of using existing directory information (such as users), applications also frequently require additional data to support their operations. Directory vendors generally provide means to extend the directory schema to provide support for additional objects and properties. This does mean, however, that in practical terms each specific installation of a given directory service may not be compatible—at least on a schema level—with other installations of the same directory service.

Another growing area of application and directory integration is that of groupware applications. These products commonly use the directory to store everything from information about users' mail accounts to security information used for document sharing, and rely heavily on the directory in their operations.

As more applications become directory-enabled, the extent to which application directories interact directly to provide interoperability decreases. For those applications that do interact, interoperability is commonly provided via the following methods:

- **Directory gateways**—Integration of multiple application-specific directory namespaces requires the implementation of directory-based gateways. A directory-based gateway can either enable a connection between two directories for data exchange; or, one directory can subsume the other, managing the subsumed directory's resources.

- **Federated naming**—For application-specific directories to exchange data, effective inter-namespace name resolution must be provided. *Federated naming* (also called *federation*) refers to the capability to perform name resolution across different namespaces, a core process of the interoperability of application-specific directories.

- **Meta-directory integration**—Some enterprise networks are using meta-directory products to facilitate interoperability among the disparate directories on their network. A meta-directory manages information that is a superset of all the integrated application-specific directories. Meta-directory products can perform directory operations across diverse namespaces. A meta-directory product can provide support for the transition from multiple application-specific directories to a unified directory environment.

Directory and File Systems Integration

In the current NOS directory services, the integration of existing file systems, as well as the selection of which file systems and operations to support, is clearly implementation specific.

In some cases, the network vendor has vested interests in selectively providing support for their proprietary file systems, and secondarily providing support for common file system namespaces. Although some NOS directory service vendors provide support for installable file systems, none yet provide a scalable namespace operating in a heterogeneous network environment with extensible multi-namespace integration of all common file systems.

In addition to the question of which file systems are supported by the directory service, there is the consideration of the extent to which file system operations are supported by and integrated with the directory tools. Some directory services provide access to substantial file system functionality via the directory administration tools, although others are limited to a specific subset of management tasks. A tool might provide the capability to control file system access rights in the same interface and using the same information as when controlling user rights to other resources on the network, for example, but not allow file operations such as copying, moving, and so on. File system integration is one of the least developed pieces of existing directory services, with many vendors choosing to continue managing file system resources independent of the network directory. In any case, most of the networks that provide any support for file system management via the directory do not support the full range of file system administrative tasks.

The Quest for the Ultimate Directory

There is substantial movement toward more directory interoperability, fueled in no small part by the explosion of Internet use and the adoption and enhancement of open standards, including X.500, LDAP, and DNS.

Most current distributed directory service implementations use the set of specifications collectively referred to as the X.500 standards as a starting point; however, the degree of adherence to those specifications is vendor specific. A major strength of the X.500 specifications has proved to be its design for managing complex information systems by establishing well-defined information models and formats for information exchange among different directory components. Some aspects of the X.500 specification, such as the default object set, are widely supported for interoperability reasons, although other aspects (such as the protocols) are less widely used.

The most promising development for directory interoperability is the widespread support for LDAP. LDAP uses the X.500 information models and defines a standard method for a client to access and modify directory information. In addition, LDAP provides a standard protocol and set of APIs that will enable software vendors to develop directory service platform-independent versions of their applications.

Although LDAP does not address many aspects of directory operation, it does provide a starting point for more widespread directory interoperability. Continued work on extensions to LDAP, which will provide a richer protocol and schema, are ongoing. Most major directory service vendors have announced support for LDAP in their current or future directory offerings.

An increasing number of directory services are using DNS to perform name resolution and location service functions, allowing directory service operations across enterprise-wide WANs as well as the Internet. For example, the latest version of Windows NT (a.k.a. Windows 2000) *requires* the use of DNS to locate directory servers. Microsoft is leveraging the new DNS resource records identifying services, to allow location of LDAP servers. DNS also provides name resolution for the domain portion of an LDAP URL.

`<dream sequence>`

Logically, the eventual convergence of directory technology should be expected, such that an enterprise will have a single directory that delivers all the functionality of multiple current directories, and which is flexible enough to add support for future network and application growth.

In an enterprise network with fully integrated directory service capability, management and client applications will present all network users, groups, printers, and servers in the same user interface with files and directories.

Optimally, when directory services are integrated with the core NOS operations and every required application, the complete array of informational and network resources can be managed through a single unified administrative interface and no administrative tasks will *ever* be duplicated.

`</dream sequence>`

Sigh.

From that rather lofty set of aspirations for the "ultimate" directory of the future, it's necessary to step back just a bit. The next chapter examines the fundamental structures of a directory service and reviews how each of these aspects has evolved to meet the increasing demands placed on the directory.

*...that which does not evolve
loses market share...*

2

Evolution of Directory Structures

THIS CHAPTER LOOKS AT THE BASIC INFORMATION STRUCTURES used in directory services and explains the relationship between directory service operations and directory service design. This chapter also reviews the evolution of directory information structures and describes how the functionality required has helped to shape the design of directory services.

Thinking about Directory Information

To a large degree, when examining directory service implementations it becomes apparent that need drives design—where a given directory service has been designed to fulfill some specific set of requirements within an organization. The overall requirements of a directory service can be viewed from several basic perspectives:

- What information is the directory service going to manage?
- How is the directory service going to be administered?
- What services does the directory need to support?
- What are the operational requirements of the directory service?

The following sections examine each of these factors in a bit more depth and examine how each of them influences the overall directory design.

What Information Is the Directory Service Going to Manage?

Directory services are an information management system, capable of dealing with a wide variety of information. Directory services in networks provide a critical infrastructure role by supplying the information required for user authentication and management, directory-enabled applications, network configuration, device management, and content services.

Directory services can also reach far beyond being a management tool for corporate IT departments. They can support the business infrastructure by managing information related to the company's overall business. In this kind of application, the information set managed by a general-purpose directory service can exceed that used by even the most comprehensive network-centric directory.

The issue of scale must also be considered, generally expressed in terms of number of objects that can be effectively managed by a given directory service. There is quite a bit of variance in scalability. Although network directory products may scale to one million objects or more, for example, some X.500 general-purpose directory services scale to tens or hundreds of millions of objects!

As the scope of the directory expands, both numerically and in complexity, more robust and flexible information organization capabilities are needed.

- Methods must be defined to represent abstract information and objects with no real-life analog. The directory must support the definition of many types of complex information structures and must provide secure access to that information.

- Issues concerning ownership of information must be dealt with and some sort of distributed control of directory information must be supported. This brings with it a need to organize information to facilitate this distribution and to show relationships between the distributed portions.

- The naming style must support the unique identification of the entire scope of information contained in the directory while cognitively and operationally maintaining relationships among information.

- More directory information equates to more directory entries and requires more sophisticated data management mechanisms.

Deciding the scope of the information the directory is going to contain helps shape the logical organization and presentation methods and defines naming schemes. The scale of the information the directory service will be managing determines the necessary data storage, management, and retrieval capabilities.

How Is the Directory Service Going to Be Administered?

Important business and political issues are involved in the use of directory services. One of the most important is that of ownership and administration of directory information. One critical requirement for a highly functional directory service is the ability to distribute the directory information among multiple separate entities, each of which owns its own portion of the namespace.

Depending on the purpose of the directory, this distribution of information ownership could be between the following:

- **Totally separate entities**—In a large-scale distributed directory service, different companies may each own a portion of the total directory service namespace. Consider the case of a directory service designed to serve as the consolidated white pages for an entire state. Each local telephone company owns and controls its own portion of the directory namespace, with the directory service also serving to link together the different namespaces into a cohesive directory as a whole. This is one of the fundamental aspects of the X.500 design—it is intended to function as a single logical directory service, yet consist of an inter-connected group of globally distributed and locally controlled directory services.

- **Subportions of a single entity**—On the other hand, if the entire scope of the directory service is network management, the information is likely to be controlled by different administrative groups within a single corporation. Frequently this sharing of information ownership takes a somewhat less complete form than that previously described, with a primary administrative group delegating particular management tasks while ultimately retaining control of the entire directory namespace.

- **Sole ownership**—In a limited directory implementation, ownership of the directory namespace may not be shared at all, but lie with a single group. This type of directory tends to be fairly small, serving a single application or server. This type of directory is considered *centralized*.

A directory service that is going to support distributed ownership of the directory information must organize the information in a way that both facilitates the distribution of information ownership and clearly maintains the relationships among those distributed portions. The distribution of namespace ownership is best accomplished within a hierarchical directory structure, because the ownership structure can then define the directory tree structure and provide a built-in framework for naming, location, security, and administration.

What Services Does the Directory Need to Support?

Directory services can act as much more than information management systems, they can also provide critical supportive information services to the enterprise. Directory services offer robust search and management capabilities, store security credentials, and provide customizable control of who can view or manipulate the directory information.

One of the most fundamental services a directory service must provide is security for the information contained within the directory. This requires the directory to provide a way to authenticate users as well as to enforce access control on the directory information. Directory services are acting in critical roles to enable e-commerce, PKI, and to support applications that require security services.

Publicly available X.509 certificate repositories are one increasingly common use of a directory service. One example of this is VeriSign, which has a public repository of the individual (personal) public key certificates it has issued at:

```
https://digitalid.verisign.com/cgi-bin/Xquery.exe
```

Even within a single organization, the need to manage PKI certificates brings with it the need for a straightforward administration method. Network directory services frequently provide the same sort of PKI support as VeriSign, just on a substantially smaller basis.

One of the longer-term uses of X.500 distributed directory services is that of a . global business white pages. Many businesses are listed in the white pages, providing a centralized point of access to look up business contact information. Because the individual businesses control their own directory namespaces, varying degrees of information are available from different companies—some have little information on staff; others have the entire staff email listings (and maybe even pictures of employees).

You may want to explore this directory to gain both a better understanding of the initial intent of X.500 and an appreciation for the complexity of interconnecting (both operationally and administratively) such a service. A public access point to the root of the X.500 tree is provided by Dante's NameFLOW-Paradise site at this *uniform resource locator* (URL):

```
www.dante.net:8888/?=+
```

Directory services are also moving into service provision in the personal arena. One interesting new direction is Internet-based identity and relationship management for individuals. Strong security and a fine degree of control over the display of personal information are provided. Tools allow customization of how and when Web forms will be automatically completed, for example, and with what information. This capability may even extend to e-commerce data such as credit card information and PKI certificates.

This style of directory provides a truly portable solution for people who must manage personal, professional, financial, and Web-related information across multiple machines, perhaps even from various locations around the world. The ability to custom manage an increasingly Web-centric personal life makes this style of directory service a powerful personal relationship and information manager. One such product is Novell's **digitalme**™, which is examined in more detail in Chapter 8, "Novell Directory Services."

What Are the Operational Requirements of the Directory Service?

Another issue should be considered when looking at how the capabilities required from a directory service have shaped the overall design and functionality. Operational requirements of the directory service such as performance, reliability, distribution, availability, and interconnectivity have also influenced the design of directory services.

These operational aspects of the directory are particularly relevant in relationship to the data management mechanisms employed by the directory service. These requirements help determine the necessary directory data storage and retrieval mechanisms and physical data distribution and replication methods.

As people have demanded higher functionality from directory services, vendors have employed a number of different approaches to issues of data storage and management. Some directory services, notably the network-centric ones such as *Novell Directory Services* (NDS) and *Active Directory* (AD), incorporate proprietary data management functionality into their directory products. Other directory services, typically the massively scalable general-purpose style, such as those developed by Open Directory and Nexor, use a powerful relational database that is either directly incorporated or interchangeably plugged in.

Operational requirements can also affect the selection of protocols. The need to allow Web-based access to the directory may prompt you to choose *Lightweight Directory Access Protocol* (LDAP) as a necessary client access protocol, for example. A growing number of directory service products support LDAP, a protocol that allows client access to directory information over TCP/IP. LDAP is becoming the salient directory access protocol, particularly for accessing directory information over the Internet.

Scope of the Directory Service

As stated before, one of the most important considerations in the design of a directory service is the scope of its contents. The *scope* of the directory determines the directory namespace boundaries and contents and is programmatically defined by the directory schema.

A number of fundamental categories of directory service products exist on the market. Directories can be differentiated by the *scope of their information and services*— the range of information they hold, who they provide that information to, and the types of network or business functionality they support. These include the following:

- Directories that can manage the network operating system user accounts and resources such as printers and file shares (NOS directory services).

- Directories that can support a single application (an application directory service).

- Directories that provide a specific information service (a limited-use directory service).

- Directories that can manage the entire range of information relating to a business, whether related to the network or not (a general-purpose directory service).

- Directories that can manage other directories (meta-directories).

Some directories are rather limited as to the range of information they can contain. For instance, an email directory has information on users, mail accounts, email servers, and perhaps other information related to mail or scheduling applications. It does not contain information about network resources such as printers, however, even though you may use printers from your email client. If your email application needs information about printers, it must find that data elsewhere, usually in a NOS directory.

The scope of a directory may be finite—that is, the vendor determines what you can put in the directory and the list of valid directory objects is not modifiable. Alternatively, a directory may have an *extensible* schema, meaning that you can add new objects and change the scope of the directory. An extensible schema means you can customize the directory to hold information usually stored in separate directory services, thereby consolidating directories and eliminating redundancy in administrative tasks.

Obviously, a directory designed to manage a finite and limited range of objects has a different purpose from one that can contain any resource on the network. The broader the scope of the directory, the more powerful it will be as a management tool.

Network Operating System Directories

One of the most familiar forms of directory services is those that are integrated into the major NOSs as network management tools. At a minimum, a network directory contains and manages the following:

- Network resources (servers, printers, and so on)
- Network security principals (users and groups)
- Associated network security information

Early NOS directories had a very limited scope, only containing information on users, groups, computers, and devices on the network. These NOS directories (such as those provided in Windows NT 4 and Novell NetWare 3.x), provided limited search functionality or none at all, and did not scale well in enterprise implementations. Although these NOS vendors may refer to their directory storage and service operations as a "directory service," there are substantial differences in scope and functionality between these early NOS directories and current NOS directory services.

The NOS directories are evolving and integrating directory service technologies to unify and streamline the management of user accounts and control access to network resources. Current NOS directories are enhanced to contain application-specific information in addition to the information used to manage the network—the most sophisticated NOS directories may contain just about any type of information, from the oft mentioned email accounts to public key certificates.

By using a NOS with integrated directory services, network administrators can simplify resource management and facilitate the distribution of administrative tasks while maintaining effective security. Network clients (whether a person or an application) primarily use the directory to locate and access resources, a task at which a NOS-integrated directory service excels.

The more powerful of the NOS directories, such as NDS and the emerging AD, are also extensible via a scripting language or an administrative application. This capability to extend the NOS directory contents and operations provides a method for developers to integrate application management into network management tools and leverage existing user account and network resource information. Network administrators can also customize the directory to hold additional information required by their organization, such as HR data or ID pictures.

Chapters 8 and 9 examine these leading network directory services (NDS and AD) in more depth.

Application-Specific Directories

Other widely deployed directory service technologies are those centered on application-specific directories such as the directories used in email and other messaging services. *Application-specific directories* are designed to support a very limited set of information and operations. They cannot integrate or centralize the information from other types of directories, and usually cannot support the integration of foreign naming conventions.

As NOS directories become more robust, application developers are leveraging them to provide the services that have traditionally been handled by application directories. Existing network resource and account information can be accessed and, as previously mentioned, many products also enable developers to extend the directory schema to support the specific data requirements of the application. This provides an advantage to developers who can just use existing directory functionality instead of creating yet another application-specific database. Network administrators also find this highly preferable to maintaining individual directories for each application in use on the network.

Because not all NOS directories allow modifications to the schema, and because NOS directories have historically been tied to a specific NOS platform, this is only a partial resolution to the directory integration issues discussed at the end of Chapter 1, "Introduction to Directory Service." This is likely to change in the future as AD is deployed and as NDS is ported to additional operating system platforms.

As application directories span a range of implementations, examining email and instant messaging can highlight some common application directory uses.

Messaging Directories

Because the messaging directory is the most widely deployed application-specific directory, it merits a closer look to understand what an application directory can and can't do.

Messaging directories, at a minimum, contain email account information such as username and password. Frequently, additional data is added to support advanced communication functionality, such as email/fax/voice integration or groupware applications. Messaging directories are used to maintain and synchronize changes to messaging systems, sometimes combined with groupware products.

These messaging products rely on client and server software agents for communicating between individual users and the directory to perform operations such as address lookups. The administrators of messaging directories use product-specific tools to monitor and analyze the messaging flow between the clients and server and to evaluate and manage the application-specific directory database.

Email directories are becoming more integrated with those used in scheduling applications, requiring expansion of the related directory and naming conventions to support the additional functionality. Although many different naming formats are used in messaging applications, the explosion in Internet email usage has driven the widespread adoption of the naming convention specified in RFC 822 (for example, `kiernan@mythical.org` or `alexis@monstrrrs.com`).

Early messaging models commonly revolved around either the X.400 specification or proprietary schemes. Yet the X.400 messaging specifications were still lacking in comprehensive directory functionality. The initial concept behind the X.500 standards was to design a fully operational directory model for the telecommunications carriers to provide widespread deployment of a "white pages"–style directory that would also support X.400 operations. Even though most messaging directories use some of the X.500 standards as a conceptual framework, little or no direct interoperation occurs between messaging platforms.

Chapter 4, "X.500: A Model for Directory Services," discusses the X.500 standards in detail, including how they form the base for much of today's directory design and development.

Instant Messaging Directory Services

Another type of an application-specific directory is that used by a variety of instant messaging services (such as Mirabilis ICQ, AOL Instant Messenger, and others). This style of directory holds not only static information about Internet users (such as their name and email address), but also provides support for dynamic attributes such as the currently logged on IP address, which can be used to locate users for chat and similar Internet conferencing services.

Limited-Use Directories

Some highly limited directories are in use today, some of which are arguably *not* truly a directory service. These services generally offer clients the ability to look up existing information but not modify it at all. These limited-use directories may provide specific services (such as name resolution, or verification of security certificates), or may provide public information lists of one sort or another.

By taking a look at two very different limited-use directories, you can get an idea of what such a tightly focused directory does.

The Domain Name System

The *Domain Name System* (DNS) is the most successful and widely used distributed directory service available. Although DNS is a highly specific and limited-use directory, primarily performing name-to-IP address resolution for domain names, it nevertheless is the most scalable directory implementation to be employed in the largest existing distributed network environment (the Internet).

Compared to most other directory services, the DNS schema is exceedingly simple, and its scope of content is very limited (containing domain and host names and their corresponding IP addresses). Until recently the DNS schema has not been extended much, nor have DNS records been dynamically updateable. With the addition of the SRV record (defined in RFC 2052), however, the schema has been effectively extended to include the identification of hosts that provide specific services (most notably LDAP servers). A *Service Resource Record* (SRV) is a DNS entry that maps the name of a network service (such as LDAP) to the TCP/IP address of the server providing the specified service.

In addition, the implementation of *Dynamic DNS (DDNS)* now allows the DNS resource records to be dynamically updated to reflect changing server availability and IP addressing. The addition of DDNS is a major step forward in the capabilities of DNS because it allows dynamically assigned IP address/host names to be resolved by DNS. As many network environments rely on the *Dynamic Host Configuration Protocol* (DHCP) to supply IP addresses, DDNS can be integrated with DHCP to provide a way to dynamically include *all* network hosts in the DNS database.

For more detailed information on DNS, refer to Chapter 6, "Domain Name System."

Public Directory Services

Another highly useful way in which limited-use directories are being deployed is as global locator services. These providers are just part of an ever-expanding list of companies leveraging directory technology to provide consumers with new services. Many of these directories provide for the cataloging of a wide range of individual information to assist people in finding others who hold memberships in professional or other associations, such as having attended the same high school or college. A few examples of this type of directory service include the following:

- InfoSpace
- BigFoot
- Four11
- VeriSign
- WhoWhere
- Switchboard

Significant restrictions apply to the functionality of most public directories, in that the scope of information is specialized and limited, and the information is not readily changeable by users.

General-Purpose Directories

A *general-purpose directory* is designed for use in a wide range of implementations and environments. A general-purpose directory commonly supports integration of sets of information that would normally reside in different directories and databases, and allows schema extensions for customization of the directory content.

A general-purpose directory is commonly designed to support existing standards for directory services (most notably X.500), and is the most flexible of directory implementations. For instance, a general-purpose directory could manage a single directory and make it look like an application directory, an email directory, or a network directory depending on the need.

One of the hallmarks of a truly general-purpose directory is its ability to scale. Admittedly, one million directory objects seem like a lot when you think in terms of manageable network objects. It's not such a huge number, however, when the directory information concerns the entire business operation, business partners, clients, and frequently much more. Directory services in this class scale to the tune of tens or hundreds of millions of objects. Two examples of general-purpose directories are DXServer by Open Directory (www.opendirectory.com) and Isocor's Global Directory Server (www.isocor.com).

Novell Directory Services provides another interesting perspective on general-purpose directory development. NDS is currently being ported to more operating system platforms—NDS now runs on Windows NT, Linux, and Solaris in addition to NetWare. Because NDS no longer depends on NetWare as the required OS platform, Novell is repositioning NDS in the marketplace. NDS is a mature directory product, which can now run almost anywhere, and is being promoted as a "full-service directory" by Novell. It will be interesting to see how Novell's **digitalme**™, and this transition of NDS to a more general-purpose directory plays out in the marketplace.

Meta-Directories

Enterprises today are using heterogeneous networks, commonly comprised of Windows and NetWare-based LANs and UNIX servers of some derivation (Linux, Sun Solaris, and others). In this environment, most network administrators have to integrate multiple NOS directories with messaging directories, application directories, and more. Administrators must then coordinate these directories in the context of thousands (or tens of thousands) of network users and many more resource computer systems, printers, servers, routers, gateways, and workstations, which comprise the network. The need for integration of disparate directory information is a key factor that makes a clear argument for some combined network management capabilities.

Meta-directory products aren't always actually a directory service, but are sometimes tools that provide a method to unify and integrate portions of the network resources, users, and security policies in an enterprise network environment. This technology may enable users to provide just one password to gain access to all types of network resources, whether email, corporate intranet data, or needed human resources information.

A meta-directory product must address several technical issues:

- Naming discrepancies between disparate namespaces must be eliminated or, at a minimum, a translation mechanism to allow interdirectory communication must be provided.

- A meta-directory implementation must also manage schema discrepancies between directories. Directories may support only a single schema for all objects in the directory. To support the integration of multiple directory services with different schema, however, either the directory model needs to be extended to accept more than one schemas per directory tree, or some method of resolving differences between schema must be implemented.

- Security issues are a critical concern. Access control must be correctly maintained when information is accessed via a meta-directory connection.

A meta-directory application uses namespace-specific software components to communicate with each directory in its native protocol. A meta-directory product may enable a network administrator to manage foreign network and application resources, or provide users with an integrated and consistent view of many different directories. Yet meta-directory tools may provide limited support for replication or synchronization between the directories, or none at all.

Some network administrators and corporate executives will find meta-directory technologies useful for overseeing network management and for simplifying user access to corporate network resources. This is particularly true for meta-directory technologies integrated with the NOS server platform, such as Novell's DirXML.

The integration of disparate directory data is not without administrative costs, however, in terms of directory service management and tool implementation as well as increasing administrative task requirements for the smooth integration of discrete sets of directory information. Careful consideration must be given to the possible outcome of a poorly implemented meta-directory product, which could simply add an additional layer of directory management requirements without adequately compensating long-term gains.

As the core NOS directory services become more capable, and as more businesses adopt X.500-style general-purpose directories, you can expect to see directory service products more directly incorporating meta-directory capabilities. Novell is already working on DirXML, for example, and Microsoft has purchased ZOOMIT so as to incorporate its meta-directory technology into later versions of AD. Standalone meta-directory products will likely be seen more as a migration tool and a temporary measure than a long-term solution.

At the time of writing, a number of meta-directory products are available to support the distributed computing requirements of enterprise networks, such as Netjunction from Worldtalk Corp. (`www.worldtalk.com`) and Zoomit Via from the ZOOMIT corporation (`www.zoomit.com`).

Structural Characteristics of a Directory Service

The capabilities required of the directory service and the scope of the information to be managed determine the best design for a particular directory implementation. As directory services become more powerful and handle more information, the information structures are having to change to keep pace with the demands placed on the directory service.

Three critical aspects of directory information structures are *logical organizational methods, naming scheme*, and the *information and data management mechanisms*. The combination of these aspects determines the directory service's capabilities, and points to some of the important reasons why network administrators praise the arrival of AD and NDS (years earlier) as the means of managing a distributed network.

The organization of directory information must be designed to support the expanding scope and corresponding need to organize large amounts of information, to interconnect discrete namespaces, to provide structure for administration, and to enhance security and data management. Directories can be categorized by the structure of their namespace:

- **Flat namespaces** are those in which all objects are held below a single superior object, as if in a common container.

- **Hierarchical namespaces** provide a means to logically organize the resources in the directory to facilitate access and management, enable the distribution of information ownership, and support data management and security boundaries.

The directory naming model must support the need to uniquely identify information by name, maintain relationships between directory information, enforce information ownership, and perhaps even make a context-dependent selection from multiple names for one object. This set of tasks becomes more involved as the set of information managed by the directory grows and the organizational structure becomes more complex. Directory services can also be described by the naming model that they use:

- A **physical naming model** dictates that a directory uses actual network device names, which places a number of constraints on directory capabilities.

- A **logical naming model** uses symbolic names transparently mapped to physical device names. This naming method is flexible enough to support the needs of large, distributed directory services using abstract objects.

Directory information storage methods are determined by scale of information and operational needs such as performance, reliability, and distribution requirements. The directory information can be stored in various ways:

- A **centralized directory** holds the entire directory namespace on a single server. Copies of the directory information *may* be stored on additional servers.

- A **distributed directory** subdivides the directory namespace it holds, and multiple copies of the *subset* of directory information are spread throughout the network. These subsets are logically linked into one directory, as in NDS or AD. General-purpose X.500 directory services are designed to extend this distribution to the entire world.

When it comes to network-focused directory products, you can see that these basic characteristics tend to be combined in particular ways:

- The NetWare 2.x-3.x bindery and Windows NT 4.x domain are examples of the less-sophisticated directory approaches. Implemented in a flat namespace, directory objects directly correspond to users and physical network resources such as servers, printers, and file shares.

- More sophisticated directory designs, such as NDS and AD, use a more abstract design, with a logical naming model, hierarchical structure, and distributed information store. This provides a much more robust and scalable solution than the bindery and domain-style implementations.

As an individual vendor's directory products mature, a general progression becomes noticeable: from physical to logical naming, from flat to hierarchical organization, and from centralized to distributed information storage, as well as an increase in the scope of objects managed via the directory. This evolution is intended to provide more powerful network management capabilities, improve network performance, and provide additional fault tolerance. Yet it also leads to increased complexity and an increasingly steep learning curve for the IT professionals who must master the technology.

Although each aspect of a directory is presented here as an either-or choice, the delineations are not necessarily as absolute in practice. The Windows NT 4 domain model, for example, uses a two-tiered, but internally flat, namespace and a centralized database with copies distributed to backup servers. Keep this ambiguity in mind as the major aspects that determine the overall directory design are discussed.

Organization: From Flat to Hierarchical

Another critical aspect of the directory design is the overall structure of how the directory is logically modeled and presented. In general, directories are either *flat*, holding all network resources in one large group, or *hierarchical*, modeling the directory into a tree of some sort. The rules specified in the directory schema determine the structural characteristics of the directory namespace.

Flat namespaces, such as the NetWare 3.x bindery, display all the network resources in a single container along with the users who need access to those resources. Flat namespaces frequently contain a relatively small set of network resources and users, and were mostly used in early NOS directory implementations. Although this design can be effective for small networks, it can rapidly become unwieldy as the number of network entities that must be managed increases.

Most current directory service products employ some sort of a hierarchical model, with at least a nominal capability to model the network as a tree of containers populated with objects (resources and users). This hierarchical model of the directory information is referred to as a *Directory Information Tree* (DIT).

Directory services implemented in a hierarchical namespace must define general object categories of *container objects* (used for organization) and *leaf objects* (which represent network entities), and define rules that control how they are placed in relationship to each other.

When forming a directory into a hierarchical tree, container objects are used to logically subdivide and structure the directory. Container objects are arranged hierarchically, and may contain other container objects or leaf objects. Leaf objects represent network resources, services, users, and so on. Leaf objects cannot contain other objects, but may appear to do so because they reference other objects as attribute values, as in the case of groups (which contain a list of users as an attribute of the group object).

In network directory services, the DIT is commonly used to reflect a company's internal structure by creating container objects corresponding to business units and other corporate divisions. In a company with multiple locations connected via WAN links, it is common to design the top levels of the DIT along geographic boundaries to facilitate management and control network traffic.

Figure 2.1 shows a simple DIT for a company with two offices (one in the United States, the other in Europe). As you can see, the top layer of the DIT is divided by physical locality with business divisions contained in the appropriate geographic subdivision.

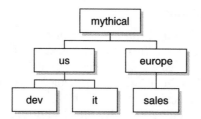

Figure 2.1   A hierarchical directory provides a treelike
structure for organizing and managing the network.

Hierarchical namespaces also provide the structure for the flow of inherited security
rights and administrative privileges. By using the DIT to model the business
organization, network administration and security control can be logically assigned and
managed within a familiar framework.

Naming: From Physical to Logical

A fundamental characteristic (and key usability factor) of a directory namespace is the
conceptual foundation on which network resources are named. The basis for object
naming is commonly divided into *physical naming models*, which use network device
names, and *logical naming models*, which use symbolic names to represent network
resources.

The implications of the naming model a directory is designed on are far reaching,
affecting far more than just how object names are assigned. A few less obvious factors
in using a particular naming model are

- **Flexibility**—A design that requires every entry to have a corresponding real-
  life object (that is, a printer or file volume) limits the overall flexibility of the
  directory.

- **Ease of use**—Logical naming models are easier to use because easy-to-remember
  names based on common language can be employed.

- **Reduction in administration**—Administration for physical naming models is
  generally more time consuming when compared to a directory using logical
  names.

- **Stability of network resources**—With a logical naming model, an object's
  name seldom changes, obviating the need to constantly update network users
  with a new device name every time a resource is relocated.

To help you understand the design and operational differences, the following sections
focus on the capabilities and contingencies of physical versus logical naming models.

Physical Naming Models

Physical naming models are based in the names of the physical devices attached to the network (commonly, server names). In a physical namespace, shared file and print resources are known and accessed by the specific server and or server/resource location.

Figure 2.2 illustrates the usage of a physical naming model. This example uses a familiar model, the *Universal Naming Convention* (UNC), used by Windows. The mars server has two printers attached, laser and inkjet, and one file share, SRC. As you can see, the printers are known on the network by the combined server and printer names: \\mars\laser and \\mars\inkjet. Similarly, the SRC file share is identified on the network as \\mars\SRC.

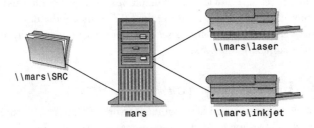

Figure 2.2   Physical naming models use actual device
names to identify resources on the network.

Clearly, with any network (irrespective of the naming model used) every user has to determine the name of each resource on the network prior to being able to access it. On a small network, with only a few resources, this may be simple—people memorize the names of the resources they use regularly, manually maintain a list, or ask the person at the next desk.

Networks using a physical naming scheme add a layer of complexity, however, in that resources are renamed when they are relocated. Therefore, network users are confronted with the requirement of relearning the location (and therefore the name) of resources whenever the resources are moved to a new network location. When the name of the network resource changes when the object is moved, it is said to be a *location-dependent name*.

Now take another look at the server from the preceding example to illustrate the primary shortcoming of location-dependent naming. In Figure 2.3, the mars server has become busy enough that the inkjet printer must be moved to another server, neptune. As you can see, this means that the printer name changes from \\mars\inkjet to \\neptune\inkjet, and every reference to that printer must be modified to reflect this change.

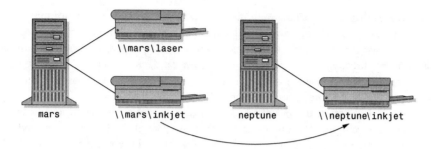

Figure 2.3   If network names are location-dependent, when a resource moves, its name changes (creating extra work for administrators and confusion for users).

Network administrators must not only ensure that network resource names are changed in *every* instance they are referenced (whether by NOS, messaging, or other system components), but must also inform network users of all changes that may affect them. Every person and application which references that printer must now be provided with the new name, and make appropriate configuration changes to reflect the current printer location. This adds considerable overhead to the administration of a large or complex network.

Many types of networks use physical naming models in their directory implementations, including the NetWare 3.x bindery, and the Windows NT 4 domain. These networks generally implement a single or multitiered namespace that is not truly hierarchical (commonly referred to as *flat*). Windows NT 4 further organizes resources into *NT domains* (which adds another tier), usually representing a subdivision of the company.

Logical Naming Models

When the scope of the directory is just the physical devices and users on a network, naming can be very simple. When the directory scope expands to more than a small object set, however, naming must be approached from a somewhat different perspective.

The naming models in more powerful directory services must contend with issues such as the following:

- Names must be delinked from physical objects so that abstract objects and information can be represented.
- Names must uniquely identify objects across broad directory namespaces.
- The directory service may need to provide numerous names for the same object depending on requestor or context.

Namespaces that use logical naming models enable you to create a relationship between a physical network device and a symbolically named directory object that represents that device. Network users can then access any network device by using the name of the directory object rather than the physical device name and/or location. The directory is responsible for transparently mapping the logical resource name to the actual physical resource for the client.

Figure 2.4 illustrates the use of a logical naming model on the same server as in the previous two examples. Because these resources are part of the Development division, the printers are now named devLaser and devInkjet, and the file share is named devSRC. These names no longer designate the physical location of the network resource; they now point to directory objects. The directory maintains the relationship between the logical name used to identify the network resource and the physical location of the resource.

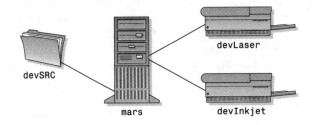

Figure 2.4   Logical naming models use symbolic
names to identify resources on the network.

One of the main advantages of using an abstract name to represent network resources is that resource names can remain unchanged, even if the physical location of resources do not. When the name of a network object remains consistent when the physical location of the resource changes, the naming model is referred to as a *location-independent model*. Location independence simplifies network management in one critical way: After a resource is named, there is seldom a need to rename it.

Figure 2.5 reexamines the process of moving a printer from one server to another. In this case, the directory entry for devInkjet is edited to reflect the new physical location of the printer. Because the name used to identify the printer on the network does not include information regarding its location, however, moving it does not affect the name by which it is known on the network.

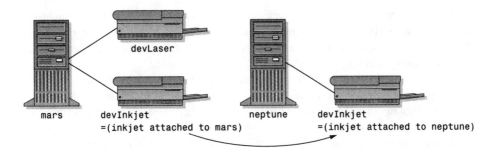

devLaser

mars   devInkjet   neptune   devInkjet
        =(inkjet attached to mars)   =(inkjet attached to neptune)

Figure 2.5   Location-independent names provide a means for network
names to remain the same, even when a resource physically moves.

This approach is clearly advantageous for network administrators and users alike. Administrators are required to change the information regarding the printer's physical location in one place only, the directory. Even better, the people and applications that access that printer need not make any configuration changes, nor even necessarily know that the printer is attached to a different server.

Logical naming models do not require a one-to-one relationship of physical resources to directory objects, a feature allowing increased flexibility through the use of objects without a real-world corollary. Because directories using a logical naming model are generally formed as a hierarchical tree, for example, container objects that have no corresponding physical objects can be created solely for structure or to create security boundaries. Other objects can be created to hold specific information, such as application settings, or to provide access to an area of administrative functionality.

Logical naming models provide greater flexibility for network administrators and easier access to resources for network clients. Logical naming models are clearly desirable in a network environment, especially when compared to using physical device names that change and require clients to adjust their resource mappings.

Clearly, physical namespaces are less advantageous than logical namespaces, require more network management, and increase the amount of information a user needs to access available network resources. Conversely, logical naming models reduce administrative overhead and simplify user location of, and access to, network resources.

Common Naming Conventions

To locate resources on the network, every network resource or entity included in a directory must have a name. One of the key factors in helping people identify network resources and their locations is the style in which network objects are named, variously referred to as the *naming convention, naming format,* or *naming model.* The naming convention is the structure that determines how objects within a directory are named.

Each directory service uses a specific naming convention, which can be thought of as a particular "style" of naming a network object. Each naming convention specifies the number and legality of characters that can be used within names, and the delimiter used to denote different parts of the name.

All objects in the directory have to be named in accordance with the specified naming model. This naming model is used consistently for all the objects within the directory. For an object to be located within a given directory, the object must have a name that conforms to the designated naming convention.

The naming convention used in a distributed network environment can make a critical difference in how easily people can identify and find network resources they need. The naming style can also make a big difference to those who have to manage and support the enterprise network environment, providing cognitive organization and logical structure to distributed network components.

Some naming conventions, notably those rooted in DNS, are nearly universally used and relatively simple to remember. Others, such as those derived from X.500, are more cognitively difficult and, although widely used, can present challenges to the people who must contend with long and complicated name strings. Recently more directory products are being designed to mask the intricacies of the naming model from the client whenever possible and to provide support for a number of naming conventions, simplifying at least one aspect of network usage.

The following section reviews the naming of network resources and users from the perspective of different naming conventions, including UNC, X.500, LDAP, HTTP, RFC 822, and DNS naming. For the purposes of this illustration, the discussion focuses on how a specific person and her computer would show up in the various directories. These examples assume that the Netmages organization has an employee named Brynna with an account in a number of different directory services and examine how she and her computer are identified using each naming convention.

X.500 Naming

Many directory implementations provide support for X.500 or X.500-style naming formats. X.500 natively uses a formalized style of designating each directory entry by type, name, and placement in the directory tree.

Each X.500 object class designates a property to serve as its *naming attribute*. For example, the Common Name property is frequently designated as the naming attribute for leaf objects. The naming attribute also supplies an abbreviation used in the name of each object; in the case of Common Name, the abbreviation is cn. The abbreviation for the naming attribute is used when forming the X.500 RDN; therefore, the name is considered *attributed* or *typed*.

Each entry in a directory tree has both a local reference called a *Relative Distinguished Name* (RDN), and a fully qualified name referred to as the *Distinguished Name* (DN). Although the RDN is not guaranteed to be unique within the directory, the DN is and thus unambiguously identifies and positions an object within the directory tree. The RDN is just the name of the object paired with the appropriate name type attribute. In this example, the RDN of the user object would be cn=brynna.

The DN of a directory entry is constructed of the object's RDN concatenated with the names of its superior objects in the path to the root of the directory tree. A DN is written starting with the root and continuing down the directory tree to the leafmost object. For a user named Brynna in the Wizards subdivision of the Netmages organization, for example, the RDN is cn=brynna, and the DN is this:

```
o=netmages,ou=wizards,cn=brynna
```

For more detailed information on X.500 naming conventions, refer to Chapter 4.

LDAP Naming

LDAP uses the X.500 naming convention referred to as typed naming, where each part of the name is delimited by commas and linked to the abbreviation for its name attribute by an equal sign (cn=brynna). An LDAP DN is written starting with the leafmost object, however, and continues up the directory tree to the root.

Therefore, although an LDAP DN appears, at first glance, highly similar to an X.500 DN, it is in fact reversed. So the user object referenced in the preceding example would look like this when referenced by an LDAP client:

```
cn=brynna,ou=wizards,o=netmages
```

RFC 2253 describes the mechanism by which X.500 names are converted to LDAP names.

LDAP URL Naming

Directory services that provide access to the directory via Web browsers can support the LDAP URL *naming model*. DNS is used in the LDAP URL resolution for the domain portion of the object's name. LDAP URLs are designed to leverage the existing DNS infrastructure as a means of locating LDAP directory servers for a particular DNS domain (defined in RFC 2255).

A LDAP URL name is constructed in the following form:

```
LDAP://host.domain.tld/path-to-object
```

To continue with the example, with the DNS domain netmages.org, the LDAP URL referencing the same object would be as follows:

```
LDAP://ldapsrvr.netmages.org/cn=brynna,ou=wizards,o=netmages
```

Spaces in X.500 Naming

X.500 names, as well as many naming forms derived from X.500 (such as LDAP), can optionally contain spaces after the comma or other separator character. Spaces are normally used only to make it easier for humans to read the object name and are stripped by the directory when processing the DN.

NDS Naming

The NDS naming model accepts a dot-delimited *typed* or *typeless* derivation of the X.500 naming model. Typeless naming does not use the name attribute, which reduces the amount of data required to specify the object. NDS names can either take the typed form of

```
cn=brynna.ou=wizards.o=netmages
```

or the typeless form

```
brynna.wizards.netmages
```

UNC Naming

The UNC common to the Windows networking platform, specifies a network server and share location, and uses a \\server\share format. To access a share named docs on a server named merlin, for example, you would use the UNC designation \\merlin\docs when connecting.

DNS Naming

Perhaps the most common naming format is that used by the DNS, which is used to locate objects on the Internet (and most other TCP/IP networks). The most basic form of the DNS name is comprised of the organization's domain name, in this case netmages.org. Specific servers (hosts) can be located on a network using DNS resolution by preceding the domain name (netmages.org) with the machine name (merlin), as shown here:

```
merlin.netmages.org
```

One advantage of DNS and other naming schemes based on it, is the widespread and increasing user familiarity with the format. Directories that support DNS names enable network administrators to leverage existing user knowledge instead of having to teach a new style of object naming.

RFC 822 Email Naming

Another style of naming familiar to most people is the email name, with a user and domain address separated by the at symbol (@) using an emailname@domain.tld format, as shown here:

```
brynna@netmages.org
```

This naming format is specified in RFC 822 and is most commonly employed in email applications. Directories supporting these email names rely on DNS for resolution of the domain portion of the name. The messaging directory service is then responsible for resolving a specific username to an email mailbox and providing delivery information.

Use of Multiple Naming Conventions

As has been shown, most networks are designed in such a way that a single user is identified by several names, depending on which location service is being used to find the user. A person can have an email address (brynna@netmages.org), another name for identification within an NDS directory (brynna.wizards.netmages), and another name used by an LDAP client:

```
LDAP://ldapsrvr.netmages.org/cn=brynna,ou=wizards,o=netmages
```

Although each of these names refers to Brynna, the format that will be successful in locating her depends on the naming support provided by the directory and client. Clearly the more naming conventions supported by a directory, the more flexible and easy to use it will be.

Storage: From Centralized to Distributed

Another distinction between directory types can be drawn based on whether the directory information is contained on a single server or whether the information can be subdivided and distributed to multiple servers across the network.

Centralized Directory Information

If all the directory information resides on a single server, the directory service can be considered *centralized*, as opposed to when the directory namespace is distributed among multiple directory servers. The scope of resources controlled by a centralized directory is usually fairly narrow, and may be restricted to the resources directly attached to the single computer containing the directory information.

One salient example of a centralized flat directory is the NetWare 3.x bindery. This early implementation of a network directory was maintained on a single server, and required the user to attach individually to every server whose resources the user needed to access.

A centralized directory, with the sole copy of the directory information contained on a single server, presents some obvious problems for the network administrator. Fault tolerance and performance are both areas deserving special attention when using such a configuration.

- A single copy of the datastore provides no fault tolerance; therefore, if the directory server becomes unavailable, operations that depend on the directory stop functioning. Networks that rely on a directory with centralized information require extra diligence on the part of the network administrator to ensure regular backups of the directory information.

- There are also performance implications when using a single copy of the directory information. This creates a situation requiring all network users to be validated from a single copy of the directory, slowing access for all users and causing delays in network and user access operations.

Of course, there are also advantages to the simple design of a centralized directory. You can be sure that there will be no data inconsistencies and there is no network traffic associated with maintenance of the directory information. This is a small benefit, however, when contrasted to the liabilities of a single copy of directory information.

A directory that uses a single copy of the directory information may provide adequate performance for small networks, but is generally inadequate for larger networks. Centralized directory services also fail to provide the kind of fault tolerance and the performance enhancements possible with a distributed directory design.

Another perspective on whether the directory information can be considered centralized versus distributed is based on whether the information contained in the DIB references resources that are attached to (or controlled by) a single server or multiple servers. The NetWare bindery holds information about one server's resources only, and is also limited to a single copy. Clearly, unless a network is extremely small, with a limited number of users, printers, and so on, this is a rather impractical method of network resource management.

Centralized and Replicated Directory Information

Some networks, such as Windows NT 4, which uses a centralized set of information, also implement one or more backup servers to provide some degree of failover and performance enhancement. When a directory database is replicated (that is, copied) to multiple network servers, each directory server can handle lookup requests for workstations on its local network, thus reducing response latency.

In the NT 4 design, a *primary domain controller* (PDC) supplies a copy of the entire *Security Accounts Manager* (SAM) database to all the *backup domain controllers* (BDCs) within the domain. The BDCs can then take care of some of the network traffic associated with requests from member users, servers, workstations, and remote domains.

The centralized and replicated directory design does provide some performance benefits, supporting more robust and responsive user authentication and access control, but only the single master database (in the case of NT, the copy on the PDC) can be added to or modified. If the PDC fails, a BDC can be manually promoted to take over the role of PDC so that full network functionality can be restored.

NT 4 domains are not implicitly integrated, however, and operate as discrete directories. Although trust relationships (allowing interdomain authentication) can be established between NT 4 domain controllers, obviating the need for each user to have an account in every domain's SAM database, administration of a large network still involves significant duplicated overhead when compared to a distributed directory. Although this is better than no redundancy or load balancing at all, it is still a far cry from meeting the needs of today's enterprise networks.

Distributed Directory Information

In X.500, the core storage location for directory data is called the *Directory Information Base* (DIB). In the X.500 directory model, the DIB is distributed across multiple directory servers, each providing localized directory lookup and authentication services.

The use of directory services allows the search for network resources to be distributed over diverse physical and logical topologies. Multiple servers in WAN and LAN environments can share the DIB as well as the lookup and administrative loads for their local network. Distributed directory services can contain many different types of information and are commonly extensible, allowing for new directory object types. The functionality of a truly distributed directory service provides the foundation for new forms of organizing and managing your network.

Most current directories are implemented in a logical object-based namespace containing a distributed database of objects structured in a hierarchical tree. Many of these implementations of distributed directory services are derived from the X.500 specification, which specifies a number of directory models delimiting the information contained in the directory and management of the directory tree. X.500 also defines the structure of the database containing the directory, the protocols and services provided, the directory search model, client and server agents, and the exposed APIs. Because it provides the foundation on which much of current directory services are built, Chapter 4 examines X.500 in depth.

Distributed directories must be designed to address a number of issues regarding multiple server operations, data consistency, fault tolerance, and performance. Partitioning and replication are two important mechanisms used to manage the subdivision and updating of the directory services database, and are discussed in the following sections. In brief, *partitioning* is the subdividing of the directory, and *replication* is the copying of partition contents to other directory servers.

Partitioning the Directory Information

A *partition* is a subdivision of the directory. All directories start out as a single partition, and the smaller ones may stay that way. However, this may not always be an adequate method of managing directory data. Current directory services can hold just about any kind of data, and some of that information may be sizeable. If you decide to have a picture of each employee as an attribute of the employee's user object, for example, and you have 5,000 employees, the DIB will quickly grow quite large.

Partitioning allows different subsets of the directory to exist on different physical computers, for security or performance reasons. Subdividing an enterprise-wide directory into organizational or geographically delineated partitions, can allow those subsections of the database to be managed by regional administrators, and provides for faster directory lookup services to regional users.

Replicating the Directory Information

In a distributed directory, the DIB can be *replicated* across multiple network servers where the contents of the DIB partitions are copied (replicated) to other directory servers. Using replicas of the DIB provides a way to distribute directory service loads across multiple servers to increase performance and improve fault tolerance.

Replication ensures directory service availability by distributing copies (replicas) of directory partitions to multiple directory servers; therefore, if one replica becomes unavailable, users and applications can still access the directory contents by querying one of the other replicas. Replication can also be used to balance network traffic and speed up directory lookups by distributing the client requests to multiple servers.

Depending on the specific implementation, there may be some limitations on network functionality when certain replicas are unavailable. If a single master replication scheme is used and the master replica becomes unavailable, for example, people should be able to log on using other replicas, but directory changes may not be possible.

A distributed directory can (in its most basic form) provide an exact duplicate of the entire DIB to each designated server on the network. This is an example of a single partition with multiple replicas.

More commonly, the directory is partitioned and then replication is performed on a per-partition basis. This allows the data in the directory to be subdivided for security or management purposes and then replicated for performance and fault tolerance.

Searching in a Distributed Directory

When the directory database is distributed, the entire directory may not be held by any one server, a situation that has implications for directory searches. A directory server can only provide information regarding the network resources that it contains or has the means to locate. This means that a directory that holds only information about a subset of resources can generally only provide support for searches within that subset of data.

When the DIB is partitioned, directory servers must be capable of resolving user queries within the scope of the partitions (directory subdivisions) contained locally or, if the data is not available locally, providing access to other directory servers to continue the search process. To provide this capability, the directory servers must be able to find other directory servers to handle requests outside the scope of the portion of the DIB managed by that server.

To provide this functionality, the following three methods are used:

- When using *chaining*, a directory server attempts to satisfy queries locally and, if necessary, passes the query to other directory servers. The results from multiple directory servers are compiled and returned to the client as if a single directory server had provided all the returned information.

- The *referral* process offloads more of the work to the client by only requiring the directory server to fulfill the request as far as possible within the directory partition it holds. After it has done so, the directory server returns the results, and the names of other directory servers to query, to the client. The client must then contact other servers to complete its directory operation.

- A single request can also be submitted to multiple directory servers at once in a process called *multicasting*. Directory servers that can provide results to the query will do so; servers that cannot will discard the request. Multicasting is not commonly used to make directory queries by most current directory service implementations.

The primary difference between these methods is which software agent is responsible for controlling the process and performing most of the work. Public service providers frequently prefer chaining because it ensures a single point of access by all clients into the directory. By contrast, corporate networks frequently prefer referrals because it offloads more of the work and control to the client process. Most directory service implementations use both chaining and referral.

Use of Directory Catalogs in Queries

Directory searches on large networks can still be time consuming even when the directory database is distributed and replicated. In an attempt to speed up directory searches, most vendors have provided some type of a catalog (or index) of network resources. A *catalog* usually holds a subset of the data contained in the directory, commonly just the basic identifying information about all objects in the directory and a pointer to the directory server holding the object.

One of the most common implementations of a directory catalog is a sort of "network white pages," referencing users and machines on the network. Catalogs can also be an index to all the objects in the directory, enabling users to conduct high-speed searches of the index so that they don't have to search the entire directory.

Directory catalogs are not without their tradeoffs, however. Catalogs that contain too much data are cumbersome and slow to search, and catalogs that do not contain adequate data to satisfy most queries fail to provide optimal performance. You should also keep in mind that directory catalogs are only as good as their last update. This means that if your directory data changes frequently and your directory updates its catalogs infrequently, searches using the catalogs may return incorrect or incomplete information.

Because many functional aspects of a distributed directory are affected by the information storage methods, the next chapter looks at those aspects in depth.

*...the petals are scattered to the wind,
yet the flower remains intact...*

3

Storing Directory Information

At its core, a directory is an information repository, and how that information is stored and managed is of critical importance. What is perhaps not quite as obvious is that the methods used for the storage and management of directory information impact many aspects of directory functionality. How effectively information is stored, retrieved, and distributed can directly impact the overall scalability, performance, and reliability of the directory.

This chapter examines how directory data is stored and managed in a distributed directory environment, and it discusses how directory information is subdivided and replicated to multiple directory servers. This chapter also examines the methods of maintaining data consistency among the distributed portions of the *Directory Information Base* (DIB).

The Directory Database

The unified collection of objects managed by the directory is stored in a database, commonly called the DIB. The DIB contains the directory objects representing users, network resources, applications, and so on along with the administrative data (such as security settings) needed to manage and control access to those objects.

The methods used in database storage and retrieval mechanisms are implementation specific and can vary widely. Because there will always be vastly more queries than updates performed on a directory, many vendors optimize the search engine and provide highly available catalogs to speed up resolution of client queries.

Some vendors, such as Novell, write proprietary database engines to meet the specific needs of their directory service. Other vendors have chosen to use a relational database as the repository for directory information.

Although the DIB is generally spoken of in the singular, it should be noted that this is only true in a logical sense—frequently more than one file makes up the DIB. A directory database may be contained in a range of storage structures, from a single file containing the DIB information, to a collection of files containing subsets of directory data with a table of pointers used to link and organize the files.

As this is described, keep in mind that right now the discussion is *not* about partitioning the directory, rather, it's about the *actual data storage mechanism*—how the information is written to disk. The description that immediately follows assumes a unified (nonpartitioned) directory.

A directory that has a specialized and small information set is more likely to use a single file than a large general-purpose directory. A quick look at two extremes will help illustrate why.

- **Single file**—At one end of the spectrum is a directory with a relatively simple and small dataset—the Domain Name System (DNS). DNS, in most implementations, stores its information in text files that are very small and consist of a small dataset that can be searched quickly. Of course, DNS has one of these text files for each zone (a zone is analogous to a partition); therefore, the *DNS directory* is made up of a distributed database of millions of these little text files.

- **Multiple files**—At the other extreme is Novell Directory Services (NDS), a more general-purpose directory that commonly contains a large amount of information of varied types. For example, you can store a graphic image as an object attribute in NDS (something that is not possible with DNS's text file approach). To support the flexibility needed by NDS, Novell has devised a storage method that uses a series of files, each containing a particular portion of the data that makes up the DIB. One file stores basic information about directory objects; a variable number of others store most of the actual property value information (that is, the data) associated with those objects.

Whatever the specifics of a particular DIB implementation, directory service designers must contend with some fundamental data management issues. Obviously, support for the distribution of the DIB must be explicitly defined for a directory to function with a distributed datastore. This support is implemented via partitioning and replication of the DIB. Concomitantly, a directory design must define a method of linking the partitions into a complete directory tree, as well as a means to pass queries and other information between partitions.

DIB replication presents other critical issues of data access and information consistency. When using multiple copies of the directory datastore, data integrity between copies of the information must be maintained. All replicas must (eventually) be updated whenever changes are made to any replica. Additionally, to maintain the consistency of the directory information, some form of data synchronization must be performed.

The next section describes partitioning, and later sections examine replication and data consistency concepts and operations.

Partitioning the Directory

The DIB can be subdivided into smaller datasets called *partitions* (described as a *naming context* in X.500). A partition is a physical subdivision of the directory database stored on and managed by a specific directory server.

A partition is implemented at the container level and consists of the container object and its associated subtree. The *partition root* is the container object at the root of the directory partition and usually names the partition. The subtree that begins at the partition root is a single partition, unless another container object within it is designated as the root of a new partition.

To help you see how all these things fit together, take look at Figure 3.1. In this example, the Mythical organization has a directory with two partitions. The first partition is named by its partition root o=mythical and managed by the Phoenix server. The second partition is ou=US and is managed by Unicorn. Phoenix and Unicorn each have operational information indicating the location of the other partition.

Even when the DIB is partitioned on many servers throughout an enterprise, the directory is still represented as a unified tree when viewed by users of directory information. This means that although the DIB is physically stored on separate directory servers, the information contained in it must be combined somehow before presenting it to the user. The directory is responsible for keeping track of where all the data is actually stored and assembling it into a single tree for presentation. Therefore, even though the DIB itself may be in many pieces spread around multiple locations, the user's view of the directory information is seamless.

Example Companies: Mythical and Netmages

This section uses two example companies: a multinational firm called the Mythical organization; and a small, single location firm called Netmages. These examples highlight directory service factors from the perspective of both the small and centralized networks, as well as the large and distributed networks.

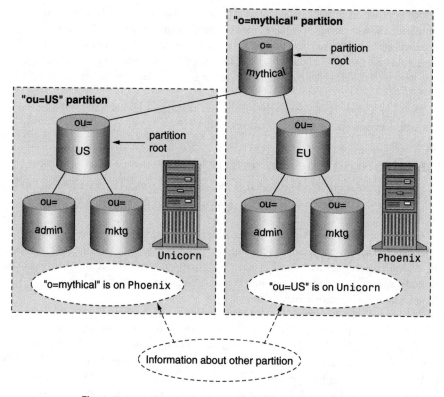

Figure 3.1   A directory tree can be divided into partitions,
each of which is a contiguous subtree of the DIT.

...of Servers and Partitions

Although it's discussed that way for simplicity, the relationship between directory servers and partitions is not necessarily one to one. In fact, it is somewhat more complicated than that. For instance:

- Copies of partitions (called *replicas*) are almost always held by more than one server for performance and fault-tolerance purposes.

- In many directory implementations, servers can hold more than one replica. This is particularly useful—if you can store replicas of multiple partitions on a single server, you can distribute adequate partitions to service requests without the expense of a separate server for each replica.

- A directory server may well have different roles in relationship to each partition it manages. A single directory server may hold the master replica of one partition, and a read-only copy of one or more others.

Managing Partitions

From an administrative perspective, partitions are created for a number of reasons. Use of partitions:

- Provides a key element in scalability by allowing the DIB to be subdivided into many parts.
- Can be used to limit replication traffic across WAN links or to any single server.
- Can divide the server load from queries to improve directory performance.

Some partitioning decisions—such as subdividing the DIB when the directory tree spans WAN links—are relatively clear, but others take considerably more thought. If you need to implement additional partitions for scalability, for example, you probably have several possible partition boundaries from which to select. Choosing the best partition design should involve identifying critical operational contingencies of both the directory and the entities that use it.

When deciding where you want to place partition boundaries, you should take some less-obvious aspects into consideration, such as the following:

- Partition constraints
- Operations across partitions

The next sections discuss each of these footers and the related implications for partition design.

Partition Constraints

You should carefully evaluate the capabilities of the directory product you are deploying, and the sort of partition design intended by the vendor, early and often in the directory design process. The partitioning approaches of various vendors differ significantly. Don't assume that partitioning will always work a particular way; it just may not. Active Directory has a rather nontraditional approach to partitioning and replication, for example, which Chapter 9, "Active Directory," explores.

A few of the clearer contingencies about how you partition your directory are based on the capabilities of a single partition or directory server. You will want to check your selected directory software for limitations, such as the following:

- Number of objects per partition
- Size of partition file(s)
- Numbers of references to subordinate (child) partitions
- Number of replicas per server
- Maximum number of replicas per partition

Operations across Partitions

You should also consider the effect of directory operations that span partitions as crossing partition boundaries slows the search process, even if the all the servers holding the partitions are on the same LAN. For every query that is not resolved in a local partition, referrals (redirecting the query to another server) are generated and additional servers must process the query, increasing search time.

The cross-partition delay is usually not significant enough to be problematic for users and applications on LANs. If the servers are separated by WAN links, however, the query has to span these links, which are the slowest connections on a network. What should be a fast request can be delayed or aborted as the request passes through slow links while being fulfilled.

In addition to the obvious example of user queries about objects that reside in a remote partition, directory operations will need to access multiple partitions at other times. Applications, and the directory itself, may perform operations that require access to the entire directory tree. If the directory is partitioned across WAN links, this process may take significant time and resources. You should assess the operations of your directory-enabled applications to make sure that, if they frequently traverse the entire tree, adequate replicas are available to support their operations without excessive network traffic.

The following section, "Partitioning Examples," provides several examples of partitioning for single-location and distributed directory implementations.

Consider Partitioning During Tree Design

When you are designing your directory tree, you should keep partitioning in mind. Because a partition can be implemented only at the container object level, you *must* design your directory tree to support your partitioning needs. Well, okay ... you don't *have to* design your tree to support your partitioning requirements—you can always *redesign* your tree to support the partitioning needs of your directory implementation. In any case, it will be helpful if you remember that the design of your tree determines where the possible boundaries of partitions fall.

Partitioning Examples

To help clarify how partitioning is used, consider the following examples of how and why a directory is partitioned. To begin with, consider the substantial differences between how partitioning is used on small networks and large networks.

- Small networks commonly start with a single partition because when the number of directory objects and replicas is small, the best performance and least administration overhead can be achieved with a single partition and minimal number of replicas. As demonstrated in the following examples, when the network grows to include more users and resources (and perhaps other physical sites), the directory can be partitioned to accommodate the changes.

- Large networks must use partitions for scalability. If the entire network is restricted to a single physical location, partitions may be devised solely based on allowable number of objects per partition or other criteria. In geographically distributed directory installations, the partitions at the top of the directory tree usually reflect WAN topology. If needed, additional partitions may be created within a geographic area for scalability reasons—those partitions are likely to reflect the enterprise organizational structure.

The following examples discuss some of the factors involved in partitioning decisions.

Limiting Objects in Partition

A directory might support a million or more objects in a single directory tree; however, the number of objects that can be stored in an individual partition is much smaller than that. Accordingly, a common reason for partitioning the DIB is to limit the number of objects per partition.

Even when a directory starts small, it is not necessarily going to stay that way. What starts out as a fairly small directory tree, with few enough objects that a single partition works fine, can outgrow that design and require additional partitions. As the directory grows, the existing partitions can be adjusted to provide the needed scalability. Next the focus turns to what happens when this occurs.

Assume, for example, that the Netmages directory has been operating with a single partition so far. Recently, the network has grown considerably, to the point that the limit on objects per partition is being approached. When this happens, a new partition must be created as a means of subdividing the DIB. Also assume that you know that the corp department in particular has been undergoing rapid growth. Because that department already has its own OU in the directory tree, adding another partition, rooted at ou=corp, should be simple. (Note the words *should be simple*; not all directory software makes it quite that easy, but it *should…*)

The directory tree in Figure 3.2 is divided into two partitions, one that starts at the root of the tree and another that begins with the corp OU. Each of these partitions is named by the container object at the partition root; therefore, they are o=netmages and ou=corp.

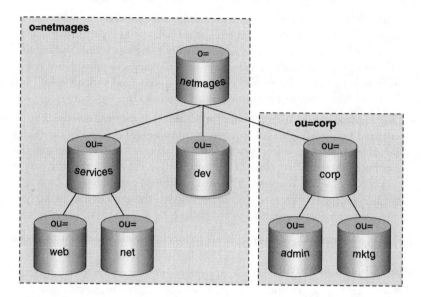

Figure 3.2   As the directory grows, partitions can be added to provide scalability.

As the directory continues to grow, the DIB can be broken into more partitions to ensure that partition limits are not exceeded and directory performance does not degrade.

The next example looks at implementation of a partition as a means of managing replication traffic (the data sent across the network to replicate directory changes).

Controlling Replication Traffic

Another reason for partitioning is to control replication traffic by restricting the distribution of directory information to locations where that data is needed. This is usually done when the directory spans multiple locations and, thus, WAN links. It may also be desirable (or necessary) on a LAN when the directory is updated frequently.

After you have determined that replication traffic needs to be controlled, more questions arise:

- Where is the replication traffic being generated?
- Who needs access to the data being updated?

If a specific department generates a considerable amount of replication traffic for information that is relevant only to that department, you may want to implement a partition to reduce network traffic.

For example, the services department of the Netmages company has decided to use a directory-enabled version of customer tracking and project management software. Accordingly, each Netmages customer has an entry in the directory that stores customer data, information related to ongoing projects, certificates used for secure communication between the customer and the development team, and so on. This is great for the people who provide services because much of their customer and project management has been moved to the directory.

However, as there is now a considerable amount of customer information stored in the directory, however, and because that information is updated frequently, it has performance implications for the network. In the case of the customer information stored in the services OU, few people outside of that division will be accessing the customer information; therefore, it doesn't make sense to replicate that information to the rest of the company. Accordingly, a partition needs to be created to segregate replication traffic.

As displayed in Figure 3.3, the tree originally shown in Figure 3.2 has now been divided into three partitions: the two that existed already (starting at the root of the tree and the corp OU) and the newly created partition rooted at ou=services.

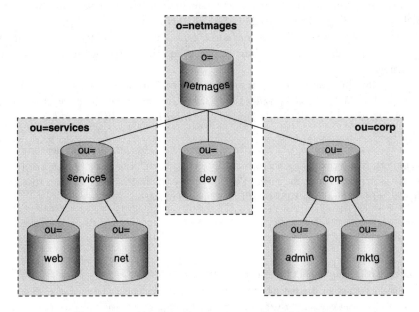

Figure 3.3   This directory tree is now divided into three
partitions to segregate replication traffic generated within ou=services.

Implementation of this partition will improve the performance of both the directory and network. The directory servers holding replicas of the `netmages` partition will not be burdened with unnecessary replication traffic for information seldom accessed by their clients. Because there will be substantially fewer updates without the information used by the services department, the server availability for client requests will also be increased. In addition, the dataset held in the `netmages` partition is now much smaller, so searches will be faster.

The next example looks at what is perhaps the most obvious reason for partitioning—WAN links.

Partitioning for a WAN

One of the most often repeated guidelines concerning partition design is "Don't span the WAN" with a partition. (In other words, don't create partitions which cross your WAN links.) This is generally a useful guideline because most administrators want to control replication traffic across slow WAN links. Because most WAN links are substantially slower than the rest of the network, the potential for replication traffic to bottleneck exists. It is probably true that, as "slow links" get faster, and vendors get more creative about replication methods, this factor will diminish—but not yet.

In many large network directory installations, partitions in the upper levels of the directory reflect the WAN topology. In this case, partitions in the lower levels of the directory might reflect company structure, such as departments. This is a common method of dividing a directory when the contents span different geographic regions. Partitions are kept physically proximate to the resources represented within them and the users who will be accessing those resources to minimize WAN traffic in service fulfillment.

To explore how directory partitioning works on a network consisting of LANs connected via WAN links, consider the example of a different company. This example uses the Mythical organization, a large multinational firm with offices on several continents.

As shown in Figure 3.4, the Mythical organization has added more sites and decided to further partition the directory tree along the same lines as the LAN/WAN border. This will restrict the bulk of the directory traffic for each partition to a single physical site, minimizing WAN traffic for both replication and lookups.

Does Partitioning Impact Directory Operations?

Optimally, users of the directory should be blissfully unaware of all this partition creation and rearranging. Some directory services require that the DIB be locked so that no other changes can be written to it during partitioning operations. This may unavoidably interrupt some directory functionality (most things that require write access to the DIB) briefly, but it won't affect most users because most of the directory use by nonadministrators requires read access only.

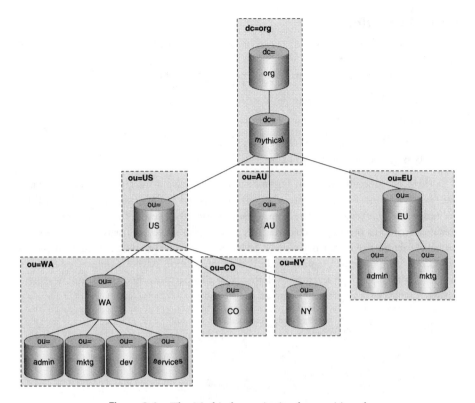

Figure 3.4   The Mythical organization has partitioned
their directory along geographic boundaries.

As you can tell, a large, geographically distributed company can have an elaborate
partitioning scheme for their directory. In addition to the first level of partitions, more
partitions could be added within a specific location if needed for scalability or other
reasons.

If you choose a partitioning scheme that breaks the DIB along WAN links, as
described in the preceding scenario, you may want to consider a couple of factors:

- If a WAN link goes down, portions of the DIB may become unavailable. To
  provide for this, you may want to place a replica of any critical partition in a
  secondary location such as a dedicated replica server in the IT department.

- The type of replica placed at each location may limit the operations that can be
  performed locally. If people frequently modify directory information from a
  particular location, you may want to place a writeable replica of the relevant
  partition(s) there to minimize referral traffic to a master replica. Of course, this
  entails additional traffic for updates, but allows for faster query responses.

Invalid Partitioning

Now that you have reviewed what can be done with partitions, take a look for just a moment at what *can't* be done with them. When creating directory partitions, you should remember that partitions have some operational limitations:

- Each object in the directory must belong to exactly one partition.
- Partition boundaries cannot overlap.
- Each partition must contain a complete, connected subtree.
- Two peer containers cannot be in the same partition without their parent.

The directory tree illustrated in Figure 3.5 does *not* have a valid partitioning scheme for several reasons. To begin with, the partition rooted at o=netmages and the partition rooted at ou=services have overlapping boundaries. As a result, the o=netmages partition contains the object ou=services, which also serves as a partition root for another partition (which can't work). In addition, ou=admin and ou=mktg are peer containers and, therefore, cannot be in the same partition without their common parent, ou=corp. (It's not even possible to name this partition because it functionally either has two partition roots, or none at all!)

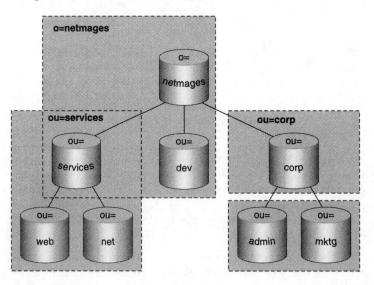

Figure 3.5   The examples shown here display two partition designs that *cannot* work in directory partitioning: overlapping partitions and peer containers without their parent.

But I Can't Do That, Can I?

Most directory software is intelligent enough that it won't actually let you create invalid partitions. However, you *should* be planning your directory long before you open the shrink-wrap and discover the functional limitations (and intelligence) of your selected directory software you should be aware of the basic rules beforehand.

Now that you have learned how the DIB is broken into smaller pieces and spread around the network, take a look at how it's linked together again. The next section discusses how objects are located when the directory is partitioned.

Name Resolution across Partitions

When the directory database has been divided into partitions, two problems present themselves:

- Multiple partitions must be logically linked together to form the complete directory tree.
- Servers holding different partitions must have a means of locating each other to communicate.

To provide the linkage necessary for both of these functions, directory servers maintain internal references to partitions whose data is not stored locally. These internal pointers to other DIB subdivisions are named differently in different models (*knowledge references* in X.500, and *name server records* in DNS), but all distributed directories have them.

When a client request exceeds the scope of the current partition (that is, the object sought is not contained in that partition), these references are used to direct the query to a directory server with the appropriate partition to fulfill the request. After the appropriate partition is found, the object is located and the desired operation is completed.

At a minimum, a partition maintains references to any partitions immediately above and below it. Additional references may be maintained for other reasons, such as directing all referral traffic to a specific server or speeding location of frequently accessed partitions by specifically maintaining references to them. Even if every directory server cannot directly locate every other directory server, the assumption is that by following a series of references, any entry in the directory can eventually be located. The process of following a series of references from partition to partition is frequently called *tree-walking*.

Knowledge Information

Although the types of knowledge information supported are implementation specific, knowledge references fall into some general categories, namely the following:

- **Superior**—The partition immediately above this one, which is used to walk *up* the tree
- **Subordinate**—The partition directly below this one, which is used to walk *down* the tree
- **Root**—The partition at the root of the Directory Information Tree (DIT), which is used to locate the tree root
- **Other**—Can be anything other than the preceding ones, which might be used to speed lookups to frequently accessed partitions, control directory referral traffic, support replication, and so on

Figure 3.6 shows the information used to link the servers holding the partitions in the Netmages tree. In this case, the directory servers maintain only the name of the immediately superior and subordinate partitions. By consulting a series of these references in sequence, any entry in the Netmages tree can be located and accessed.

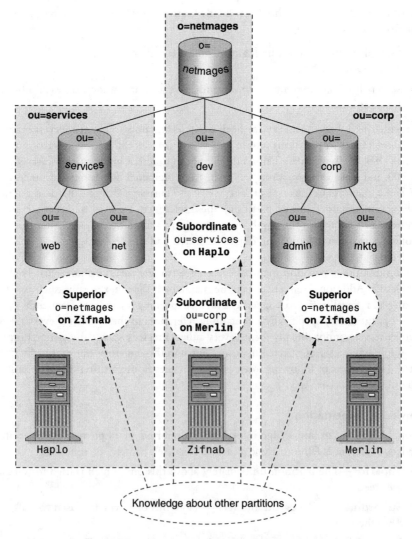

Figure 3.6 The directory stores *knowledge information*,
which is used to connect separate partitions into a single DIT.

How the directory obtains the information about servers holding other partitions varies considerably. Most directory services automate the process entirely and build the appropriate references whenever partitions are created; however, others require manual configuration of the information used in name resolution.

A knowledge reference commonly contains the following data:

- **Type of reference**—Superior, subordinate, and so on
- **Identification**—Description of the partition subtree
- **Server**—Name and address of server holding the specified partition

A single directory server may store references to multiple replicas of the same partition, each of which is stored on a different server. When servers store multiple references to a single partition, additional information may be added to the knowledge reference to support differentiation between types of partition replicas (such as master or shadow).

How Knowledge References Are Used

Now that you know that the directory contains information used to link the various partitions together into a single tree, you might be wondering how it actually works. Consider how the name resolution process is handled during a typical client query. Well, okay, *almost* typical, because the example shows a *generic* representation of the name resolution process. An actual directory service operation would likely use a different *specific* path to resolve the name and provide the results back to the client.

In this example, Natashia (who works in marketing) needs to get the phone number of Kara Stone, a customer (information stored in the `services` partition). Because Natashia is a member of the marketing team, her default directory server is in the `corp` partition. For Natashia to obtain Kara's phone number, the directory will first have to find the object representing Kara. Figure 3.7 shows the name resolution process across partitions.

User Authentication across Partitions

When directory queries span partitions, some method must be chosen to handle user authentication to the directory server holding other partitions. In general, this is handled one of two ways:

- The referring directory server passes the user's credentials to the secondary server.
- The directory client resubmits the user's credentials directly to the second server.

If you are going to be dealing with directory operations in a non-secure environment, you should see how your directory service product handles authentication across partitions. If unencrypted information is passed between directory servers, security information may be inadvertently exposed.

The following list explains what is going on during the pictured name resolution process in a bit more detail:

1. Client submits query to local (default) directory server. In this example, the query submitted is "What is Kara Stone's phone number?" The question may be "asked" in various ways, depending on the client implementation; via a form that enables you to specify query parameters and filters, or maybe even a natural language query that enables you to just *ask* the question.

2. The local directory server determines whether it holds the object, and processes the query accordingly. Natashia's default directory server, Merlin, examines the name of the referenced object (cn=Kara Stone, ou=net, ou=services, o=netmages) and determines the object is *not* contained within the local partition.

   Merlin then checks its knowledge references to determine which partitions it can locate directly. In this case, it's o=netmages.

   The query is then passed to Zifnab, the directory server holding o=netmages.

3. The next server determines whether it holds the object and processes the query accordingly.

   Zifnab examines the name of referenced object and determines the object is *not* held locally.

   Zifnab next checks its knowledge references and determines that Haplo holds the ou=services partition.

   The query is then sent to Haplo.

4. The directory server *does* hold the target object; therefore, the query is serviced and the results are returned to the client.

   Haplo, the services directory server, examines the object name and determines that it *does* hold the object in a local partition replica.

   The query is then fulfilled and Kara's phone number is returned to Natashia.

Note

Remember, this diagram denotes the logical return of the data (Kara's phone number) to the client (Natashia). The actual methods by which these processes are accomplished vary according to directory service implementation. In X.500, these methods are called *chaining*, *referrals*, and *multicasting*, and they are discussed in more detail in the "X.500 Operations" section of Chapter 4, "X.500: A Model for Directory Services."

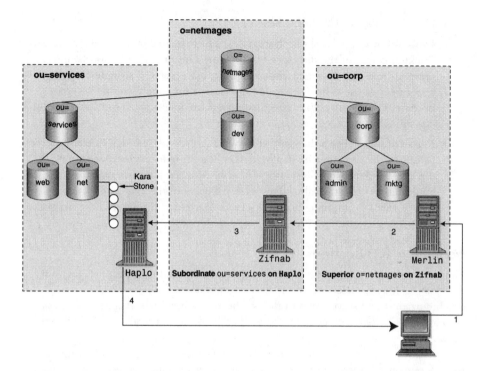

Figure 3.7   The name resolution process across partitions.

Now that you understand partitioning in some detail, it's time to switch to a related aspect of distributed storage: replication of directory data between distributed directory servers.

Directory Replication

As mentioned earlier, the DIB can be distributed to multiple directory servers to improve network responsiveness and provide the redundancy necessary for a robust directory service. These copies of the directory database are called *replicas*, and the process of creating and updating these copies is referred to as *directory replication*. Replication is performed on a per-partition basis—that is, each replica is a copy of a single partition.

Replicas provide two substantial benefits:

- **Fault tolerance**—Replication increases fault tolerance by providing secondary (backup) copies of the directory information. This provides the mechanism to prevent the entire directory from becoming inaccessible if a single directory server goes down. With a replicated directory, when one directory server becomes inaccessible, other directory servers holding replicas for that partition can still fulfill any requests.

- **Performance**—For a directory to provide fast service, enough directory servers to handle the task must be deployed. Replication reduces response latency in directory lookups and authentication services, and it increases directory availability. Replication also supports distribution of the task load for directory data retrieval to multiple directory servers distributed throughout the network.

Managing Replication

You must consider many things when determining replication approaches for your directory, such as the selection of the data to replicate, periodicity of data synchronization, and server roles in the synchronization process. Replication factors such as these can have implications for the performance and manageability of your network.

You should consider a number of replication factors in conjunction with the specific operating contingencies of the directory software and network environment. These replication factors include the following:

- Types of replicas supported
- The replication strategy
- The specific dataset and amount of data sent with each update
- The synchronization latency period (that is, the length of time it takes for changes to reach all directory servers)
- The data synchronization method employed
- The bandwidth of the network connections used for replication

One Replica of a Partition per Server

Although many directories allow a server to hold more than one replica and, therefore, more than one partition, a single server can have only one replica of any specific partition.

When managing a directory-enabled network, you may have limited options when it comes to fine-tuning replication traffic because much of the replication methodology is predetermined by the design of the directory service. Even if you cannot change a specific replication factor, however, you should be aware of the implications of the directory's replication design on your network operations. By having a thorough understanding of a particular vendor's approach, you can discover which factors can be manipulated to optimize replication in your particular environment.

The next section describes the different types of replicas you can use while working with a directory services implementation.

Types of Replicas

All replicas are *not* created equal; replica types and the operations that they support vary widely. At the most simplistic level, replicas can be divided into two types: those that can be written to, and those that cannot. In X.500, these are referred to as *masters* and *shadows*, respectively.

Although the differentiation between writeable and non-writeable is stark, in practice there are variations on each of the fundamental replica types. An examination of the different replica types will help you to better understand what functionality each provides.

What is The "Right Number" of Replicas?

In any directory service implementation, the directory processes a substantially higher number of queries in contrast to the number of changes or updates to the directory database. This means that, in almost all cases, the network traffic generated by queries will be of a much greater magnitude than replication traffic. You need to keep this ratio in mind as you plan your directory and make sure that you are placing adequate numbers of replicas to service requests promptly.

This doesn't mean that you should put a replica of every partition in your directory on every directory server. Especially when no WAN links are involved, however, you should not hesitate to put an extra replica in places where they seem useful. You can always remove them if replication traffic proves to be more of a detriment to network performance than expected.

Writeable Replicas

A *writeable replica* supports complete (or almost complete) directory functionality. A server holding a writeable replica can accept directory modifications and is responsible for replicating those changes to other servers holding a replica of that partition. Although the specific capabilities of the replicas supported by any given directory will vary somewhat, writeable replicas come in two basic flavors.

- **Master replicas** are fully functional, allowing all directory operations. Everything in the directory—objects, tree design, the schema, and so on—is updateable via a master replica. At least one master replica must exist per partition. Whether there are more writeable replicas than that depends on the directory implementation.

- **Read/write replicas** allow most operations, but they may restrict a few high-level operations such as schema modifications or tree-level changes. Read/write replicas provide additional points of administration for day-to-day directory operations. There are no requirements for read/write replicas—they are totally optional.

Non-Writeable Replicas

A *non-writeable replica* is a read-only copy of the master replica. Although there is generally no requirement for read-only replicas of any kind, their use can greatly enhance directory performance by providing additional replica servers for load-balancing purposes.

This type of replica has limitations, some of which may not be as apparent as the inability to update objects directly. If a replica is not writeable, for example, any operation that requires updating the directory cannot be performed on that server. Therefore, a directory server maintaining a non-writeable replica may perform the lookups needed for locating network resources, but not provide logon authentication because properties of the user object are updated at logon (such as workstation address).

The following few basic types of non-writeable replicas exist:

- **Read-only replicas** contain a complete partition and are frequently distributed throughout the network as needed to support directory lookups. Because, from the user's perspective, a read-only replica is indistinguishable from a writeable one, a server holding a read-only replica commonly has a way of transparently redirecting write requests to an appropriate replica.

- **Catalogs** are a read-only copy of a *subset* of directory objects and attributes; generally those properties commonly used in queries. Catalog servers usually hold a partial set of data from every directory partition, so that they can provide high-speed lookups for the entire directory. Catalogs are not considered authoritative (that is, they are not usually allowed to provide object information); they are just a high-speed index.

- **Cache replicas** are less well-defined, implementation-specific collections of directory information. Information obtained during client lookups is stored for a specified period of time and used to satisfy repeated requests for the same data.

Figure 3.8 shows the various replica types. The replica types display in a continuum of replica capability, ranging from less to more functionality and completeness of the dataset. As shown, the functionality of a replica grows as its dataset grows.

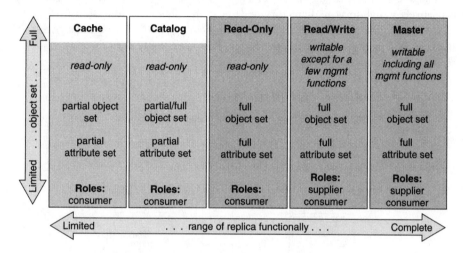

	Cache	Catalog	Read-Only	Read/Write	Master
	read-only	read-only	read-only	writable except for a few mgmt functions	writable including all mgmt functions
	partial object set	partial/full object set	full object set	full object set	full object set
	partial attribute set	partial attribute set	full attribute set	full attribute set	full attribute set
	Roles: consumer	**Roles:** consumer	**Roles:** consumer	**Roles:** supplier consumer	**Roles:** supplier consumer

Limited . . . range of replica functionally . . . Complete

Figure 3.8   The various types of replicas have different read/write status and contain different sets of directory data.

Replicas interact in different ways depending on the replication strategy used. The following section examines the different strategies used for replication.

Replication Strategies

The number, capabilities, and status of the master replicas for a directory determine how replication operates. In general, a directory supports one of these three variations:

- Single master
- Multimaster
- Floating single master

To explain the sort of functionality each of them provides, the following sections focus on the basic styles of replica design.

Single Master

Many directory vendors use a *single master* model when designing their replication strategy. This is primarily because, from a programmatic perspective, it is by far the easiest method. When a directory has a single master, data can be modified on one server only—although copies of the DIB usually reside on other servers. The directory server holding the master replica is also responsible for updating all other replicas whenever there is a change to the directory.

The directory replication process in a single master model, as shown in Figure 3.9, is relatively straightforward. Directory updates are transmitted unidirectionally from the server holding the master replica to the servers holding read-only and catalog replicas. Because those replicas do not accept changes from users (only from the master replica), they do not need to transmit any directory updates.

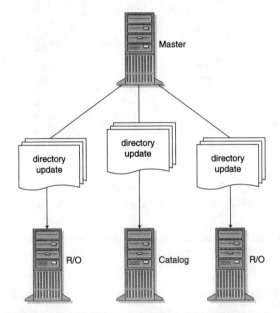

Figure 3.9   Single master replication operates in one direction, from the master to all subordinate replicas.

Single master replication is the easiest style to implement because no real data integrity issues arise—all updates come from a single supplier, so no possibility of conflict exists. This method has its drawbacks, however, primarily that this scheme requires that the master replica be available for all modifications to directory information. If the master replica becomes unavailable, directory operations will be limited until the master is brought back online or another replica is designated as the new master.

Single master replication offers a simple model for managing replication, such that the X.500 standards still define only a single master replication model. Individual vendors have overcome the obstacles raised by the single master design, however, and have independently developed a number of (highly similar) multimaster replication models, as discussed next.

Multimaster

Replication of directory information can also be implemented in a multimaster style, where more than one replica can accept changes. Use of multimaster replication ensures that non-availability of a given replica will not impede the use or administration of the network.

In multimaster replication, all writeable replicas might be considered equivalent and perform exactly the same functions, or there may be a mix of master and read/write replicas. In this model, most (or all) replicas can perform all directory functionality for that partition. Changes usually can be written to the directory on any available directory server, instead of needing access to the server holding the single master. Any server holding a writeable replica is responsible for accepting changes and propagating those changes to the other master replicas as well as any servers containing down-level replicas (such as catalog servers). Figure 3.10 shows a directory using a multimaster replication scheme with three master replicas and a catalog. As you can tell, the paths taken by directory updates have increased.

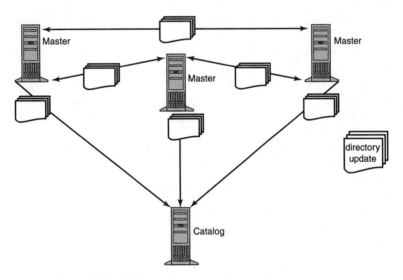

Figure 3.10   With multimaster replication, directory update traffic takes many different paths.

Of course, multimaster replication is much more complicated than single master. Because multiple writeable copies of the same information exist, some form of data synchronization must be employed to reconcile multiple updates to the same object, as discussed later in this chapter.

Floating Master

You might come across less-common variations on the single master model. The designation of the master replica may not be static, for example, but may be assigned to different directory servers as needed. This is considered a *floating master* (FM) or *floating single master* (FSM). A floating master operates exactly like a single master—just a temporary one. A directory may use a floating single master all the time, or only to provide support for a specific operation.

A directory service can compensate for loss of the server holding the master replica by allowing selection of a new master from among the existing replicas. This selection may be done automatically by providing for election of a new floating master upon failure of the current one, or it may require the network administrator to manually promote a replica to serve as the new master.

Another use of FSMs is by directories that normally use a multimaster model. When more than one replica is writeable, some operations require temporary designation of a single master to guarantee directory integrity. Operations such as schema modifications and partitioning (which change basic directory parameters) must ensure that the replica being operated on is the *only* one currently accepting any changes. Accordingly, a floating single master is designated for the duration of the operation.

Figure 3.11 demonstrates how this works. On the left side of the figure, a multimaster directory with four master replicas is shown. If an operation that requires selection of an FSM occurs, the directory will effectively switch to the operational mode shown on the right side of the figure. After the FSM determines that the operation is complete, the directory will return to the mode on the left with multiple masters.

An operation that requires the election of a single master is called a *floating single master operation* (FSMO). The FSM functions just like a single master for that period, and it is responsible for replicating changes to all appropriate servers prior to relinquishing its floating master status.

The details of how replicas exchange information are defined in the *replication agreement* established between the servers holding the two replicas, which is examined in the next section.

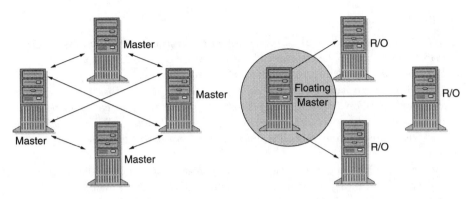

Figure 3.11   Some directory operations require
election of a temporary floating single master.

Replication Operations

For replicas to exchange information to keep the directory updated, they must first
enter into some sort of replication agreement. This agreement specifies the parameters
that will govern the replication process, including factors such as the following:

- **Roles**—The roles that each server will take during the replication processes
- **Replication dataset**—The information that is to be replicated
- **Replication schedule**—The periodicity of replication transmissions

The following sections explore these aspects of replication agreements, starting with
roles.

Roles

As mentioned during the discussion of replica types, a directory server can take the
following two roles during a replication process:

- **Supplier**—The directory server that will be sending the update
- **Consumer**—The directory server that will be receiving the update

A single replica can be a supplier, a consumer, or both (yet only one at a time).
Although a server is designated as either a supplier or consumer for a particular
replication agreement, servers can have reciprocal agreements.

   In a multimaster environment, every server holding a writeable replica of a
particular partition is likely to have a pair of replication agreements with every other
server holding a writeable replica, one for each role. The servers may transfer data in
both directions during a single replication session, or require a separate process for
each update.

   The following section explains how the dataset that will be sent during a replica
update is determined.

Replication Dataset

One of the things that directory servers must agree on prior to replication is the information set that will be transferred. This is sometimes referred to as the *unit of replication*—that is, the dataset sent with each directory update.

Of course, the primary delineation of the replication dataset is that it is the contents of a partition. Many agreements between servers will specify this as the unit of replication because most replicas need to be fully updated with all the changes to the objects in the partition. Not all replicas need the entire partition contents, however.

Consequently, although the *initial* scope of replicated data is tied to the partition boundary, some directory services provide methods of fine-tuning the dataset to be sent during replication. Filters can be established to selectively transmit updated directory information, usually based on object or attribute type. This enables an additional level of control over replication—you can determine that information will be not be replicated, even if it has changed.

Filtering replication information can be useful in several ways:

- Catalogs of directory information can be maintained for high-speed lookups.

- Replication traffic is reduced because directory information is not unnecessarily updated.

- Filtering the information available to replicas in less-secure environments can strengthen security (such as replicating only username and email address, and not salary or other sensitive data).

This means that the amount of data a server sends can vary from one replica of the same partition to another. This variance is part of what is specified in the replication agreements. For example, if an update is being sent to another master replica, every piece of updated information is likely to be sent. If the same server were sending the "same" update to a catalog server, however, the dataset sent would be greatly reduced via the use of filters.

Catalogs, which are supported by many directories, are probably the primary use of this capability. By providing an index of objects, along with a few commonly searched for attributes, catalog servers can service the name resolution needs of many lookup requests. However, this means that catalog replicas typically need to contain only a small subset of the possible attributes of any object type.

Replication Granularity

Replication granularity is a continuum—a directory server can send anything from a complete copy of the DIB to only a single attribute-value pair (an attribute and the data paired with it, such as Username=Lisa) when transmitting updates to another directory server. The amount of data sent with each directory update can significantly impact the performance of the directory and your overall network.

Of course, the catalog server could just accept a normal replica update and ignore, or discard, the extra information. By filtering data prior to replication, however, network traffic and directory update time is reduced, and the target DIB remains as small as possible, speeding responses to directory searches.

After the replication dataset has been defined, some kind of replication schedule must be arranged between the directory servers. The following sections examine the scheduling of replication.

Scheduling Replication

Most directory updates are "scheduled" to be replicated in relationship to when the change took place—that is, 15 or 30 minutes after the modification occurs. The schedule for most replication processes is predetermined by the vendor (and, thus, unchangeable); however, you may be able to customize replication scheduling somewhat.

Directory services that support differential scheduling priorities for discrete types of directory changes provide greater flexibility in directory management and help minimize the traffic caused by directory updates. A specific directory service may schedule replication based on the following:

- **The property being updated**—Different properties can be replicated according to different schedules, based on the "importance" of the information related to that property. A directory may replicate a password change immediately, for example, to ensure integrity of critical security information. In the same directory, and for the same user a change to a home phone number may not be propagated to other replicas quite as quickly as the password change. This type of prioritization provides a means of allowing rapid updates for the truly important information while not incurring too much unnecessary traffic in the DIB update process.

- **Destination of the update**—Replication across WAN links may be scheduled on a slower schedule than updates to other directory servers on the local network. This may be done to allow more time for aggregation of directory changes, minimizing the number of individual updates. Replication across WAN links may also leverage store-and-forward protocols usually used for email, such as the *Simple Mail Transfer Protocol* (SMTP), to handle replication traffic between physical sites.

Modifying Filters

Many directories allow modification of default filters, like the one used for replication to catalog servers. However, filtering is a capability that should be used carefully. Make sure that you thoroughly understand the ways that any specific directory data is used before you exclude it from being updated during replication.

You may also want to add properties to the set that is replicated to the catalog. For example, an application might need frequent access to objects not normally included in catalog replicas. Without catalog entries, every lookup of one of these objects would require referrals to another directory server just for name resolution (and, thus, increase server and bandwidth consumption). By adding these objects to the catalog, queries may be fulfilled more quickly and without unnecessary referrals to other directory servers.

After scheduling of the replication is established, another aspect to consider is the variation in the set of information transmitted during replication. The actual set of data sent will depend on whether the directory service uses complete or incremental replication, as discussed next.

Complete versus Incremental Replication

Another factor in replication is whether the directory server sends the entire contents of the unit of replication even if it has not been changed. Two basic methods are used:

- **Complete replication** sends a copy of the entire directory database, sometimes including schema information and other overhead as well as all objects, to each server with every directory update. To cut down on network traffic, updates may be scheduled infrequently, perhaps only once a day, preferably at a time when network traffic is light. Because of this, the data contained in the various replicas will generally be somewhat more "out of sync" than usual.

- **Incremental replication** sends only a subset of the DIB, containing the data that has been changed. The update information sent may be only the data that has actually changed, or a superset of the changed objects and attributes. Obviously, incremental replication is a much more efficient method of synchronization than complete replication.

As you can imagine, complete replication is a bandwidth-intensive method of transmitting directory changes. If you just add a user, for example, sending the entire DIB to every directory server will consume unnecessary network bandwidth and take longer to synchronize the DIB contents across the enterprise.

Most current directory products use incremental replication for normal operational updates and reserve the use of complete replication for special cases such as initial population of a new replica or repair of a damaged replica.

Replication Processes

As mentioned earlier, directory servers perform replication using supplier/consumer roles. It's largely the same process for most directory services with a few variations in specific behavior. In general, the replication process follows these steps:

1. The directory servers connect and authenticate. Either the supplier or the consumer may trigger this.

2. The supplier assesses what directory information needs to be updated (by an implementation-specific method).

3. The supplier then transmits data to the consumer, which updates its replica.

4. The information used in Step 2 is updated with the values that will be used in the next replication process.

The information used in Step 2 is used to ensure data consistency, and it is based on the data synchronization method used. The following section discusses data consistency.

Data Consistency

When more than one copy of a piece of information exists (as happens with a replicated partition), it is critical to ensure that the information contained in those multiple copies is the same and that they contain the correct dataset. When multiple replicas of a directory partition exist, changes made in one replica must also be made in all other replicas.

When all replicas of a partition contain the same data, the replicas are considered *synchronized* (this is also called *convergence*). Synchronization of the replicas ensures directory data consistency throughout the network.

When a directory uses a single master design, ensuring consistency when multiple users are making changes to one directory object is comparatively easy. Simply put, the server holding the master copy of the information accepts all the writes and is the sole supplier for all the update operations.

When using *multiple* writeable copies of a directory partition, however, data consistency among the different replicas on the network becomes a key issue. Clearly a method of providing updated information to all directory servers has to be addressed, while also guaranteeing the integrity of the data contained in the DIB.

Approaches to Data Consistency

Data consistency can be thought of as the degree of correlation between the directory data contained within the replicas. *Convergence* is the state achieved when the contents of the replicas are identical. Approaches to replication can be viewed by the required degree of consistency between directory servers and how quickly changed data is replicated. For a fuller understanding, consider replication from the "consistency-of-the-data" perspective, ranging from tightly consistent to loosely consistent.

Approaches that require all replicas to always have the same data are defined as *tightly consistent*—that is, all replicas of the partition are quickly updated when changes are made to any master replica. Tightly consistent replication may work in a transactional fashion, requiring that all replicas of a partition be updated before a directory modification is successfully completed. This guarantees that all the data in every replica of a partition is always exactly the same. If a single replica becomes unavailable, however, no directory updates can take place until it is once again available, or removed from the replication group.

Failed Replication Processes

Some replication processes are designed in such a way as to require the completion of replication to *every* server holding a replica of that partition before replication is considered a success. If a particular replica is not available, it could stall the replication process (for directory servers sharing that partition), possibly requiring administrative intervention to remedy the situation.

With *loosely consistent* replication, the data on all directory servers does not have to be exactly the same at any given time. Changes to the DIB are replicated more slowly and network servers gradually "catch up" to the changes made on other directory servers. Loosely consistent replication does not immediately replicate changes to other servers. Instead of sending each individual directory update, numerous small changes to the directory can be aggregated and replicated as a group. Directory services that use a loosely consistent process for most DIB updates may nonetheless use an immediate update method for certain types of data (such as data used in authentication and access control).

Most modern directory service implementations, including Active Directory and Novell Directory Services, are considered to be loosely consistent.

Synchronization Methods

In a distributed directory that allows writes to multiple replicas of a partition, the potential for conflicting updates of the same directory information always exists. The directory server must have some way of resolving these update conflicts. Where multiple changes to the same directory objects occur, the directory server must then evaluate the submitted changes and select the *correct* change to commit to the DIB.

A directory synchronization method is commonly based on one (or more) of these three approaches:

- Time of change
- Sequence number of change
- Changelog file

Defining Propagation and Synchronization

Although propagation and synchronization are often used as synonymous terms when describing directory operations, they actually refer to two distinctly different processes used to update directory replicas, as follows:

- *Propagation* is an unconfirmed process where a server unilaterally sends directory updates to other servers containing partition replicas. The servers may or may not receive the data and update their copy of the DIB; in any case, propagation does not provide a means of knowing whether the directory update completed successfully.

- In contrast, *synchronization* is a transaction-like process in which a master replica updates a subordinate replica, where a successful update must be confirmed by the other replica before the update replication is considered completed.

Interdirectory Data Synchronization

Data synchronization factors must be given serious consideration in directory implementations that support operations on multiple directories at the same time. For example, the question of synchronization between a directory that uses *Update Sequence Numbers* (USNs) for synchronization and a directory that uses time stamps can become complex and should be considered carefully before applying an enterprise-wide solution.

Time Stamps

One common method of resolving multiple updates to the same object is comparison of the time of the change to ensure that the latest change is the one written to the DIB. When a change is made to the directory, the information is marked with the time of the modification. When directory replication occurs, the time stamp of the change is checked against the time stamps of other changes to the same object or property to ensure that the latest change is written to the DIB.

In a network using time-based synchronization, all servers must share the same time, requiring the network to provide time services. Time servers may provide time to network servers, client systems, or both. The time may be based on either an arbitrary network time or external clocks representing the "actual" time. In addition, adjustments must be made for WAN networks that span time zones.

Novell Directory Services uses a time-based synchronization method, which is discussed in more depth in Chapter 8, "Novell Directory Services."

Sequence Numbers

A directory implementation may use another kind of event stamp, such as an Update Sequence Number (USN), to indicate the order of the directory changes. The directory maintains internal counters on each entry, and generates the next number in sequence when a change occurs. During the replication process, the consumer replica is provided all changes with any USN later than the last USN received.

Using sequence numbers to mark updates and synchronize directory data can be substantially more complex than using time stamps because each change must be tracked, and reconciled, on a per-server basis. Because Active Directory uses a USN-based synchronization method, it is discussed in more detail in Chapter 9.

Changelog File

Another method of updating directory information is done using a *changelog* file. A changelog is essentially just that—a file containing a log of all the changes that have been made to the directory. When a replication process is initiated, the supplier just "replays" the changelog to the consumer, effectively processing every directory update just as it was received by the supplier server.

Although this is a straightforward approach, and doesn't require the sort of extensive behind-the-scenes work of the preceding two methods, it also has the disadvantage of sending a raw list of updates. This means that if a single object has been updated multiple times, the same property may be updated several times during a single directory update. This won't generally be an issue unless you have a large network with a substantial number of replicas and frequently updated directory objects.

These preceding three chapters have covered the basics of directory services. The next chapter reviews the industry-accepted archetype of directory services, the X.500 standards.

DIB Management—Flexibility Matters!

<rant>

If serious thought has been given to the overall robustness of a directory service, flexible partitioning and replication will be seen as essential. Directories intended to meet the requirements of modern businesses must allow customization of partitioning and replication schemes. By doing so, vendors will provide the means to optimize DIB management for a particular organization.

Some directory services provide a default replication and partitioning configuration that works surprisingly well for many businesses. This is a great start; intelligent defaults are always to be hoped for. However, it is seldom that simple—networks change, business reorganizations happen, and the network directory service needs to change right along with everything else. This may mean rearranging partitioning because of changing security concerns, changing where replica servers are placed, or rearranging where specific replicas reside.

This does not mean that the actual management of the DIB must be complicated; in fact, it needs to be *easy* to configure the desired replication and partitioning scheme because errors can be costly (in terms of recovery time if nothing else). What is most critical is that a directory service design enables you to use a customized partitioning and replication scheme and that you be able to do so without an inordinate amount of hassle.

</rant>

...study closely the ancient runes...

4

X.500: A Model for Directory Services

T HE X.500 STANDARDS ARE THE BASIS FOR MUCH OF THE CURRENT development in directory services technology, so it's important to take a look at the major aspects of a directory service and its operations from the perspective of X.500. This chapter describes the X.500 standards for distributed directory services, explores the X.500 models, and examines the underlying structures and operations of an X.500 directory.

As you look at X.500, it will become clear that, for concise review purposes, some parts of the X.500 specifications are more significant (from a theoretical standpoint) than others. Because of this, some portions of the X.500 design (such as the X.500 protocols) are discussed only briefly; other areas (such as models) are covered in substantially more detail.

Introduction to X.500

The X.500 standards collectively specify the design of a distributed directory service for managing information. These standards define a global directory service that contains and manages a logical set of information which is distributed within an array of supporting servers. X.500 directories were initially proposed for an international 'white pages' to support messaging applications. X.500 was designed to provide a distributed, network-independent directory service for the messaging systems described in the X.400 specification.

X.500 is actually a set of standards, although people generally use the singular "X.500" as a reference to the entire collection. The collected specifications in the X.500 standards define the information structure of the directory service and the protocols required for access to the information contained in the directory. Table 4.1 lists the complete set of documents comprising the X.500 standards.

Table 4.1   **The X.500 Standards**

Document Number	Title	Year Introduced
X.500	The Directory: Overview of Concepts, Models, and Services	1988
X.501	Models	1988
X.509	Authentication Framework	1988
X.511	Abstract Service Definition	1988
X.518	Procedures for Distributed Operation	1988
X.519	Protocol Specifications	1988
X.520	Selected Attribute Types	1988
X.521	Selected Object Classes	1988
X.525	Replication	1993
X.530	Use of Systems Management for Administration of the Directory	1997

The X.500 standards are the common industry reference for the fundamentals of directory services, and most directory implementations derive their base taxonomy and architecture from these standards. Although the X.500 standards are the common starting point for many directory service designs and models, they are only baseline definitions allowing for different design interpretations and divergent implementations.

X.500: An Evolving Set of Standards

The X.500 standards should be considered an evolving set of specifications. They were initially developed by the *International Standards Organization* (ISO) and the *International Telecommunications Union* (ITU) in 1988, and revised in 1993 and 1997. Therefore, you will sometimes hear X.500 (or an X.500 component) referred to as *1988 X.500, 1993 X.500*, and so on—this just indicates compliance with, or reliance on, a particular revision.

Since 1988, new models have described many additional aspects of directory information and operations. Revisions have also addressed key areas of management and control of the DIB, security mechanisms for effective access control, interactions between *Directory System Agents* (DSAs), use of collective attributes, and internationalization.

X.500 directory services operate as an OSI application layer process with directory servers and clients communicating via OSI-defined protocols. X.500 relies on the following three additional OSI-defined standards:

- **Access Control Service Element (ACSE)**—X.500 uses ACSE to create and tear down associations between directory agents, essentially managing the *bind* (connect to a DSA) and *unbind* (disconnect) processes.

- **Remote Operation Service Element (ROSE)**—ROSE provides support for the request/reply style of interaction between X.500 protocols.

- **Abstract Syntax Notation One (ASN.1)**—ASN.1 defines the syntax used for storing information that will be exchanged between different systems. ASN.1 stores data in a series of type-value pairs.

X.500 describes a rich set of directory models and functionality, but a comprehensive understanding of all the details is well beyond the scope of this book. Entire books have been written on X.500—if you are going to be focusing primarily on X.500, you should buy one. If you are interested in a more comprehensive look at X.500 directory services, excellent books are available (some of which are listed in this book's Appendix, "References").

Defining a Distributed Directory Service

The X.500 models define a hierarchical directory that operates within a unified namespace and stores information in a distributed DIB. X.500 uses a structured method of naming that allows an object to be unambiguously identified and accessed.

The X.500 directory stores objects, which represent the components of the information system the directory is designed for. As X.500 was initially designed to contain a distributed 'white pages', the base object set included few objects (such as users) and attributes (such as name and telephone number) needed to provide the 'white pages' lookup functionality. In contrast, current general-purpose directory service products provide a customizable object set which can be focused on a wide range of information systems management.

Networking vendors have integrated some of the directory service functionality described in the X.500 standards, and extended the scope of objects managed by the directory to include the information needed by distributed networks and their users. In a network context, the directory would contain objects representing the logical organization of the directory (OUs, Os, and so on), as well as network resources including computers, groups, or individual users, and the corresponding network and security properties for each object. The management of network resources can then be performed via operations on the associated directory objects.

The directory is represented as a number of objects arranged in a hierarchical *Directory Information Tree* (DIT). Container objects are used to form the structure of the DIT, with objects representing network resources placed in the containers, providing access to network resources within an intuitive structure. The directory tree structure is also utilized as a framework for assignment of access rights, security permissions, and other administrative controls.

The X.500 standards specify storing the directory data in a distributed datastore called the *Directory Information Base* (DIB). This database structure allows for partitioning the directory into multiple naming contexts. The DIB is distributed across multiple directory servers, to reduce lookup latency and increase fault tolerance. The standards support a single master replication strategy.

X.500 directory services operate by using a client/server exchange between a server agent, which accesses the DIB, and an agent providing services to the network client. The server agent also provides a means for communication between server components to allow multiple physical servers to act as one logical directory.

X.500 Client/Server Agents

The directory services specified in X.500 use a client/server approach in which a client agent interacts with a server agent to perform directory operations. This architecture provides for information exchange between a network client and the directory server managing a specific portion of the directory. It also affords a method for directory servers to communicate with each other to collectively provide access to the entire directory.

Directory System Agents

An X.500 DSA is an OSI application layer process that accesses one or more naming contexts, responding to requests from directory clients and other DSAs to perform directory searches, modifications, and so on. DSAs interoperate as a system, where multiple DSAs are logically linked to transparently provide client access to the distributed directory.

The term DSA does not refer to a single protocol or piece of software, but is rather a system of services and protocols working with the portion of the DIB they manage. Most DSAs in common use support the 1993 X.500 extensions, providing enhanced management functionality (over 1988 DSAs).

Directory User Agents

A *Directory User Agent* (DUA) is the network client application that constructs and verifies queries, communicates with the requisite DSAs, and provides query results to the user or application. A DUA sees the directory as a single unit that is accessible through a local DSA and will generally use that DSA as a starting point when performing directory operations. DUAs are frequently designed to mask the intricacies of the directory from the person interacting with it, most commonly by simplifying complex X.500 names.

Some DUAs are more powerful than others and participate more actively in directory operations such as searches, allowing the DSA to return referrals back to the client for completion. A DUA can take many forms, because the term refers not to the design or user interface of the agents but to conformance with the *Directory Access Protocol* (DAP). DAP, along with the rest of the X.500 protocols, is discussed next.

X.500 Protocols

The X.500 standards specify a set of network protocols for operating the server and client aspects of the directory service. All the X.500 protocols operate at the application layer of the OSI stack. The DAP is the single protocol that provides client access to the directory; the three others support operations between DSAs.

To understand what functionality each one provides, take a brief look at each of the following X.500 protocols:

- **Directory Access Protocol (DAP)**—DAP functions as the communication channel between the client DUA and the server DSA. DAP supports a number of operations, allowing the contents of the directory to be read, searched, and modified. DAP is also responsible for managing the association between the DUA and the DSA.

- **Directory System Protocol (DSP)**—DSP supports the interaction between DSAs necessary for distributed directory operations. DSP is essentially DAP with chaining operations and is (not surprisingly) used by DSAs to chain operations to other DSAs. DSP may be configured to allow the caching of query requests and responses by the DSA, speeding lookup response time for frequently accessed directory objects.

- **Directory Operational Binding Management Protocol (DOP)** —A pair of DSAs use DOP to establish a binding agreement for use in distributed operations. These binding agreements define knowledge references and replication agreements. Each DOP entry is comprised of data including the identity of each DSA, the nature of the agreement, and additional parameters such as information governing replication (frequency, role definition, and so on). The two DSAs involved in the agreement have reciprocal DOP entries.

- **Directory Information Shadowing Protocol (DISP)**—DISP is used by a DSA to replicate a partition to another DSA. DISP is also used to transmit information during replica update operations. DSAs that are establishing an agreement to shadow the DIB must enter into a DOP agreement prior to DISP being used for actual data exchange.

Figure 4.1 illustrates how these protocols interoperate to provide directory services. The client and DSA uses DAP to communicate, and the DSAs use DSP for servicing directory requests and DISP for replication. DOP is used to form agreed upon relationships between DSAs.

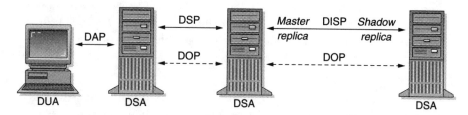

Figure 4.1   X.500 directory services use different protocols depending on which agents are communicating and why.

Application Programming Interfaces in X.500

X.500 defines *Application Programming Interface* (API) support, enabling application developers to use the directory and the directory service functionality. Two methods of access to programmatic interfaces for X.500 directory application development follow:

- XDS (Open Directory Service) was initially developed by X/Open (now the Open Software Foundation) and the XAPI Association as a programmatic interface to X.500 DSAs. XDS provides the same set of functions, arguments, and results as the X.500 DAP. The XDS API has also been used as the basis for other proprietary directory APIs such as those used by Novell Directory Services.

- The LDAP C API (specified in RFC 1823) is a low-level programming interface used in the development of directory applications written in the C language. The LDAP C API supports all DAP operations, albeit sometimes with slightly different names (such as `modify` versus `modifyEntry`).

Lightweight DAP (LDAP)

To provide a simplified access to X.500 directory services, an alternative access protocol called *Lightweight DAP (LDAP)*, was implemented as an open standard. LDAP was originally designed to support all DAP-compliant directory services operating over TCP/IP (instead of OSI-based protocols).

LDAP is gaining widespread acceptance, not only as an additional access method, but also as the *native* access method. Chapter 5, "Lightweight Directory Access Protocol," examines LDAP in detail.

X.500 Models

The X.500 standards use a number of models to describe various aspects of the directory structure and operations. Each model takes a snapshot of one dimension of the directory service, abstracting a particular layer of directory functionality to provide a distinct view of the directory's contents and operations.

The combined X.500 models describe the data structures, operations, administration, and security framework of the directory service. By examining these models one at a time, individual aspects of an X.500 directory service can be understood and then related to each other to gain a clearer picture of the overall directory functionality.

The original 1988 X.500 specification defined only the *Directory Information Model*, which deals with the most basic view of directory—that which a typical directory user sees. Since then, notably in the 1993 X.501 standard ("The Directory: Models"), a number of additional models have been defined. Some of the significant X.500 models are as follows:

- **Directory Functional Model**—Provides the "big picture" of how the directory works
- **User Information Model**—Illustrates what the directory looks like to a user
- **Operational and Administrative Information Model**—Shows what the directory looks like to an administrator
- **DSA Information Model**—Describes how DSAs interoperate to provide directory access
- **Directory Distribution Model**—Defines the rules for distributing information among DSAs
- **Directory Administrative Authority Model**—Defines how the directory is administered
- **Security Model**—Defines the authentication/access control framework

`<visualization>`

Think of the different layers of models as different colored transparencies—each layer adding its particular "hue" to the perception of the directory.

`</visualization>`

The following sections discuss these models. Keep in mind that only the most significant models are examined here—X.500 contains a number of other models, some of which explain only a single small subset of administrative detail.

Directory Functional Model

The *Directory Functional Model* states that the directory is one or more DSAs that collectively provide DUAs with access to directory information. How the DSAs interact with each other is transparent to this model—it is not concerned with the fine points of how this is accomplished, just the big picture.

Figure 4.2 shows the directory from the perspective of the Directory Functional Model. This is clearly an oversimplified view of the directory, but that is the approach of the X.500 models—dividing the directory information, administration, and operations into abstracted layers as a means of explaining them.

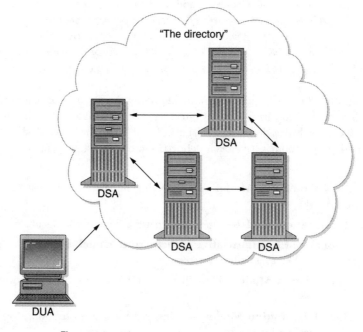

Figure 4.2 The Directory Functional Model sees the directory as a collection of servers responding to clients.

User Information Model

The *User Information Model* describes the directory as a typical directory user would see it. The entire directory tree seems to exist just as the logical representation describes it—one large tree with no boundaries. All objects in the directory can be seen and manipulated (subject to appropriate access rights), without consideration as to where the information about those objects is stored.

The User Information Model does the following:

- Determines the relationship of objects, attributes, and syntax as described by the schema.

- Defines how individual directory objects are named and how X.500 names are constructed.

The information visible by this model is referred to as *user attributes*. User attributes store the information about a directory object that is accessed and manipulated by most people using the directory. As shown in Figure 4.3, the user attributes make up only a portion of the total attribute set of any given object. This means that although a directory user can see some object information, the user is blocked from viewing administrative and operational data.

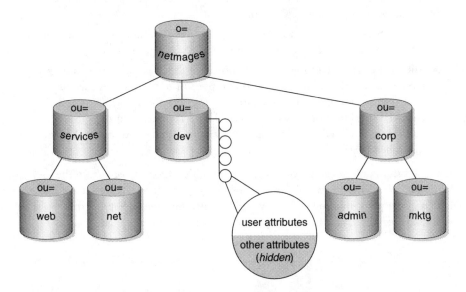

Figure 4.3   Only user attributes are visible according to the User Information Model.

The current User Information Model has replaced the former Directory Information Model. The User Information Model is one of the two models that make up the Extended Information Model, the other is the Operational and Administrative Information Model, discussed next.

Administrative and Operational Information Model

The *Administrative and Operational Information Model*, as you might guess from the name, is essentially the directory as the network administrator sees it. As in the User Information Model, the entire directory is seen as a single large DIT with no regard for actual DIB distribution. In fact, only one substantial difference exists between these two models—operational attributes and subentries are visible in the Administrative and Operational Information Model.

Take a look at what information the two additional categories of attributes provide:

- **Operational attributes** contain information used internally by the directory to keep track of directory modifications and subtree properties. Typical operational attributes would include such things as schema information, access control data, and information used in directory replication. Operational attributes are unlike user attributes in that they are not returned as part of a normal directory query, but must be specifically requested. There are three types of operational attributes:

- **Directory operational attributes** are used for operational parameters that apply to every DSA, such as access control.

- **DSA-shared operational attributes** store information used between DSAs to perform replication.

- **DSA-specific operational attributes** contain information that applies to a single DSA, such as the time of the last replica update.

- **Subentries** are used to select a subportion of the directory and define specific properties that should be applied to that portion of the DIT. A subentry contains the description of a directory subtree and the security controls, collective attributes or subschemas that should be applied to the subtree. Subtrees are defined under the Directory Administrative Authority Model (described later).

Figure 4.4 shows more of the total attribute set of the directory object. In the Administrative and Operational Information Model, operational information that was hidden in the preceding model is now visible. With the additional properties available to the directory user, management operations can now be performed.

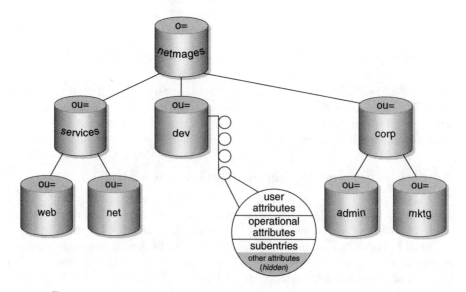

Figure 4.4   The Administrative and Operational Information Model provides access to the additional directory information required for administration.

DSA Information Model

The *DSA Information Model*, which is based on the X.518 Distribution Model, states that the directory entries should be structured into a DIT. The model also acknowledges that the contents of the DIT are held in a database that is divided into multiple naming contexts and shared among DSAs. The information contained in this model describes the DSA's location in relationship to other DSAs and how various DSAs interact to control the directory information.

The information seen by this model includes *DSA operational attributes* in addition to all the attributes viewable by the two previous information models. DSA operational attributes identify where a particular naming context fits in the directory tree. They also control interaction between DSAs during the replication process.

Knowledge Information

A DSA uses *knowledge information* to identify and describe the relationship of one DSA to another. *Knowledge references* hold references to portions of the DIB that are not contained within a local naming context. X.500 defines both mandatory and optional knowledge references.

The four mandatory knowledge references are as follows:

- The **Immediate Superior knowledge reference** contains a single pointer to the DSA holding the naming context that is the parent of the naming context held by the current DSA. Obviously, first-level DSAs will not contain an Immediate Superior reference because there is no actual root object to reference. First-level DSAs contain Subordinate references to all other first-level DSAs as a means of locating all the naming contexts subordinate to the DIT root.

- The **Subordinate reference** specifies naming contexts that are children of the naming context held by the current DSA. A Subordinate knowledge reference contains the *Relative Distinguished Name* (RDN) of the child naming context as well as the access point for the DSA holding it.

- A **Supplier reference** contains information used in replication to identify the DSA that will be providing the update, specified in the replication agreement that has been made with the supplier DSA.

- The **Consumer reference**, as you might guess, holds information on the replication consumer. This information is the reciprocal of that in the Supplier reference.

It should be noted that the Superior/Subordinate and Supplier/Consumer references occur in pairs. Figure 4.5 illustrates the relationship between the different types of knowledge references. Merlin has a Supplier reference to Zifnab; therefore Zifnab has a Consumer reference for Merlin. Likewise, Zifnab contains a Superior reference to Haplo, and Haplo has a Subordinate reference to Zifnab.

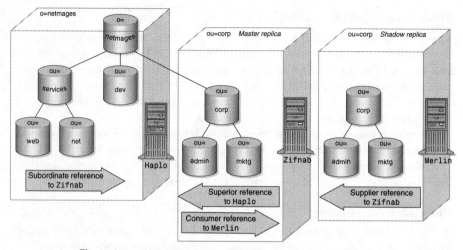

Figure 4.5 Each DSA uses knowledge references to locate other naming contexts for object location and replication.

Two additional (optional) knowledge references are defined by X.500:

- **Cross references** are used to point to another naming context that is neither superior nor subordinate to the current naming context. Cross references can be used to speed referrals to frequently accessed DSAs.

- **Non-Specific Subordinate references** (NSSRs) are a special type of subordinate reference containing the name of a DSA holding a child naming context, but not the RDN of that context. NSSRs were designed as a method of protecting the data in a subordinate naming context that is handled by another administrative authority.

DSA–Specific Entry

Each entry (object) in the directory tree is likely to be referenced by multiple DSAs. The information stored with the object in each of these DSAs will probably be at least somewhat different. To reflect this difference, the term *DSA-specific entry* (DSE) is used. Essentially, a DSE is an entry in the DIT as held by a specific DSA.

An object with its complete set of attributes, for example, will be stored by the DSA holding the naming context containing the object. Any shadow replicas will also have a copy of that object, with most of the same attribute values, except for a few DSA-specific attributes. In addition, a reference to that object with a partial set of its properties may exist in other DSAs as part of a catalog, cache replica, and so on.

The DSA Information Model describes a *DSA Information Tree*. A DSA Information Tree is comprised of the complete set of names (and associated DSEs) known by a specific DSA.

Directory Distribution Model

The *Directory Distribution Model* makes the rules controlling how directory information is shared by multiple DSAs. According to the Directory Distribution Model, a single DSA shall hold the master copy of each directory entry—the copy of the object considered authoritative. That DSA is called the *master DSA* for that entry. Correspondingly, a DSA holding a shadow copy of an object is considered the *shadow DSA* for that object.

Each DSA manages one or more naming contexts, which are collectively referred to as a *DIB fragment*—that is, the portion of the DIB that is held by a single DSA.

As shown in Figure 4.6, Haplo has a single replica, the master of o=netmages, making Haplo the *master DSA* for the entries in that naming context. The ou=corp naming context has two replicas, one held by each of the DSAs Zifnab and Merlin. Likewise, Zifnab is the master DSA for ou=corp. Merlin has two replicas, ou=corp and o=netmages, both shadows, making it the *shadow DSA* for both naming contexts. Each of the DIT fragments contained by Zifnab and Haplo consists of a single naming context, while Merlin has two naming contexts in its DIT fragment.

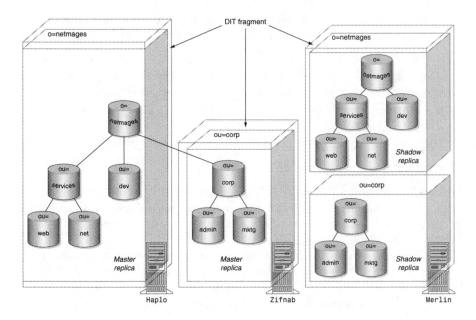

Figure 4.6   The Directory Distribution Model defines how DSAs interact to share management of directory information.

The Directory Distribution Model defines a *naming context* as a subtree of the DIT that is held on a single DSA and managed by a common Administrative Authority, which is part of the next model discussed.

Directory Administrative Authority Model

The *Directory Administrative Authority Model* acknowledges that different people or organizations will administer different parts of the directory tree. This model provides a way for the DIT to be divided into *subtrees*, management of which can then be delegated as needed.

A directory subtree starts at a container object and extends downward until another subtree definition is encountered. The subtree description can also be filtered by object type so that, for example, a subtree could consist of only the User objects within a directory subtree.

The subtrees defined within this model are as follows:

- **Autonomous Administrative Areas (AAA)** are managed by independent organizations, each of which is completely responsible for its portion of the directory tree.

- **Specific Administrative Areas (SAA)** are subtrees of autonomous administrative areas in which entries are viewed from a specific administrative perspective.

- **Inner Administrative Areas (IAA)** are defined within an organization to designate an area with delegated administrative tasks or collective attributes.

Each administrative area has a corresponding *administrative point*, which is the node (container object) at the root of the administrative area. By attaching subentries to the administrative point, different types of administrative control may be defined. The name denotes the type of administrative area it begins:

- Autonomous Administrative Point (AAP)
- Specific Administrative Point (SAP)
- Inner Administrative Point (IAP)

Figure 4.7 shows how a DIT is divided into administrative areas. In this figure, a single AAA encompasses the entire `netmages` tree. The entire tree is also defined as one SAA. Because the AAA and the SAA are congruent, the same node (`o=netmages`) is used as their respective administrative points, the AAP and SAP.

The tree also has two IAAs defined, one at `ou=services` and one at `ou=web`. The IAP for the two IAAs are at `ou=services` and `ou=web`, respectively. Unlike the SAA, IAAs can be nested inside each other, because the IAA boundary is somewhat permeable (allowing settings to cross IAA boundaries).

Administrative Areas Are Not Naming Contexts.

The boundaries of administrative areas and naming contexts do not necessarily coincide, although they may. Administrative areas describe logical zones of administrative control, but naming contexts are physical subdivisions of the DIB. Both AAAs and SAAs may span naming context boundaries, and therefore DSAs.

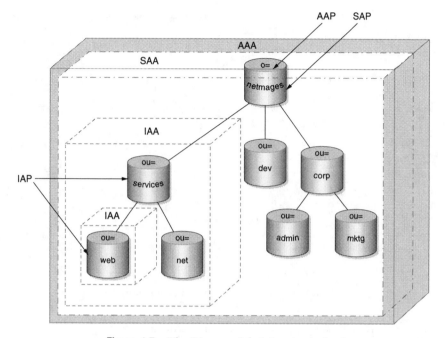

Figure 4.7 The Directory Administrative Authority
Model divides the DIT into delegable zones of authority.

When an AAA is created, three SAAs are also implicitly created, mirroring the AAA
boundary. Each type of SAA controls a single aspect of administration. A Specific
Administrative Area is defined in one of three forms:

- **Access control**—An *Access Control Specific Area* (ACSA) manages some portion
  of the security policy for this portion of the DIT.

- **Collective attributes**—A *Collective Attribute Specific Area* (CASA) administers
  those attributes applied to an entire subtree.

- **Subschema**—A *Subschema Specific Area* (SSA) defines the schema that applies to
  this portion of the DIT.

Within an AAA, there are always three SAAs—one each of the three types just listed.
The AAA may be further subdivided into additional SAAs. The boundaries of a
specific type of SAA cannot overlap. Figure 4.8 expands on the preceding example of
administrative areas by showing the individual SAAs. Where the borders of the three
different SAAs were first shown as congruent, this is not necessarily the case. Although
it is true that SAA borders cannot overlap, it is only true for the same type of SAA. As
you can see from the figure, each type of SAA can have its own set of boundaries.

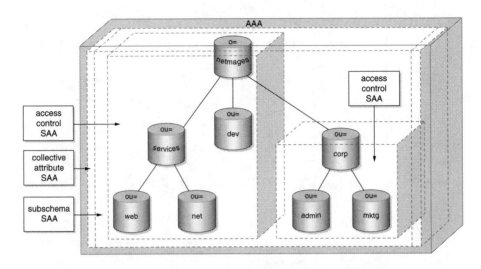

Figure 4.8 Each AAA contains three types of SAAs,
which may or may not have the same boundaries.

Later extensions to X.500 provided the following distinctions to support policy-based
management:

- A **DIT Domain** is the section of the global DIT managed by a specific
  administrative authority, referred to as the *Domain Management Organization*
  (DMO). A DIT Domain consists of one or more AAAs, which may be
  disjointed (unconnected). Policies applied to the DIT Domain apply to
  information, like those that govern subschemas.

- A **Directory Management Domain** (DMD) consists of a set of DSAs and
  DUAs administered by a specific organization. DMD policies apply to DSA
  operations and can be used to limit the operations and services provided by one
  or more DSAs.

There is a one-to-one correspondence between DMDs and DIT Domains—they are
the same things looked at from two perspectives. As shown in Figure 4.9, a DMD is
a management area concerned with the directory *operations*, while a DIT Domain
is a management area over directory *information*. Policies can be applied to each of
these management areas.

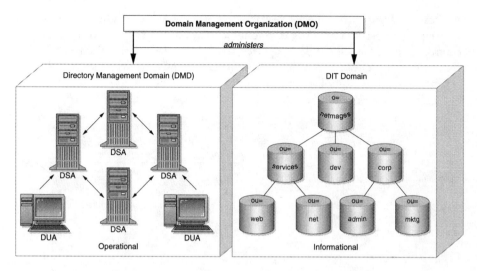

Figure 4.9 A DMO manages both the informational and operational aspects of the directory.

Security Model

Security within the X.500 framework is defined by application of the Directory Administrative Authority Model to security provision within the directory, supporting delegation of security administration. The security divisions within the directory exactly parallel the administrative divisions.

When viewing an administrative area from a security management perspective, the relationships shown in Table 4.2 apply.

Table 4.2 **Correlations Between the Security Model and the Administrative Authority Model**

Administrative Model	Security Model
Specific Administrative Area (SAA)	Access Control Specific Area (ACSA)
Inner Administrative Area (IAA)	Access Control Inner Administrative Area (ACIA)
Specific Administrative Point (SAP)	Access Control Specific Point (ACSP)
Inner Administrative Point (IAP)	Access Control Inner Point (ACIP)
Administrative Authority (AA)	Security Authority (SA)

As shown in Figure 4.10, an AAA contains one or more ACSAs that have non-overlapping borders. An ACSA is an autonomous area of security, such that access control information will not be recognized across ACSA boundaries. Each ACSA can contain one or more ACIAs, which may be nested. An ACIA provides for *partial* delegation of access control administration.

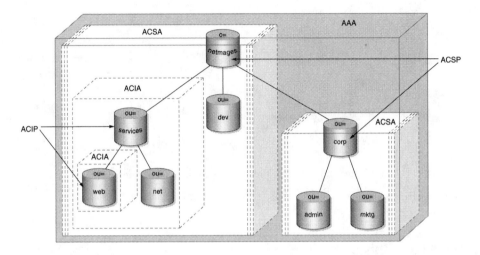

Figure 4.10   The AAA is subdivided into ACSAs, and can be subdivided into further ACIAs.

Authentication and access control mechanisms are applied within the access control area by adding a subentry to the administrative point (either ACSP or ACIP). The subentry has *access control lists* (ACLs) containing the access control polices. When determining access control for an object, the directory assesses the collection of permissions from all ACIPs above the object location *up to and including the first ACSP or AAP encountered*.

Take another look at Figure 4.10 and the two examples that follow to see how this works.

- If an object exists in ou=web, its inherited security permissions will be the combination of the *access control information* (ACI) attached to ou=web, ou=services, and o=netmages. The first two administrative points are ACIPs, which are both used in the evaluation of security information. o=netmages is the first ASCP encountered, so the collection of ACI stops at that point.

- An object in ou=admin will inherit access control information from the ACSP ou=corp only. Because the first administrative point (ou=corp) is an ASCP, the administrative point at o=netmages will *not* be included in the evaluation of security information.

An access control area can also be subdivided into sets of directory entries, in a form called a *Directory Access Control Domain* (DACD). This enables the administrator to apply security policies to a diverse set of directory objects within a subtree, by collecting them into this logical access control domain.

X.500 Directory Objects

Directory objects are commonly thought of as being limited to those objects used to represent tree structure and network entities. However, a directory service also uses many "invisible" objects for internal operations.

X.500 defines three major types of object classes, based on their purpose in the directory. Each object is constructed from one or more class definitions. The three major class categories in X.500 are as follows:

- **Abstract**—The use of abstract classes is very limited, although they are critical to the directory. There is currently one abstract class defined by the X.500 standards: top. top provides a basic set of properties used by every object in the directory.

- **Auxiliary**—Auxiliary objects are sometimes called *non-effective objects* because they are not used in the formation of directory trees. Auxiliary classes are used internally by the directory service to create the actual objects used in the formation of the tree. An auxiliary object contains a set of attributes defined to support a specific derivation of an existing object. As an example, an application vendor might add objects defining the additional properties needed by various entities using their application. The auxiliary classes can be thought of as the building blocks for structural class objects.

- **Structural**—The structural (or effective) object classes are those objects that form the directory tree and are commonly viewed and manipulated by network users and administrators. When a structural object is created, certain properties are required and must contain valid information. New directory objects cannot be created unless all mandatory attributes have valid entries. The structural classes that are generally used by all X.500 directory services can be subdivided into three major types based on their intended functionality:

  - **Container objects**—Provide structure and organization for the directory objects contained within

  - **Leaf objects**—Represent an actual entity available on (or using) the network, or other information set

  - **Alias objects**—Secondary representation of existing object which merely function as pointers to the original object

The base set of structural directory objects (and attributes) is actually rather small, a couple of dozen types of *structural* objects in all. The CCITT X.521 specification contains the object definitions of the fundamental classes, or types, of directory objects. Clearly the class definitions published in the standards consist of a rather minimal set of objects.

The X.521 object set is considered to be a base set of internationally standardized objects. The standards state that national administrative authorities and other entities are expected to implement additional object sets. Therefore, the object classes described in the base X.500 schema are not usually the entire set of objects allowed for a particular directory service. Vendors extend the X.521 object set to include all the classes needed to support the basic scope of directory operations for their implementation. Objects may also be added, or modified, by directory-enabled software, network administrators, and so on. All of this is also true of the attribute set described in X.520.

Container Objects

The *container objects* are a collection of objects that may contain other objects. In a directory, container objects are used to create and structure the hierarchical tree within the directory namespace.

The container objects were designed with fairly specific purposes in mind. Accordingly, they have different limitations on where they can reside and what kinds of objects they can contain. The container objects fall into the following classes:

- **Country (C)**—A Country object is used to organize a DIT into international subdivisions, and can be contained only within the root. Country objects are optional and are most frequently used when placing an organization in a global X.500 directory. Country designations are two-letter character codes ("us" for United States, "de" for Germany, and so on) and are defined in ISO 3166.

- **Locality (L)**—The Locality object is used to organize directory trees into geographic subdivisions, and can be contained within the Country, Locality, and Organization classes.

- **Organization (O)**—An Organization object is used to specify the top-level organizational node in the DIT, and can only be contained within the root or Country. The Organization object is the top-level object in a DIT that can contain leaf objects (users, servers, printers, and so on). An Organization object is subdivided by creating Organizational Units within it.

The Root

The root is a fictitious object; although it is referred to and treated as though it were a normal directory object, it is actually made up of entries in each of the DSAs that hold naming contexts immediately subordinate to the root. The root object is a DSA-Specific Entry in that it may be different in each of the DSAs that references it.

- **Organizational Unit (OU)**—An Organizational Unit is used to subdivide a DIT into logical administrative units, and can be contained within an Organization, Organizational Unit, or Locality object. The OU is the most commonly used container object in the directory, and is used for most logical subdivisions of the DIT.

Leaf Objects

The *leaf objects* in an X.500 directory service represent resources and entities on a network. As previously mentioned, the defined X.500 object set is small—leaf objects correspond primarily to variations on people, groups, and objects used for directory operations. But remember, in a commercial directory service product, the schema will be extended so that leaf objects correspond to a wide range of individual network elements (printers, servers, users), as well as logical groupings of resources, properties, and processes.

The following list shows the set of leaf objects defined by X.521:

- Application Entity
- Application Process
- Certification Authority
- Certification Authority-V2
- CRL Distribution Point
- Device
- DMD
- DSA
- Group of Names
- Group of Unique Names
- Organizational Person
- Organizational Role
- Person
- Residential Person
- Strong Authentication User
- User Security Information

If a Leaf Can't Contain an Object, How Can You Have a Group of Users?

Leaf objects may not contain other objects, although some, such as groups, appear to contain other objects (in this case, users). However, the users contained in that group are actually values of an attribute that holds a members list.

Aliases

An *alias* is an object that functions solely as a pointer, or reference, to another object within the directory (roughly analogous to a shortcut in Windows). An alias is placed in the directory as a reference to an existing object instead of creating a new object to represent the same resource. Aliases are particularly useful for providing multiple references to a single object.

Suppose that an enterprise wanted to make a single person from the development unit easily available to the entire corporation. As the network administrator, you might create an alias for a development contact and place it in the directory tree at an easily found location. By assigning the alias to point to a particular developer, you would ensure that everyone could use a single point of contact for development and changes to the *actual* contact would be transparent to end users.

Figure 4.11 shows a possible implementation of this idea. Brynna exists as a user in the dev OU and is also referred to by the alias devcontact in the net OU. In this example, the actual user object for Brynna is considered the *target object*. By using an alias, when Brynna is promoted, and someone else replaces her as the development contact, only the internal reference on the alias must be updated to point to the person taking on those responsibilities and the devcontact name remains unchanged.

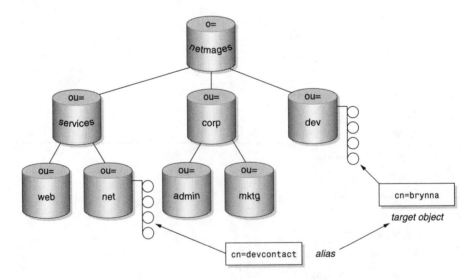

Figure 4.11 The devcontact alias object just contains
a reference to o=netmages, ou=dev, cn=brynna.

Directory Information Tree

In the X.500 specifications, the objects in the directory are organized into a DIT—the complete collection of directory objects logically represented in a hierarchical tree. A set of container objects is used to create the tree structure.

A DIT provides logical organization of the directory content for display in both management and user applications. The DIT structure can simplify the location of directory resources, especially for people using resources on large networks.

The directory access control methods use the DIT to delimit differential areas of directory security. In addition to access control, the DIT is also used for other administrative subdivisions (such as subschema or collective attribute), as well as for administrative delegation.

In a network environment, a DIT is generally structured to represent the underlying network infrastructure and/or corporate structure, as a means of organizing directory management and simplifying object location.

The Global Tree

An assumption of the original X.500 design was that a single tree would define a global namespace subdivided by nation and region. Each country would have the administrative authority for its section of the namespace, and could delegate the administrative authority on a regional, state, or organizational level.

The DIT was originally conceived from a "global directory" model, consisting of a root entity at the top of the DIT, with each country on the second level, and states on the third, as shown in Figure 4.12.

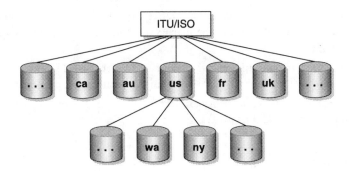

Figure 4.12   The X.500 tree was originally designed to support a global namespace.

DIT Functionality May Vary

The specific process and limitations of DIT organization are highly dependent on the vendor implementation. The functionality of DIT operations will vary among vendors and may vary among different implementations by the same vendor.

The national representatives to the ITU/ISO manage the subportions of the global DIT. These administrative authorities delegate administration of a portion of the DIT to each organization as they request a name for their enterprise.

Structuring the DIT

The directory tree is built according to the structure defined in its schema. The *structure rules* determine the relationship between objects in the directory, and how an object can be named.

Structure rules can be broken down into two major components:

- **Superior rules**—Define a set of container objects where each object can possibly reside
- **Name form**—Determines how the object is named

DIT Roles in X.500 Models

The DIT is a logical structure that provides the basis for the representation of directory information for multiple X.500 models. When you look at the DIT as viewed in each of the models, its role in the directory service operations becomes clearer:

- The DSA Information Model defines structuring directory entries into a distributed DIT with multiple naming contexts shared between DSAs.
- In the User Information Model, the DIT is used to organize and display usable objects such as printers, servers, users, and so on.
- In the Organizational and Administrative Model, the DIT display includes both the usable objects as well as the management functionality on those (and other) objects.
- In the Directory Administrative Authority Model, the DIT provides the structure used in administrative subdivisions of the directory objects.
- The Security Model describes using the DIT structure for access control subdivisions of the directory.

DIT Permissions Flow

The directory tree also provides the structure for the flow of security settings. Particular types of properties may be assigned to a container, and via inheritance, to all objects within it. When a directory object is created within a container object, it inherits the security attributes of its parent container objects.

Most directory implementations also allow for the blocking of rights inheritance at the container object level. This is usually done through an *Inherited Rights Filter* (IRF), which enables the network administrator to select which rights should not be inherited by objects in a particular container. IRFs are described in more detail later during the NDS discussion.

This inheritance of security control is enabled by the assignment of access control areas. Access control areas may be defined as a permeable (ACIA) or non-permeable (ACSA) portion of the DIT which has associated access control information. This is discussed in more detail in the "Security in X.500" section later in this chapter.

X.500 Naming

One of the more familiar naming models is the one defined in the X.500 specification and its derivatives. Many directory implementations provide support for X.500, LDAP, or other X.500-style naming formats. X.500 naming starts with a very simple premise, that each directory object has both a name assigned to it and a specific location in the DIT. By concatenating the series of object names between the specified directory object and the root of the tree, the object's *Distinguished Name* (DN) uniquely identifies each object in the DIT.

Each directory object has a name assigned by the network administrator at the time the object is created. The object name is the contents of one or more attributes designated by the class definition as its naming attribute.

Every naming attribute uses its own abbreviation in typed naming of directory objects:

- **C** = Country
- **L** = Locality
- **O** = Organization
- **OU** = Organizational Unit
- **CN** = Common Name (any leaf object)

The X.500 standards describe a naming convention in which each object in the directory has an RDN. The RDN is just the name of the object combined with the appropriate abbreviation with no additional information identifying its place in the tree (for example, cn=angela). In general, a directory may contain objects with duplicate RDNs as long as the RDN is unique within a specific container object.

Each entry in a directory tree also has a fully qualified name, referred to as the DN, which uniquely identifies and places the object within the directory tree. A DN is the comma-delimited string of RDNs starting with the object name closest to the root and continuing down the directory tree to the object. Each component of a directory object's DN is the RDN of the object it is referring to.

In the tree represented in Figure 4.13, the DN of the PR Manager named Angela is o=netmages,ou=corp,ou=mktg,cn=angela. As you can see from this example, DNs in a large tree could easily become long and confusing. For this reason, you may want to consider using short names or abbreviations as container names when feasible.

When Is a CN Not a CN?

Some directory implementations are not in exact compliance with the X.500 usage of these abbreviations. For example, Active Directory uses CN as the name type attribute for a default set of container objects.

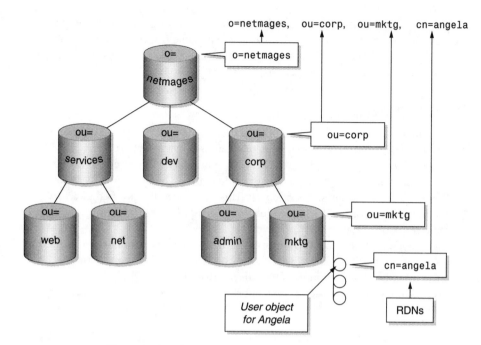

Figure 4.13   The Distinguished Name uniquely identifies
both the object and its location in the tree.

Typeless Naming

If the name type abbreviation is used when forming an X.500 name, it is considered *typed*, or *attributed* naming; whereas X.500-style names without abbreviations are considered *typeless*. The X.500 specifications do not support typeless naming, although some X.500-based derivations, such as NDS, support both typed and typeless naming. From the user's perspective, the obvious advantages of typeless names are their simplicity and "friendliness."

X.500 Directory Schema

The objects contained within an X.500 directory are specified in a set of data structures and rules called the *schema*, which defines the directory objects and their properties. The schema delimits the contents and structure of the directory service in the definitions of its objects.

The X.500 schema definition is distributed throughout the documents comprising the X.500 standards. There are system schema component definitions in X.501 describing operational attributes and other schema information in the documents defining the relevant portion of the directory.

An internationally standardized base schema for a core set of structural objects is defined in two documents:

- **X.520: Selected Attribute Types**—Defines attributes and matching rules
- **X.521: Selected Object Classes**—Defines object classes

The schema in the standards documents is meant to be supplemented by additional schemas devised by various national administrative authorities, vendors, and so on.

Most current X.500 directory products store the schema as objects in the directory. This allows the directory to dynamically accommodate schema changes, easily replicate those changes to other DSAs, as well as provide support for differing schemas in discrete directory subtrees. This is a significant improvement over earlier X.500-based directory implementations that stored the schema in a text file that was loaded when the DSA was initialized. In this configuration, the schema was generally static until the DSA was shut down and restarted.

The X.500 directory schema has three major components that link together to form the internal structure of the objects in a directory tree. The three components of the directory schema are as follows:

- The *classes* are the set of objects allowed within the directory.
- The *attributes* of each object class are the set of properties allowed by that class of object.
- The *attribute syntax* determines syntactical constraints of the attribute and matching rules.

These components follow rules, which are used to constrain the contents of the directory objects and allow their appropriate placement in the directory tree.

- *Content rules* define the attributes each object class contains. These rules are governed by the contents of the `Must Contain` and `May Contain` fields of the object class definition.
- *Structure rules* define the logical tree structure of the directory and determine where objects can reside and how they are named. These rules are governed by the contents of the `Superior Rules` and `Name Form` fields.

In many directory implementations, only one directory schema is allowed to exist per tree. As noted in the section on X.500 models, however, the 1993 extensions to X.500 define subtrees as a method to attach differing schemas to some portions of the DIT. LDAP also supports this method of attaching subschemas. This is particularly useful, at least theoretically, as a means of facilitating data exchange between directories with different schemas.

Object Class Definitions

Object class definitions specify which objects can appear in the directory tree, what information is required to create the object, and how those objects work in relationship to other objects in the directory. Every object in the directory belongs to one class, and each class has *superclasses*. Superclasses serve as a means of adding template-like sets of properties to objects within the directory.

An object is defined via a set of subdefinitions, which are linked to provide the complete object description. The components used to define an object class are as follows:

- **Object class**—Defines the attributes the object must or may contain, as well as *kind* and *subclass* information
- **Name form**—Designates which attributes are used for naming
- **Structure rules**—Determines the name form and superior rules

This information works to define each object, its possible placement in the directory tree, and its purpose in the directory. The following complete object definition is examined in more depth to clarify how the subdefinitions work together to form the directory objects and constrain how the objects can be formed into a tree:

- **Object identifier**—Each object type has an *object identifier* (OID) that uniquely identifies the object class.
- **Kind of object**—The 1993 standards added a designation of the *kind* of object the class is defining: structural, auxiliary or abstract.
- **Name form**—The name form defines the allowable RDN values for a specific structural object class. Name form definitions contain at least one attribute whose value is used to form the RDN of a directory entry. A name form may also contain the names of additional attributes whose values may optionally be used to form a multi-valued RDN.
- **Superior rules**—The superior rules define the possible structure of the directory tree, by delimiting which container objects can hold a specific object class. The superior rules list for a specific object is the list of containers the objects may be created within.

- **Mandatory attributes**—As you can imagine, the mandatory attributes of an object must have values assigned to them at the time of object creation. Mandatory attributes, listed in the Must Contain field, must be maintained for the life of the object for the object to be recognized by the directory. If an object loses a mandatory attribute, it becomes an unknown object and must be re-created. Most objects have only a few mandatory properties that are used for critical functionality (such as the attribute used for naming).

- **Optional attributes**—Optional attributes are those properties for which values may be assigned, but which are not required for object creation. The May Contain field of the object class definition lists the optional attributes. Many directory objects have a large number of optional attributes that are used to track information about the object that, although useful, are not required for the object to function correctly.

- **Superclasses**—Superclasses act as building blocks for directory objects by providing logical sets of properties to add to an object definition. An object is comprised of the information contained in the definition of the object class, and the definitions of its superclasses (and their superclasses, and so on). For example, all objects have top as a superclass, either directly or via inheritance from another super class. Superclasses are denoted in the schema as entries in the Subclass Of attribute.

Objects have a hierarchy, in that they go from more general to more specific. Therefore the person object contains attributes common to all persons (surname, for example); organizationalPerson contains information specific to a person within a business context (such as title).

As shown in Figure 4.14, the organizationalPerson object is constructed from the combined definitions of the top, person and organizationalPerson objects. The person object is also used as a superclass of the residentialPerson object and contains the attributes needed for all objects representing persons.

You may notice that rather than solely specifying individual attributes, the organizationalPerson definition lists several attribute sets (LocaleAttributeSet, PostalAttributeSet, and so on). These sets provide a convenient way of adding a collection of attributes to an object class, and are discussed in more detail in the following section.

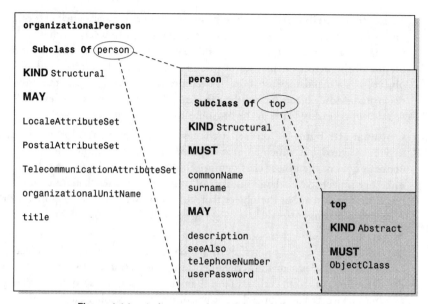

Figure 4.14   A directory object is built from the collected definitions of the object class and all the object's superclasses.

Attribute Definitions

An *attribute definition* in the directory schema specifies the structure (as opposed to the content) of an attribute. Each property (or attribute) that can be assigned to an object in the directory must first be defined in the schema. The attribute definition includes the attribute syntax and any constraints placed on the attribute, such as whether it is limited to a single value.

Each attribute has a particular syntax that constrains the data type of values entered into it and defines how the attribute value is processed. The matching rules used when comparing values are defined by the attribute definition.

Attributes have a `Subtype Of` field, which operates a lot like the object `Subclass Of` field. An attribute's super type provides portions of the attribute definition, usually the acceptable syntax and matching rules.

Useful Attribute Sets

X.500 designates several collections of attributes as *useful attribute sets*. These sets are designed to provide a way of quickly adding a logical collection of attributes, providing support for a particular functionality, to an object. As you saw in the illustration of how the `organizationalPerson` object class is built (Figure 4.14), the attribute sets make it easier to define a new structural object class.

There are four such sets of attributes:

- **Telecommunication attribute set**—Defines a set of attributes containing information used for business communications.

- **Postal attribute set**—Provides a set of attributes related to the physical delivery of mail.
- **Locale attribute set**—This attribute set identifies a location geographically.
- **Organizational attribute set**—Contains attributes an organization typically possesses. This attribute set includes properties such as passwords as well as the three previously defined attribute sets.

Attribute Syntax Definitions

The *attribute syntax* defines how the attribute value is constrained by data type and syntax limits set within the schema. Attributes which are of the same syntax type can be compared for ordering, equality, and substring matches. The attribute syntax is defined in two parts—ASN.1 syntax and matching rules.

Although a directory schema will usually be extensible, the syntax list is often fixed when the base schema is developed. This means that although you can add new object types and extend existing objects by adding new attribute types to them, you may not be able to define a new type of syntax for the values contained within that attribute. If a wide variety of attribute syntaxes are already defined, however, this constraint may not be problematic.

Extending the Schema

X.500 directory schemas are easily extensible, allowing the integration of new objects and attributes into the directory as needed. The method used to extend the directory schema varies with the specific directory service implementation, yet most commercial directory implementations provide some sort of tool(s) used for schema extension.

Many directory-enabled applications will modify the schema as part of the installation process. This provides a method for implementation of specific objects to support extended application functionality.

Directory administrators who need to customize existing objects can also perform schema modifications. This is a powerful capability because it provides a way to directly customize the directory contents to support new directory functionality.

Removing Objects from the Schema

It is important to remember that removal of a class definition from the directory schema can have substantial consequences. Removing the class definition of an object that has been added to the schema, for example, will turn objects of that class currently in the directory into unknown objects. This would have substantial ramifications for the performance of applications that rely on those objects, a factor which should be considered prior to removing schema extensions or restoring the original schema.

Note that certain directory repair operations can return the schema to its default configuration. In such a case, objects that belong to classes added via extensions to the basic schema will appear as unknown objects.

Directory Information Base

X.500 specifies the structuring of the directory data into a distributed DIB, which provides for replication of the directory datastore to reduce lookup latency and increase fault tolerance.

X.500 doesn't specify back-end storage methods, so many different approaches are used by vendors. In its simplest form, the DIB can be stored as sequential ASN.1 entries in a text file. On the other end of the spectrum, however, using a relational database (such as Oracle) for directory storage is not uncommon.

Naming Context

A *naming context* (*partition*) is a portion of the DIB that is stored and managed by a specific DSA. A naming context is a subtree of the directory with the metadata used by the DSA to place the naming context within the DIT. Multiple naming contexts are linked together to form a large directory tree, managed collectively by multiple DSAs.

The complete contents of a naming context are as follows:

- The *subtree* of the directory containing the entries managed by this DSA.
- The *context prefix* identifying the placement of this naming context in the tree.
- The *superior reference* identifying the DSA holding the parent naming context.
- The *subordinate reference(s)* pointing to any naming contexts that are children of this one.
- *Cross references* are optional for any naming context.
- *Supplier/consumer references*, which are used for replication.

Root Context

There is no actual directory object representing the root of an X.500 directory tree—the root is a fictional node. Still, the directory must store information concerning the root of the directory tree to support name resolution and communication between DSAs at the top of the tree.

This information is held in the *root context*, which is not an actual directory object but rather a logical construct referring to the entries immediately subordinate to the root of the directory tree. These entries, which refer to one or more naming contexts, may be held by a single DSA or, frequently, distributed across multiple DSAs.

DSAs that hold naming contexts immediately subordinate to the root of the tree store cross references to peer-level DSAs rather than a superior reference to the nonexistent tree root. By using these cross references during the referral process, DSAs can locate entries held by other naming contexts. DSAs are not required to have a cross reference entry for every peer-level naming context; however, all naming contexts must be reachable via a series of cross references within the root context.

Replication in X.500

As discussed in previous chapters, *replication* is the copying of all or portions of the DIB to another DSA; synchronization, on the other hand, is the process of keeping the contents of the DIB consistent.

This section briefly examines how X.500 approaches directory replication and synchronization, and is discussed from the organizing perspective of replication used in Chapter 3, "Storing Directory Information." This chapter also summarizes each key point of how X.500 defines replication. For more information on directory replication and synchronization, refer to Chapter 3.

Replica Types

Replication for X.500-based directory services is explained in X.525, which describes the types of replicas and replication operations (referred to as *shadowing*).

- **Master**—The master replica in X.500 is referred to as the *master DSA*, which contains the writeable master copy of the data held within the naming context.

- **Shadow**—A shadow is a read-only copy of the naming context held by the master DSA. Only Read, List, Search, and Compare operations can be performed on a shadow.

- **Cache**—Although X.525 describes caching, caching is considered beyond the scope of X.525, and it does not attempt to supply a definition.

Each replica contains the naming context of a specific master DSA.

Replication Strategy

X.500 defines a replication mechanism called *shadowing*, which operates on a single master model. Shadowing in X.500 uses a single master DSA that has administrative authority for the naming context and replicates changes to shadow DSAs. A shadow DSA is a read-only replica of the naming context held by the master DSA.

Replication Operations

The two forms of shadowing are called *primary* and *secondary* shadowing. As shown in Figure 4.15, *primary shadowing* is where the shadow consumer gets data directly from the master DSA. In *secondary shadowing*, a shadow consumer becomes a shadow supplier for other shadow consumers. In secondary shadowing, instead of receiving updates via the master DSA, the update comes from another shadow.

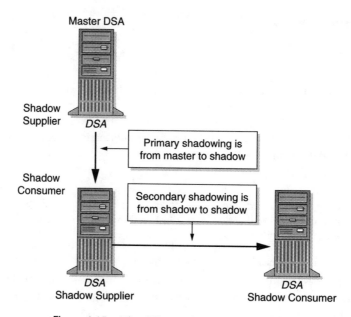

Figure 4.15 The difference between primary and
secondary shadowing is the source of the data.

The key aspects of how X.525 defines replication can be viewed in the following
summary:

- **Replication agreement**—Before shadowing can occur, a shadowing
  agreement must be established between DSAs. The shadow operational binding
  defines the DSA roles, and a shadowing agreement defines the update mode
  and unit of replication.

- **Roles**—Shadowing always operates between two specific DSAs who are
  assuming reciprocal shadowing roles, where a DSA is either a *shadow supplier* or a
  shadow consumer.

- **Replication dataset**—The replication dataset is derived by factoring the
  specified scope of the DIT to replicate, and the attributes selected for
  replication.

- **Scheduling replication**—The update mode specified in the shadowing
  agreement defines the update scheduling which sets the periodicity of the
  update refresh.

- **Total versus incremental**—X.500 defines two methods of supplying shadow
  updates. *Total refresh* is where all the contents of the naming context are copied
  from the shadow supplier to the shadow consumer. *Incremental refresh* is where
  only the contents of the naming context that have changed are copied.

- **Replication processes**—The X.525 specification describes both "push" and "pull" replication operations. Push replication is where the shadow supplier initiates the update to the shadow consumer. Pull replication is where the shadow consumer initiates the update.
- **Data consistency**—X.500 uses time stamps on directory changes for synchronization of directory updates.

X.500 Operations

In the X.500 models for directory services, operations revolve around DSAs that handle client queries and perform search operations on behalf of clients (and other DSAs). Core operations include authentication, object location, object manipulation, and searching the directory. In addition to the basic set of operations, directory operations can be enhanced to allow for further directory functionality using service controls and extensions.

Binding and Authentication Operations

For a DUA to communicate with a DSA, they first have to agree to talk. A `DirectoryBind` operation (commonly called a `Bind`) is used to establish an association between a DUA and a DSA.

The `DirectoryBind` establishes an application-layer association between a DUA and a DSA, and is also used to perform authentication. Authentication can be done using simple or strong authentication (as per X.509), or via an external mechanism. To end the association, the DUA sends a `DirectoryUnbind` message to the DSA.

In addition to `DirectoryBind`, the `Compare` operation also has been used in authentication, by comparing the stored value of a particular attribute to a client-provided value. The intended use of `Compare` was as a mechanism for verifying passwords without retrieving the data.

Object Name Resolution

Every directory operation must start by locating the object or objects which are the focus of the operation. In a distributed directory, DSAs work together to determine the location of any object in the directory. This object location process is referred to as name resolution.

The methods used by a DSA to provide name resolution include *chaining, referral, and multicasting*. The primary difference between these methods is which software agent is responsible for performing most of the work and verifying completion of the task. Both DUAs and DSAs should support all three modes of agent interaction, with the default being the referral style. DUAs may request a particular mode of operation, which can be accepted by the DSA or rejected in favor of the DSAs selected mode.

Chaining

When a DUA submits a query to the local DSA, it can request that the query be processed using chaining. A chaining request tells the DSA to provide the DUA with a complete response to the query rather than referrals for the DUA to pursue. If the server does not support chaining, it will override the client request and handle the request using the referral process.

In the *chaining* process, after a query has been submitted to a DSA, it attempts to satisfy the query locally and, if necessary, passes the query to other DSAs. This process will be repeated by each receiving DSA until the entire scope of the directory operation has been explored and a definitive result for the originating query is obtained. The query may pass through many servers, collecting data at each one, before being able to access the entire scope of the directory query. At that point, the last DSA in the chain returns the query results back through the chain of DSAs to the originating DSA, which forwards them on to the DUA.

Chaining includes a mechanism to allow compilation of data from multiple sources, deletion of duplicate data, and transparent delivery of the results to the client. The results from multiple DSAs are compiled and returned to the DUA as if one DSA had provided all the returned data.

As shown in Figure 4.16, the chaining process is commonly conducted by a DSA on behalf of the DUA, and occurs in a sequence of directory operations.

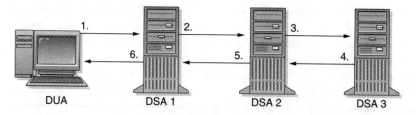

Figure 4.16   During the chaining process in query resolution, the DUA requests the DSA to return definitive results from all available DSAs.

The process is as follows:

1. The DUA sends a query to DSA 1.

2. DSA 1 doesn't have the object or the entire scope of the query, and sends the query to DSA 2.

3. DSA 2 also does not have the object or the entire scope, and sends the query to DSA 3.

4. DSA 3 completes the scope of the query, results are compiled, and returned to DSA 2.

5. DSA 2 compiles cumulative DSA results, and returns the results to DSA 1.

6. DSA 1 compiles cumulative DSA results, and returns the results to DUA.

Referrals

Referrals are a more efficient mechanism that requires the client to perform most of the work involved in a search and frees up the DSA to service other client requests.

When a DSA cannot fulfill a query, it can provide referrals to other DSAs. With referrals, after a DSA has attempted to fulfill a request from its portion of the DIB, it will return any results to the client. If the DSA cannot complete the request locally, it will also provide locations (or "hints" about possible locations) of other DSAs that may be able to fulfill the request. The client is then responsible for contacting other DSAs to satisfy the directory request, as the DSA will not try to contact the other DSAs for the DUA (see Figure 4.17).

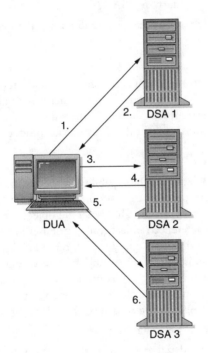

Figure 4.17 The referral process requests data that the DSA has available, yet does not request the DSA to pursue query resolution beyond the scope of the naming contexts held locally.

As shown in Figure 4.17, the referral process occurs in the following sequence:

1. A DUA submits a query to DSA 1.

2. DSA 1 first tries to resolve the query within the local naming context. If the query can be resolved via the naming context held on DSA 1, the server returns the requested data. This example assumes that the query cannot be resolved locally, and that DSA 1 returns data (partial answers) as well as a reference to the closest relevant DSAs (that is, DSA 2). The DUA would then use these DSAs to pursue the query.

3. The DUA sends the query to the DSA 2.

4. DSA 2 tries to resolve the query locally (and would return the results if available). Again, this example assumes that the query is not resolved locally, and again DSA 2 may return data and reference to the other DSAs (that is, DSA 3).

5. The DUA sends the query to DSA 3.

6. DSA 3 successfully resolves the query and returns the query results to the DUA.

Multicasting

Multicasting is where a network client simultaneously sends information to multiple servers. DUAs using multicasting submit a single query to multiple DSAs at the same time. DSAs that can provide results do so; all others discard the query. Multicasting is not commonly used by most current directory service products.

Dereferencing Aliases

One aspect of X.500 operations is the capability to specify special handling options for aliases as part of the query process. An alias object is a pointer to another object located elsewhere in the directory. An alias is *not* the object it represents, and does not contain attributes of the referenced object (only attributes of the alias itself).

Sometimes, however, a directory query must locate the *aliased object* itself (not the alias). *Dereferencing* an alias is a process whereby the directory goes to the underlying object to which the alias is referring and continues the operation from there. The indication of whether to dereference aliases is specified as part of the query (if the operation supports it). Dereferencing is used by the following operations:

- **Read**—Aliases are always dereferenced.

- **List**—Aliases are not dereferenced by default, but can be on user request.

- **Search**—Aliases are not dereferenced by default, but can be on user request.

No other DAP operations support dereferencing, and as a result, you can perform actions such as Add and Remove on the alias itself.

An example alias, and how it might be processed during a search, should make this a bit clearer. This example uses the devcontact alias described earlier to demonstrate how the dereferencing process works. If a search that includes the devcontact object within its scope is requested, the DSA will handle the search operation differently depending on whether dereferencing is requested by the client.

In Figure 4.18, a DUA has requested a search of the entire DIT for all objects with a name starting with the letter *B*. The `devcontact` alias does not meet the search criteria, but the target object `brynna` does.

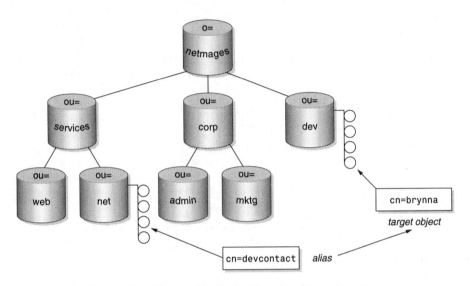

Figure 4.18   The actual information returned in response to a directory query varies depending on how aliases are handled.

Depending on whether the client requests alias dereferencing, one of two things will happen:

- If the object is *not* dereferenced during the search, the alias object `cn=devcontact` will be examined during the search. Because the alias name starts with *d*, it will not be returned as part of the search results.

- If the object *is* dereferenced during the search, the alias will be examined, and the referenced object name is retrieved. The referenced object is then examined, and the information returned will refer to the aliased object `cn=brynna`. In this case, the object does match the search criteria and will be included in the query results.

Directory Access Operations

A set of operations can be performed on directory objects, including searching, adding, deleting, modifying, as well as other operations. DAP provides most of the commonly used directory operations.

Table 4.3 displays the DAP operations for accessing directory objects.

Table 4.3 **Directory Access Operations**

Operation	What This Operation Does
Read	Reads information from a single directory entry, and enables you to specify a range of attributes to be returned.
List	Lists the contents of a single container (all subordinate entries). List is analogous to a dir command in MS-DOS or ls in UNIX.
AddEntry	Creates a new directory object in the selected container. The object must meet schema restrictions to be created.
ModifyEntry	Changes the value of one or more attributes of a single directory entry. Attribute values may be added, deleted, or replaced by this function. The ModifyEntry operation is atomic, in that if all changes are not successfully completed, none of the changes are applied.
RemoveEntry	Deletes a single directory object, either a leaf or an *empty* container. Subtrees can not be deleted using this operation.
ModifyRDN	Changes the RDN of an object.
Search	Searches can be performed on a single directory entry, a single container and its contents, or an entire subtree. Additional information contained in the search query defines the treatment of aliases and filters.
Abandon	Used in conjunction with other object operations to signal query termination. Abandon is sent by a client to tell the DSA to stop servicing an outstanding request, and can only be sent for operations that may involve multiple DSAs—Read, List, and Search. A DSA receiving an Abandon request ensures that no results are returned to the DUA. Abandon terminates a *single* operation only and does not close the association between the DSA and DUA.

Mechanisms in X.500 provide support for per-query constraints on operations called *service controls*, as well as *extensions* to the base set of operations. This capability may be used for directory enhancements ranging from special handling of query results to security measures. Service controls and extensions are invoked with parameters attached to the original DAP request.

A *service control* is a method of specifying constraining information for a single query. Service controls can be used to specify preferred modes of functionality or restrictions on how the DSA handles a particular request. Some of the things service controls indicate are as follows:

- Selection of chaining or referrals
- Alias-handling preference

- Limits on time allowed for query completion
- Limitations on amount of data to be returned

Extensions allow the use of arguments to support new operations, and may be defined by either vendor or specification. Extensions rely on a pre-arranged agreement between the communicating directory components on the set of new operations, along with the methods used to invoke the functionality. Extensions can be designated as critical or noncritical by using the *criticality subcomponent*. If a request contains a critical extension unknown to the server, the query is not processed and an error code is returned to the client.

Security in X.500

Specifications for X.500 security models and operations are defined in multiple documents, most notably the X.500 and X.509 specifications.

In the X.500 security design, the directory is both a security provider as well as a user of the security services. As a security provider, the directory provides authentication and access control services to applications and other network services. As a user of the security services, the directory uses authentication and access control over its objects.

Security on network resources and directory objects can be assigned on a very granular basis. Security descriptors can be assigned to an object and will remain with the object even if it is moved or renamed, which allows a high degree of flexibility in security administration.

As discussed earlier, in X.500 the Directory Administrative Authority Model is applied to security provision within the directory, where the DIT is divided into security divisions that directly parallel the administrative divisions. When viewed from a security management perspective:

- Each ACSA is an autonomous area of security, where access control data doesn't cross ACSA boundaries. An ACSA can be subdivided into multiple discrete ACSAs. The root of an ACSA is an ACSP.
- An ACIA can be nested inside of an ACSA, providing for delegation of access control administration, and each ACIA can each contain nested ACIAs within itself.
- The *security authority* is the specific administrative authority for the area.
- A DACD is an access control area subdivided by sets of directory entries.

Authentication and access control mechanisms are applied within the ASCA or ACIA. The access control policies that will be applied are contained in access control lists, which are subentries attached to the administrative point. The access by a DUA to any specific directory object is controlled by the entire set of permissions specified in the chain of superior ACIPs, up to and including the first ACSP or AAP.

Authentication

Before a directory can allow a user to access or manipulate an object, it needs to validate the user's identity. The directory uses the *authentication* process, which is the set of operations that verify the user identification.

The X.509 specification documents a framework for authentication in a directory service and defines three security services: *simple authentication, strong authentication, and digital signatures.*

Both simple and strong methods of user authentication provide the basic functionality of authenticating the user to the directory. The following sections discuss these in more detail. First, however, it's important to describe the basic differences between the cryptographic approaches used in the authentication methods.

Approaches to Cryptography

X.509 describes both symmetric and asymmetric cryptographic methods used in the authentication process. Although the simple authentication does provide basic user identification, the symmetric cryptographic methods used are not considered secure. X.509 is clearly focused on the use of asymmetric public key cryptographic methods and certificates for strong authentication.

- **Symmetric cryptography**—With *symmetric* (also called *shared-secret* or *private-key*) cryptography, the sender and receiver share the same key. In symmetric cryptography, the user provides the secret key that is stored and used to authenticate that user in subsequent processes.

- **Asymmetric cryptography**—*Asymmetric* (or *public-key*) cryptography uses pairs of keys (public/private) to encrypt information. *Permutability* is a property of some asymmetric encryption methods, where either key in the pair can be used to encrypt the message contents, and the other key can be used to decrypt the contents.

Simple Authentication

In the simple authentication process, the directory uses clear text names and passwords to verify the identity of its users. Simple authentication may use Bind or Compare operations, in which the submitted name and password are checked against the directory contents, but the name and password are not encrypted. Simple authentication processes are characterized by DSAs that store DN/password pairs, and DUAs that transfer username and password in clear text. There are two derivations of simple authentication:

- **Protected password**—Protected password authentication transfers the name in clear text, but the password is encrypted via a one-way hash function.

- **Mutual authentication**—Both the simple and protected password methods involve a one-way authentication process where the DUA authenticates to the DSA. In mutual authentication, the DSA returns its credentials with the results of the DUA's authentication request, and is also authenticated by the client. This ensures that the client can trust the DSA.

Strong Authentication

Strong authentication uses *public-key* (PK) cryptography to produce security credentials, providing controlled access to the directory. Because it uses PK encryption, strong authentication is considered far more secure for transmission of sensitive data.

Public keys are stored in the directory so as to be accessible to applications, users, and directory operations. For users to access other public keys, the DUA must trust the DSA providing the public key. Strong authentication uses a point-to-point scheme utilizing a chain of trust between DSAs. An example of a chain of trust is where a DUA trusts a specific DSA (DSA 1), and that DSA trusts another DSA (DSA 2), and as a result the DUA will trust DSA 2.

Authentication takes place when an association between DSA and DUA is established. In strong authentication, the user credentials are established via the user's public key, using one of three different methods:

- **One-way exchange**—The sender provides explicit validation, but only implicitly validates the receiver.
- **Two-way exchange**—This is the same as a one-way exchange, but the receiver sends a reply token back explicitly confirming the identity of the receiver.
- **Three-way exchange**—In addition to the two-way communication, a third exchange is used for synchronization between the DUA and DSA.

Although X.509 does not specify an encryption algorithm, it does require permutable public-key encryption algorithms be used. An example is the RSA algorithm (named after Rivest, Shamir, and Adleman, 1978).

Access Control

In addition to verifying the identity of the directory user, you also need to be able to control access to directory elements based on that identification. *Access control* mechanisms are used to provide differential levels of access to directory objects and operations, and directory data is available only when a DUA has access permissions. The initial X.500 specifications described two models for providing this differential access control:

- **Basic access control**—X.500 specifies a basic access control model that delimits entry access and attribute access permissions, and the use of these permissions to control categories of directory operations (such as Add, Read, and so on). Application of permissions is segregated via access control administrative areas.

- **Simplified access control**—Simplified access control is functionally a subset of the basic access control scheme. Simplified access control does not support ACIAs.

In addition to these two forms of access control, later revisions of the X.500 specifications include a *rules-based* access control model. The rules-based model focuses on the access control decisions and regulates directory access via user clearances and security labels on directory objects. Rules-based access control applies rules of the security policy, denying or granting access based on congruency between security labels and clearance. The rules-based model determines access control by comparing the security labels and clearance values in the access control decisions of each operation.

Basic Access Control Model

The *basic access control* (BAC) model describes mechanisms for controlling access to the contents of the directory. The BAC model defines a set of access control components and categories of access types.

The initial X.500 specifications defined *access control schemes* for managing access to directory information. An access control scheme is set as an operational attribute, and defines the procedures to specify the access control information and to manage access control operations. The BAC model specifies access control information controlling user access to protected items in the directory via assigned object permissions.

- **Objects to be protected**—A *protected item* is any directory element that can be individually controlled (that is, names, entries, attributes, and values).

- **Access control information**—The *access control information* (ACI) is the data stored with each protected item in the directory and is used to determine which users are granted access, and what kind of access is granted. *ACI items* are the operational attributes that collectively control access to protected items in the directory. All ACI items have a range of priority called *precedence*, where higher-precedent ACIs overrule lower-precedent ACIs. Each ACI item also has an *authentication level* value indicating the type of DUA authentication required. A group of ACI items implemented as a set is known as a *security policy*.

- **Distinct classes of users**—*User classes* are used to distinguish different categories of directory users, and the DUA which is initiating the operation is termed the *requestor*.

- **Permissions to access objects**—*Permissions* can be thought of as the right to complete an operation, and are stored with directory objects as ACI items. Permissions are divided into categories by type of access (*entry* or *attribute*) and are applied to directory elements to control access. An ACL contains sets of ACI items used to specify the user classes and types of access to provide a directory object. Because directory operations need to make programmatic access control decisions regarding protected items, the *Access Control Decision Function* (ACDF) is the algorithm used to determine access. The access control decisions are processed by the ACDF algorithm, which determines whether to *grant* or *deny* access based on the content of the ACI items of both the object and client.

Access Control Permissions

In this model, access control types are subdivided into *entry access* and *attribute access* categories:

- **Entry access**—Entry access is when the access to the directory entry is as a named object.
- **Attribute access**—Attribute access is when the access is to the attributes, or to the attribute values (containing operational and/or user data).

The two categories of permissions correspond to their related forms of access control, *entry access permissions* and *attribute access permissions.* In the BAC model, access to the directory information is regulated by the DSA granting or denying permissions to the requested object. Access to data in the directory is effectively controlled by the permissions assigned to the directory entry or attribute, and the permissions of the requestor attempting to access it.

Entry Access Permissions

The following entry access permissions apply to objects (entries) within the directory, as shown in Table 4.4.

Table 4.4 **Entry Access Permissions**

Permissions	These Permissions Allow
Read	Read access to specifically named objects
Browse	Access to operations using non-explicit names
Add	Creation of a new directory object
Remove	Removal of a directory object
Modify	The contents of an object to be changed
Rename	The renaming of a directory object
Disclose on Error	The object name to be disclosed upon error
Export	An object to be moved out of the present location to a new location in the directory
Import	An object (and subordinates) in another location to be moved into the present location
ReturnDN	The DN to be returned as the result of a directory operation

Access Control Constraints Vary

Not all directory operations share the same access control constraints. For example, some directory operations require that all access control decisions succeed for the operation to succeed. In contrast, other directory operations do not require that all access control decisions be successful for the operation to be completed.

Attribute and Value Access Permissions

Table 4.5 shows the attribute access permissions that apply to attributes and values within the directory.

Table 4.5 **Attribute and Value Access Permissions**

Permissions	These Permissions Allow
Compare	Operations to be compared to the values or attributes the permissions are applied to
Read	Values or attributes to be provided in search or read operations
FilterMatch	Filter processing with applied search parameters
Add	Creation of a new attribute (for attributes), or allows the creation of a new value (for values)
Remove	Removal of an attribute or value
Disclose on Error	Attribute or value to be disclosed upon error

Access Control Precedence

ACI items are evaluated based on precedence, where higher-precedence ACI items override lower-precedence ACI items. This effectively allows a "weighted value" to be assigned to each ACI item, providing a method to implement an access rights hierarchy.

The precedence of ACI items is a value between 0 and 255 that is applied to all ACI items. This allows ACI items to be evaluated along an axis of precedence. In brief, the rules of precedence are as follows:

- High-precedence ACI items override lower-precedence ACI items.
- If multiple ACI items have the same precedence, but dissonant access permissions (granted and denied), denied access overrides granted access.

Digital Signatures

Digital signatures are a means to verify that transmitted information was validly received, and to confirm the identity of the sender. A digital signature is essentially a summary of the data produced by a one-way hash function encrypted with the sender's public key.

Digital signatures provide the following functionality:

- **Message integrity**—Ensures that the data didn't change in transmission (via comparison of hash values)
- **Message authentication**—Verifies the source of the data (via the public key)

A quick review of the basics of how digital signatures are created might help you to better understand them. The phrases "signing the data" and the data is "signed" refer to the process of creating an encrypted summation of the specific set of data and appending the encrypted value to the data. The data is signed in the following three-step process:

1. Data is hashed (mathematically represented).
2. Hash value is encrypted with the sender's public key.
3. Encrypted hash is appended to the data.

The encrypted hash value is referred to as the *digital signature*. The sender and receiver agree upon the specific hash algorithm prior to transmission.

Next, it's important to briefly examine how a digital signature is used to verify message contents and authentication. Digital signatures are used to validate the integrity of the transmission of the data across the network. Note that this ensures data integrity only (that is, proving that the data is unchanged); it does not encrypt or protect the data during transmission.

The following process describes the common steps of how a digital signature is used:

1. The data (unencrypted) and the digital signature are transmitted.
2. The data and signature are received and separated.
3. The digital signature is unencrypted using the sender's public key, and the hash algorithm is determined.
4. The receiver re-hashes the (unencrypted) data.
5. The receiver compares its generated hash value to the hash value transmitted by the sender.
6. If hash values are the same, the message is considered authenticated; otherwise, the data is rejected.

X.509 Certificates

The X.509 standards define certificates based on PK technology, also referred to as *asymmetric cryptography*. To encrypt and decrypt data, PK (or asymmetric) cryptography uses a key pair comprised of a published *public key* and a secret *private key*. Key pairs are implemented in such a way that any messages encoded with either key may be decoded only by the other key.

The certified public keys are contained in certificates. A *certificate* is essentially a collection of data that associates the public key of a network user with their DN in the directory, and is stored within the directory as an attribute of their user object. A certificate serves as validated identification to the directory.

Directory services use certificates to provide client authentication, where the identity of the network client is established by examining the certificate provided. This provides bilateral authentication—the directory provides validation while receiving the client validation. When authentication is performed, DAP is used to access the directory to obtain the public key certificates, and DSP is used to access certificate data when communicating with another DSA to complete the authentication.

In a public key encryption methodology, the user works with a *Certificate Authority* (CA) to create a certificate that validates the user's private and public keys. The CA is used to generate and validate CA certificates, user certificates, as well as server certificates. For more information on certificates or CAs, check out the VeriSign site at: www.verisign.com

...leveraging is the sincerest form of flattery...

5

Lightweight Directory Access Protocol

ALTHOUGH X.500 PROVIDED THE MOST WIDELY ADOPTED directory service model, the access protocol defined by the X.500 standards has not been as widely implemented. Notably, the X.500 *Directory Access Protocol* (DAP) has been supplemented, and in some cases replaced, by the *Lightweight Directory Access Protocol* (LDAP). LDAP has become the access protocol of choice for many directory vendors and has accelerated directory interoperability efforts.

This chapter examines LDAP in some detail. This chapter relies on information contained in Chapter 4, "X.500: A Model for Directory Services," and assumes an understanding of the general structure and operations of X.500. If you're not familiar with X.500, you may want to read Chapter 4 before reading this chapter.

Introduction to LDAP

LDAP is a dedicated client access protocol for communicating with a directory and viewing or manipulating the objects contained within the directory. LDAP was designed as a simplified subset of the X.500 DAP to provide basic access to X.500-based directories. LDAP was targeted at management and browser applications that provide interactive access to directories. LDAP can be implemented as a protocol to access most X.500 directories or as a standalone server.

A key goal of the initial LDAP design was to minimize the complexity of the access protocol in order to encourage widespread implementation of directory-enabled applications. As such, it succeeded admirably.

LDAP is now considered the leading directory access protocol and has been adopted as an open standard for directory services. Most vendors offering directory services have released, or announced plans for, directory products that support LDAP. Among vendors supporting LDAP v.3 are Microsoft, Novell, Netscape, and Sun.

You should keep in mind that the LDAP specification is contained within a series of *Request for Comments* (RFC) documents. Some portions of the LDAP specifications are mandatory for implementation; others are recommended or totally optional.

RFCs are first written as drafts, and then enter an open review process during which different people advocate for divergent versions of the proposed RFC. Most directory vendors are represented in the LDAP working groups that are continuing work on LDAP. As you can imagine, this means that although quite a bit of agreement occurs among vendors as to core aspects of LDAP, it is still a little less "standardized" than some standards. Novell is working on one set of LDAP replication methods, for example, and Microsoft is working on another; they may both be accepted as standards. Therefore, although both vendors would comply with "LDAP standards," the standards they comply with would still differ.

Features of LDAP

Although the X.500 specifications defined a powerful data model and protocols to support a robust directory, the original DAP described in the X.500 specifications has had somewhat limited acceptance. LDAP has been designed to compensate for the perceived disadvantages of DAP while leveraging the strengths of the overall X.500 directory design.

Low Overhead Protocol

The X.500 specified DAP operates at the application layer level of the *Open System Interconnect* (OSI) stack, mandating a considerable amount of processing for each interaction between the directory client and the DSA. By comparison, LDAP maps its messages directly onto the TCP byte stream, bypassing much of the handling required by DAP (newer versions of DAP also map directly to TCP). In addition, *Connectionless LDAP* (CLDAP) has been defined to provide some of the functionality of LDAP over a connectionless protocol, in this case UDP.

TCP/IP Based

The X.500 design was focused on the directory service being comprised of many Directory System Agents (DSAs), connected via OSI-defined networking protocols. With the explosion of Internet usage and the concurrent demand for TCP/IP support in almost every networking environment, the TCP/IP protocol has emerged as the clear enterprise networking protocol of choice.

The decision to design LDAP predicated on using TCP/IP has proven to be a wise one. Most networks run the TCP/IP protocol stack, if not because it is required by the network operating system, then at least for Internet connectivity purposes. Because of LDAP's dependency on TCP/IP, LDAP will operate only on networks employing TCP/IP as a protocol.

Uses DNS for Global Namespace

Another assumption of X.500 was the establishment of a widely accepted and utilized global namespace. The worldwide X.500 directory tree requires an assigned authority to manage the top level of the tree, both within each country and internationally. Although some companies currently using X.500-based directories choose to have a corporate presence registered in the worldwide X.500 tree, not all have chosen to do so.

Yet, there is currently a worldwide namespace in widespread use and supported on virtually every platform: the *Domain Name System* (DNS). Again, the designers of LDAP have made a wise decision to employ widely implemented Internet technologies and have begun to define methods by which LDAP can use DNS. This allows LDAP to leverage the worldwide use of DNS as the top layer of its directories, obviating the need for an additional set of registrars and namespaces.

Two primary LDAP and DNS integration methodologies are proposed:

- A DNS service (SRV) record entry provides a way of locating LDAP servers. This allows clients to query their local DNS server as a means of locating an LDAP directory server.

- LDAP is also incorporating DNS name components as part of LDAP names. This means that the DNS domain "`mythical.org`" could be given an LDAP name of "`dc=mythical, dc=org`" ensuring congruence between an organization's directory tree naming structure and the DNS domain name.

Because these are not a part of the initial LDAP v.3 specifications, it is important to note that all vendors will not necessarily support all the DNS/LDAP integration proposals. The integration of DNS and LDAP is discussed in more depth in the LDAP naming section of this chapter.

Widely Accepted APIs

LDAP provides APIs that are easy for programmers to write to and are widely supported by vendors. The need for a widely accepted API was initially addressed with the adoption of the LDAP C API (RFC 1823). RFC 1823 defines a simple method of interacting with an LDAP directory using the C programming language. Since then, several more APIs have been proposed either as an open standard, or via proprietary methods. The LDAP Programming section of this chapter discusses the current state of LDAP APIs.

The Evolution of LDAP

The International Standards Organization Development Environment (ISODE) Consortium at the University of Michigan designed LDAP v.2 as a lightweight protocol replacement for DAP as specified in X.500. The LDAP v.2 protocol was published in March 1995 as RFC 1777, making RFC 1487 (LDAP v.1) obsolete. LDAP v.2 defined a small set of simple, yet powerful, operations and provided a common starting point for the much broader design of LDAP v.3. Common programming language API support was provided when the LDAP C API was specified in August 1995 in RFC 1823.

The Internet Engineering Task Force (IETF) accepted the core set of LDAP v.3 protocols in December 1997. Although these RFCs serve as the basis for LDAP v.3-compliant implementations, they do not address all areas of directory functionality. The portions of LDAP that have been agreed upon and published as RFCs include the basic protocol structure and operations, a minimal schema, and definitions of LDAP names and search filters. Table 5.1 lists the RFCs that form the base of LDAP v.3.

Table 5.1   **The Core LDAP v.3 RFCs**

RFC Number	Name
2251	Lightweight Directory Access Protocol (v.3)
2252	Lightweight Directory Access Protocol (v.3): Attribute Syntax Definitions
2253	Lightweight Directory Access Protocol (v.3): UTF-8 String Representation of Distinguished Names
2254	The String Representation of LDAP Search Filters
2255	The LDAP URL Format
2256	A Summary of the X.500 (96) User Schema for use Use with LDAP v.3

Much like the 1993 extensions to X.500 broadened the scope of the defined directory design and operations, LDAP v.3 expands on the very simple LDAP v.2 base. In fact, the expansion of LDAP in many ways mirrors the 1993 X.500 extensions:

- LDAP v.3 fully supports all LDAP v.2 protocol elements.
- A data model that encompasses many aspects of the multiple X.500 information models has been introduced.
- Support has also been added for referrals, schema and security enhancements, and operational attributes.

All Versions of LDAP v.3 Are Not the Same

By design, each time LDAP is modified by any means other than extension, the newly modified version will be assigned a new version number. This information will be sent to a client when a Bind operation is performed.

The following are some of the more important aspects of LDAP v.3:

- **Referrals**—LDAP v.3 is enhanced to provide support for referrals as a mechanism of resolving directory queries for data not contained in the local copy of the DIB.

- **Schema publishing**—The schema for an LDAP v.3-compliant directory is contained in the directory as a series of objects, providing easy access to the schema entries for modification or extension.

- **Subschema**—Another significant improvement to LDAP v.3 is the capability to use subschemas to support different schemas for subtrees within a directory tree and facilitate the exchange of information with other directories.

- **Extensible operations**—LDAP v.3 provides a mechanism for extending many aspects of the directory, including directory operations.

- **Improved security**—LDAP v.3 supports the Simple Authentication and Security Layer (SASL), Secure Sockets Layer (SSL) and Transport Layer Security (TLS). These changes address a major deficiency of LDAP v.2: security mechanisms limited to plain text and Kerberos 4 authentication.

- **Internationalization**—Another enhancement to LDAP v.3 is Unicode support, which allows text to be represented in virtually any language. Distinguished names and attribute values will use the ISO 10646 character set.

The published RFCs are the basis for LDAP v.3 implementations, but they do not address some key areas of directory functionality. Because of this, work is ongoing on a variety of LDAP extensions, from schema extensions to replication strategies. Some of the most important directions for the future of LDAP are discussed in the "Proposed LDAP Extensions" section at the end of this chapter.

LDAP v.2 Is Still Being Enhanced

Interestingly enough, even though LDAP v.3 has been an accepted standard for some time now, LDAP v.2 is still being improved. Two proposed standards to support public key security have been released as the following RFCs:

- RFC 2259 "Internet X.509 Public Key Infrastructure Operational Protocols — LDAP v.2"

- RFC 2587 "Internet X.509 Public Key Infrastructure LDAP v.2 Schema"

LDAP Models

Like X.500, LDAP includes models that describe individual aspects of LDAP structure and operations. Because LDAP was designed to support DAP (and thus X.500-compliant operations), these models cover areas somewhat similar to the X.500 models, as you might expect. The following two models describe the two basic LDAP perspectives:

- The Data Model
- The Protocol Model

The following sections examine each of these models.

Data Model

The LDAP Data Model essentially combines most of the significant elements of the X.500 information models to describe the structure and contents of the LDAP directory. The Data Model defines the object set used by the directory as well as how those objects will be organized. The LDAP data model includes the entire directory schema, including both user and operational attributes and other information.

The structure of object class definitions is basically the same as in X.500. Directory objects are comprised of attributes that are either required or optional for the object class. Attributes can contain one or more data values, each of which is of a designated syntax type. The syntax type definition constrains the data type of the attribute value.

The Data Model also defines how information contained in the directory is named and organized. The LDAP naming structure roughly corresponds to the X.500 naming model, with each object having a *Relative Distinguished Name* (RDN) and the RDNs being concatenated into a *Distinguished Name* (DN) to uniquely identify each object in the tree. An LDAP DN is constructed in reverse order from an X.500 DN, however, with the leafmost object first. RFC 2253 defines a method of translating an X.500 name string to an LDAP DN.

As in X.500, *entries* are organized into a *Directory Information Tree* (DIT), which may be subdivided into multiple naming contexts and distributed to multiple directory servers. Each of these naming contexts (partitions) is written into a portion of the DIB called a *replica*. More than one server may hold a replica of a particular naming context, and the replicas may be of the master, shadow, or cache type.

Protocol Model

The Protocol Model defines LDAP query and update operations. LDAP assumes a client/server model, where directory clients perform protocol operations (queries and so on) against directory servers. In this model, the LDAP client transmits a request for a directory operation to a server that performs the necessary operation on the specified directory objects and returns a response to the client. Client/server communications in LDAP are *asynchronous*, meaning that multiple client requests can be sent while the results from earlier requests are still pending.

A directory server that supports LDAP operations must listen on port 389, the designated standard port for LDAP communications. Specific implementations may use additional ports for communication, allowing the network administrator to designate the ports selected for use. This allows the use of non-standard ports with proxy servers, for security or other purposes.

The LDAP Protocol Model specifies operations to perform basic directory functions, including create, delete, modify, rename, or query a directory entry.

The Protocol Model also defines the methods by which DSAs handle requests for directory objects that are outside the scope of their naming context. LDAP v.3 supports both referrals and chaining as a means for a directory server to resolve requests for directory operations on objects it does not hold; LDAP v.2 provided chaining support only.

The "LDAP Operations" section of this chapter takes a look at LDAP protocol operations in more detail.

LDAP Directory Objects and Schema

As you might expect, the LDAP schema is highly similar to the X.500 schema. Two RFCs combine to provide the basic schema for LDAP directories:

- RFC 2256 lists the minimum supported X.500 object set expected from an LDAP v.3 server. RFC 2256 draws upon the X.500 standards X.501, X.509, X.520, and X.521 as the basis for its definitions.

- RFC 2252 defines additional *LDAP-specific* objects, attributes, syntax, and matching rules that should also be supported.

As with X.500, the schema designed for LDAP clearly indicates vendors are expected to expand the base schema as needed to support their specific directory implementations. Further IETF draft documents can be written to define additions to the schema. Since the adoption of LDAP v.3, a number of draft proposals for LDAP schema additions have been written, and it is expected that many of these will be adopted over time. For example, representatives from Microsoft and Netscape, as well as Critical-Angle Inc., have been working together to definine the schema additions necessary to support an Internet white pages.

The schema for an LDAP v.3 directory is published in the directory instead of being stored in a text file as in earlier directory implementations. Each schema entry (object, attribute, and so on) has a corresponding directory object in a special container object within the root *DSA Specific Entry* (DSE). Schema publishing allows easy access to all schema entries for modification or extension. Changes to the schema can be sent to other DSAs using the directory's usual methods for updating replicas.

LDAP Directory Objects

Because LDAP was initially designed to operate as a replacement for DAP in an X.500 directory service, the X.500 schema forms the base for the LDAP object set. The actual requirements for LDAP schema contents are rather minimal, however. LDAP servers are *required* to support only two objects: `top` and `subschema`. Neither of these objects is structural; they are used internally by the directory.

It is recommended (although not mandated) that LDAP servers support 21 additional X.500 structural objects, essentially the base X.500 schema. The structural objects defined in X.521, along with the `alias` object, form the suggested LDAP schema. RFC 2256 provides the framework for the objects that should be recognized by an LDAP server. The recommended LDAP schema consists of the same entries as those listed in the "Objects" section of Chapter 4.

RFC 2252 has defined two additional object classes for use by LDAP v.3 servers: `subschema` and `extensibleObject`. As mentioned earlier, support for the `subschema` object is mandatory, while the `extensibleObject` is optional. The following sections take a brief look at each of these objects to show how they fit in the LDAP schema.

The subschema Object

One of the major improvements in LDAP v.3 is the incorporation of mechanisms that allow directories with different schemas to communicate more effectively. While X.500 uses operational attributes to support subschemas, LDAP uses the `subschema` object to accomplish the same thing. Each directory subtree has a single `subschema` entry containing the schema definition for that portion of the directory tree.

By using `subschema` entries, the directory can define schema information for a subtree and exchange schema information with other directories. This exchange of schema information takes place before any information about objects in the directory is exchanged. If a server holds a writeable replica, it is required to provide access to `subschema` entries. Clients use these entries when querying the directory for the list of supported objects, attributes, and syntax.

The `subschema` object is an auxiliary object and has seven attributes:

- `objectClasses`
- `attributeTypes`
- `dITStructureRules`
- `nameForms`
- `dITContentRules`
- `matchingRules`
- `matchingRuleUse`

Each of these attributes is multivalued, listing all the classes, attributes, and so on supported by a DSA. The first two attributes are mandatory because they define critical aspects of the schema contents. The other attributes can be used to provide additional information regarding the schema description, tree structure, and directory operations.

The `extensibleObject` Class

The `extensibleObject` class is an auxiliary class that adds *every* attribute in the schema to the `May Contain` list (that is, the list of the attributes an object may contain) of the object it is added to. The `extensibleObject` does not actually have every attribute in the schema listed in the `May Contain` list of its class definition. Because there are likely to be hundreds of attributes defined in a directory schema, the additional attributes are *implicitly* added as a function of assigning this auxiliary class to an existing object.

Adding this class to a class definition has no effect on attributes already defined as mandatory for the object class. Any attribute that is mandatory for the structural object prior to the `extensibleObject` being added will still be mandatory after the `extensibleObject` definition is added to it.

It is important to note that all LDAP servers may not support this object class. Any LDAP server that does not support the `extensibleObject` class will refuse to add entries that contain it as an auxiliary class.

In addition to the classes defined in the relevant RFCs, vendors and developers may decide that they need additional objects to support directory operations. LDAP allows for schema extensions, whether by vendors of commercial products or by developers and administrators in an enterprise.

Additional objects may be supported as long as the following conditions are met:

- Class definitions must not conflict with existing LDAP RFCs.
- Class definitions must be published in the `subschema` entry.

The `Root` "Object"

As mentioned during the discussion of X.500, the root of the DIT is not an actual object, but rather a DSE held by each server holding a naming context immediately subordinate to the root of the tree. In LDAP this entry is called the *root DSE*. Information contained in the root DSE identifies critical operational factors that apply to a specific LDAP server.

LDAP defines LDAP operational attributes, which are only found in the root DSE. An LDAP server is required to recognize these attributes, although there is no requirement that the attributes exist or have values. The attributes found in a root DSE are as follows:

- `altServer`—Lists other servers to contact in the event that this server becomes unavailable. Clients can cache this information in case it is needed.
- `namingContexts`—Contains a list of naming contexts held by the DSA.

- supportedControl—Contains a list of the *Object Identifiers* (OIDs) of controls the DSA supports. An OID is a globally unique identifier for objects and attributes assigned by various international standards organizations including American National Standards Institute (ANSI) and the Internet Assigned Numbers Authority (IANA).

- supportedExtension—Contains a list of the OIDs of the extensions the DSA supports.

- supportedLDAPVersion—List of LDAP versions supported by an LDAP server.

- supportedSASLMechanisms—Names of SASL mechanisms supported by a DSA. The *Simple Authentication and Security Layer* (SASL) framework is discussed in the "LDAP Security" section of this chapter.

In addition to these attributes, a root DSE entry is likely to contain vendor-specific information used to identify the capabilities of the directory and to manage it. A root DSE in Active Directory, for example, contains entries for a dnsHostName and an ldapServiceName.

The root DSE is likely to differ in each DSA that holds a reference to it. As this may seem odd—that multiple references to the same root DSE could differ—take a quick look at how this works.

The root DSE entry holds some information that will be common to all the LDAP servers holding a naming context immediately subordinate to the root. Generally, operational information, such as supported LDAP versions, controls, and so on will be the same across multiple directory servers. However, some of the information contained in the root DSE is specific to a particular directory server. For example, the list of naming contexts held by a server is likely to vary from one LDAP server to another.

The root DSE is named with a zero-length DN and can be queried by performing a search on the base object of the root DSE with an objectClass of *. An LDAP URL that performs this query on the unicorn.mythical.org server would look like:

```
ldap://unicorn.mythical.org/?*
```

Dynamic Objects

RFC 2589 defines an extension that provides a mechanism to implement dynamic directory objects. *Dynamic directory entries* are non-persistent directory objects that, if not periodically refreshed, disappear from the directory after a designated length of time. These objects are essentially standard structural directory objects that have been modified by the addition of a *Time-To-Live* (TTL) value.

Three schema additions are defined to support this functionality:

- The `dynamicObject` is an auxiliary object that adds the `entryTtl` attribute to an object.
- The `entryTtl` property is an operational attribute that contains the TTL of the object measured in seconds. If no value is supplied for this property, the server will assign one.
- `dynamicSubtrees` is an attribute that defines the portion of the DIT that can contain dynamic entries. If this entry is contained in the root DSE, dynamic entries are permissible anywhere in the DIT.

Dynamic objects can be used to represent transitory resources that both require a directory entry and have a finite life span. The intent is that dynamic objects will be used for entries that are useful for only a limited period of time. Some examples of this might be a person who has an entry only when present on the network, or a meeting that disappears when it is over.

As an administrator, the advantages of having such objects automatically delete themselves when they are no longer needed is obvious. When such objects are used within a directory, however, administrative concerns also arise. What happens if the TTL of a dynamic object expires while it still contains a child object with an unexpired TTL, for example? Concerns of this type can confound the process of performing a simple modification (adding a TTL) to an existing directory object.

Attributes

Not surprisingly, like in X.500, LDAP attributes can also be divided into user and operational categories. These attributes are defined in the same way for LDAP as for X.500. Therefore, only the following quick review is called for:

- **User attributes** are those that appear in the directory when viewed through common administrative tools. User attributes contain information used by the network administrator, applications, services, and clients in day-to-day directory operations. A wide range of information is contained in user attributes— everything from names (such as a CN) to security information (such as a `userCertificate`) to custom information (such as employee photos) may be found in an LDAP directory.
- **Operational attributes** are used internally by directory management processes. These attributes identify the operational capabilities of a DSA and track directory changes. Generally, operational attributes are maintained invisibly by the directory and are not directly modifiable by an administrator, although they may be viewable by someone with appropriate security permissions.

As the base LDAP schema contains about 70 attributes, it's impractical to go into detail on each attribute in this chapter. If you would like to review the complete list of LDAP attributes, you should refer to RFC 2252.

Syntax

Most LDAP attribute values are encoded as alphanumeric strings. Even so, each attribute is assigned a specific syntax type as part of its definition. The syntax definition constrains the value of the data that may be entered for a given attribute, ensuring that a value is entered and interpreted correctly.

The LDAP v.3 schema specifies 33 syntaxes for use in an LDAP directory. The syntax definitions for LDAP include a variety of methods for interpreting numbers (such as phone numbers, OIDs, and so on), text (Boolean, country codes, and so on), as well as binary definitions.

As with attributes, the number of syntax definitions in the base LDAP schema makes it impractical to go into detail about each one here. RFC 2252 also contains the complete list of LDAP attributes.

Matching Rules

In addition to the syntax type, an attribute definition may include *matching rules* instructing the directory on how to handle filters used in directory queries. Matching rules contain information concerning how to handle the value of a property when a filtered directory operation is presented.

There are matching rules defined for both different filter types and some specific attribute types. The core LDAP schema contains matching rules for `Equality`, `Inequality`, and `Substring` filters as well as rules used for subschema attributes.

Again, you should refer to RFC 2252 for more complete information on this aspect of the LDAP schema.

The Directory Information Tree

In keeping with its initial goal of accessing X.500 directories, LDAP uses essentially the same type of DIT structure as X.500. Container objects are arranged to form the tree structure, and leaf objects representing network resources and entities are distributed into the appropriate containers. DNs are derived by concatenating the RDNs of the referenced object and its parents.

However, critical differences exist between both the structure and naming methods used by X.500 and LDAP. The differences are essentially the following:

- **Structure**—The possible arrangement of objects within the tree is much looser than that implemented by X.500, where an object class may only exist within specified container objects (such as OUs within Os, but not vice versa). In the LDAP schema, an object class has *no* constraints regarding the container objects classes in which it can reside. This doesn't mean that an LDAP server cannot place additional constraints on DIT structure, just that the RFCs defining LDAP do not. If an LDAP directory is a front end to an X.500 directory, however, the more restrictive X.500 structure rules will apply.

- **Naming**—LDAP DNs are written starting at the leafmost object and proceeding to an entry immediately subordinate to the root. This is the *opposite* of X.500 naming, which starts at the root of the DIT and proceeds to the referenced object.

Unlike X.500, LDAP does not make assumptions about the existence of a global directory tree structured to facilitate the location of X.500 servers. Instead of creating an LDAP-specific global namespace as a means of locating LDAP servers, LDAP vendors have chosen to approach the issue from a different angle (such as using the *Service Location Protocol* (SLP) or DNS). The exact resolution to the problem of locating distributed LDAP directory servers in an environment such as the Internet is still under consideration. However, there is some ongoing discussion in the IETF working groups concerning methods of locating LDAP servers.

One method currently being used relies on the existing DNS namespace as a form of top-level locator service. DNS has been extended to support service (SRV) records, which supplies a means of locating a server providing a specific service via DNS lookups. Of course, this requires that the top of an organization's DIT mirror the organization's registered DNS domain name. Concomitantly, LDAP supports a method of using DNS name components as part of an LDAP DIT. (Microsoft has chosen this approach for AD.) The "DNS Domain Names in LDAP" section later in this chapter discusses in more detail how DNS names work with LDAP.

LDAP Naming

The primary method for LDAP naming is defined in RFC 2253 and is modeled on typed X.500 naming. Additional RFCs describe an LDAP URL format used by clients such as Web browsers and a mechanism to use DNS domain names in LDAP directories.

The following RFCs define LDAP names:

- RFC 2253 "Lightweight Directory Access Protocol (v.3): UTF-8 String Representation of Distinguished Names"
- RFC 2255 "The LDAP URL Format"
- RFC 2247 "Using Domains in LDAP/X.500 Distinguished Names"

The following sections explain what each RFC specifies in the way of naming support.

LDAP Names

Because LDAP was designed to support X.500 directories, the ability to map an X.500 DN to an LDAP DN accurately is of critical importance. RFC 2253 describes a way to convert X.500-distinguished names from the X.500 format to a UTF-8 string for use by LDAP.

At first glance, an LDAP DN may look like an X.500 DN—it is constructed of a series of X.500-style RDNs separated by commas. On closer examination, however, you'll notice that an LDAP DN lists the string of RDNs in *reverse order* when compared to an X.500 DN.

To illustrate how this works, take a look at an example directory entry from the perspective of both X.500 and LDAP. Figure 5.1 shows the directory object for a user named Michael.

The LDAP DN for this directory object is as follows:

```
cn=michael, ou=mktg, ou=corp, o=netmages
```

However, the X.500 DN for the same object is as follows:

```
o=netmages, ou=corp, ou=mktg, cn=michael
```

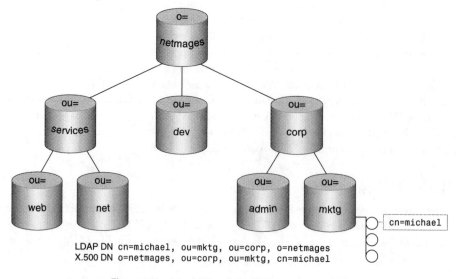

LDAP DN cn=michael, ou=mktg, ou=corp, o=netmages
X.500 DN o=netmages, ou=corp, ou=mktg, cn=michael

Figure 5.1 The order of the RDNs in an LDAP
DN is the reverse of that in an X.500 DN.

RFC 2253 also specifies the actions to take in special cases such as when encountering a multivalued RDN, when RDNs contain special characters, or when the RDN attribute type is not recognized by LDAP. This can be rather complex in practice, and you may want to read RFC 2253 if you will be working with many directory implementations that use special cases in naming. The following sections briefly look at a few examples to show how this works in general.

Multivalued RDNs

Sometimes an object has more than one naming attribute designated. This might be done to distinguish between objects that would otherwise have the same name, or as a means of adding additional information for location or management purposes.

Multivalued RDNs are just concatenated with a + symbol as in the following example:

```
cn=michael+l=seattle, ou=dev, o=netmages
```

Unrecognized Attribute Type

As mentioned earlier in this chapter, a typed RDN is created by combining the abbreviation for the naming attribute with the object name, resulting in an RDN such as ou=dev or cn=michael. However, sometimes a directory object uses an attribute type that is unknown to a particular directory server for its name. In such a case, it is not possible for the directory server to create an RDN using the name type abbreviation.

Every attribute in the schema has an OID that can be used to identify the attribute type. When an LDAP server encounters an unknown name type attribute, it uses the OID to form the RDN rather than the unknown attribute type abbreviation.

The next example assumes that an object uses a portion of a DNS domain name as an RDN component. The OID for the *Domain Component* (dc) attribute, which names this type of object, is 0.9.2342.19200300.100.1.25. Because this is not a mandatory part of the LDAP schema, however, all LDAP servers might not recognize it. If a server did not contain the dc attribute in its schema, it would use the following RDN to refer to the object named by the dc name type:

```
0.9.2342.19200300.100.1.25=mythical
```

And if that RDN were part of a DN string, it might look something like the following:

```
ou=us,0.9.2342.19200300.100.1.25=mythical,0.9.2342.19200300.100.1.25=org
```

As you can see, OIDs are not very friendly and are not easy to use or remember. Therefore, using an OID when naming directory objects is undesirable; but this mechanism does at least allow LDAP servers to cope with unknown attributes.

Special Characters

Some characters require special handling when they are used in an object name. If the CN structure chosen for user objects is "lastname, firstname," for example, a problem presents itself. As LDAP uses commas to separate the components of a DN, the comma might be part of the CN attribute or it might be the separator between RDN components. The directory must have some way to distinguish between the two uses of the comma.

To facilitate this distinction, LDAP uses a process called *escaping* to identify such characters when they occur as part of a RDN rather than as part of the DN structure. The following characters occurring within an RDN require escaping—that is they must be preceded by a backslash (\):

- A space at either the beginning or end of an RDN string
- A # at the beginning of an RDN string
- A comma (,), semicolon (;), plus sign (+), double-quotation mark ("), backslash (\), less than (<), or greater than (>) occurring anywhere within the string

Some organizations may choose to use these special characters within the attributes used to name an object. Consider the example of a username in the format "lastname, firstname"—that is, cn=smith, michael. If you wanted to reference this object in an LDAP name, you would need to escape the , character in the RDN, like this:

```
cn=smith\, michael, ou=mktg, ou=corp, o=netmages
```

This example points out the need to carefully consider the ramifications of your naming models when constructing your directory. If you expect that your clients will be performing lots of queries using LDAP URLs, you may want to minimize the use of special characters to minimize confusion.

Compatibility Factors in LDAP Names

Naming compatibility issues exist between LDAP v.2 and LDAP v.3. RFC 1779, which defines LDAP v.2, is considerably more lenient than RFC 2253 when it comes to naming objects. However, compatibility issues between LDAP v.2-compliant names and LDAP v.3 are also addressed in RFC 2253. An LDAP v.3-capable DSA will accept any name that is compliant with LDAP v.2, but it will not generate LDAP v.2 names.

LDAP v.2 naming constraints differ from LDAP v.3 in the following ways:

- Semicolons as well as commas are acceptable as RDN separators.
- Whitespace characters are allowed on either side of the separator characters, equal signs (=), and plus signs (+) used in multivalued RDNs.
- Quoted RDN strings are allowed by LDAP v.2.
- Some normally escaped characters within quoted strings do not require the leading backslash.
- OIDs used in place of attribute name in RDNs were prefixed with the text OID.

LDAP v.3 implementations must accept any of this syntax. When an LDAP v.2 style name is encountered, semicolons are replaced by commas, whitespace is ignored, and other processing is done as needed to create an LDAP v.3-compliant DN.

LDAP URLs

Accessing directories via a Web browser is becoming more common, whether it is done on a corporate LAN to find employee information or across the Internet to a publicly accessible database of names and phone numbers. An *LDAP Uniform Resource Locator* (URL) format has been defined to provide access to LDAP directories using a client such as a Web browser.

LDAP URLs were originally defined at the University of Michigan under a National Science Foundation grant and were first released as RFC 1959. RFC 1959 has been superseded by RFC 2255, which updates LDAP URLs for LDAP v.3 and also defines an extension mechanism for use as a means to enhance the LDAP URL format.

An LDAP URL begins with the protocol designator `ldap` and may designate a host name as well as the DN of the directory object being referenced. The URL can also specify search parameters, authentication data, and other information needed to complete the query.

The most basic form of an LDAP URL follows:

```
ldap://[hostport]/[dn]
ldap://netmages.org/cn=felisha,ou=dev,o=netmages
```

The complete LDAP URL syntax is as follows:

```
ldap://[hostport][/dn[?[attributes][?[scope][?[filter][?extensions]]]]]
```

This breakdown of the components in an LDAP URL is as follows:

- `ldap`—The URL begins with a *scheme* prefix denoting the protocol to be used when handling this URL. The `ldap` designation indicates that the URL references one or more entries in the directory held by the specified LDAP server.

- `hostport`—The `hostport` specifies the LDAP server that should be contacted and, optionally, the TCP port that should be used. If no `hostport` is specified, the client must have information telling it which LDAP server to contact. The default LDAP port of 389 is assumed unless otherwise noted. If a TCP port is specified, it is separated from the host name by a semicolon, as in `zifnab.netmages.org:389`. The `hostport` specification is defined by RFC 1738, section 5.

- `dn`—The `dn` is an LDAP DN identifying the base object to be used in the search. The DN should be constructed as a `distinguishedName` defined by RFC 2253, section 3, as discussed in the previous section.

- `attributes`—This part of the URL indicates which attributes should be returned as a response to the directory search. This is formatted as an attribute description, as defined by RFC 2251, section 4.1.5.

- scope—The scope indicates the range of the directory entries to be searched. The options for scope are as follows:
    - base—Only the specified object should be searched.
    - one—Indicating a search of single level of the directory tree.
    - sub—The entire subtree, starting at the specified object should be searched.
- filter—This portion of the URL indicates the filter to be applied in this search. It is constructed as defined in RFC 2254, section 4. If no filter is specified, the default value of * is assumed and all user attributes should be returned by the directory server.
- extensions—This construct allows URL extensions to be specified as part of a query. Extensions are written as a type=value string, with the value being optional unless required by the specific extension. Multiple extensions can be written on a single query by separating them with a comma. Extensions are discussed in the "LDAP Operations" section of this chapter.

The structure of the attributes, filter, and extensions is discussed in a bit more depth in the section on LDAP searches later in this chapter.

As you can see, the LDAP URL provides a powerful mechanism for performing queries using a Web browser. This enables you to examine the directory from any computer with an LDAP-enabled Web browser. Internet Explorer v.4 and Netscape Communicator v.4 and later provide LDAP support, although the method by which information is handled may vary.

Examples of LDAP URLs

The following URL will query the DSA at netmages.org and return the entire set of user attributes for the specified user:

```
ldap://netmages.org/cn=felisha,ou=dev,o=netmages
```

The next query will only return the surname (sn) attribute of the same user.

```
ldap://netmages.org/cn=felisha,ou=dev,o=netmages?sn
```

This query will return the objectClass attributes for all the objects in the subtree under ou=dev,o=netmages.

```
ldap://netmages.org/ou=dev,o=netmages?objectClass?sub
```

These are just a few examples of how LDAP URLs can be used to query a directory. If you are going to be using LDAP queries extensively, you should refer to the appropriate RFCs for more detailed information. The Appendix of this book includes information regarding the location of the RFCs.

Processing

According to RFC 2255, an LDAP URL should be processed in the following manner:

1. The client must obtain a connection to the LDAP server specified in the hostport of the URL or, if no server is specified, an LDAP server selected by the client. If a session already exists with an appropriate LDAP server, it may be reused.

2. If required, the client is then authenticated to the LDAP server. This step is optional unless a critical bind name extension is specified within the URL.

3. The search operation specified in the URL is performed and the results returned to the client.

4. After receiving the results of the search, the client may maintain the connection to the LDAP server or disconnect.

LDAP URLs commonly use DNS names to identify the DSA that the query should be sent to. LDAP also uses DNS domain names in other ways, however, as discussed in the following section.

DNS Domain Names in LDAP

Mechanisms have been adopted to allow the use of DNS domain names within an LDAP directory. RFC 2247 specifies a means of using DNS domains as part of LDAP DNs. This was designed to provide a simple method of translating DNS domain names for use within an LDAP DN.

The algorithm for converting DNS names to LDAP DNs is straightforward. Start with an empty DN and add an RDN for each component of the DNS name, in the same order as the DNS name. These RDNs are named with a dc naming type attribute and have a value of one component of the DNS name.

Using this method, the DNS domain netmages.org can be translated to the following LDAP DN:

    dc=netmages,dc=org

A DN that consists solely of dc components, or that subportion of a longer DN, can be mapped directly back to a DNS domain name. This is done by concatenating the value of each RDN that corresponds to a portion of the DNS name, using a period (.) to separate them. Therefore, the LDAP distinguished name dc=netmages,dc=org can be easily translated back to the DNS domain netmages.org. The dc name type makes it easy to determine which portion of the LDAP DN corresponds to the DNS domain.

To support this functionality, two new object classes have been created: dcObject and domain. There is one critical difference between a dcObject and a domain—the domain class is *structural* and can appear in the directory, but the dcObject is *auxiliary*. This means that the dcObject is used for extending the functionality of objects that correspond to an existing directory object, and the domain object is designed for objects that exist primarily as a placeholder for the DNS name component. A dc attribute has also been created, which is used to name the domain object. The following sections explain these new objects and attributes.

dcObject

The dcObject is an auxiliary class that has been defined to allow the addition of the dc attribute to a standard container object, such as an Organization or an Organizational Unit. There is a single user attribute, dc, which is mandatory for the class dcObject. The dc attribute has as its value a single component of a DNS name and is used to name an object that has the dcObject added as an auxiliary class. In fact, the addition of the dc attribute to the definition of an existing container object is the only function of the dcObject. Although this may not seem like a lot of functionality for an entire object class, this simple change provides a mechanism for congruence of the LDAP directory and DNS domain names.

domain Object

On the other hand, the domain class is a structural object that, although its basic function is the same as the dcObject (providing a way to use DNS names in a directory), also provides a more complete object definition. As with the dcObject, the domain object requires the dc attribute only; it does have a number of optional attributes, however, that provide additional information about the object represented.

The optional attributes of the domain object include telecommunications, postal, and other attributes. This information is useful when performing directory administration and queries.

dc Attribute

The dc attribute type has as its value a single component of a DNS domain name. The value of the dc attribute is used as the name of the domain object or the container object to which the dcObject auxiliary object has been added. In keeping with the DNS standard, the value of the dc attribute is not case sensitive.

Notes on DNS Names in LDAP Names

As previously mentioned, DNS domain names are also used when constructing an LDAP URL. This can lead to portions of a DNS name being referenced multiple times when constructing an LDAP name, which may get a bit confusing. If you are using an LDAP URL to access a directory that uses dc components, such as an Active Directory server, for example, you could run into a URL like this:

```
ldap://netmages.org/ou=dev,dc=netmages,dc=org
```

The first time the domain name is used (netmages.org), it is as the host portion of the URL, and it is resolved by a DNS server to locate the appropriate LDAP server. The second time the domain name is used, (dc=netmages,dc=org), it is as part of the LDAP path and is resolved by the LDAP server as part of the path to the directory object.

Also note that some directory implementations use DNS domain names in a variation of the method described in RFC 2247. For example, Active Directory masks portions of the domain name in some instances. No *top-level domain* (tld) name is presented via AD clients; therefore, netmages.org appears as just netmages when viewed via some AD tools.

Given these factors, it is important to remember that the path to the same directory object may differ, depending on how that object is accessed—that is, which tools are used.

The Directory Information Base

As LDAP is an access protocol that was designed to support X.500 directories, it relies on the underlying directory to define its own methods for storage and handling of DIB functionality. Therefore, LDAP doesn't address most aspects of the DIB that are dealt with by the X.500 model. Synchronization, replication, partitioning, and actual DIB structure are not currently addressed by any of the RFCs that define the core LDAP protocol.

Although this approach has simplified the protocol design, it is not without its drawbacks. Because there is no standardized method for replication, severe limitations are placed on the type of interoperation between LDAP directories. This is likely to change in the future as vendors recognize the need to allow directories to work together.

The LDAP protocol design does acknowledge that there will be multiple copies of the DIB, however, and that the access protocol must address security constraints. Most importantly, servers that hold shadow or cache replicas are required to place the same constraints on data access as the server holding the master replica.

There has been significant work taking place in this area. The IETF has a working group that is currently determining the replication requirements, the first step in designing actual replication methods. Several Internet drafts have been offered as options for replication, including a draft from Microsoft and Cisco, which is the basis for the multi-master replication being used in AD.

LDAP Operations

LDAP supports operations to perform the directory functions previously performed by DAP. Because of this, most LDAP operations are essentially the same as DAP, although the names may differ.

Table 5.2 lists the LDAP operations defined in the core LDAP RFCs.

Table 5.2 **LDAP Operations**

Operation	What It Does
`Bind`	Functions like a DAP `directoryBind`. Bind operations were required by the LDAP v.2 specification but are optional under LDAP v.3.
`Unbind`	Functions like a DAP `directoryUnbind`.
`Search`	Functions like a DAP search request. Searches are discussed in more detail later in this chapter.
`Modify`	Functions like a DAP `modifyEntry`. This operation will not remove any portion of an object's Distinguished Name; that must be done with a `ModifyDN` operation, described later.
`Add`	Functionally the same as a DAP `addEntry` operation.
`Delete`	Equivalent to a DAP `removeEntry`.
`Compare`	An LDAP `Compare` operation is the same as a DAP `Compare`.
`Abandon`	Functionally the same as a DAP `Abandon` request.
`ModifyDN`	The `modifyDN` operation can be used to do two things: change the RDN of an object, or move an object or subtree to another location in the directory tree. This operation changes one or more components of an object's DN. The LDAP v.3 `modifyDN` request is essentially the same operation as an LDAP v.2 `modifyRDN` with the addition of one parameter, `newSuperior`. The `newSuperior` value is used to designate the DN of the object that will become the new parent of the entry being modified.
`Unsolicited notification`	An unsolicited notification is sent by the server to signal a condition of which the client should be aware. The only unsolicited notification defined in the core LDAP v.3 specification is a notice of disconnection, which is sent to notify the client that the server is closing a session. This would be used in the case of the server receiving an LDAP message it cannot parse, underlying security failures, or the server becoming unavailable for some reason.
`Extended operation`	The extended operation provides a mechanism for adding new operations to the LDAP protocol. These extensions may be created for a specific implementation or defined as an RFC. The extended operations are discussed in more detail later in this chapter.

Name Resolution

An LDAP server processes queries in much the same way as an X.500 DSA. The server receives a request, evaluates the DN, and fulfills the request or hands the query off if it cannot be fulfilled locally. Like X.500, LDAP also uses either chaining or referral as the mechanisms for completing queries beyond the scope of the naming contexts held by the contacted DSA.

Both of these processes were discussed in detail in the "Name Resolution" section of Chapter 4. Therefore, it's not necessary to go into them in detail here. Briefly, the two processes work as follows:

- Using referrals, a DSA resolves its portion of directory query, and then passes the results back to the client, as well as pointers to other DSAs with which to continue the search. LDAP v.3 supports referrals as a mechanism of resolving directory queries for data not contained in the local copy of the DIB.

- Chaining requires that directory servers pass a query down a line of servers and back via the same path to resolve queries. Using chaining results in more work for the directory server and can be used with less-intelligent client software. You should remember that LDAP v.2 does not support referrals, however, so only chaining operations will be performed by an LDAP v.2 DSA.

LDAP Searches

Because most of the use of LDAP will be for queries, a powerful, yet simple search mechanism has been defined as part of the LDAP v.3 specification.

LDAP searches can be performed on a single directory entry, the contents of a single, or an entire subtree. Each LDAP search request contains a `baseObject` that is the LDAP DN designating the starting point of the search. Additional information contained in the search query defines the scope of the search, treatment of aliases, filters, and so on. Although many of the following parameters are similar to those used in LDAP URLs, there are some differences.

The syntax for a search request is as follows:

```
[baseObject], [scope], [derefAliases], [sizeLimit], [timeLimit], [typesOnly],
[filter], [attributes]
```

The definitions of the search parameters are as follows:

- `baseObject`—The LDAP DN of the object at which to start the search.
- `scope`—Specifies the scope of the search request.
    - `baseObject`—Search only the `baseObject` for matching attribute values.
    - `singleLevel`—Search only the immediate subordinates of the `baseObject`, *not* including the `baseObject`.
    - `wholeSubtree`—Perform the search on the entire subtree, *including* the `baseObject`.

- derefAliases—Specifies alias-handling preferences. The process of dereferencing aliases is discussed in the "Name Resolution" section of Chapter 4.
  - neverDerefAliases—Do not dereference aliases for purposes of either locating the baseObject of the search or performing the search.
  - derefInSearching—Dereference aliases when performing the search, but not for locating the baseObject.
  - derefFindingBaseObj—Dereference aliases when locating the baseObject, but not when performing the search.
  - derefAlways— Dereference aliases for both baseObject location and searches.
- sizeLimit—This parameter restricts the number of entries that may be returned by search results. A sizeLimit of 0 means that no limitations are requested by the client, although servers may restrict the number of entries returned. Valid values for sizeLimit are any positive integer.
- timeLimit—timeLimit is a value indicating the number of seconds allowed for completion of a search. The value can be any positive integer. An unlimited search time is indicated by a value of 0.
- typesOnly—This parameter accepts a Boolean value. Setting the typesOnly value to TRUE tells the server to return only attribute types and no values. A setting of FALSE indicates the server should return both attribute types and values on the search.
- filter—Possible filter entries are: equalityMatch, substrings, greaterOrEqual, lessOrEqual, present, approxMatch, and extensibleMatch. Additional filter operators of and, or, and not may be used to form queries using combinations of the above filters. These filters are evaluated in exactly the same way as in the 1993 X.511 standard (section 7.8.1) and return a value of either TRUE, FALSE, or UNDEFINED. If the evaluation of the filter results in a TRUE response, the appropriate attributes are returned in the search results. Otherwise the entry is ignored during the search operation. For more detailed information on the use of filters in LDAP queries, refer to section 4.5.1 of RFC 2251.
- attributes—A search request can identify a subset of attributes to be returned by specifying the names of those attributes as part of the query. Two special values are also used: a null value, and the asterisk (*), both of which return all *user* attributes. Although a client can request that all attributes be returned, normal access control and other directory restrictions will limit actual search results. An attribute description of 1.1 is used to specify that the client does not want any attributes returned in the search results. Due to the large number of values for some operational attributes, they are never returned in search results unless they are requested by name. The * is used when requesting all user attributes in addition to specific operational attributes.

Extended Operations

Extended operations allow new directory functionality to be defined and existing operations to be extended. Mechanisms have been added to LDAP v.3 to provide support for extensions to the base set of LDAP operations and query handling. The extended operations can be defined either as a lasting extension to the directory or dynamically (as part of a directory query, for example).

These extensions can be used for enhancements ranging from special handling of query results to security measures. One area in which a great deal of operation extension work has taken place is on various mechanisms to customize the delivery of directory query results to the client. Methods to allow a directory server to incrementally deliver subsets of a large query have been devised as a way to allow the client agent more control over the directory search process.

Not surprisingly, the methods used for the extension of LDAP operations are essentially the same as those used by X.500 extensions and controls, but the names of these mechanisms aren't quite the same between the two specifications:

- **Operational extensions**, which correspond to X.500 *extensions*, provide a method of defining new LDAP operations, either privately or by RFC.

- **Controls**, which are analogous to X.500 *service controls*, are a means by which extended handling information can be specified for a single query.

Extensions

The extension mechanism provides a way to dynamically add functionality to query strings. Operational extensions allow the use of predefined syntaxes and methods to support operations not included in the basic LDAP specifications. A likely use of an operational extension would be for additional security measures, such as digitally signed operations. Operational extensions may be defined via RFC or by an individual vendor or developer.

Operational extensions can be designated as critical or noncritical (that is, whether the extension is *required* for the operation). Extended operations are marked as critical by a prepending an exclamation mark (!) to the extension syntax portion of the request. It is important to remember that extensions may or may not be supported by the system processing the URL. LDAP servers should follow these rules when processing URL extensions:

- Supported critical extensions *must* be processed.
- URLs with unsupported critical extensions *must not* be processed.
- Supported noncritical extensions should be processed.
- Unsupported noncritical extensions may be ignored during URL processing.

The operational extensions supported by a given LDAP server are listed in the `supportedExtension` attribute of the root DSE entry.

Controls

A *control* is a method of specifying extension information for a single LDAP request. Controls can be used to support added functionality such as sorting, paging, or other special handling of search results. A list of supported controls is located in the `supportedControl` attribute of the root DSE entry.

Controls can be designated as critical or not, either by the developer or at the user's discretion. Unlike operational extensions, however, controls are marked as critical (or not) by a Boolean value in a criticality field within the control syntax. Controls are evaluated and handled according to the same rules as operational extensions.

LDAP Security

One of the most important considerations for any network service is security. LDAP defines some of the methods by which secure access to data and network resources is provided.

Both LDAP v.2 and v.3 provide a mechanism for simple authentication and support for Kerberos. LDAP v.2 supports Kerberos v.4.1 or a simple authentication method using clear-text passwords.

LDAP v.3 also adds support for the Simple Authentication and Security Layer (SASL), which is a powerful means of providing secure communications using a variety of methods, including Kerberos.

Many drafts related to security are circulating in the LDAP Extensions (LDAPExt) working group of the IETF. To review the current status of the work on security, you should visit the LDAPExt page at:

`www.ietf.org/html.charters/ldapext-charter.html`

The following sections briefly look at each of the LDAP security mechanisms. Because the security mechanisms used by LDAP are varied and complex, however, you may want to refer to the relevant RFCs for more complete information.

Access Control

There has not been agreement on an access control model for LDAP, leaving individual vendors to implement proprietary methods to manage this aspect of security. This is clearly a significant gap in the current state of LDAP. Drafts defining access control requirements and models are currently under discussion, and it can be hoped that some agreement will be reached soon, allowing work in this area to move forward.

Authentication

Unlike the access control factors, LDAP has defined authentication mechanisms. LDAP supports non-authenticated access (access by anonymous entities), as well as the following three authentication methods:

- Simple Authentication
- Simple Authentication via SSL/TLS
- SASL-based authentication

Anonymous Access

LDAP allows anonymous (non-authenticated) access to the directory, providing a means for anyone to access the information managed by an LDAP server if so desired by the network administrator. This is very useful if the LDAP service is being used to provide information for something like an Internet directory of email addresses. Non-authenticated access does not require an entry in the directory.

Simple Authentication

LDAP supports a simple authentication method that allows connecting to the directory and authenticating with a clear text password (where the password is transmitted unencrypted across the network). Although this method does provide a modicum of security, it is not recommended in most environments unless some other security mechanism is in place to prevent inadvertent disclosure of passwords and other security information.

The simple authentication method is also used for non-authenticated connections. In this case the password is set to a zero-length entry, as is the distinguished name portion of the authentication string. LDAP v.2 clients often use this method for non-authenticated access to the directory.

Simple Authentication via SSL/TLS

By combining the convenience of the simple password authentication method with the added security of an encrypted connection, the authentication process can be made more secure. This can be accomplished by using the *Secure Sockets Layer* (SSL) or *Transport Layer Security* (TLS), the successor to SSL. Of course, this approach requires that both the client and server obtain public key certificates for use in the SSL/TLS process. Because public key certificates require management, this method is not quite as simple for the administrator, but it does add some security to the process.

Simple Authentication and Security Level

LDAP v.3 implements an extensible security model using *Simple Authentication and Security Layer* (SASL), which allows for the use of different security providers. SASL provides a way for connection-oriented protocols to specify an authentication method and optional security layer (encryption) for protocol interactions.

When using SASL, the client specifies the desired authentication mechanism (or method). If the contacted server supports the specified SASL mechanism, it will initiate the authentication process. Authentication then takes place in accordance with the specified authentication mechanism. If the client also requests that the optional security layer be implemented, this encryption takes place immediately upon completion of the authentication process.

As defined in RFC 2222, mechanisms used with SASL must be registered with the *Internet Address and Naming Association* (IANA). SASL currently supports the following mechanisms:

- Kerberos v.4
- GSSAPI
- S/Key
- External

The next sections briefly examine each of these SASL mechanisms.

Kerberos

Kerberos technology was developed by MIT in response to the need for secure communication across what is essentially an insecure environment, the Internet. Kerberos operates by authenticating clients and then issuing tickets to be used for authentication of the client to the service. The ticket consists of the client identity and a temporary *session key*, which is then sent to the service by the client. This session key contains a unique shared encryption key that is used by both the client and service during that one session. The client and service can then encrypt all communications using the session key, thus providing a means to operate securely over a public medium such as the Internet.

Kerberos uses both an *Authentication Server* (AS) and a *Ticket Granting Server* (TGS), collectively referred to as a *Key Distribution Center* (KDC). Network clients and services each have a secret key (password) that is registered with the AS. When the client is authenticated by the AS, a *Ticket Granting Ticket* (TGT) is granted to the client by the AS. This key, which is essentially a session key for use between the client and the TGS, is presented to the TGS, which then issues the actual ticket and session key for use between the client and service.

This method of ticket management ensures that user passwords are used only once, at the beginning of a session, and need not be reentered or cached, removing a possible weakness in the security implementation. As a additional layer of security, Kerberos tickets are valid for a short period of time only, further limiting the ability of a third party to intercept the ticket and use it to impersonate someone with access rights that the third party does not have.

Generic Security Service API

Generic Security Service API (GSSAPI) defines an interoperable security system for use on the Internet and is another one of SASL's principal providers. GSSAPI provides a protocol- and mechanism-independent interface to underlying security methods based on public key and secret key technologies. RFC 1508 defined GSSAPI and was obsoleted by RFC 2078, the current version of GSSAPI.

S/KEY

The *S/KEY One-Time Password system*, described in RFC 1760, was designed to prevent intruders from obtaining user passwords via packet sniffers and so on. The S/KEY system is designed to counter a replay attack, where an intruder captures and then replays a username and password to gain entry to the network.

The S/KEY One-Time Password system uses a secret pass phrase factored with a server-provided seed value, and then applies a secure hash function multiple times to produce a sequence of one-time passwords which are used to implement secure communications. The S/KEY hash function is based on the MD4 Message Digest algorithm.

Using the S/KEY system, only a single-use password is ever transmitted across the network. The user's originating secret pass-phrase is never transmitted and is, therefore, not exposed to compromise.

External

The use of an external SASL mechanism enables you to plug in a security protocol or method that is otherwise unsupported by SASL. This can be used to provide support for a variety of security approaches such as TLS, SSL, or IPsec.

LDAP Programming

One of the critical factors for widespread support of the LDAP protocol is the availability of APIs. In August 1995, RFC 1823 was published, defining the LDAP API. RFC 1823 defines a C language programming interface to perform queries and modifications on an LDAP directory (commonly referred to as the *LDAP C API*).

The original LDAP API was written for LDAP v.2. Since then there have been several proposed additions and extensions to the original LDAP API issued as Internet drafts. This includes, most importantly, `draft-ietf-ldapext-ldap-c-api-04.txt`, a basic update of the LDAP C API to support features new to LDAP v.3 such as extended operations.

Synchronous and asynchronous modes of operation are both supported. Synchronous operations return the actual results of the operation to the client. Asynchronous routines return the message ID of the operation; this message ID can be used by the client when querying later for results.

Interfaces that support the functions listed in Table 5.3 are provided.

Table 5.3 **LDAP API Functions**

API Name	Function
ldap_init()	Opens a connection to the LDAP server
ldap_simple_bind()	Authenticates the client to the directory using simple authentication
ldap_sasl_bind()	Authenticates the client via SASL mechanisms
ldap_unbind()	Unbinds and closes the connection
ldap_search()	Searches the LDAP directory
ldap_modify()	Modifies an existing LDAP entry
ldap_modrdn()	Modifies the name of an existing LDAP entry
ldap_add()	Adds a new entry to the directory
ldap_delete()	Removes and entry from the directory
ldap_abandon()	Abandons an operation in progress
ldap_result()	Obtains results of a previous asynchronous operation

There are also provisions for routines to parse the results returned by these operations. Entry names and attribute values can be retrieved and the viewing of results can be managed by these routines.

LDAP Data Interchange Format

The *LDAP Data Interchange Format* (LDIF) has been defined as a means of describing LDAP entries in a standardized text format. LDIF facilitates the exchange of directory data by implementing a simple text listing of a directory entry.

LDIF can be used to import and export directory data as well as describing information to be applied during a directory update. Many LDAP utilities read and write LDIF, as do most development tools designed for use with LDAP directories.

In addition to the LDAP C API, a number of other APIs to access LDAP directories have been developed.

- There are several IETF draft proposals for a Java API for LDAP, implemented as a set of Java classes.

- ADSI is Microsoft's proprietary API designed around Active Directory.

- Netscape has a freely available Java SDK that fully supports LDAP v.3.

- PerlLDAP is a Netscape product that provides support for Perl scripting as an interface to LDAP directories.

- JNDI is SunSoft's proprietary API that provides access to LDAP, NIS+, NDS, and other directory services.

Proposed LDAP Extensions

It is important to remember that *X.500 is a set of standards* that define directory service structures and services, and *LDAP is a protocol* that is designed around the X.500 information models and supports X.500 DAP operations. The initial intent of LDAP was purely as an access protocol for X.500 directories. Because of this focus, many aspects of directory design were not specifically addressed but just assumed to be X.500 compliant.

The scope of LDAP is broadening, however, to the point that some directory products (such as Active Directory) are being built around LDAP, with no underlying X.500 directory. This means that much more than client access methods need to be defined. DSA-to-DSA interaction does happen with LDAP v.3; it just requires that one of the DSAs be seen as a client by the other DSA. As LDAP develops, it is likely to expand to provide more direct support for a broader range of interactions between disparate DSAs.

The RFCs that define the LDAP v.3 protocol are just a starting point for what are sure to be highly variant LDAP implementations. Literally dozens of IETF drafts have been proposed as additions to LDAP. Many of these drafts address simple topics such as the definition of a single new object or a simple operation extension; others address considerably larger issues such as replication. You can check on the status of any IETF working group by visiting their Web site at:

`www.ietf.org`

It is worth taking a brief look at a few areas of the LDAP protocol which (although they have not been finalized yet) have been circulating in draft form for an extended period of time. These drafts address some of the key issues that still face the developers of directories, especially as they relate to directory interoperability.

Replication

One of the more difficult aspects of an open directory standard or protocol is the exchange of information between different vendors' implementations. Although a number of other facets of LDAP v.3 have been resolved, no consensus has been reached on a standard method of directory replication. In fact, there is currently vigorous debate about the IETF draft that defines replication *requirements*, a much broader topic than an actual replication mechanism.

In the meantime, vendors have proceeded with implementation of proprietary replication approaches, limiting interoperability. Some of these proprietary designs have been proposed as solutions to the LDAP replication question. Microsoft and Cisco proposed a multi-master replication scheme to the IETF, and although it has not yet been accepted as part of the standard, it does form the basis for Active Directory's replication design.

Broader Schema

The LDAP v.3 schema, as described by the core LDAP RFCs, does not go much beyond the basic X.500 schema. In fact, the LDAP object set contains only two classes in addition to those defined by X.500; and both of these classes define objects used internally by the directory. This limited schema provides the basic directory objects and properties that all directories require as a starting point.

Numerous IETF drafts describing additions to the LDAP schema have been published by a wide variety of organizations and businesses involved in directory development. Some of these drafts propose extensions to existing objects; others define new object classes and associated property sets. As you might expect, support for extensions to the LDAP schema will be vendor specific.

LDAP also makes it possible for programmers and administrators to independently extend the directory schema; therefore, if a needed class or property is not defined within the vendor's product, it can be added. This is not without complications, however, and should be carefully considered in the context of the corporate network before implementation. If two DSAs have different schemas and try to replicate data, for example, some objects may be unrecognized and unusable.

The next chapter looks at the third significant standard being used in directory services: the Domain Name System.

...simplicity belies the breadth...

6

Domain Name System

DOMAIN NAME SYSTEM (DNS) PROVIDES NETWORK CLIENTS THE ABILITY TO FIND network servers and services via their logical name instead of having to know and use the server's IP address. The location services provided by DNS have become integral to the directory service operations of most network operating systems.

This chapter describes the DNS from a directory service perspective. This chapter covers DNS from domain namespace design and name resolution to zone files and resource records. The coverage of DNS is based on RFCs, and vendor-specific approaches are not discussed. For details on specific DNS implementations, refer to the DNS references listed in the Appendix.

Introduction to DNS

The DNS is the service used to locate network servers on the Internet and many corporate networks. DNS is a network name service that enables you to find a server's network address by supplying the server's host name. This process of locating a server's IP address via its host name is referred to as *name resolution*.

DNS is a client/server implementation that uses two fundamental components:

- A network server providing DNS services (the *name server*)
- The client running the DNS *resolver* (which may be either a workstation or another DNS name server)

DNS servers provide lookup services for DNS clients. They perform name resolution for requested DNS domain names and supply IP addresses for the servers within the specified domains.

DNS is a service designed to operate on TCP/IP-based networks, allowing network clients to use the names of network servers (as opposed to having to use IP addresses). A DNS server translates the "friendly name" of a network server (for example, www.mythical.org) into its corresponding IP address (for example, 192.168.111.90).

DNS implements a hierarchical naming strategy to associate a logical DNS host and/or domain name to a corresponding IP address. The DNS namespace is organized in a logical tree structure, arranging network servers within a hierarchical tree of domain nodes. DNS is designed to support the delegation of management, a clear necessity in such a large implementation as the Internet.

DNS operates by storing (and providing) domain name information in a distributed database contained on DNS *name servers* located within the TCP/IP network. The name servers store their portion of this distributed database in DNS *zone files*. Each DNS zone file stores the domain name information (for the pertinent DNS region or *zone*) in DNS *resource records* (RRs).

From a general networking perspective, DNS corresponds to the application layer of the OSI model, and it can be implemented over either the TCP (RFC 793) or UDP (RFC 768) protocols on port 53.

Prior to DNS, the association of IP addresses and the server's host name was done via storing the server names and corresponding IP addresses in a HOSTS.TXT file. The Internet name–to–IP address mapping was initially centralized with network servers periodically downloading the updated HOSTS.TXT file. When the number of servers exceeded the design capacity of this strategy, DNS was adopted.

One of the core goals in the design of DNS was to replace the centrally administered HOSTS.TXT file strategy with a distributed database that provided a hierarchical namespace, extensible data types, distribution of administration, and no operational limits on database size. The central specifications for DNS (RFCs 1034 and 1035) were accepted as standards in 1987.

DNS as a Specific-Use Directory

Although DNS is not a general-purpose directory, it does share many of the basic characteristics of a directory service—that is, a defined namespace, distributed data storage, client/server agents, and delegated directory servers that process client queries.

From this perspective, DNS looks very much like a directory service. Even though much of the high-level design and functionality of DNS is similar to an X.500-style directory service, however, the specific mechanisms that DNS uses differ somewhat.

An important distinction between DNS and the directory services discussed to this point is the language used to describe their components and operations. Unlike many directory service implementations, which may use a term or two a bit differently from each other, DNS uses a vocabulary almost entirely different from X.500, but it still describes functions that closely parallel X.500. Being able to connect the two sets of terminology may help you to more fully understand how DNS is both similar to and different from most directory service products on the market today.

To highlight the difference in vocabulary, this discussion reviews DNS, examining the parallels between DNS and X.500, and draws connections between the terminology employed. To start, an (admittedly) over-simplified analogy between terms used in DNS and X.500 follows. Table 6.1 shows the correlation between terminology.

Table 6.1 **Vocabulary Correlations**

Functionality	DNS Term	Analogous X.500 Term
Directory entries	Resource records (RRs)	Objects
Object subentries	Fields	Attributes
Definition of directory contents	Resource record definitions	Schema
Logical representation of directory	DNS domain namespace	Directory Information Tree
Data storage	Zone files	Directory Information Base (DIB)
Subdivision of directory	Zone	Naming context (partition)
Data updates	Zone transfers	Replication
Server agent	Name server	Directory Service Agent (DSA)
Client agent	Resolver	Directory User Agent (DUA)
Query resolution	Recursive and Iterative	Chaining and Referral

Although these analogies may be only somewhat helpful, a summary of the basics of DNS may prove instructive.

DNS is a highly specific, limited-use directory, primarily used to locate servers on the Internet and other TCP/IP networks. DNS operates as a network service that performs name–to–IP address resolution for domain and host names. DNS contains records used to locate various hosts (servers), frequently those performing specific roles (mail servers, name servers, and so on) or using a generic name to advertise a service (i.e. WWW, FTP).

A RR is a single entry in the DNS database that is analogous to a directory object. A RR consists of a series of fields (analogous to attributes), including information that identifies what type of RR it is and the identification of the network host represented by the record. Each type of RR is designed to represent a particular resource or service and contains the fields required for that type of record.

The *DNS schema* is comprised of the entire set of all possible RRs. These RRs are defined through the RFC process and may or may not be eventually implemented by industry vendors. Compared to general-purpose directories, the traditional DNS schema has historically been very simple with a limited scope of content—a small set of RRs describing hosts on the network. Multiple RFCs and drafts propose ways to enhance the functionality of DNS, from storing security data to service location. These new RFCs are discussed in the "DNS Schema" and "Evolution of DNS" sections later in this chapter.

The *DNS domain namespace* describes a hierarchical tree of domains. Each individual domain component, like an X.500 RDN, is a single component of the DNS name. Each domain component is separated by a single period (.) between the host, subdomain, and domain names. The highest level of the domain namespace tree structure is called the *root*, the nodes on the next level are referred to as *top-level domains* (tld), and the next level nodes are called *second-level domains*.

The information base for DNS is distributed as sets of RRs divided into zones, which are generally stored in text-based *zone files*. Each zone file contains a set of RRs and is limited in size to 64KB. A zone is a functional subdivision of the DNS database and, like a partition, each DNS zone contains a contiguous subtree of the DNS namespace.

Similar to X.500 replicas, DNS makes copies of the data it maintains in the zone files, using a single-master style replication model. There is a single *primary name server* for a given zone, which holds the master copy of the DNS data, and generally functions much like a directory server holding a master replica. There are also additional *secondary name servers,* which act much like read-only replicas and provide redundancy for load balancing and fault tolerance for DNS services.

Replication of DNS data (called *zone transfers*) commonly transmits the entire zone, but support for incremental transfer of just the zone data that changed is also supported. Although zone transfers traditionally required the secondary name servers to request updates at predetermined intervals, a notification mechanism (defined in RFC 1996) allows a primary name server to initiate the process.

DNS uses name servers to provide DSA-like functionality—that is, name servers process client queries, return results, and referrals to other name servers (but with a much more limited capability than X.500 DSAs).

Analogous to an X.500 DUA, the client-side software component in DNS is referred to as a *DNS resolver.* Although many general-purpose directories do have an application or interface to view the DIT as a hierarchical tree, DNS implementations do not commonly provide this.

Although the specifics of the name resolution and query resolution process differ, the basic approach is similar to that of X.500 in that DNS provides both a client-intensive (iterative) and a server-intensive (recursive) process. These processes are described in the "Name Resolution" section later in this chapter.

DNS Client/Server Agents

Like other directories, DNS is based on a client/server network model and employs specific software agents to conduct client and server operations. The following two software components are used by DNS:

- **Name servers** provide the server-side functionality of DNS.
- **Resolvers** act as the client component of DNS.

DNS is implemented such that a DNS client requests services of a name server by submitting a query, requesting information about a specified node within the DNS namespace. Each DNS name server manages a specified portion (that is, a zone) of the DNS domain namespace and related RRs. When a DNS server cannot provide a resolution to a query, it will commonly use a list of referrals to other DNS servers in order to locate a name server that can provide an authoritative response to the submitted name query.

The following sections review each of these components in a bit more detail.

DNS Name Servers

A DNS name server is a network server that handles information about a specific portion of the DNS domain namespace. A name server is designed to store, manage, and provide DNS information to network clients. A name server is responsible for one or more DNS zones (analogous to partitions) for which it is required to respond to name queries.

A name server is specified in the domain zone file via the Name Server (NS) RR, and it designates the DNS server that is performing authoritative name resolution services for the assigned zone. Name server records should always point to authoritative name server for the designated zone. The use of *authoritative* by DNS has a specific meaning— for a name server to be authoritative, it must contain current RRs for the designated zone.

The DNS server component is provided as a network service and can be implemented in a variety of server roles. The following terms are used to describe the roles a name server can take:

- **Primary**, **secondary**, and **master** apply to replication roles.
- **Authoritative** and **caching-only** refer to operational roles in the name resolution process.

Each of these roles is discussed later in the appropriate section of this chapter.

Correctly configured primary and current secondary name servers are authoritative for the designated DNS zone by default. From a lookup perspective, there is no operational distinction between primary and secondary name servers because the algorithm used in DNS name resolution uses the NS RRs for the referenced domain in the submitted order. The distinction between primary and secondary is important to the replication process, however, and these roles are discussed in more detail in the "Replication of DNS" section of this chapter.

DNS Resolvers

A *resolver* is the DNS client component that interacts with the name servers to obtain DNS domain, host, or service information. A resolver is commonly built in to the operating system's TCP/IP protocol stack. Both DNS clients and name servers provide resolver functionality, managing DNS communications between clients and servers as well as server to server.

DNS resolvers format data submitted by the client into DNS query packets to be sent to DNS name servers, and they handle and interpret DNS reply packets from DNS name servers, passing the results back to the requesting client. DNS resolvers can also cache results from previous name queries for use in subsequent name query resolution.

A DNS resolver commonly requests the following three types of operations for DNS clients:

- A **name-to-address translation** is a process of deriving the corresponding IP address from a submitted DNS domain name. The name-to-address translation is sent to the DNS name server as a request for a host address RR.

- An **address-to-name translation** is the reverse process of deriving the DNS host and domain information from a submitted IP address. To resolve an address-to-name translation request, the octet values of the IP address are reversed and concatenated with the reserved domain name suffix, `in.addr.arpa`, by the resolver. The address-to-name translation is then sent to the DNS name server as a request for a type PTR RR (referred to as a *pointer record*).

- A **general lookup function** is an operation involving searching the DNS zone files for records of a particular name, class, or type. General lookup functions are not commonly used, but they are employed by DNS utilities (such as NSLOOKUP) for troubleshooting DNS configuration problems.

How a Browser Uses DNS

A Web browser provides a familiar example of a DNS client using a DNS resolver, the client component in the DNS client/server implementation. When a browser is provided the URL of a Web site, the browser passes the domain portion of the URL to the resolver, which processes and forwards it as a DNS name query to the locally assigned DNS name server.

The name query refers to the host or alias (in the case of a Web site, www) which exists within a designated DNS domain (such as, `mythical.org`), and is specified in URL format as www.`mythical.org`.

The DNS name query is referred to an authoritative DNS name server for the specified DNS zone, which responds to the name query by returning the corresponding IP address of the host to the resolver (which then passes it back to the client application, the browser). The browser then uses the host IP address to initiate direct communication with the host server.

Models/Views in DNS

Unlike X.500, the DNS RFCs do not specifically define informational or functional models. Yet, similar to the way that X.500 describes models from the perspective of users, administrators, DSAs, and so on, DNS describes both components and views employed by DNS (RFC 1034).

The components defined by DNS include the domain namespace, RRs, name servers, and resolvers. In addition, three *views* of DNS are described:

- DNS defines the **user view**, which is analogous to X.500's User Information Model because it views the DNS directory from the user's perspective where the DNS namespace is comprised of a single unified tree. Users can query any portion of the DNS tree without having to understand the structure of the underlying distributed database.

- DNS also defines a **resolver view**, which doesn't correlate directly to an X.500 model, although it does provide some of the functionality described in the X.500 DSA Information and Distribution Models. The resolver views the DNS namespace as an unknown number of name servers, each of which contains a static portion of the DNS database.

- DNS also defines a **name server view**, which roughly corresponds to the X.500 DSA Information Model. The name server sees individual zones and recognizes that the information contained in those zones is somewhat dynamic, requiring refreshing to remain current. A name server maintains internal references to child and parent domains and provides query resolution services by using those references for referrals.

DNS Objects: Resource Records

All the information in a DNS database is stored as entries called RRs, which contain information about network hosts and services. These RRs are defined by the RFC process and, as a result, are an evolving set of entries providing ever-increasing functionality.

A dozen or so RRs are in common use, although many more are defined in the collected RFCs. Table 6.2 shows the RRs most often found in DNS.

Table 6.2 **The Set of Commonly Used Resource Records**

Resource Record Type	Content	RFC Number
A	Address	1035
CNAME	Canonical name	1035
HINFO	Host information	1035
MINFO	Mailbox or mail list information	1035

continues

Table 6.2 **Continued**

Resource Record Type	Content	RFC Number
MX	Mail exchange	1035
NS	Name server	1035
PTR	Pointer	1035
SOA	Start of authority	1035
TXT	Text	1035
WKS	Well-known service	1035
ISDN	ISDN	1183
NOTIFY	Notify	1996
SRV	Service	2052
UPDATE	Dynamic update	2136

We will look at some of the most important RRs in more depth later in the section titled "Defining the DNS Schema."

The DNS Tree

DNS is a system comprised of a distributed database of names logically structured as a hierarchical tree called the *domain namespace*. The DNS namespace is represented as a structure of domain nodes organized in an inverse tree. Each node in the DNS tree represents a domain that can contain one or more child nodes representing subdomains.

Each node in the DNS domain tree database (with all its child nodes) is defined as a *domain*. A domain may contain multiple subdomains or servers (hosts). Every DNS subdomain is "owned by" its parent domain. Every host, service, or subdomain that is owned by a specific domain is considered to be contained within that domain's namespace.

Organizations that register domain names are assigned (delegated) authority for that portion of the DNS domain namespace, and they manage the subdivision, naming, and administration of that subtree of the domain tree structure.

DNS domain references consist of logical components of the DNS name separated by a dot (that is, ".") delimiter. The five possible components of a DNS domain name are as follows:

- The root of the domain tree
- The top-level domain
- The second-level domain
- A subdomain name
- A host name

The Root Domain

The root of the DNS tree is a reserved value that is unnamed (null) and, as mentioned earlier, is referenced in DNS RRs via a trailing period (.), designating the highest level of the domain tree hierarchy.

At the heart of DNS operations (and the top of the DNS tree), the root name servers contain the zone information for all top-level domains. The root name servers are the authoritative servers for most top-level domains and can identify authoritative servers for the remaining top-level domains.

The root DNS servers control the core of the DNS database for the Internet. Many of these servers and the IP addresses they manage are, in turn, managed by Network Solutions (previously known as the Internet Networking Information Center— InterNIC). Root name servers for other top-level domains are managed by the registrar for that domain.

The root name servers play a key role in DNS name resolution, as DNS servers on the Internet are usually configured to refer name resolution requests to the root name servers whenever local name resolution is not possible.

When a DNS name server cannot resolve a name query, it performs the DNS referral process from right to left, beginning at the root. The name server forwards the query to a root name server, which replies with the address information for the authoritative server of the appropriate top-level domain. The name server then queries the top-level domain name server, requesting information on the second-level domain name provided in the query. This process continues until the query has been completed.

Top-Level Domains

Top-level domains are divided into the following three primary subdivisions of domain types:

- **Organization types** are associated with a corresponding three-letter abbreviation. These top-level DNS domains are primarily used for U.S. organizations and are subdivided by type of organization.

- **Geographical/country top-level domain names** are implemented by using the two-character country codes established in the ISO 3166 specification and are administered by agencies in each country. For example, the `.us` domain is managed by the U.S. Domain Registry at the Information Sciences Institute of the University of Southern California.

- **The `in.addr.arpa` top-level domain** is a special domain reserved for use in reverse name lookups, where the normal lookup process (DNS domain name to IP address) is inverted, and an IP address is resolved to a DNS domain name.

Figure 6.1 shows some of the currently available top-level domains. This figure does not, however, show any representation of the `in.addr.arpa` domain in the DNS tree.

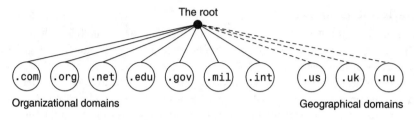

Figure 6.1 The top-level of the DNS domain namespace.

The most familiar (and coveted) top-level domains are those used by businesses and other organizations. These domain names comprise the most commonly used top-level domains, including the following:

- **.com** is for *commercial* organizations.
- **.org** is for *non-commercial* organizations.
- **.net** is for *networking* organizations.
- **.edu** is reserved for *educational* institutions.
- **.gov** is reserved for *governmental* organizations.
- **.mil** is reserved for *military* organizations.
- **.int** is for *international* organizations.

Various organizations manage the top-level domains:

- Network Solutions (NSI) currently manages the most common organizational top-level domains (.com, .org, .net, .edu). Until 1999, NSI enjoyed a monopoly on the domains they manage. However, NSI is beginning to share the responsibility for these domains with newly appointed registrars.
- The Department of Defense manages the .mil domain.
- The General Services Administration manages the .gov and .fed.us domains.
- The IANA manages the .int domain, which is used only for registering organizations established by international treaties.
- Other top-level domain registries (based on country code) have begun providing registration and name resolution services, such as registries using the .nu (Nuie) and .tm (Turmekistan) top-level domains.

Second-Level Domains

Second-level DNS domains are domains created by, and assigned to, specific organizations or people. The second-level domain name is a single DNS name component, like an X.500 RDN. However, a second-level domain is usually referenced by combining the selected second-level domain name (such as `mythical`) and the top-level domain (`.org`), into a single domain name expression, as in `mythical.org`. When the term *domain name* is used in common parlance (as in seeking a Web site), it is commonly the combined domain names being referred to.

Figure 6.2 shows two second-level domains as they are delegated to the organization(s) that created and registered them.

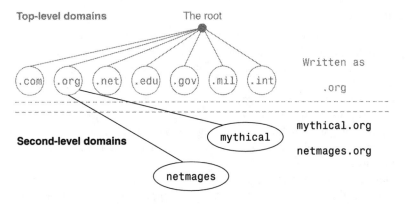

Figure 6.2 The second level of the DNS domain namespace is where various registrars register and delegate DNS domains to organizations.

Proposed Additional Top-Level Domains

The International Ad Hoc Committee (IAHC) has approved seven new top-level domain names. The new top-level domains provide wide new subdivisions of the DNS namespace. The introduction of these (and other) new top-level domains will ease the existing namespace constraints on domain names (especially in the `.com` domain). These new proposed top-level domains include the following:

- `.web` is for *web-centric* sites.
- `.store` is for *online sales* sites.
- `.firm` is for *commercial* sites.
- `.info` is for providers of *information services*.
- `.arts` is for *cultural and artistic* sites.
- `.rec` is for *recreational* sites.
- `.nom` is for *personal nomenclature*.

When an organization registers a second-level domain name with NSIInterNIC, the responsibility for managing the DNS namespace from that second-level domain downward through the DNS tree is delegated to that organization or their assigned technical contact. Organizations can then define DNS subdomains and hosts to match their actual network configuration and usage requirements.

After the domain is divided into subdomains, local administrators can further delegate the management of those subdomains. This structure of namespace management, where NSIInterNIC delegates DNS namespace control to organizations, and the organization delegates to subdivisions within the organization, provides for decentralized administration of DNS domain names.

Subdomains

The use of *subdomain names* is optional within the DNS namespace. Subdomains are specified to the left of the second-level domain name and are commonly used to specify organizational subdivisions (for instance, `sales.mythical.org`), as shown in Figure 6.3.

Subdomains can be multiple levels deep, allowing for detailed subdivisions within the DNS namespace controlled by an organization (for example, `oem.sales.mythical.org`). Subdomain names are not managed by NSIInterNIC and are entirely controlled by the organization that has registered the second-level domain name.

Although technically, any domain is a subdomain—even the top-level domains are subdomains of the root—the term *subdomain* is generally used to describe domains *below* the second level—that is, the section of the DNS tree created and managed by the organization delegated responsibility for a second-level domain.

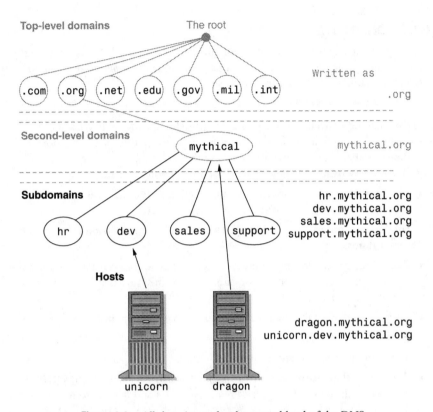

Figure 6.3   All domains under the second level of the DNS domain namespace are subdomains assigned and administered by the organization registering the second-level domain name.

DNS Hosts

In DNS, a *host* is a computer—generally a server supplying some sort of network service for the specified domain. Each host has at least one name and may also have aliases to allow location via multiple names. This is particularly useful because some of the common network services have universally accepted names associated with the server providing the service (such as www for web servers).

In DNS naming, the host name appears on the leftmost side of the DNS name, separated from subdomain and domain names by the dot (.) delimiter. If a server named dragon were providing DNS services for the mythical.org domain, for example, the DNS name would be constructed as dragon.mythical.org. Similarly if the unicorn server were providing DNS services for the dev subdomain of mythical.org, the DNS name would be constructed as unicorn.dev.mythical.org.

DNS Naming

The names of each of the domain components are used in the DNS name string, except the root, which is represented by a period. These components are combined to form a DNS name in the following manner:

```
<host>.<subdomain>.<second-level domain>.<top-level domain>
```

The DNS naming convention specifies a dot (.) delimiter to separate name components. The number of dot delimiters in the construction of a DNS domain name indicates the relative domain position within the DNS hierarchy.

DNS has a few basic rules governing the construction of names:

- The minimum information required to resolve a DNS name is
  ```
  <host>.<second-level domain>.<top-level domain>
  ```

- Subdomain components of a DNS name must be unique within the containing parent domain.

- The character set allowed is only A–Z (uppercase and lowercase), 0–9, and the hyphen character (-). DNS is not case sensitive, meaning that a *Z* and a *z* are considered equivalent.

- Components of a DNS name can be up to 63 characters in length (with the exception of the root domain).

DNS names are evaluated as either of the following:

- **Fully qualified domain names**—A *fully qualified domain name* (FQDN) is specified with the complete set of required values and has the terminating root delimiter (.) as the rightmost value (that is, `host.domain.tld.`). FQDNs are typically constructed by starting with the host name and specifying the domain components from the host up to the root of the DNS tree, and concatenating the host (or alias) and domain components with the dot delimiter, as follows:
  ```
  host.subdomain.domain.tld.
  ```
  For example:
  ```
  www.dev.mythical.org.
  ```

- **Relative domain names**—All DNS domain names that do not end with a trailing (.) delimiter are not FQDNs, but they are referred to as *relative DNS names*. Relative DNS domain names are more commonly used and are constructed by starting with the host name and specifying all domain components up to the top-level domain (rather than to the root of the DNS tree as an FQDN does). Relative DNS domain names are structured as `host.domain.tld`, as in `www.mythical.org` (which does not have the trailing period). A host name may be omitted if a null host address record is written to the zone file for the local host.

Defining the DNS Schema

Like other directories, DNS has to define a schema of some sort. In the case of DNS, the schema is the total set of possible RRs defined in RFCs. The DNS RFCs do not explicitly define the set of RRs as a *schema*. (The use of the term here is borrowed from the X.500 specifications.)

The schema has been defined via the RFC process, which has kept the number of RR types supported by all DNS servers relatively low. Compared to general-purpose directories, the DNS schema has historically been very simple with a limited scope of content—a limited set of RRs describing hosts on the network. Unlike many other directory services, DNS does not publish its schema as part of the available DNS information.

Although there have been a number of RFCs proposing additional DNS RR types over the years, few have been widely adopted by industry vendors until recently. Now a number of proposed standards for new RRs will effectively extend the DNS schema. RFCs have been written proposing ways to enhance the capability of DNS to manage security, both for the DNS service and the network in general. Several of these RFCs define ways to allow DNS to hold security tokens (such as X.509 certificates, Diffie-Hellman keys, and so on). These RFCs are listed in the "Evolution of DNS" section later in this chapter.

Only certain ASCII characters are considered valid within DNS RRs, specifically the characters A–Z, a–z, 0–9, and the hyphen (-). In addition to this base character set, special characters are used within a zone file's RRs, characters that are used to denote defaults (default domain), wildcards, or other special properties within a zone file. These characters are as follows:

- The (@) symbol is used within DNS zone records as a shortcut reference to the current default domain.

- The parentheses () are used to encompass arguments that span multiple lines.

- The asterisk (*) is used for wildcard expressions.

- The semicolon (;) is used to begin a comment line, where everything after the semicolon is ignored.

DNS Resource Records

DNS RRs are entries in DNS zone files containing specific information about the domain or host, and can be categorized by RR *class* or *type*.

A RR *class* indicates the class of network. The most commonly used RR class type is the Internet class specified by the IN class record entry. Although RFC 1035 also defines the following three additional classes, they are rarely used:

- CS—CSNET class (obsolete)

- CH—CHAOS class

- HS—Hesiod class

A RR *type* indicates the nature of the RR, type of data contained within each record, and specifies the data format employed for that RR type. For example, the host address RR type accepts a host name and IP address parameters.

This section describes the most common RR types employed in conventional DNS zone files including the *start of authority* (SOA), name server (NS), mail exchange (MX), host address (A), and the canonical name (CNAME) records. In addition, the DNS service resource (SRV) record is employed to indicate TCP/IP services locatable via DNS queries.

Start of Authority Records

A SOA record is the first entry within a DNS zone file, and refers to the primary DNS server that is authoritative for the specified DNS domain.

A SOA RR entry in the DNS zone file is structured as shown here:

```
<domain> IN SOA <source> <contact> <serial#> <refresh> <retry><expire> <TTL>
```

- `<domain>`—The fully qualified DNS domain name. A common shortcut used in DNS zone files is the @ symbol referring to the default domain.

- `<source>`—The `source` argument specifies the host upon which the zone file is stored.

- `<contact>`—The `contact` argument specifies to the email address for the zone file administrator. This email name format requires replacing the customary @ symbol with a period.

- `<serial#>`—The `serial#` argument specifies the version number for this zone database file, which is a number that should be incremented every time it is updated.

- `<refresh>`—The `refresh` argument specifies the amount of time (in seconds) that a secondary DNS server delays before checking with the primary DNS server to see whether a zone transfer is needed.

- `<retry>`—The `retry` argument specifies the amount of time (in seconds) that a secondary DNS server delays before retrying a zone transfer that did not complete.

- `<expire>`—The `expire` argument specifies the amount of time (in seconds) that a secondary DNS server will continue attempting to perform a zone transfer. If the time limit expires without a successful zone transfer, existing zone information for this specific zone is discarded.

- `<TTL>`—The `TTL` argument specifies the amount of time (in seconds) that a DNS server is permitted to store RRs from this specific zone file in its cache.

Order of DNS records

The order of entry of the RRs in a zone file is not preserved in the operation of DNS.

Following is an example of an SOA RR entry:

```
@ IN    SOA    dragon.mythical.org. info.dragon.mythical.org.(
8
10800
3600
604800
86400 )
```

Name Server Resource Records

A *name server* (NS) RR is used to specify a name server for a designated zone and is always specified within a zone file, as well as in the reverse lookup zones defined in the `in-addr.arpa` DNS domain.

The NS RR specifies the DNS server responsible for authoritative name resolution for the designated zone. NS records should always point to authoritative name servers.

The NS RR entry in the zone file is structured as shown here:

```
<domain> IN NS <host>
```

For example:

```
@ IN NS dragon.mythical.org
```

Host Address Resource Records

A *host address* (A) RR is used within a zone file to specify the linkage between a host name and its corresponding IP address. The host address RR is one of the most common RRs used in DNS forward lookup zone files.

Every zone file must contain at least one host address RR for every host within the DNS zone and for every IP address assigned to that host. The host address records may comprise a substantial number of the entries contained within the zone file.

The host address entry in the DNS zone file is structured as shown here:

```
<host> IN A <IP address>
```

For example:

```
dragon IN A 192.168.111.90
```

A reserved host record address is defined that refers to the local host—which is implemented in the same format as host address RRs—and is created in most zone files by default. This address record for the local host provides a means to perform lookups on the local computer by associating the local host name with a standardized IP address (`127.0.0.1`) commonly used to perform loopback testing on host network adapters. *Loopback testing* is used to verify that the TCP/IP protocol is installed and functioning on the local machine. The format for the local host RR entry is structured as follows:

```
localhost IN A 127.0.0.1
```

Canonical Name Resource Records

A *canonical name* (CNAME) RR is used within a zone file to specify an alias for a host name. CNAME records specify only the host and alias names; therefore, CNAME records depend on existing host address (A) RRs already defined within the zone file for the designated host. Using aliases via CNAME RRs provides a mechanism to isolate client access to resources from the details of network server implementation.

The CNAME RR provides a way to associate multiple logical names with a single host, allowing a single server to host multiple services. A common use of the CNAME record, for example, is to specify the server providing FTP services for a domain (that is, `ftp.mythical.org`). The CNAME RR entry in the DNS zone file is structured as follows:

```
<alias> IN CNAME <host>
```

For example:

```
ftp IN CNAME dragon
```

Should the FTP services for the designated domains be required to move to a new host server, the new server's host address RR could be added, and the CNAME alias updated to reference the new server. The change of host servers would be transparent to the FTP clients.

Glue Records

In DNS deployment, a condition arises in which references to the name server for a domain exist only within the domain it is the name server for. For example, when the only reference to a name server for a subdomain is within the zone file of the subdomain name resolution cannot be completed.

To accomplish effective address resolution, a *glue record* must be used to append the host address to the name server reference in the parent domain. The glue record is employed only in the name server delegating the domain, and it is not employed in the target domain.

Assume you are referencing a name server for `dev.mythical.org` from the parent `mythical.org` name server, for example, and that the name server for `dev.mythical.org` is `unicorn.dev.mythical.org`. In such a case, the NS record and glued A record would be specified as follows:

```
dev.mythical.org.      NS unicorn.dev.mythical.org.
unicorn.dev.mythical.org.    A 192.168.111.83
```

Service Resource Records

The *service* (SRV) RR is a new DNS record type introduced in RFC 2052 and is used to specify the location of named TCP/IP-based network services. SRV records enhance the capability of DNS to locate network resources by identifying the specific *services* provided by a particular server. The SRV record maps the name of a network service to the IP address of the server providing the service.

From the perspective of directory services, the SRV record is one of the more important new RRs because it supports the identification of service hosts such as LDAP servers. This is one of the ways DNS and LDAP are being integrated to provide directory service functionality—DNS acts as the location service, and LDAP provides the structured query support.

The DNS service RR entry in the DNS zone file is structured as shown here:

```
<service>.<protocol>.<name> SRV <TTL><priority><weight><port><target>
```

- `<service>`—The `service` parameter accepts the symbolic name of the service provided, which is specified in accordance with the standardized abbreviated code specified in RFC 1700 (such as `http`).

- `<protocol>`—The `protocol` parameter specifies the transmission protocol to be employed for network communications. The protocol types most commonly specified in this parameter are the Transmission Control Protocol (`tcp`) and the User Datagram Protocol (`udp`).

- `<name>`—The `name` parameter is optional and is commonly employed to indicate additional domain name data to be prefixed to the domain name of the current DNS zone.

- `<TTL>` The `TTL` parameter sets the time in seconds that a DNS server is permitted to cache SRV records from the zone.

- `<priority>`—The `priority` parameter is used to establish a priority scale (0–65,535) for each host of a named domain target.

- `<weight>`—The `weight` parameter is designed to effect load balancing between target domain hosts for the specified service.

- `<port>`—The `port` parameter is used to specify the TCP/IP service port number for the specific type of service. Standard assigned service port numbers are specified along with their abbreviations in RFC 1700.

- `<target>`—The `target` parameter of the service RR specifies the host domain name supporting the server lookup requests. A corresponding host address (A) record must exist in the appropriate zone file for every host listed in the target parameter of an SRV record.

The Distributed DNS Database

The logical DNS tree of domains and subdomains is stored in a distributed database contained on servers spread throughout the network. In its Internet implementation, the network spans the entire world. The DNS database is subdivided via domain delegation and is partitioned using DNS zones.

Partitioning the DNS Database

To store the DNS data, the RRs of the domains and subdomains are grouped into zones. A *zone* is a set of RRs representing a single contiguous subdivision of the DNS namespace. A zone is comprised of DNS RRs managed in a specific file, referred to as a DNS *zone file*.

The key distinction between a DNS domain and a DNS zone is that a DNS domain represents the logical structure of the DNS namespace, whereas zones represent the physical distribution of DNS information to specific name servers.

Every zone is anchored to a specific domain node referred to as the zone's *root domain*. DNS servers can manage one or more domains contained in one or more zone files, as shown in Figure 6.4. A zone must be a contiguous subdivision of the DNS namespace (a subtree) because a zone may not contain records from discontiguous domains.

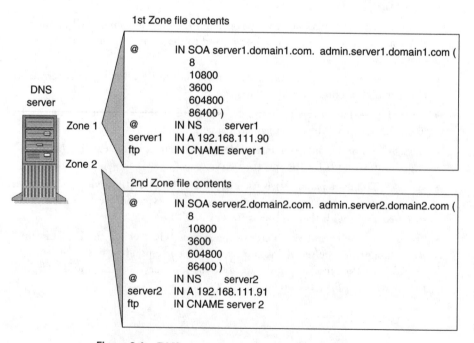

Figure 6.4 DNS servers support one or more DNS zones
(a collection of RRs representing a contiguous subtree).

Subdividing the logical DNS domain namespace and defining corresponding zones can facilitate management of distributed DNS services. RRs contained within each zone can be replicated from primary to secondary name servers via a *zone transfer*. Secondary name servers are employed to provide backup DNS name servers for the zone. Distributing secondary name servers throughout the network can provide load balancing for heavily utilized DNS services.

Zone Delegation

Zone delegation is the process by which a name server is delegated responsibility for handling a specific subzone. This is specified in the zone file by the use of the delimiting name server (NS) and address (A) RRs following the SOA record.

DNS Zone Files

DNS is commonly configured via text-based zone files that contain the necessary RRs defining host, domain, and DNS services. A zone file describes a specific portion of the DNS database and contains the specific set of RRs defining that zone. Other standard DNS files include the cache and reverse lookup files. These distributed zone, cache, and reverse lookup files are collectively referred to as the DNS database.

DNS Boot File

A *DNS boot file* is not specified in the RFCs for DNS, nor are they required for RFC-compliant DNS operations. Implementations of DNS either support the use of a boot file to specify startup parameters, however, or provide other support for the DNS startup command functionality. A BIND-compliant DNS boot file is a text file that allows startup commands controlling DNS behavior, including the `directory`, `cache`, `primary`, `secondary`, `forwarders`, and `slave` commands. The following sections briefly look at each of these commands.

Lame Delegation

When a DNS name server is delegated as authoritative for a specific DNS zone and yet does not respond to name queries with authoritative results, this is referred to as *lame delegation*. The condition of lame delegation usually results from incorrect configuration of the DNS name server, where the name server is not configured to respond authoritatively for the specified zone but should be.

BIND is a UNIX DNS Implementation

BIND stands for *Berkeley Internet Name Domain*, a vendor-specific version of DNS that specifies the use of a boot file for startup functionality.

directory

The `directory` command is used to specify the location of external files referred to within the boot file. A directory command entry is structured as follows:

```
directory <directory path>
```

For example:

```
directory d:\nt\system32\dns
```

cache

The `cache` command identifies the DNS cache zone file specifying the root name servers. A cache command entry is structured as shown here:

```
cache . <DNS cache filename>
```

For example:

```
cache . cache.dns
```

primary

The `primary` command specifies both the DNS domain for which the name server is authoritative and the zone file containing the RRs for the designated domain. A DNS boot file may contain multiple `primary` command entries, one for each configured primary zone. A `primary` command entry is structured as shown here:

```
primary <domain> <zone filename>
```

For example:

```
primary mythical.org mythical.dns
```

secondary

The `secondary` command is used to specify the DNS domain for which the server is authoritative, the master server IP addresses from which to download zone information, and the name of the local file used for caching transfered zone information. A DNS boot file may also contain multiple `secondary` command records, one for each secondary zone. Each `secondary` record can contain more than one host IP address. A secondary command entry is structured as follows:

```
secondary <domain> <IPaddressesOfHosts> <local cache filename>
```

For example:

```
secondary mythical.org 192.168.111.90 mythcache.dns
```

forwarders

The `forwarders` command is used to specify the IP addresses of name servers that will perform name resolution on forwarded name queries. A `forwarders` command entry is structured as shown here:

```
forwarders <IPaddressesOfHosts>
```

For example:

```
forwarders 192.168.111.98 192.168.111.99
```

slave

The `slave` command is used to specify that using the forwarders is the only method of name resolution. Versions of BIND will support the use of the `option forward-only` command as equivalent to `slave`. A `slave` command can be used only subsequent to a `forwarders` command and is a single-word entry, as shown here:

```
slave
```

or

```
option forward-only
```

DNS Cache File

The *DNS cache file* contains host address RRs for the root DNS name servers. The DNS cache file is required to resolve name queries for DNS names for which the local name server is not authoritative (that is, domains not contained in the server's zone files). The Internet root name servers are the most common entries contained within a DNS cache file; for networks not connected to the Internet, however, the DNS cache file should contain host address RRs for the root servers of the local network.

Reverse Lookup Files

The *DNS reverse lookup files* are zone files referenced when a DNS name server is searching the `in-addr.arpa` domain to perform a reverse lookup (finding a host name based on IP address). One reverse lookup file per subnet exists, containing the information necessary to resolve an IP address to its corresponding host name. Similar to forward lookup zone files, a reverse lookup zone file will also contain NS and SOA records. However, reverse lookup files differ in their use of pointer (PTR) records rather than address (A) records. Two uses of pointer records are employed in reverse lookup operations: to either identify a specific host, or to identify a specific network.

PTR Records to Identify a Host

A PTR RR is used within a reverse lookup zone file to associate an IP address to a host name in a reverse lookup zone within the `in-addr.arpa` domain.
The PTR RR is a counterpart to the host address (A) RR specified in a forward lookup zone.

To create a PTR RR, the IP address values are written in reverse order with the `in-addr.arpa` domain concatenated to the end of the reverse IP address. The PTR record is structured as shown here:

```
<reverseIPaddress>.in-addr.arpa IN PTR <host>
```

For example, the PTR record for `dragon.mythical.org` at `192.168.111.90` is as follows:

```
90.111.168.192.in-addr.arpa IN PTR dragon.mythical.org
```

Gateway PTR Records

Gateways for a specified network can be located using the `in-addr.arpa` domain. Although gateways are specified with PTR RRs in the same manner that hosts are specified, they also have additional pointer records used to find them solely by network number.

These additional PTR records will use one, two, or three octets of the IP address in the construction of the `in-addr.arpa` domain name, depending on whether they are Class A, B, or C networks. Therefore, a gateway PTR record would look like the following:

- `10.in-addr.arpa` for a Class A network
- `18.128.in-addr.arpa` for a Class B network
- `111.168.192.in-addr.arpa` for a Class C network

Replication of DNS Data

The replication of DNS data follows the single-master replication model discussed in Chapter 3, "Storing Directory Information." This section describes the replication roles used by name servers and the replication operations they use to propagate the changes to the DNS data.

Replication Roles of DNS Name Servers

DNS name servers can be implemented in a range of roles and functionality:

- Primary
- Secondary
- Master

Although DNS name servers are commonly referred to by their role (as a primary name server, or just primary), the server component remains the same (just the tasks the server performs differ).

Primary Name Servers

A *primary name server* is the server containing a master copy of all the DNS information files used in supporting the services for the specified zone. All changes to zone information, including adding hosts, services, or domains, are performed at the primary name server. The primary name server is commonly also the master name server—that is, the source of the RRs transmitted during a zone transfer.

A primary name server acquires its zone information by accessing local DNS information files (zone files), as shown in Figure 6.5. The primary name server for a specified zone is an authoritative name server for that zone.

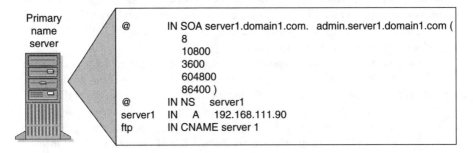

Primary
name
server

```
@           IN SOA server1.domain1.com.  admin.server1.domain1.com (
            8
            10800
            3600
            604800
            86400 )
@           IN NS    server1
server1     IN   A   192.168.111.90
ftp         IN CNAME server 1
```

Figure 6.5   The primary name server obtains zone
information direct from local zone files.

Secondary Name Servers

A *secondary name server* is essentially a backup name server for a DNS zone that receives its zone information from an authoritative name server (typically the primary name server for the zone). Secondary name servers are commonly used as backup servers to heavily utilized DNS servers, providing name resolution support on a distributed basis.

Secondary name servers obtain their zone information via periodic replications (that is, zone transfers). During a zone transfer, the secondary name server receives the zone's RRs, typically from the primary name server for that zone (which sends current zone data to the secondary zone server), as shown in Figure 6.6.

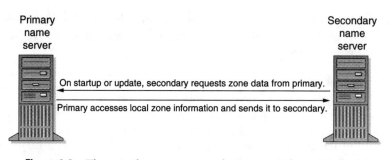

Figure 6.6   The secondary name server obtains zone information from the primary name server during period updates (zone transfers).

A secondary name server initially requests the zone information from the primary name server upon startup and, from then on, periodically checks for updates by comparing its serial number in the SOA record to the serial number in the primary's SOA record. When the primary's serial number differs from the secondary's, the secondary initiates a zone transfer request.

The periodicity of secondary updates is controlled by three key fields in the SOA record, specifically the `refresh`, `retry`, and `expire` fields. Every `refresh` number of seconds, the secondary name server will check the primary name server. If the secondary name server fails to complete the update check, it will retry the update check every `retry` seconds until it succeeds. If it does not complete the update check within `expire` seconds, the zone records are discarded, and the server returns errors to queries in that zone.

Master Name Servers

The designation of a name server as a *master name server* merely specifies that it is the *source* of the DNS zone RRs during a zone transfer. For a secondary name server to acquire its zone information, a name server from which to obtain the zone records must be specified. Although this can be either a primary or secondary zone, in either case it is referred to as the master name server.

Name Servers Can Be Both Primary and Secondary

From the description of the roles performed by name servers, you may have gotten the impression that these are exclusive roles, but that is not the case. Because a name server can support more than one zone, it can be a primary name server for one zone and a secondary name server for another.

Replication Processes

Replication in DNS takes place using some kind of zone transfer. Originally, DNS supported only complete replication—where the entire zone file is sent with each zone transfer. With newer DNS implementations, zone transfers can be performed in an incremental fashion to minimize the bandwidth used in DNS data replication.

Zone Transfers

A *zone transfer* is the process whereby a secondary receives a complete copy of the zone information from an authoritative name server. A zone transfer essentially transmits a copy of all RRs of a specific zone to the receiving (secondary) server.

Figure 6.7 shows the zone transfer process, which is as follows:

1. By default, the secondary name server will periodically check with the master name server to determine whether zone records have been changed. The secondary will request the SOA record to evaluate the serial number (the version number) of the zone records.

2. The master name server sends the SOA record to the secondary.

3. The secondary server compares version numbers and requests zone transfer if the version number has changed.

4. The master name server begins the zone transfer, transmitting zone file contents to the secondary name server.

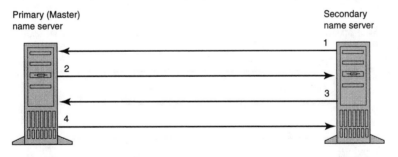

Figure 6.7 DNS zone transfer from primary to secondary server.

To accomplish a zone transfer, the secondary name server must specify the name server from which to obtain the zone information. Although the source of the zone transfer can be either a primary or secondary name server, it is always referred to as the master name server.

Incremental Zone Transfers

Initially all zone transfers required transferring the entire set of RRs for the zone during every zone transfer. RFC 1995 described an incremental method for propagation of zone file update information. Incremental zone transfers allows the master name server to send only the RR information that has changed since the last zone transfer with that secondary server. Because substantially less information must be transmitted, incremental zone transfers are a far more efficient method of DNS zone replication.

Incremental zone transfers require the master name server not only to maintain the updated master zone file, but also a recent history, logging changes to RRs that occurred with each update of the zone file (and its corresponding version number). When the master name server receives an incremental zone transfer request, it compares the version numbers; if they differ, the master name server sends the RR changes that have occurred between versions.

Zone Transfers with DNS Notify

RFC 1996 defines a push mechanism for a master name server to notify selected secondary name servers of changes to zone files. DNS Notify allows name servers to push the zone changes to secondary name servers as they occur. Although secondary name servers commonly "pull" (`refresh`) zone updates from master name servers, the DNS Notify "push" implementation provides more timely updates and ensures consistency of DNS zone information (see Figure 6.8).

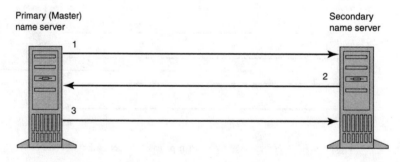

Figure 6.8 DNS zone transfer from primary to secondary server using DNS Notify.

1. A DNS Notify process occurs when zone records on the master name server change, and the serial number field in the SOA record is incremented. The master name server sends a DNS Notify message to servers contained within the notify set, and those servers respond with an SOA type query to check the zone file version.

2. The secondary name server compares version numbers; and if the master name server's zone file version exceeds the secondary's zone version number, the secondary name server requests a zone transfer.

3. The master name server copies all RRs for that zone to the secondary name server. When complete, the secondary name server is again authoritative for the designated zone.

For DNS Notify to operate, the IP address of every secondary name server must be contained within the master name server's notify set. After the secondary name server IP addresses are listed in the master name server's notify set, the zone information will be pushed to that set of secondary name servers only.

DNS Operations

DNS provides the operations necessary to support resolution of domain names to IP addresses, as well as to identify hosts of network services. DNS name servers can be assigned different operational roles and can be configured to perform different degrees of query processing (such as when configured with `forwarders` or `slave` entries).

Similar to X.500, DNS provides two forms of query resolution:

- One that requires the client to perform most of the lookup processing (iterative queries)

- Another that offloads the query process management to the server (recursive queries)

This section discusses the fundamentals of name resolution, and describes how each of the query types is handled.

DNS Name Resolution

DNS name resolution is the process by which a DNS name server resolves a DNS name to its corresponding IP address. Typical DNS approaches to resolving a name query are referred to as *recursive name resolution* and *iterative name resolution*, prompted by the corresponding type of query. In addition, a special kind of name query allows for reverse name resolution process (from IP address to name), commonly referred to as *reverse lookups*.

A naming system strategy such as DNS, which uses a distributed database, is commonly presented with a condition in which a name server receives a client query that can be resolved only by another name server. A DNS name server that receives a name query but cannot perform the name resolution itself will refer (or provide) the name query to another name server.

The following section discusses the different roles that a name server may operate in, and then describes how DNS name queries work. The section also reviews the specific recursive and iterative name resolution processes.

Operational Roles of Name Servers

Fundamentally, DNS name servers operate in one of two operational roles:

- Authoritative
- Caching-only

Authoritative Name Servers

A DNS name server may control one or more zones containing one or more domains. A name server has *authority* for each zone that it controls and is referred to as an *authoritative* name server. For a name server to respond positively to a name query, it must be an authoritative server for the zone containing the queried name.

The primary name server for a specified zone is an authoritative name server for that zone. If the secondary name server's zone data is current, the secondary name server is also authoritative for the specified zone.

The authority for a DNS name server to provide name information within a specified zone is defined using an SOA record. When a name server contains the SOA record in its zone file for a particular DNS domain or subdomain, that name server is referred to as *authoritative* or as an *authoritative server* for that zone.

Caching-Only Name Servers

A *caching-only name server* is not linked to any specific zones and does not contain its own zone files. When a caching-only name server initializes, it has no information on zones or domains and relies exclusively on other primary or secondary name servers for its information. A caching-only name server builds its DNS information from queries passed to primary or secondary name servers and stores the information in its local name cache.

The caching-only name server (see Figure 6.9) directly processes additional queries referencing the DNS information stored in its local cache. The sole function of caching-only name servers is to perform name queries, store the responses in their local cache, and return the query responses to the client submitting the query. The cached DNS data remains in the cache until the Time-To-Live (TTL) expires or the next reboot of the server.

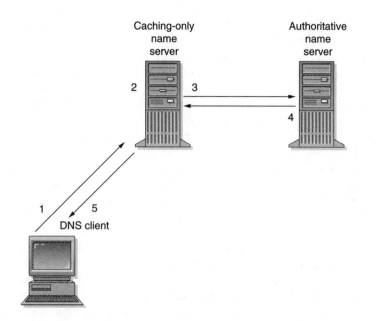

Figure 6.9 A caching-only name server does not have local zone files and builds its cache from name query requests it handles.

Figure 6.9 shows how a caching-only server performs, which is as follows:

1. A DNS client submits a recursive query.

2. The caching-only DNS server is not linked to any zone (and does not contain local zone files) and, therefore, looks in cache for RRs matching query.

3. If a match is not found in cache, the name server queries other name servers.

4. The authoritative name server for the zone returns query results to the caching-only name server.

5. The caching-only name server stores the query results in its local cache for future access and returns the results to the client.

DNS Name Queries

A typical DNS name query (forward lookup) is initiated by a client resolver requesting name resolution for a specific host or domain name. The DNS client resolver (or a name server) may submit either iterative or recursive name queries to the name server. The key difference between an iterative name query and a recursive name query is that when a client passes a *recursive query* to the name server, it requests the name server to complete the name resolution process on its behalf (by querying other name servers). With an *iterative query*, however, the client requests the server to provide only whatever local information it has (and not to query other name servers).

A DNS name query is resolved starting from the left side of the submitted DNS name (containing the most specific portion), proceeding through the domain components to the right side of the submitted DNS name (containing the most general portion of the domain name). The name resolution process uses each component of the domain name in an effort to locate an authoritative name server for the submitted name query.

When a name server receives a resolver query for a specific domain name, it first checks the zone files for which it has authority. (If it finds the name, it provides the authoritative result to the client). If it does not have the name in its zone records, it checks its local cache to see whether it has resolved the query before. (If it has, it provides the authoritative result to the client.)

A name server will commonly pass DNS requests it cannot resolve to a higher-level server in the DNS tree (using the NS records of the parent domain to locate the right servers to query for the requested domain). If the DNS server is presented with a query for an unknown domain name, the resolver may query other name servers higher in the DNS tree or may redirect the query to the root name servers. The resolver typically will continue to query other name servers until it receives an authoritative response to the query.

Caching DNS Query Results

DNS name servers temporarily store name query information results in a local cache, allowing the name server to retrieve commonly requested DNS information rapidly, without having to access other name servers. DNS information that is stored in the local cache has a TTL value applied to the cached RRs. Although all DNS name servers will cache the results of name queries that have been submitted to them, *caching-only* name servers will not be authoritative for any domain and will merely contain DNS query results for name queries that they process.

Iterative Name Resolution

Iterative name resolution is like the X.500 referral process because the name server receiving the name query either answers the query authoritatively or refers the client to another name server. When the information requested in an iterative name query is not found in local zone files, the name server does not query other name servers on behalf of the client.

An iterative name resolution request instructs the name server to attempt to complete name resolution from within its own DNS dataset (see Figure 6.10). If the contacted name server contains the requested information, it will provide it to the client; otherwise, it may return pointers to other name servers that may contain the queried data (but will make no attempt to contact the other name servers on behalf of the requesting client).

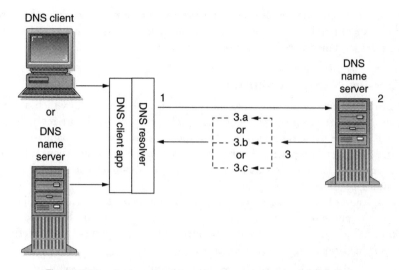

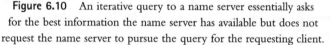

Figure 6.10   An iterative query to a name server essentially asks
for the best information the name server has available but does not
request the name server to pursue the query for the requesting client.

Figure 6.10 shows how an iterative name query to a name server occurs, which is as
follows:

1. DNS client resolver (can be a DNS client or another name server) submits an
   iterative query to a name server.

2. The receiving name server first tries to resolve the name query within local
   zone records.

3. The name server provides one of the following three responses to client:

   - **3.a**—If the query can be resolved via local zones and cache file, the name
     server returns the zone data (zone RRs with corresponding host names
     and IP addresses) in query results to the client.

   - **3.b**—If the query cannot be resolved locally, the name server returns a
     referral (best guess at closest relevant domain name server) to the client,
     for the client resolver to use in further name queries.

   - **3.c**—When an authoritative name server for the zone cannot resolve the
     query from its zone records, it will return an error to the requesting client
     specifying that the requested data is not found.

Iterative name resolution is also referred to as a *nonrecursive name resolution* because the name server responds to the query based on its own DNS information and does not recursively send the query to other name servers.

Recursive Name Resolution

Recursive DNS queries are similar to the X.500 chaining process, in which query resolution is pursued on the server side and only complete results are returned to the client. Recursive name resolution is where the server receiving the name query pursues query resolution with other name servers on behalf of the client submitting the query. DNS name servers must be specifically configured to allow recursive forwarding of name queries.

Submission of the recursive query tells the name server to provide the client with a complete response to the query—not just a reference or a pointer to an alternative DNS name server. The name server will query other name servers until a definitive result for the originating query is obtained:

- A definitive positive response to the name query occurs when an authoritative name server verifies that the target exists and provides the requested results in the query response.

- A definitive negative response to the name query occurs when an authoritative server verifies that the target of the name query does not exist.

Recursive DNS server operations are commonly employed by *stub resolvers* (a resolver component that provides a minimum functionality) and rely on recursive operations for name resolution and address translation. Stub resolvers are frequently configured to query a specific set of servers, and they expect to receive an authoritative response to queries (as opposed to referrals).

Figure 6.11 shows a specific example of recursive name resolution, in which the client submits a recursive name query on the domain name www.mythical.org to a local DNS name server that queries the DNS root name servers to resolve the domain name. This process is as follows:

1. The DNS client resolver submits a recursive query for www.mythical.org.

2. The local name server fails to resolve the name query within its zone records.

3. Because the query cannot be resolved locally, the name server submits an iterative query to the DNS root name servers.

4. The root DNS name server is not authoritative for zone, so a referral to the .org domain name server is returned.

5. The local name server queries the .org name server.

6. The .org name server is also nonauthoritative, but it does contain reference to the authoritative name server for mythical.org and, therefore, returns a referral to the mythical.org name server.

7. The local name server queries the `mythical.org` name server.

8. The `mythical.org` name server is the authoritative name server for the zone that includes `www.mythical.org` and, therefore, returns the requested host IP address, `192.168.111.90`, to the local name server.

9. The name server then returns definitive query results (the IP address of `www.mythical.org`) to the requesting client.

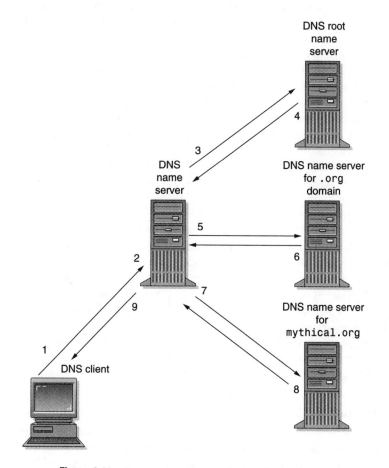

Figure 6.11   In recursive name resolution, the local name server pursues a query on behalf of a client until it is resolved.

Reverse Lookups

In most DNS queries, the client submits a DNS host and domain name, requesting the corresponding IP address (a forward lookup). Yet sometimes a resolver will submit an IP address to receive the assigned DNS host name from a name server. A DNS query that requests this address-to-name resolution is referred to as a *reverse name query*, or *reverse lookup*.

There is no structural correlation in the assignment of DNS domain names and IP addresses, a factor which by default would require a search of all domains within the namespace to provide a resolution to a reverse lookup. To provide the capability to effectively perform reverse lookup operations, a special domain called **in-addr.arpa** was created within the DNS namespace. The in-addr.arpa domain functions by naming its nodes with the numbers used in IP addresses.

DNS domain names become less specific from left to right, with the most specific (host name) information on the left side, to the least specific (top-level domain name) on the right side. In contrast, IP addresses become more specific from left to right, with the network number represented in the first octet(s) and the host identifier represented in the remaining octet(s). This differential direction of specificity in the ordering of DNS names versus IP addresses requires the reversal of the IP address octets in the delineation of the `in-addr.arpa` tree.

Like address records used in forward lookups, in the `in-addr.arpa` domain PTR records are used to correlate IP addresses to host names in reverse lookups.

As an example of the reverse lookup process, consider this: To locate a host name for the IP address `192.168.111.90`, a client resolver would submit a query to a DNS name server for a pointer record indicating `90.111.168.192.in-addr.arpa`. If the submitted IP address is not contained within the local DNS domain, the name server will begin at the DNS root and perform sequential domain node name resolution. When the sequential name resolution reaches `111.168.192.in-addr.arpa`, the zone records would be searched for a pointer type RR for host `90`, which would resolve to the domain host `dragon.mythical.org`. At this point, the reverse lookup process would be completed and the results returned to the client.

Name Resolution with *forwarders*

DNS servers can be configured with `forwarders` entries to control DNS lookups to name servers. `forwarders` enables you to specify the order and the scope of a DNS lookup process and provides a means to control the flow of DNS query traffic for security or other operational reasons. Generally, in an enterprise network with connectivity to the Internet, direct DNS lookups to external servers would be restricted to specific internal name servers.

If a name server has `forwarders` specified, it can also specify that it should only use `forwarders` via a `slave` command. `forwarders` and `slave` commands are optional entries in the DNS boot file.

DNS Servers Configured with *forwarders*

`forwarders` are essentially a list of name servers to query first. The `forwarders` entries are added to the beginning of the list of name servers to query if the requested domain information is not available in local files. If the `forwarders` command is present, other name servers (such as the root name servers) will only be queried if the `forwarders` provide no response within a short period of time.

`forwarders` are commonly used in enterprise networks to provide a means to have all DNS lookups search the internal DNS namespace first, and to access external name servers only after internal resources have been exceeded. In common configuration, only specified internal name servers would be allowed to forward name queries to external DNS servers. Depending on results received, the name server will respond in one of two ways:

- If a name server receives a name query that it cannot resolve, it first forwards the query to the other name servers specified in the `forwarders` command. The specified name server then processes the forwarded name query and returns the query results to the requesting name server.
- If the forwarder does not answer the query within a specified period of time, the originating resolver will transmit the query to other name servers.

DNS Servers Configured with the *slave* Command

A name server configured with the `slave` command requires an existing `forwarders` entry. A name server configured with the `slave` command must either use only the name servers specified in the `forwarders` entry or return a failure message if they cannot resolve the name query request. A DNS server configured with the `slave` command does not further attempt to contact alternative name servers if the name servers on the `forwarders` list cannot resolve the name query.

The DNS `slave` command works in combination with the `forwarders` entry, specifying that the list of name server records will replace (instead of being added to the beginning of) the list of name server records to query when queries cannot be resolved locally. The `slave` command effectively prevents referral of DNS name queries to the name servers other than those specified in the `forwarders` command. Using the `slave` command, if the query cannot be resolved by the specified list of `forwarders`, the query will not be resolved at all.

> **Slave Operations in BIND**
>
> Some DNS implementations, notably later versions of BIND, use the syntax **option forward-only** to indicate that the name server should function as a slave.

Name Resolution Processes with *forwarders*

In Figure 6.12, two forms of name resolution are displayed with the lookup processes using `forwarders` and `slave` commands specified in the DNS boot file. The diagram begins a DNS client submitting a name query for a DNS host name, as follows:

1. A DNS client submits a name query.

2. The name server attempts to resolve the query within local zone records. When a name server fails to resolve a name query, it performs different name resolution processes (depending on whether it has `forwarders` or `slave` commands specified). These variations on name resolution are demonstrated in A and B:

A) **If configured with `forwarders` command**—You can specify that a DNS name server is required to first use a designated list of forwarders to resolve all queries outside of the local zone, *before* attempting to contact other name servers (including the DNS root name servers). DNS name servers to query first are specified in the `forwarders` command entry in the DNS boot file and are operationally prefixed to the NS lookup records.

   3. The name server first queries the name server(s) specified in the `forwarders` command

   4. The name server receives a response indicating query failure.

   5. The name server then queries the DNS root name servers.

B) **If configured with `slave` command**—A name server configured with the `slave` command (in the DNS boot file) forwards DNS queries to designated forwarders *only* and does not attempt to contact DNS name servers outside of the designated forwarders list. A `slave` name server depends entirely on the specified list of forwarders to provide query resolution, whereas name servers without a `slave` command are allowed to relay DNS queries to name servers in the DNS cache file (usually the DNS root name servers on the Internet).

   3. The name server first queries the name server specified in the `forwarders` entry.

   4. Upon receiving a response, the name server makes no further attempt to contact other name servers.

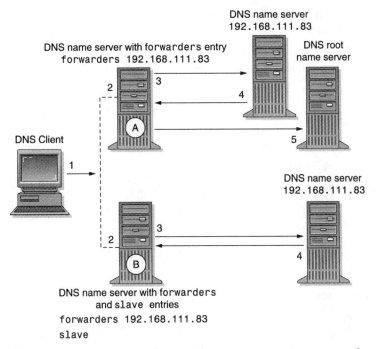

Figure 6.12 DNS name resolution with `forwarders` or `slave` commands.

Proposed DNS Extensions

DNS is an evolving technology with new functionality and operations being continuously proposed. In addition to the base DNS operations, proposals for dynamic updates, IPv6 support, network service location, and security mechanisms are being considered. DNS is also being integrated into directory service implementations such as Active Directory and Novell Directory Services.

Support for dynamic updates of DNS data (Dynamic DNS) is described in RFC 2136, "Dynamic Updates in the Domain Name System (DNS UPDATE)."

Integration of network service location is described in RFC 2052, "A DNS RR for Specifying the Location of Services (DNS SRV)."

Additionally, extensions to DNS to provide IPv6 support are proposed in the following RFCs:

- RFC 1886, "DNS Extensions to Support IP Version 6"
- RFC 1884, "IP Version 6 Addressing Architecture"

DNS Security

Although accepted DNS standards do not specify security mechanisms for DNS operations and are not commonly implemented, the following RFCs suggest support for public key (PK) technology and DNS security operations. Given the widespread support for use of X.509 certificates in network security operations, implementation of PK technology in DNS seems likely.

- RFC 2065, "Domain Name System Security Extensions"
- RFC 2137, "Secure Domain Name System Dynamic Update"
- RFC 2230, "Key Exchange Delegation Record for the DNS"
- RFC 2535, "Domain Name System Security Extensions"
- RFC 2536, "DSA KEYs and SIGs in the Domain Name System"
- RFC 2537, "RSA/MD5 KEYs and SIGs in the Domain Name System"
- RFC 2538, "Storing Certificates in the Domain Name System"
- RFC 2539, "Storage of Diffie-Hellman Keys in the Domain Name System"
- RFC 2540, "Detached Domain Name System Information"
- RFC 2541, "DNS Security Operational Considerations"

DNS in Directory Services

DNS is being integrated as the location service (and more) into many networking directory service products such as Active Directory. Because LDAP is the most widely accepted directory service protocol, the integration of DNS and LDAP is significant in that DNS provides the location services and LDAP provides the query functionality. Use of DNS domains in LDAP and X.500 is proposed in RFC 2247, "Using Domains in LDAP/X.500 Distinguished Names." Directories will be containing, managing, and distributing DNS information, reducing the need for standalone DNS servers, and cutting the cost of DNS network administration.

DNS Is Providing More and More Functionality

DNS has lacked a number of things one would expect of a full-featured directory service: schema flexibility; adequate security; and most critically, DNS had an extremely limited set of possible objects (or in DNS terms, RRs). In any case, whatever you call it, DNS didn't have very many different things it could manage.

This wasn't really a problem. DNS wasn't supposed to manage many different things; it was just supposed to provide the most highly accessible, massively scalable, distributed directory ever. And it succeeded amazingly well.

```
<consider>
```

Take just a second and consider what DNS actually does, as a global directory, and how well it works, and how seldom it breaks. Then consider that it is managed by a collection of hundreds of thousands of people (of widely varying skill levels and experience) who almost never communicate with each other. And the data is stored in *text files*, not a fancy database, but *text files*....

Pretty impressive, huh?

```
</consider>
```

Dynamic DNS

Dynamic DNS (DDNS) allows the DNS RRs to be dynamically updated to reflect changing server availability and IP addresses. The addition of DDNS is a significant improvement because it provides the functionality to resolve host names to dynamically assigned IP addresses. Traditional DNS RRs are static records written in the DNS zone file. All changes made to DNS zone records had to be individually and manually modified.

However, network environments commonly rely on the *Dynamic Host Configuration Protocol* (DHCP) to supply IP addresses to network clients. Unfortunately, there has not been a way to include the dynamically assigned TCP/IP addresses within the static DNS files. DDNS provides this critical mechanism, enabling administrators to dynamically include DHCP clients in the DNS database.

As proposed in RFC 2136, DDNS specifies a new RR type called UPDATE, which provides a means of performing dynamic updates of RRs on a zone's primary name server.

Using a network with DDNS implemented provides certain key advantages, most notably that changes to DNS zone data can be automatically performed by the DNS name servers (thus minimizing DNS administration). Another advantage to using DDNS is that it can work with DHCP and other dynamic registration services (such as WINS) to synchronize all name-to-address mapping throughout the network.

The updating method used in DDNS is consistent with earlier static DNS in allowing zone updates to be performed on a zone's primary name server only. Using dynamic updates, a primary name server can be provided a list of authorized name servers that are allowed to initiate the zone updates. These authorized dynamic update servers can include secondary name servers as well as DHCP servers.

There are controls over how updates take place in DDNS. In its application, DDNS allows the specification of a set of conditions that must be met for the dynamic update to be performed. DDNS is effectively atomic in nature. Therefore, only if all conditions are met, will a DNS update be allowed. For a DNS update to occur, the following conditions must be met:

- The request must confirm that the required RR (or RR set) exists or is in use.

- The request must confirm the requesting server is allowed to update the specified RR.

- The request must confirm the requesting server is allowed to initiate dynamic update of the specified zone.

After all conditions are satisfied, the primary name server will proceed with updating the specified RRs.

*...investigate in detail,
contemplate at length,
act with caution....*

7

Evaluating Directory Services

T HIS CHAPTER SWITCHES FROM THE FOCUS ON DIRECTORY theory and technologies
and takes a step back to look at how to assess your directory service needs. The
discussion begins by examining key factors to assess in your existing network and
explains how to determine what you need a directory service to do. This chapter also
presents ideas about how to evaluate the various directory service products in the
context of your network.

There are no fixed "right answers" to directory implementation questions. Each
section of this chapter does, however, try to highlight key questions that you should
ask about your network, your business, your needs, and the directory service that you
are considering.

<set context>
A lot of questions are asked while examining assessment and evaluation criteria in this chapter. These
questions can be usefully answered only in the context of *your specific* network and business environment.

How to Examine Directory Services

The deployment of a directory service represents a significant investment of time, money, and other resources. Such a project requires a substantial amount of corporate effort to research, plan, and deploy. When deployed, the directory service needs to work well for an extended period of time—businesses often rely on the directory service for core operations and don't change them lightly. Given this, you should evaluate and plan carefully before committing to a particular solution.

Directory service products vary significantly in the scope of services provided and the industry standards supported; the underlying mechanisms of each directory service implementation also differ.

It can be difficult to sort out the competing claims of directory vendors and derive a clear understanding of the technologies and functionality supported by each directory product. It can be particularly difficult to assess the "unseen implications" of the vendor's architectural decisions on the resultant directory service product.

You must, however, evaluate directory service products in the context of the requirements of your networking environment. (How does it work with *your* existing NOS, key applications, networking infrastructure, etc.?)

To do this, you need to look at three basic areas:

- **Assess your network environment**—Determine the current state of your network in detail.

- **Assess your directory service needs**—Analyze your enterprise requirements and goals.

- **Evaluate key directory service factors**—Determine which products provide the critical directory service features your network requires.

Assess Your Network Environment

The most fundamental step in assessing the usefulness of a directory service product to your network is evaluating your current information and networking environment. You'll need to carefully assess your IT infrastructure and operations with regard to the effects and implications of implementing any directory service.

If you are familiar with the current state of your network, you will be better able to determine what is desired from the directory service and, ultimately, how to achieve your goals.

<set context>
The questions presented in this section must be answered in the context of your specific *networking environment and business operations.*

Network Infrastructure Factors

The capabilities of the underlying network components can substantially affect the overall performance of any network service. This is particularly true for a network directory service, because they tend to concentrate traffic on particular network segments, and on new directory servers. Ascertain the state of your core network components by evaluating the following:

- **Network topology**—Start your assessment by looking at the physical topology of the network. You need to know the bandwidth of the local segments as well as each WAN connection. These values are useful in assessing the impact of replication traffic for local and remote partitions. You should also note any IP subnetting structure in use.

- **Network hardware**—Identify hardware that is part of the network infrastructure, such as routers and bridges. These devices may be manageable via a directory service. For instance, there is an initiative called Directory Enabled Networking (DEN), spearheaded by Cisco and Microsoft, focused on developing the technology to allow directory services to manage network devices.

- **Servers**—Determine the quantity, distribution, and nature of your servers—how many servers, where are they physically located, and what services are they providing to your network? How many logon servers, application servers, print servers, and file servers do you have on your network? Determine which network operating systems are in use on your network—do you have more than one core NOS, and if so, how are the different NOS types connected, and what kinds of data or services are shared?

- **Workstations**—You will need similar information about the clients on your network—how many and what operating systems are they using, which servers do they access? You will want to pay particular attention to where clients are in relationship to critical servers, such as email. Do people log on or access resources across dial-up or WAN connections?

- **Other network factors**—Does your network tend to be more static or dynamic? Do you have test environments that need to be isolated from the production environment? What else is planned for the network? How will this impact your directory service plans? Do you have outsourced services (such as Web hosting or call-center management) that will be affected?

Having a Map Can Be Useful

If you don't already have one, you might want to create a network map including bandwidth, WAN links, and national (language) boundaries. You can then add the number and location of important components and management functionality to the map as a means of drawing a complete picture of your network environment. This will prove helpful when it is time to plan your directory because you will be able to sketch both needed services and proposed configurations on the network map.

Factors in Network Services

Many network services are required for core network operations and applications. You need to identify all critical services being used by your network and applications. Examine how the various services are being managed, paying particular attention to duplicated tasks. Services you should gather information about include:

- **Network services**—Evaluate the network services used in your network environment, what they are used for, and what depends on the service. Make a list of the network services (DNS, DHCP, WINS, and so on) so that you can determine whether services will be supported, ignored, or obsoleted by the new directory service product.

- **Security services**—Your network probably uses multiple security methods and protocols, requiring you to determine the degree to which a directory service supports or replaces them. Make sure that you evaluate the use of Web security services such as Public Key Infrastructure (PKI) certificate management, Secure Sockets Layer (SSL), and others. Are you using security identifiers, such as SmartCards, photos, or biometrics that you want to store in the directory?

- **Application services**—Identify the key applications used in your business. Do you have critical applications that rely on a specific NOS or directory service? Custom applications should also be carefully assessed; they are frequently among the most important, and yet, because they are custom written, may have integration issues.

Information Organization Factors

One of the common reasons for moving to a network-wide directory service is the desire to consolidate existing management and resource information. This frequently means subsuming existing directories and the associated information as part of the integration/migration path. Existing information management processes should be reviewed, as much of the information currently managed by various entities around your network will eventually be contained in and managed by the directory service. Look at such information management factors as the following:

- **Namespace organization**—The primary directory in your current network is probably the one associated with your NOS—Is the namespace flat or hierarchical? Will it need to be restructured? If so, is there a migration path from your current namespace to your proposed directory structure?

- **Current naming schemes**—You'll want to identify the naming schemes in use in your networking environment; there are likely to be several. What naming schemes (such as those used in your NOS or email) does your network currently support? Will the directory provide support for these naming schemes (or will it replace them)? For example, Active Directory uses the DNS naming conventions for its core naming scheme but provides backward compatibility to the NT NetBIOS-based services.

- **Resource location**—Determine how network resources are currently located. Do network users commonly browse to locate printers and file shares, or are static mappings done when they log on to the network? As an example of one approach—when a user logs on to an NDS server, needed network and application directories are mapped to logical drives via logon scripts.

- **Existing directories**—You probably already have a number of directories and directory-like products already on your network, either as standalone applications or integrated into another piece of software. Determine exactly what information is being managed by current directories, and what is relying on their services. Assess the different management products in use and determine whether their functionality can be consolidated via the directory service.

Business Aspects of the Network

Although implementing a directory service is an IT operation, it is clearly also a business process, affecting the entire company. Business considerations should also be taken into account while planning the directory deployment and implementation. Aspects to consider include:

- **Corporate organization**—Because it is probable that at least some portions of your directory tree will be modeled on your business organization, you should make sure that you have a current company organizational chart. You should also collect information on critical business subdivisions and collaborative efforts so that any additional requirements can be accommodated in the directory design.

- **Impact of implementation on your business**—Consider the impact that a network-wide directory service implementation would have on your business operations. What is planned for the business in the near future? Times of major business flux usually are not a good time to be overhauling the corporate network.

- **Degree of business flexibility**—Assess the flexibility of your business operations. Is your business organization static or dynamic? Does your company buy other companies often? Are there frequent departmental shuffles? Consider the impact of such things when designing your directory tree. If you design your DIT around a corporate organization chart that changes every 18 months, you will spend a lot of time reorganizing your directory (in this case, geographical divisions might be useful). Likewise, if staff changes that affect the use of network resources are common, you need to take this into account in your directory design to streamline user management.

- **Relationships with business partners**—Evaluate the impact of the directory service implementation on the relationships with your business partners. Do you share information with business partners, vendors, or others either electronically or otherwise? Do you have outsourced partners (such as Web hosting services) that will be impacted by the planned directory service? Although discontinuing certain outside services may be one goal of the directory implementation, management should be aware of the impact on important business relationships.

After you have thoroughly assessed your current network environment, the next task is to assess what your business needs from a directory service.

Assess Your Directory Service Needs

After you have details concerning the current state of your network, you are prepared to take the next step: determining your needs and goals. Directory services are a general-purpose approach to network management, but operationally the needs of each network are individual. Chapter 2, "Evolution of Directory Structures," talked about how the operational needs drove the design of different sorts of directory services. With this perspective in mind, you will want to think about how your business needs drive the design of a directory service for your network.

As with any significant change in the operation of your business, it is imperative to have clearly defined goals—in this case, the goals for what your enterprise is trying to achieve by implementing directory services. Some of these goals will be operational (network management, for example); others may be political (such as control of information).

You need to carefully identify, in the context of your specific network(s), the business, operational, and network needs you are trying to address. As Melinda (see sidebar below) would ask, "*What functionality are you lacking…?*"

The Melinda Question

One day, an enterprise customer was complaining that the software from Melinda's company was crashing. Unclear as to the exact nature of the problem, Melinda asked about the process that led to the software failure:

Melinda: Hmmm, when does it crash?

Customer: When I am opening and closing it.

Melinda: Both opening and closing? Every time?

Customer: Well I lined up my icons so that I can click to open your program and then click to close it without moving my mouse ... real fast, you know? That's when it crashes, when I open and close it a bunch of times in a row real fast—that's when it crashes!

Melinda: Sir, *what functionality do you feel our program is lacking that you are attempting to add by doing this?*

You can view the implementation of every technology from this kind of perspective—when you apply this perspective to directory services, the question becomes:

What functionality is your network lacking that you attempting to add by implementing a directory service?

Define Your Goals Carefully

A common goal for network directory services is "simple network access and management." Although this is a useful goal, more specific answers are required for a successful transition to a network directory service. Look carefully at what you are trying to achieve.

You have to examine closely what information management and networking functionality your existing network is lacking that your business *needs* and the degree to which a directory service product can supply that functionality. You should first consider "big picture" issues such as the following:

- What is the scope of information that you need the directory service to manage?
- What administrative capabilities do you need? Are you planning on centralized or delegated administration?
- How will the directory information be used in network operations and applications?
- What are your baseline operational requirements for the directory service?
- Which groups need to access what ranges of directory information?

Different entities will have significantly different (as well as overlapping) goals and requirements. It is critical that the needs of all involved be considered when determining what the directory service should do. For the directory service implementation to be successful, the common requirements and goals need to be met, and any unique requirements addressed as needed.

The goals and requirements of the following entities should be carefully considered when deciding what the directory service should do:

- Business management
- Network administrators
- Users
- Applications

<set context>

The questions presented in this section must be answered in the context of your specific *business needs and objectives.*

Business Goals and Requirements

The overall business organization goals are likely to revolve around how the directory service can enhance their business operations—reduce cost, optimize use of network, and improve productivity. These goals are common to most businesses, but it is difficult to quantify an approach to accomplishing them, and even more difficult to measure them. More tangible business goals can take a wide variety of forms, depending on what your business does:

- **Partnerships**—Business operations may require a secure method of sharing business information with partners, clients, and vendors.

- **E-commerce**—Your business may need to provide e-commerce operation support with services such as security and certificate management.

- **Customer management**—You may also need your customer management information to be available to, and/or integrated with, your core business applications.

Who Should Participate?

An important part of a directory service deployment is putting together the planning and deployment team. As part of a distributed network management team, most administrators are directly responsible for only a portion of their network. Because directory services are generally deployed on a network-wide basis, however, administrators from across your organization will need to collectively assess the current needs of the enterprise network.

As directory services are ultimately about information, expect that nontechnical staff will also need to be involved in the planning and deployment process. You should make sure the Human Resources department is represented, for example, because so much of the directory information is about the people who work in your enterprise. Depending on your implementation and business, you may want to consider legal reviews of policies regarding directory contents, disclosure, and usage.

By inviting people from outside the IT department to participate in the project, you will ultimately improve the quality of your directory service design and implementation. Getting input from people in other departments will also help ensure that you don't plan a technically brilliant solution, only to have it run into an unseen business-related barrier.

Customer Management as a Business

Consider an ISP as one example of a business that can significantly reduce the cost of managing clients with a fully integrated, and thoughtfully designed, directory service. A directory service could allow a new user account to be created and configured in a minimum of time—something especially needed in the high client turnover environment of an ISP. Additional fee-based services can also be supported via QoS and other network management technologies that are being increasingly directory-enabled.

Networking Goals and Requirements

Networking requirements are usually concerned with resource management, network security, and monitoring, as well as the ease of management tasks and the ability to delegate administration. You will want to evaluate the required directory service functionality in these aspects of your network:

- **Network management**—Consider the administrative aspects of your network environment. Are there tasks that are needlessly difficult, duplicated management effort, or other situations you would like to address via the directory service?

- **Security**—Do you need strong authentication, access control, encryption, data control, privacy, PKI services, and/or digital certificates?

- **Network services**—Is support for location, query, dynamic addressing, management, routing, and/or QoS services required?

- **Desktop management**—Do you require robust distributed client desktop management capabilities, such as those provided in Novell ZENworks or Microsoft IntelliMirror?

User Goals and Requirements

People want the directory service to make their jobs easier—for network administrators, that usually translates to easing client access to information and network resources and simplifying management of client's network-related data. Some of the capabilities the people who use the directory service will expect are as follows:

- **Resource location**—A directory is frequently used to locate network resources such as file shares and printers.

- **Address book**—One of the most common uses of a directory service is as an address book with email, phone numbers, and other information about the people within your enterprise.

- **Client application usage**—Directory-enabled applications will allow the storage of application-related client data (such as configuration information) in the directory. This frees users from having to keep track of application information stored in multiple locations and provides support for roaming users.

- **Multi-network sign-on capabilities**—Even though most enterprise networks are using multiple NOS platforms, user logon to each of the networks has commonly not been integrated. From the user perspective, this is less than desirable and calls for some form of integration. This can take the form of simple password synchronization or more integrated solutions such as Novell's Single Sign-on.

- **Groupware operations**—The directory can also play a central role in the operations of groupware products (such as scheduling), which rely upon access to information about network clients.

Application-Related Goals and Requirements

The core applications that you use in your business operations provide another aspect of the goals and requirements for a directory service. Application-related factors you need to determine include the following:

- **Criticality**—Which applications *must* be integrated into the new directory service? Although it is nice to plan on eventually integrating everything into the directory, it's seldom a fast process. You should prioritize applications relative to the need to integrate them with the directory and assess the time involved to do so.

- **Information**—Determine what information your applications need to store and whether there is overlap between the information required by various applications. You should also determine the size of the data that an application will store. Data storage size can have multiple implications, including increases in the size of the directory and replication traffic.

- **Services**—Which services (such as security or logon) do your applications need the directory service to provide?

- **API**—Which APIs do existing applications require to operate correctly? Are certain programming interfaces needed for in-house programming or future application deployment?

How Easy Is It?

Evaluate with particular interest the question of "how easy is this directory service product for *people* to use?" Consider how many times per hour (per day, per week) people using your network are going to be attempting to carry out a sequence of directory operations to fulfill some job-related task. To clarify the ramifications, imagine what would happen to productivity if looking up each email address became *difficult* or *time consuming*.

Many corporations envision the directory service becoming the central means of access to all information on the enterprise network. If it's going to become the sole or main method of accessing information in your enterprise network, however, it had better be *very, very* easy to use.

Prepare for Compromises

One of the things that will become obvious in the process of assessment and evaluation is that you are unlikely to locate the "perfect" directory service. In the directory service implementation process, it is likely that everyone will have to make some compromises along the way. Some goals may not be attainable, some business operations too difficult, time consuming, or expensive to "directory-enable."

Assessing Performance Requirements

Determining requirements for directory performance is another important aspect of the needs assessment. By combining information about the demands that will be placed on the directory (how many clients, queries, and so on) and the performance expected of it, you gain a clearer vision of the level of service it must provide. This is central in determining the overall quantity and distribution of directory servers required for your environment.

You should consider these issues:

- **Availability**—What level of availability does the directory need to deliver? Is it going to be accessed by the public via the Internet at any time, or will it be used for a 50-hour-a-week business environment, and at what client request loads?

- **Responsiveness**—What is required in terms of responsiveness to queries? How much latency is acceptable in data synchronization? If you are controlling critical real-time security applications, for example, you have a substantially lower threshold for latency than many other businesses will.

- **Bandwidth**—Consider the amount of bandwidth available for directory traffic, both in terms of queries and replication. Do you have critical links that are already congested? Are there intermittent (dial-up) connections that must be accounted for in the directory design?

Considering Information Control Factors

A number of critical information management factors are involved in implementing a directory service. One issue that you must deal with is particularly difficult: the politics of information. Key political factors center around issues of information management, control, and privacy.

Consider the information ownership factors discussed in Chapter 2, in relation to your network and a distributed directory service. You must determine who is responsible for managing and controlling access to directory information. Information control policies must also be determined, for business security as well as protection of personal information. Consider questions such as the following:

- **Who owns which portions of the data?**—To you, as the network administrator, it may seem natural that all the information contained in the directory should be "owned" by the IT department. You can be pretty sure, however, that not everyone will be in agreement. Consider that information about employees is one of the most significant portions of directory information. Accordingly, HR may feel that *they* should own some staff information. There is no single (or simple) answer, but you must ensure that your administrative approach takes these issues into account, perhaps by delegating management of sensitive information to HR.

- **Who is responsible for accuracy of data?**—This may not be the same group that "owns" the information. You may want to make employees responsible for keeping their personal information updated, for example, and provide them with a simple Web form to do so. The ultimate ownership of the information would not rest with the individual staff member, but the duty of keeping it accurate would.

- **Who is responsible for initially providing the directory information?**— The initial population of the directory can be tedious, particularly if the information is dispersed across the enterprise. It is likely that much of the information you want for the directory is in a NOS or email database, application database, or HR management tool. Information from external databases such as these can frequently be imported into the directory via scripting or tools provided by the vendor. For the information that cannot be imported, however, you may want to consider distributing the responsibility for providing *small amounts* of information to individuals.

- **Information Privacy**—Corporations require access to a substantial amount of information about each individual they employ and, as a result, are also faced with the task of providing controlled access to the data where required, while protecting the information from unauthorized access. This is true not only for personal information but also for sensitive corporate data.

With a clear sense of your enterprise requirements and objectives, you are ready to move on to evaluating the available directory service products.

Directory Services and Privacy

Consider how moving from a simple directory to a directory service can reframe the whole issue of privacy. When phone directories were the usual printed white pages, you could look up a telephone number only if you knew the name of the person or business. Then, reverse directories enabled looking up a person by his or her phone number, providing more (but still fairly limited) capabilities.

With the Internet, online white pages provide significant advantages—the information is more likely to be current, you can access directories from any geographic area, and anyone can do a reverse lookup.

People and businesses can now be located based on their addresses, and a map with directions to the listed address can be printed with a single click. This is great for businesses—customers can find you and get directions to your business at the same time. But (on the personal side), do you want just anyone to get a map to *your house*?

This increased capability can be used for either good or bad. In whatever use, however, it has serious legal and organizational implications for your directory. Because your directory will contain sensitive information, you *must* consider the implications of access to that data. As many people object to their personal data being made available, an "opt-in" policy for controlling exposure of any personal data seems useful. Clear policies should be written and consent obtained before personal information (such as home addresses) is exposed to anyone other than the employee and the very few people who *need* to know.

Key Factors in Directory Services

Now that you have reviewed your network environment and determined your requirements and goals, you can move on to evaluating the available directory service products. It is important at this point to keep your specific network in focus, because the operational requirements will depend on size and distribution of your network resources, as well as security, administration, and integration demands. You should also thoroughly analyze the migration process prior to committing to a specific directory service implementation.

Key factors you will likely want to consider regarding the planning and implementation of a directory include the core functionality, administration, performance, security, and other directory design factors.

Core Functionality

To evaluate a directory service, begin by examining the core functionality needed in your network environment. By this time, certain aspects of your desired directory service are probably considered critical—either the product supports them or it's not for you. Look at whether the products you are considering meet your needs regarding the following:

- **Supported network operating system**—A core issue when selecting a directory service product is the NOS platform on which it can operate. To a large extent, the question of supported NOS comes down to this: Does it run on what you are currently using, and can it integrate with your current NOSs?

- **Scope of directory**—You will want to investigate the product's management scope. Determine the range of information the directory integrates and manages—including how down-level directories and external resources are handled. Most critically, make sure that whatever is *essential* to you is within the capabilities of the directory service. Extensibility is an important aspect to consider because it provides you with the mechanism to expand the directory scope as needed.

- **Server requirements**—Of course you need to consider the vendor's recommendations for minimum server hardware including processor, RAM, and storage space requirements. However, you also need to realistically assess the type of load that will be handled by your directory servers. Your actual hardware needs should include adjustments for the expected number of clients and queries, as well as the amount of data handled by the typical directory server. Don't merely accept the vendors' metrics at face value—test the product on your lab servers and monitor the performance under varying loads. Benchmarks for server metrics may be available from a number of industry sources. Dedicated servers may be required for adequately responsive directory service operations

`<set context>`

This section provides you with a range of questions to ask and perspectives to examine in the context of evaluating the utility of a directory service product.

- **Client support**—Whether your current network clients are supported is another thing you need to determine. You are likely to have a mix of client platforms and the functionality provided to some clients may well be limited. (*Limited* commonly means operating as if the server were a previous version.) You may find that some client machines require hardware or software upgrades to fully utilize the directory service. If so, verify that functionality will be adequate in the interim.

- **Dependencies**—Does the directory service require supporting services and, if so, are those services currently being provided on your network? Would existing services require substantial reconfiguration or replacement? You should make sure your directory administrators group includes people who are familiar with all the ancillary services required by the directory. Active Directory requires DNS, for example, and, although it is not required that you run Windows 2000 DNS, it is highly recommended. Because of the interrelationship between DNS and AD, a notable number of reported AD problems can be traced to incorrect DNS configuration.

Determine Your Approach to...

You will want to determine your overall approach to particular aspects of a directory service because it can make a difference in your evaluation. Every network situation differs—different approaches are desirable for different network environments, depending on how the directory is going to be used. Consider basic factors such as the following:

- DIT design—This generally comes down to a decision between designing the top of the directory tree along geographic boundaries or business divisions. Lower portions of the DIT may be divided along business functional lines or perhaps used to organize directory objects into OUs by class (users, groups, and so on) for management purposes.

- Naming—The naming model can make a substantial difference in how easy it is for people to determine and remember object names. Your naming standards should provide a clear and simple method of naming objects in a way that facilitates their identification and location.

- Administration—How is the directory going to be managed? Are you planning on centralized or delegated administration? Make sure that responsibility for backups of the directory and maintenance of directory servers are clearly assigned (with redundancy) because reliable directory operations will likely be crucial.

- Education—Decide whether administrators and users will be formally trained in classes, expected to self-study through commonly available resources (and allocated time), or some combination of the two.

Information Organization

The tree design used by a directory service has major implications concerning the degree to which the product can meet your requirements. When evaluating a directory service product, pay close attention to product constraints and inherent functional limitations. Things to consider include the following:

- **Logical organization**—The logical organization allowed by a directory service product can play a critical role in tree design, naming, as well as Directory Information Base (DIB) partitioning and replication. The directory may provide a classic X.500-style tree (NDS) or integrate other models in the tree design (AD). Directory trees may be logically subdivided for some reason, or perhaps multiple trees are linked together for management purposes.

- **Desired tree design**—How do you want to design your tree? Do you need to account for WANs, international borders, or the business organization in your DIT design? What other directories or namespaces exist on your network, and do you want to use one of them as the basis for your directory tree?

- **Tree design constraints**—Are there constraints on directory design or operations because of some aspect of the overall design? A salient example of this is Active Directory. The AD namespace integrates NT domains (complete with domain security boundary), and then uses the domain boundary to define the DIB partition. As you will see in Chapter 9, "Active Directory," this has some interesting implications. In light of the organization allowed by the directory, does your preferred DIT design work?

- **Flexibility**—Will the directory be flexible enough to support your network as it grows both in size and complexity? Does the directory provide the ability to easily reorganize to reflect company changes? Is there support for key tree functionality such as freely pruning, grafting, and moving objects within the tree?

From the Vendor's Perspective

Look at directory service products from the perspective of the vendor. Note how they intended the directory to be organized and used. What networking models, preferred technologies, and overall approach were they using in their design? If you look at how the vendor views their directory, you can get a feel for how their product will work in your environment. Chapters 8 and 9 delve more deeply into this topic.

DIB Management

You should also examine what sort of data repository is used, and how the DIB is managed. Key factors in DIB management revolve around the nature of the distribution and replications methods that are used, such as the following:

- **Partition flexibility**—Examine the degree of flexibility in partition management. Do you have the ability to subdivide or combine existing partitions? Does partition management require an inordinate amount of time or effort?

- **Degree of control over replication**—Consider replication factors such as the replication granularity, latency, and degree of control over the scheduling, protocols, and routing of replication traffic. Are there restrictions on where replicas can be placed, protocols that can be used, number of replicas per server, and so on?

- **Effect of synchronization**—Synchronization methods and costs must also be considered, especially across WAN links. You are primarily able to control the impact of synchronization traffic via how you partition your directory, and the use of routing and scheduling. The method of synchronization used may have its own implications. NDS relies on time services, for example, requiring you to monitor an additional service to ensure data integrity.

Scalability

Examining DIB management in general is useful and gives you an idea of how the directory will impact your network. You will also want to determine specific limitations on the amount of information the directory stores, however, because it directly impacts the scalability of the directory service.

The question of scalability is frequently framed as "does the directory service work as well on a large distributed network as it does on a small LAN?" But, the *relevant* question is "does it scale sufficiently for *your* environment?"

You need to assess your expected tree size—keeping in mind that you will likely have objects for users, groups, computers, services, printers, other managed hardware, volumes, file shares, services, and application information. Remember to factor in the likely future growth and partnership needs of your business.

Each directory service has metrics concerning the data it stores that place fundamental constraints on directory scalability. These factors include the following:

- **Objects per partition**—There are functional limits on the number of objects a partition can hold. This may vary widely, even from one version of a product to the next. For example, Novell redesigned the storage mechanisms for NDS 8 and now states that NDS can hold millions of objects per partition, although prior versions only handled a few thousand!

- **Partitions per server**—There may also be restrictions on the number of partitions a server can hold. For example, AD allows a domain controller to manage only a single partition. The total number of partitions in the DIT may also be limited based on operational factors.

- **Storage limitations**—There are probably also physical file storage limitations, which can be particularly significant for large networks. If you have lots of large objects in your directory, DIB partitions could exceed file or storage limits. The partition size may also be a consideration when implementing backup routines and when replicating to new DSAs.

- **Objects per tree**—One critical limitation occurs at the directory tree level rather than the partition. You should ensure that the directory supports an adequate number of objects to meet your needs in a single tree. In both AD and NDS 8, however, this number is theoretically well over a million. (Novell says an NDS 8 tree can hold a billion objects!) Therefore, it might seem that most enterprise networks are unlikely to run into this limitation (but, remember when 640KB should be enough RAM for anyone?).

Directory Administration

One key area in evaluating directory services is the degree of difficulty in conducting administrative tasks. From the perspective that effective administration is essential in a directory service, the ease of administrative task performance is a baseline consideration. Administrative aspects of a directory service to assess include the following:

- **Degree of complexity**—An important aspect of directory administration is the degree of complexity—how easy is it to perform management tasks? Complexity can take many forms: perhaps numerous tools are required to effectively manage the entire directory; it may be difficult to ascertain effective access permissions; or some functions are hidden entirely. Although complexity is not inherently bad (and it's pretty much unavoidable), it does require the vendor to pay particular attention to supplying powerful and flexible tools that streamline administration.

- **Support for delegation**—The capability to securely delegate management tasks is a significant advantage to a directory service, particularly for administrators of large or distributed networks. Assess how the directory service supports delegation and which subsets of rights or tasks can be delegated. Are tools designed to simplify delegation, perhaps by offering templates of permissions to support specific tasks, or via security equivalence to existing administrators or roles?

- **Effectiveness of management tools**—Another concern is the availability and capability of the tools used to manage the directory. Are the tools unified or distributed throughout multiple applications? Can they be extended to support custom capabilities? Are tools available to administer the directory across the Web or from other remote locations? Do administrative tools run on the necessary platforms?

- **Scope of management capabilities**—Does the directory integrate with other management tools to provide enhanced management capabilities? Is there integration of desktop management software for remote deployment and management of clients? Does it support the Simple Network Management Protocol (SNMP)—can it interface with intermediate network hardware and report on network traffic issues?

Education and Support

Any change in your network operations requires you to train your staff to some degree, and especially your IT group. The change to a directory-centric network can entail substantial training requirements. This is also true, to a lesser degree, of people who use the directory service as a client.

Educating people about new technology is always costly—in terms of both time and money. Books are purchased, classes are held (and paid for), people spend days away from their usual jobs—it's an involved and expensive process. However much this may cost, failing to provide education is likely to cost more in long-term support costs and lost productivity.

Clearly one of the goals of IT management is to encourage staff members to train themselves. By providing people with the ability to conveniently explore a new technology, in small pieces and at their own speed, you can provide them with the knowledge they need to do their job, while not overwhelming them with tertiary details. Even with all of the self-study, however, some more traditional educational expenses are unavoidable, including the following:

- **Administrator training**—Determine how much and what kind of training is going to be required for network administrators to effectively manage the new directory service? Will classroom training be required or are there adequate resources available for self-teaching or online learning? Is there a substantial community of others working with the product active in newsgroups or on a mailing list?

Your Directory Is Valuable

When the directory contains your business information, and provides the underlying infrastructure for the core of your business operations, you cannot afford to let it become nonoperational (or even problematic). Compare such problems to the cost of redundant servers (as well as switches, routers, and backup devices)—hardware is cheap when compared to what network downtime can cost your business.

- **User education resources**—Educated users require less technical assistance to do their jobs, reducing support costs. Additionally, the materials used frequently overlap enough that you can provide a trimmed down version of the IT staff's educational materials to the rest of your staff. One advantage to the explosion in Internet usage is the increased comfort many people feel when accessing information via a Web page. You can leverage this familiarity by providing Web-based interfaces for clients to access educational resources.

- **Availability and utility of documentation**—Although good documentation is always important, it is of special concern when you are planning something as complex as running a distributed network with new software. Consider to what degree documentation concerning technical and operational aspects of the directory service is available. Does the available documentation provide a *useful* and *sufficiently detailed* explanation of the needed information?

- **Availability, usefulness, and cost of technical support**—Professional-quality technical support is also important and rapidly becoming a scarce commodity. Cost-effective technical support for your directory service will likely be necessary at various times. Carefully check the vendor's support policy; it is likely to be somewhat limited (perhaps only covering installation issues for a brief period of time). Is additional support available in your area, either in the form of local consultants, or via engineers providing services from a remote location?

Directory Training and Certifications

Just as networks did years ago, directory services are becoming an area of specialization for information technology professionals. For example, Novell has started to train Directory Engineers (with periodic recertification requirements)—essentially a CNE, MCSE, or CCIE with additional focus on directory service technologies. The Directory Engineer certification requires both a written test and a hands-on style exam, with the candidate performing a set of tasks on a live system.

More information on the Novell Directory Engineer certification is available at:
`education.novell.com/cde`

Vendor Responsiveness

Once, in the course of writing a book, we sent email to two large vendors requesting information about their respective products.

In the first case, we selected an employee of the company who was publicly providing contact with the group controlling the product in question. The response was delayed and then merely routed us to another employee, who directed us to another (wrong) department. No follow-up occurred to determine whether we received the information.

In the second case, we sent email to an employee of the company about 7 p.m. We had a response the same night and email waiting from an employee in the product group the next morning offering to help. Over the next few days, we received a number of follow-up contacts with useful data about their product.

You may want to seriously gauge some of the less-tangible aspects of a vendor's approach to their customers, such as whether they actually respond to your technical and information needs.

Support for Standards and Initiatives

Another useful perspective can be gained by viewing the degree to which a directory service vendor supports widely accepted industry standards and, correspondingly, the degree to which a proprietary scheme is implemented. Many firms rely on industry-approved solutions for multiyear stability of network operations and are less inclined to use products that support proprietary technologies only. Commonly supported standards and initiatives include:

- **LDAP**—The LDAP protocol is rapidly becoming the de facto standard for client access to most directory service products. As LDAP is being used more for interoperability purposes, and many applications and tools are being written to support LDAP, clearly LDAP support is useful or needed in most directory services. Particularly if clients will be primarily accessing directory information via the Web, you will likely want to select a directory service solution with robust LDAP support.

- **DNS**—DNS is widely deployed on the Internet and, increasingly, on corporate networks. Dynamic DNS (DDNS) is also beginning to be employed in some directory service products. Consider the degree to which the directory integrates DNS/DDNS management functionality and replication processes into the directory. Integrated DNS/DDNS is particularly important to companies with distributed networks and substantial investments in DNS name server deployment. There is also the question of whether you want congruence between your DNS namespace and your directory tree. If you are doing e-commerce (or other Internet presence), you should also examine the correlation between DNS namespaces used internally (intranet) and externally (Internet).

- **Directory Interoperability Forum (DIF)**—DIF is a significant directory forum that was founded in 1999 by a group of directory vendors as a means of advancing directories based on open standards such as LDAP. Vendors participating in DIF include Novell, IBM, Isocor, Oracle, Lotus, Data Connection, and more than 25 others. The DIF Web site is at www.directoryforum.org.

- **Directory-Enabled Networking (DEN)**—Cisco and Microsoft are leading the DEN initiative to promote enhanced management of network hardware and services via directory services. This capability will provide a means of controlling use of the network infrastructure, routing, bandwidth, encryption and other functionality via policies enforced by the directory. Other partners in DEN include Intel, 3Com and Hewlett-Packard. The DEN Web site is at: www.cisco.com/warp/public/cc/cisco/mkt/enm/diren/index.shtml

An Architectural Touchstone

As the archetype of directory service designs, X.500 provides a structure that all directory designs can be compared against so that the degree of directory functionality can be assessed. Understanding the similarities and differences between a particular directory service implementation and the X.500 standards also brings architectural elements into focus. A directory service does not necessarily need to comply exactly with X.500, but it will be helpful if you understand how it does *not*.

- **Internet Engineering Task Force (IETF) working groups**—The IETF is an organization of internetworking engineers, vendors, researchers, and others who form *working groups* to focus on a particular area of Internet development. For example, IETF has two LDAP-related working groups: LDUP (LDAP Duplication/Replication/Update Protocols) and LDAPExt (LDAP Extensions). Information on both groups is available at: `www.ietf.org`

- **eXtensible Markup Language (XML)**The eXtensible Markup Language is being employed in accessing and representing directory service content. Bowstreet Software, in an alliance with IBM, Microsoft, Novell, Oracle, Sun, and Netscape, are leading the effort to develop an XML-based method of accessing, managing, and manipulating directory information called *Directory Services Markup Language* (DSML). XML is the underlying abstraction language used to create DSML. DSML will enable vendors to create applications that can use and share information from multiple distributed directories operating on different platforms. DSML allows applications to use directory information without knowledge of the specific format used by any particular directory. DSML is being developed as an IETF open standard. Novell is also developing their own version of an XML-based language, called DirXML.

Vendors for Open Standards

The Directory Interoperability Forum is a particularly interesting group as it is largely made up of vendors of proprietary directory services. It is probably a good sign that these industry players have embraced open standards. The DIF has the following stated objectives:

- Fostering the widespread adoption of open standards for directories by working with major standards bodies such as IETF, Desktop Management Task Force (DMTF), and the Open Group.

- Expanding the market for application vendors supporting open directory standards.

- Increasing customer confidence concerning directories based on open standards.

DIF has the following working teams:

- **Standards**—This group works with standards bodies to generate new proposals and to participate in the collaborative process leading to the adoption of open standards.

- **SDK**—The SDK team works with member vendors to help ensure consistent behavior across directories and a robust SDK that will be made available to the general public.

- **ISV programs**—This team works with independent software vendors (ISVs) to provide education, Open Group certification, promote the vendors' SDK, and provide support for problem resolution across directory products.

- **Marketing**—This team encourages deployment of open directory standard–enabled applications, stages promotional activities, and manages the organization's Web site.

Security Standards and Integration

A critical factor in directory service product evaluation is how the product implements security for directory objects and information. Most directory service products on the market support a mix of proprietary security schemes and open standards. You should investigate a number of aspects of the security provided for both the directory and the network. You can start by looking at the following:

- **NOS integration**—The degree to which the directory service security integrates with the security of the various NOSs used on your network is an important consideration. Seamless integration of directory security with the NOS security subsystem is fundamental for network-wide user authentication.

- **Security design considerations**—Fundamental security design should be examined for compatibility with your current (and desired) approach to security. AD and NDS approach the application of directory security from somewhat different tangents, as discussed in Chapters 8 and 9.

- **Supported security standards**—You will want to know the degree to which a directory provides support for existing security standards, such as Kerberos, SSL/PCT, X.509 certificates, and SASL. If you are going to deploy secondary security services (such as an X.509 certificate server), check the degree to which they are integrated with the directory.

- **Authentication methods**—Factors involved in the authentication method employed to identify users on your network include availability of strong authentication and the encryption technologies used. You may also need the directory to perform pass-through authentication to applications or other directories. Does the directory service need to support employee photographs, SmartCards, biometrics, or other authentication methods? If so, you may want to investigate the size of the associated information to assess the impact on data management factors such as DIB size and amount of traffic.

- **Access control**—You need to consider how the directory service handles access control. Are permissions attached to the structural DIT objects, for example, managed via groups and policies, or by some combination? What forms of permission inheritance and inheritance-blocking are provided?

Application and Programming Support

Because your business operations rely on your applications, the application support provided by the directory service product is clearly a key element. In addition to concerns about basic application compatibility issues, consider the following:

- **Compatibility with key applications**—Is the directory service compatible with all currently deployed applications that are important to your business? Will critical proprietary applications continue to work, or can they be easily upgraded or replaced?

- **Supported APIs**—Look at the degree of support the directory service provides for programming languages and APIs commonly in use in systems and application development. The support provided by a directory service for application development can substantially influence the availability of directory-enabled applications. API support is also important if you are planning on writing in-house applications that use the directory.

- **Directory-enabled applications**—Earlier in this chapter, you were asked to identify the applications in use in your environment and decide which of them are important to integrate into the directory. You should verify the availability of directory-enabled versions of those products for your preferred directory platform.

- **Scripting languages**—Directory services that provide support for scripting languages as a means of accessing and manipulating directory information are convenient from the administrative perspective. Simple, yet powerful scripts can be quickly written to automate many directory management tasks. Scripting support also means that directory information is available via languages commonly used on the Web, such as JavaScript and VBScript.

- **XML derivations**—Variants on XML are also being used to access directory information via the Web. Consider whether you need this capability, and, if so, how well the directory service delivers it. XML-based interfaces may also be a means of providing directory interoperability, as demonstrated by Novell's plans for DirXML as an enabling technology for meta-directory-like capabilities in NDS. The other important emerging directory service XML derivative is the DSML, which is a developing open (IETF) standard.

Directory Service Performance

The performance capability and fault tolerance of the directory service implementation has to be evaluated in the context of your specific network. To effectively assess the performance available from a directory service product, you have to use the baseline requirements established in your existing network and apply them to the technologies and methods used by the specific directory service implementation.

By applying the directory service product constraints to your required directory capabilities, you can determine baseline feasibility and approach with a given directory service product.

First, consider the capabilities required for your network. Examine the requirements you defined earlier, and contrast that with the directory service capabilities, as follows:

- **How well can the product handle your information base?**—Assess your expected tree size. When you are estimating your tree size, keep in mind that you will likely have objects for users, groups, computers, services, printers, other managed hardware, volumes, file shares, services, as well as application information. Keep the future growth of your business and network in mind.

- **How well can it handle your peak service demands?**—This is a combination of availability and responsiveness (as described earlier). Given the number of connections (all entities accessing the directory) that will be used on your network and the amount of bandwidth required, what kind of capability does the product DSA have to handle the load? How many queries will need to be processed (at peak loads, and minimal loads)? Factor in all users, applications, other network services—anything that requires services from the directory requires a connection. Will the DSA be supplying more than one network service to clients, and can it handle the load of all services combined?

- **Does it have effective fault tolerance?**—If a DSA fails, is there redundancy or failover support? Do discrete sections of the DIB become unavailable, or do alternative DSAs automatically handle the query?

Next, factor in the product constraints. Every directory product has constraints on a variety of aspects of operation, such as the following:

- Metrics concerning DIT and DIB (discussed earlier)
- Number of DSA servers required per network/subnet
- Client/query load limits per DSA

Review the product constraints and assess the limitations with regard to your network and business requirements.

Then, keeping both your required capabilities and the product constraints in mind, establish the baseline feasibility and "fit" of the directory service product for your environment. When you evaluate your goals and requirements, and factor in the constraints of the product, you are left with the set of information needed to assess baseline considerations for deployment:

- Determine the number of DSAs required per client (responsiveness) and the impact of replication on network traffic (bandwidth): Will you need more servers, faster servers, or more bandwidth? Excessive server load is generally dealt with by deploying more DSAs.

- Carefully assess the placement of DSAs and partition replicas in the network topology to provide adequate service to clients. You can restrict lookup traffic by ensuring that DSAs are placed in the right locations—close to the people who use those partition resources.

- Examine how catalogs are used because they typically provide a faster indexed access to the directory contents and frequently play an important role in overall responsiveness of your directory service. After determining whether the directory provides catalogs, you should examine whether you can customize catalog content, how catalogs handle access control, and how effectively catalogs work to facilitate resource location.

- Consider the impact of expected directory usage and replication traffic on the effective bandwidth of the infrastructure connecting these clients and servers. Partitioning and replication of the DIB are factors of particular concern, because the performance impact of replicating the directory information can be a significant factor, both within the LAN and across slower WAN links.

When evaluating the bandwidth usage of a directory service, assess the effect of the directory service methods used. Take a look at the following:

- Overall percentage of network utilization for client logon, directory access, and directory replication.
- How the directory partition information is replicated, the size of the unit of replication, the frequency of replication, and the effective bandwidth utilization.
- Does the directory service support QoS bandwidth metering?

Directory Interoperability

Because most enterprise networks have multiple NOS variants in use, the capability to link different directory services has become increasingly important. You'll want to evaluate the directory service's capability to share and synchronize information with other directories, and to assess issues in directory migration, such as the following:

- **Interoperability "style"**—Start by determining the style of interoperability you need—are you planning on long-term coexistence of multiple directory services or migration to a single directory? Is support for the level of directory integration required for your network environment provided? If you are planning on long-term coexistence, are directory synchronization or meta-directory tools available?
- **Support for managing the resources of other NOSs**—If you use multiple NOSs, you may decide to use each NOS directory service, and then synchronize their data (if possible). Alternatively, you might deploy a directory service on one NOS to manage the resources of both. For instance, NDS is notable in that it provides directory service functionality not only on the NetWare platform, but other leading NOS platforms as well (Windows NT, Sun Solaris, and Linux), providing a means of smoothly integrating a broad range of NOS resources.
- **Migration factors**—Because migration to a new directory service is a substantial expense and business interruption for most firms, migration factors should be seriously evaluated in your review of each directory service product. You will want to examine which of your current directories can be replaced by the new directory service. Examine what it will take to migrate *your* network to the new directory service. Pay particular attention to the availability of migration tools and mechanisms such as LDIF bulk import/export capability. Consolidating directory information manually can be costly in terms of time and effort.

Assessing Costs

After you have determined a directory service approach that effectively supplies the needed solution, you need to look carefully at what it will cost. You also want to look at the benefits to be derived from the directory deployment. Keep in mind that enterprise management (and thus you) must find a balance between the cost and the benefit of every new tool and technology used in the corporate network environment.

One of the central concerns in enterprise computing today it is *Total Cost of Ownership* (TCO). Determining TCO is an analytical process that attempts to precisely quantify the cumulative "cost" of owning and operating every computer system within the corporation. It is important to remember, however, that in addition to costs of ownership, there are also benefits of ownership. Every model of evaluating TCO is based on a set of assumptions, which may (or may not) accurately or adequately reflect the cost or benefit factors in *your* network environment.

Although many methods of cost assessment of networks and directory services exist, they are essentially beyond the scope of this book (see the following sidebar); they are described here in summary only.

...at What Cost?

The direct costs of a directory service implementation are at least partially knowable. With close evaluation, what you will pay for the software and hardware components is comparatively clear. The initial costs for a directory service include the following:

- **Software (per server/client)**—Pay close attention to the license cost structure—is it per server, per client? Are client licenses required for Internet access to the directory? Do you need to purchase other products that are required to support directory functionality?

- **New or upgraded hardware**—Do you need to upgrade existing servers or purchase new ones? Will other network components require hardware upgrades for adequate performance of the directory?

- **Documentation, training, and support**—What will adequate documentation cost? What will training and support cost?

Costing Methods Vary

Directory and network metrics are the subject of much debate, as vendors and industry analysts discuss various strategies for assessing network and information infrastructure costs. When you look at the different approaches to cost analysis, the specifics of how costs and savings are calculated vary substantially between models. Numerous TCO models point to a common core set of issues and factors in analyzing cost of ownership, however, including administration, capital investment, technical support, and end-user operations. Some sources for in-depth enterprise costing formulas are:

- Forrester Research at www.forrester.com

- The Burton Group at www.tbg.com

- The Gartner Group at www.gartner.com

Obviously, this is not the total expense for a directory service; there are additional deployment costs and ongoing maintenance expenses. The preceding list does, however, represent much of the immediately knowable aspects of the initial expense.

TCO is a much-less-direct financial measure, because it includes less directly tangible costs such as deployment, administration, maintenance, and programming. Significant industry vendors and analysts have used various TCO criteria, but these assessment criteria are often affected by technology or vendor bias, selective focus, or (our favorite) numbers fabricated from a single event and generalized from there.

Clearly, the numbers used to assess your cost of ownership should be based on your real financial and networking information, not an arbitrary set of values proposed by others. From your information, you can more closely determine the *actual* costs as they apply to *your* network and environment.

...for What Gain?

You are upgrading your network to a new directory service for a reason, right? So, setting all the directory theory aside for a moment, just how is implementing this directory service going to benefit the company? Many people think of benefits in terms of money; they plan on saving money by consolidating directories, streamlining network management, increasing productivity, and so on. Of course, you probably will see some of those benefits (...eventually).

However, buying and implementing a directory service on your network is not likely to *make* you money in the near term—and it surely will *cost* you money in the near term. Although in the long term the implementation of a directory service can save enterprise businesses substantial amounts of money, directory deployment will be initially expensive in terms of software, hardware, network infrastructure, training, and administration costs.

The Technology Is Affordable

Whatever the numbers, most companies that want to use directory services can afford to slowly integrate the technology into their network and business operations. Deliberative integration provides time for business to assess the impact of the change and to minimize the disruption of normal business operations.

The Upgrade Domino Effect

It starts slowly...you just want to upgrade a specific capability of a few servers—just a little thing really. And then you decide that just a little more RAM would really help performance and enable you to add more concurrent users. Then you discover that *now* you have enough RAM for that application you've been wanting, but the application requires more storage space (on each of the servers)...

Directory services are by no means immune to "the upgrade domino effect." In fact, they are a likely cause of it (new hardware, new versions of applications, more administrative time, user training, and so on). After all, one of the primary reasons people implement a network-wide directory service is to take advantage of applications that support it; and new applications may require additional resources. Thoughtfully consider the possible unintended consequences of a directory service deployment.

A common measure, called Return on Investment (ROI), is used to describe the
return (over time) of the value invested in such infrastructure costs. Like TCO, the
ROI for a directory service implementation is highly variable. Vendors will proclaim
substantial benefits that (should) result in a positive ROI. For the enterprise, however, a
directory service implementation is an actual expense over an extended period of
time, and returns (via productivity and so forth) are much more speculative.

Theoretical savings and other monetary benefits from the use of a directory service
typically include the following:

- **Less administration required**—Reduction of duplicated management tasks is
  frequently stated as a means by which a directory service will save you money.
  However, those administrators will probably be busy learning how to make the
  new directory service work. Therefore, although they will be doing fewer
  repetitive tasks, they will also be doing more *different* ones.

- **Reduced user-support costs**—One commonly mentioned savings is lowered
  support costs from a network that is centralized, easier to use, and that supports
  remote desktop management. Using the directory as a common storage point
  for configuration information means fewer misconfigured applications, faster
  recovery from system crashes, and perhaps a centralized means of application
  deployment.

- **Elimination of paper directories**—Your business may be able to reduce or
  cease production of hard copies of information. This proves especially useful for
  information that is widely distributed, commonly misplaced, and contains
  information that changes frequently and is, therefore, outdated quickly (such as
  employee telephone listings).

- **Other possible savings**—Some less easily measured sources of savings may
  apply to your situation, such as lowered exposure to security risks, reduction in
  process delays, or a more efficient use of the network resources.

As you can see, ROI estimations can help—they can provide focus, guidelines, and
direction. The degree of ROI really depends on what you do with the directory
service, however—how you use it and the context in which it is implemented. The
directory can become a powerful management tool, enabling you to assess and control
your business as well as your network. A directory service could also be applied in a
wide variety of valuable e-commerce implementations (and depending on the success
of the site, could substantially improve your ROI).

For most networks, however, ROI will be a more subtle set of factors that reduce
costs over time and improve user productivity via simplified information management.

Is It Going to Make You Money?

Are you planning on making money from the directory service? If so, be very specific about how, and
verify your details carefully. Unless your business is actually implementing the directory service in a for-
profit operation (such as an e-commerce site, or selling the data contained in your directory), you will
probably not directly make money from deploying a directory service.

...power derived from classic forms...

8

Novell Directory Services

THIS CHAPTER IS A CONCISE THEORETICAL OVERVIEW of Novell Directory Services (NDS). Because NDS is rooted in the X.500 standards, you will find many similarities in description and approach. Therefore, only the differences are highlighted here, avoiding a re-explanation of X.500 concepts and terms.

<set context>

Although this book is clearly not an administrative "how to" guide, we do hope to help you understand _why_ NDS and AD work the way do—from an _architectural_ perspective. By understanding the underlying directory structures and operations, you can more clearly see how the design decisions made by a particular vendor influence the resultant directory service offering.

Accordingly, we are going to examine the two most prominent network directory services; NDS in this chapter and Active Directory (AD) in the next. As we examine each product, we will describe how it implements fundamental aspects of a directory service and discuss how the architecture influences its ultimate capabilities.

Introduction to NDS

NDS has been around a long time, at least from the perspective of network directory services. Introduced in 1993 as a method of managing NetWare networks, NDS has grown significantly over the years and now manages much more than NetWare. NDS has also expanded its reach beyond just the NetWare platform, and now it runs natively on many network operating systems.

NDS is a mature product with a broad scope of network management capabilities and cross-platform support—something Novell is promoting by positioning NDS as a standalone product. Novell is supporting this focus on NDS with a number of NDS-related offerings along with active participation in industry directory service partnerships and initiatives. But before we look at NDS, let's look at where NDS came from...

`<history>`

Prior to the introduction of NDS with NetWare 4 in 1993, NetWare used a *bindery* rather than a directory service. To describe a bindery by the information organization and management aspects we discussed in Chapter 2, "Evolution of Directory Structures," and Chapter 3, "Storing Directory Information." A NetWare bindery is a flat namespace, using a physical naming model and a centralized database. A bindery manages a very limited set of objects (such as users, groups, print servers, and print queues) for a single server, requiring a separate user account on each server.

The bindery was clearly an inadequate approach to network management and Novell, recognizing this, released *NetWare Name Services* (NNS) in 1990 as an add-on to NetWare 3. NNS was designed to synchronize the binderies on a group of NetWare servers called (perhaps not surprisingly) a *domain*. Synchronization had to be performed manually and was only functional with a small number of servers in the domain. However, NNS did enable access to any server in the domain rather than only the one server a user was attached to. Still, NNS was only designed as a stopgap measure until NDS was ready. Accordingly, only one version of NNS ever shipped and Novell discontinued support in 1994.

`</history>`

What Version Is That Anyway...?

As we discuss various aspects of NDS, we will be focusing on NDS 8. However, we recognize that there are still a lot of networks using NetWare 5 without NDS 8 or NetWare 4 (which doesn't support NDS 8). For this reason, we will sometimes touch on multiple versions of NDS when significant differences between them exist. If a version number is not otherwise specified, assume NDS 8.

NDS is a networking-focused directory service originally designed to manage distributed NetWare networks. With the introduction of NDS, Novell shifted their network management focus from a server-centric view to a more general network focus. Although NDS initially managed a fairly basic set of network resources and processes, it has been extended greatly over the years.

NDS now supports management of not only basic network resources but also a broad range of applications, services, and other information concerning the network. Between Novell's enhancements to NDS, the linkage of other NetWare network management tools (such as BorderManager and ZENworks), and third-party development, NDS now provides a central point for administering not only the network, but many aspects of the business as well.

NDS Design Overview

NDS was specifically designed to be consistent with the X.500 specifications to provide compatibility with much of the directory development being done at the time. NDS has successfully implemented all directory operations, capabilities, and features described in X.500, including naming model, DIB management, as well as in DUA-DSA and DSA-DSA operations.

Again, it will be useful if the correlations between terminology are clear. Table 8.1 provides a comparison of NDS terminology to the terms used in X.500. As you can see, there aren't many significant differences between the two.

The "Full Service Directory"

Novell has defined what they call the *Full Service Directory* (FSD)—essentially the criteria for what they see as a fully capable directory service. Novell says that the FSD is "... a general-purpose database that manages discovery, security, storage, and relationships." The FSD taxonomy presents an interesting perspective on Novell's approach to a directory service. It is available at:

www.novell.com/products/nds/fsd/fsd_taxonomy.html

Table 8.1   **NDS/X.500 Terminology Comparison**

Functionality	NDS Term	Analogous X.500 Term
Directory entries	Objects	Objects
Entry attributes	Attributes	Attributes
Definition of directory contents	Schema	Schema
Logical representation of directory	Directory tree	Directory Information Tree (DIT)
Data storage	Directory database	Directory Information Base (DIB)
Subdivision of directory	Partition	Naming context
Data updates	Synchronization	Replication
Server agent	NDS server	Directory Service Agent (DSA)
Client agent	Client	Directory User Agent (DUA)
Query resolution	Tree-walking and referral	Chaining and referral

NDS leverages the X.500 models, defining a directory service containing objects comprised of a series of attributes. The NDS schema specifies a wide range of class, attribute, and syntax definitions and is easily extensible. The NDS namespace defines a single hierarchical directory tree. NDS naming is also similar to X.500.

The NDS DIB is partitioned as needed, and partitions are stored on multiple DSAs as required. NDS uses what is generally multi-master replication with a static single master for some operations, such as partitioning and schema modifications.

NDS servers provide the expected DSA functionality—manage client login, fulfill queries, and provide referrals to other NDS servers. NDS client-side software is available for Windows, Macintosh, and DOS operating systems.

NDS performs distributed operations (such as name resolution) by a form of chaining that Novell calls *tree-walking*. Referrals are also used to route clients between directory servers. NDS operations are very much like those in X.500, although using proprietary protocols.

DNS

With the shift to native TCP/IP in NetWare 5, Novell had to address the need for IP services such as DNS and DHCP. NDS 8's native LDAP also brings with it requirements for DNS to provide support for resolution of LDAP URLs. Not surprisingly, Novell decided to thoroughly integrate both their DNS and DHCP implementations into NDS.

All DNS and DHCP information is stored as directory objects and configuration is performed via those objects. Each DNS zone is stored as a directory object, for example, and replicated via the usual NDS methods. Even with this storage mechanism, NetWare DNS servers interoperate fully with other DNS implementations and are compliant with BIND 4.9.5.

DNS in NetWare supports a proprietary form of Dynamic DNS, registering DHCP clients with NDS. Each DHCP assigned DNS entry consists of several directory objects representing host names, IP addresses, and additional resource records.

Novell's DNS uses the *Service* (SRV) resource record for a range of services, such as FTP. However, LDAP is not listed in the selection for type of SRV records when one is created. NDS doesn't use DNS to locate directory servers (as Active Directory does), but rather uses the *Service Location Protocol* (SLP) as specified in RFC 2165. SLP is designed for advertising and locating services for distributed IP networks.

LDAP

As with just about every other directory service, NDS supports LDAP v.3. Novell calls their implementation of LDAP support *LDAP Services for NDS*, sometimes also called *Novell LDAP* (NLDAP). As of NDS 8, LDAP support is native. In earlier versions of NDS, LDAP support was provided as an add-on. The LDAP implementation provided with NDS 8 has been optimized for searches and (according to Novell) performance doesn't degrade with large directory trees.

When LDAP Services are installed, an LDAP Group object is created and mappings between NDS and LDAP classes and attributes are configured. The LDAP group also controls security, distributed operation mode (referral or chaining), and specifies a proxy user for anonymous LDAP access.

Individual LDAP Server objects are also created and then added to an LDAP group. An LDAP Server is configured to control server-specific operational parameters such as port settings, search limitations, and catalog usage.

Novell is active in the IETF *LDAP Duplication, Replication, and Update Protocols* (LDUP) working group. This group is focused on defining a replication architecture for LDAP to standardize the methods by which LDAP replication can take place.

Client/Server Agents

NDS is implemented via a client/server model, where a DSA services client queries and interacts with other directory servers to manage directory information. Although NDS is very X.500-like in design and operations, the protocols used are primarily proprietary.

However, they don't stray far from their X.500 design roots. Novell's version of DAP is called *Novell DAP* (NDAP), for instance, and supports all the functionality provided by DAP. Likewise, NDS does not use X.500 replication protocols, but rather employs a proprietary replication method.

DSA component

The core DSA component in NDS is just called the *NDS server*. A NDS server can manage one or more partitions of directory information, providing client access and supplying updates to other NDS servers. NDS servers perform all DSA operations, including user authentication, directory information management, partitioning, and replication. The NDS DSA component also manages the physical storage of directory partitions.

NDS is notable as a directory product because it operates on multiple networking platforms. Standalone NDS server products are available for the following:

- **NetWare**—NDS 8 requires NetWare 5, although earlier versions of NDS run on NetWare 4.

- **Windows NT**—NDS for NT supports Windows NT 4. The initial release of NDS for NT was dependent on a NetWare server for physical storage of the DIB. The NDS for NT 2.x DIB is stored on the NT server, however, eliminating this requirement. Novell plans to release a version of NDS that will run on Windows 2000.

- **Sun Solaris**—NDS for Sun Solaris supports Solaris 2.6 (SPARC version) and future versions will support Solaris 7. Although NDS does not officially support Solaris 7 in its first release, it does generally interoperate with it. The first version of NDS for Solaris is v.2 because it aligns with NDS for NT 2 in terms of feature set and functionality. NDS 8 supports UNIX applications that utilize the UNIX PAM framework APIs for login services.

- **Linux**—There is also a version of NDS for Caldera Linux in development, projected to release by the end of 1999.

Clients

In discussing NDS clients, we must unavoidably look at NetWare clients, although that is certainly not all that can talk to NDS. The growing number of LDAP-enabled products (browsers and Web applications among others) will expand the range of "clients" for NDS greatly in the future. NetWare clients include the following:

- **Novell Client for Windows**—This is the preferred client for computers running Microsoft Windows. The Novell client is designed to be high performance; the core component is a *virtual device driver* (VXD), and it employs 32-bit versions of the IPX and TCP/IP protocols. The full range of NetWare services and management utilities are supported and the client is fully integrated into Windows Explorer. The Novell client is highly configurable from either the administrator or client side and can also perform simultaneous authentication to multiple NDS trees. There are three versions of this product—for Windows 95, Windows NT, and DOS/Windows 3.1. (The functional equivalent of this client was previously called Client32.)

- **Microsoft Client for NetWare Networks**—Microsoft also provides a NetWare client for Windows. Windows 98 and NT 4 ship with an NDS-aware client, which is available as an add-on for earlier versions of Windows. Even though the client is NDS aware, however, it is still limited, primarily providing access to NetWare file and print services. Many of the NetWare management tools are not operational when using this client. Microsoft's client also requires the use of NWLink (Microsoft's version of IPX) and does not work with NetWare 5's native TCP/IP.

- **NetWare for Mac**—As of NetWare 5, Novell no longer provides a Macintosh client. Prosoft Engineering, Inc. now provides all Macintosh client support for NetWare. Prosoft's first NetWare client, NetWare for Mac is a fully NDS aware IPX client for NetWare 4 and later. Other NetWare Macintosh clients are under development. You can reach Prosoft at: `www.prosofteng.com`

- **Bindery clients**—NDS supports bindery clients by providing a bindery-style view of a portion of the NDS tree. When a client accesses NetWare via bindery services, they can only see the object classes that existed in NetWare prior to NDS. This means that only the user, group, print queue, print server, and profile objects are visible. Bindery services do *not* support a single client login to the network—connections to additional servers must still be made manually.

Macintosh and OS/2 Clients

Prior to NetWare 5, Novell supplied clients for Macintosh and OS/2 as well as Windows. Although these clients are no longer available from Novell, they will probably remain in use for some time yet. The Novell versions of these clients are

- *NetWare Client for Mac OS* is a fully NDS-aware client supporting both client and administrative functionality.

- *NetWare Client for OS/2* provides NDS client functionality to OS/2 workstations.

NDS APIs

NDS supplies numerous APIs for accessing the directory, providing a robust search capability with comprehensive object management interfaces. The following programmatic interfaces to NDS are available:

- **DSAPI**—This is the traditional method of programming NDS—is functionally a port of the XDS APIs from X.500.
- **LDAP C API**—NDS uses its integrated LDAP services to provide native LDAP programmatic access to directory contents.
- **ADSI**—Programmers can also access NDS via *Active Directory Service Interfaces* (ADSI), which is Microsoft's API for Active Directory.
- **JNDI/JNCL**—The Java Naming and Directory Interface is part of JavaSoft's API set and provides easy network resource discovery for Java clients.

The following provide scripting support:

- ActiveX
- JavaBeans
- Open DataBase Connectivity (ODBC)
- Novell script (was NetBasic 7)
- NetBasic 6/7

'Twas the Night Before Printing...

...and Novell announced two new offerings based on NDS 8 designed for managing resources on both sides of the corporate firewall. Both products run on NetWare, Windows NT, and Solaris, with future support for Windows 2000, Linux, and Compaq Tru64 announced.

NDS eDirectory is a stand-alone, cross-platform LDAP directory service that provides a means of managing information on the Internet to support e-commerce, business-to-business relationships, Web-based applications, and provide personalized Web content or services based on profiles and customer data.

NDS Corporate Edition is an additional service for eDirectory that allows for management of resources on the corporate network. NDS Corporate Edition can integrate NT domains and Solaris user accounts as well as network resources into NDS. It replaces the "NDS for..." product line.

Ubiquitous NDS Administration

There are some limitations on non-Windows clients, primarily in the availability of administrative tools. However, the lack of support for administrative tools should become less of a problem in the future as Novell has released the first version of a browser-based administrative console written in Java: ConsoleOne Web Edition. Although ConsoleOne is in its early iterations and still somewhat limited, it does hold promise as a platform and location-independent method of managing NDS.

NDS Models

Although Novell does not directly discuss directory models when describing NDS, it is clear when you examine the design and operations of NDS that the X.500 models apply.

Support for Industry Initiatives

NDS provides substantial support for interoperability with other networking platforms and is actively pursuing open standards for interoperability with other industry vendors. Industry initiatives supported by Novell include the following:

- **Directory Interoperability Forum (DIF)**—Novell is one of the leaders in the DIF, a group of vendors supporting the development of directory-enabled application development and open directory standards.
- **LDUP working group**—Novell is active in the IETF LDAP Duplication, Replication, and Update Protocols (LDUP) working group. This group is focused on the methods by which LDAP replication can take place.
- **Directory Enabled Networking (DEN)**—DEN is a collaboration between network infrastructure device vendors and directory service vendors seeking to enable directory-based control over infrastructure devices (such as routers and switches). Novell has forged partnerships with a number of leading network hardware vendors to provide directory-based management of their network devices, including Lucent, Cisco, and Nortel.

NDS Objects and Schema

The design of NDS clearly reflects the architectural models that X.500 applies to the schema and objects. NDS objects are comprised of attributes, each of which has a designated syntax. Objects have constraints on where they can be created and how they are named.

Because there is such a high degree of similarity between the objects and schema used by NDS and X.500, only some aspects of this topic are briefly touched on here.

Directory Objects

NDS directly incorporates the X.500 object model, supporting the base X.521 container and leaf objects. In addition, NDS creates many other directory objects for informational and network management purposes.

Object ID

When an object is created, each server that holds a replica with the object assigns it a unique *object ID*. This object ID is a 4-byte value that is used by most NDS operations as a unique identifier for the object. Each object also has the object ID of its parent object.

Container Objects

The NDS container objects all have analogs in X.500 objects, although the class definitions may not be exactly the same. Container objects serve the same basic function as in X.500, providing organization to facilitate information distribution, management, and security. The following container objects are available in the default NDS schema:

- **[root]**—NDS has a visible (and often mentioned) [root] object, which is functionally the root of the NDS tree. The [root] is automatically created when the NDS tree is created and is not explicitly named. Rather, it is referred to as either the [root] or (less often) by the tree name. [root] is essentially the top class instantiated as an effective object. The [root] can contain Alias, Organization, or Country objects.

- **Organization**—NDS requires the creation of one Organization object during initial NDS installation. There can be additional Organization objects directly beneath either the [root] or Country objects.

- **Organizational Unit (OU)**—An OU is used in NDS for organizing directory information to facilitate administration and use. The OU is by far the most common container in most NDS trees. An OU can be contained by an Organization, Locality, or far more often, another OU.

- **Country**—The Country object can only be created under [root]. The country class can contain a range of objects representing services and applications. However, it cannot hold OUs or the common network entities (such as computers and users). An object of the country class must be named with a two-letter code that complies with ISO 3166.

- **Locality and State**—Use of the Locality and State objects is totally optional. To create either object, you select a Locality as the class of object to instance, and then select Locality or State/Province. The Locality/State object can hold more classes than a Country, yet not as many as an O or OU. Instances of the class may be placed beneath Organization, Country, or other Locality/State objects.

Tree Root Class

The tree root class defines an *effective* (one that can be used in a tree) container object, although it is not commonly exposed by the administrative tools. However, the tree object *is* visible in ConsoleOne. A tree name (T) attribute is used to name an instance of the tree root class. The class definition for tree root is visible in the Schema Manager tool.

NDS Object Size

Although X.500 doesn't specify object size constraints, NDS limits objects to 50KB in size—although most objects are only a few kilobytes. This provides a reasonable amount of leniency in extending the schema to support properties such as pictures while still maintaining some control over the amount of information stored (and replicated) by NDS.

Leaf Objects

The leaf objects contained in the base NDS schema are highly similar to the X.500 objects, although there are quite a few more classes. Classes in the base NDS schema can be divided into some general categories based on what they are intended to manage:

- **Network resources**—The most common objects are probably those used for basic network management such as users, computer, and printers.
- **Services**—Objects are created as needed to managing services, such as DNS, DHCP, and LDAP.
- **File system**—A number of objects are used to manage file resources, including the NCP Server, AFP Server, Volume, and directory map classes.

Some objects are presented in subsets depending on the context—DNS objects are manipulated in DNS Manager, schema objects are visible in Schema Manager, and so on. DNS objects appear in the NDS tree, but their contents are hidden from within the usual tree administration tools, and they function primarily as pointers to the DNS management tool.

Interestingly enough, the tool that you use to manage the NDS tree affects the object classes that you can select from when creating a new object. After an installation of NetWare 5, NDS 8 and DNS, you can create about 23 base classes via the NWAdmin administrative tool. The other NDS administrative tool, ConsoleOne, exposes *28* additional classes!

Directory Schema

Like early versions of X.500, early versions of NDS used a static schema, which was read when the server initially loaded and remained the same until the server was restarted. However, also like X.500, current versions of NDS publish the schema in the directory as objects. Storing the schema in the directory facilitates schema replication and discovery and also allows developers and administrators to easily access the schema to modify it.

From a structural perspective, the NDS schema is similar to the X.500 schema. Obviously, the specifics of the class definitions vary; but because you know the basics of how the X.500 schema works, the NDS schema should make a lot of sense.

What Is an Unknown Object—and Why Do I Have One?

An unknown object represents an object that NDS does not recognize, usually because one of its mandatory attributes no longer exists. An object may become unknown as a transitional effect during synchronization, or the change may be permanent. One example of a permanently unknown object is what happens if a server is deleted prior to its volumes. The volumes become unknown because the object for the server they belong to (which is the value of a mandatory attribute) no longer exists.

Browsing the NDS Schema

You can browse the NDS schema with the Schema Manager, which is available from the ConsoleOne or NDS Manager Tools menu.

Object Class Definition

NDS class definitions look a lot like X.500 class definitions. The same rules for building classes apply: Classes inherit part of their definition from superclasses; containment and naming rules are largely the same. NDS class definitions are comprised of the following set of fields:

- **Class Flags**—Class flags define the type of class (effective, non-effective, or auxiliary) and the designation as a leaf or container. Ambiguous naming or containment can also be set. (In this case, ambiguous means a class without a specified named by or containment class.)

- **ASN1 ID**—Like the X.500 OID, this is an globally unique number assigned by Novell when schema extensions are registered. If schema extensions are being used for an application that is to be Novell certified, an ASN1 ID is required.

- **Super Classes**—Identifies the additional classes that should also be included in this class definition. As in X.500, all NDS classes have top as a superclass and are likely to have others as well.

- **Containment Class**—Lists the types of objects this object class can be created within, such as OU or O.

- **Named By** —Identifies one or more attributes that will be used to name instances of this object class.

- **Mandatory Attributes**—Contains a list of properties for which the object class must have values. Mandatory attributes can only be assigned to a class definition during creation.

- **Optional Attributes**—Additional properties for which an instance of the object class may or may not have values.

- **Default ACL Template**—Each class has a default set of ACL settings as well as an ACL that it inherits from top. This determines the initial ACLs for an instance of that class.

Classes can be added to the schema, and classes created via extension can be removed from the schema. To maintain base compatibility, however, classes that are part of the standard NDS schema cannot be removed from the schema.

Attribute Type Definition

NDS has quite a few attributes defined—NDS 8 without any extensions has well over 500! Just in case that isn't enough, or there isn't an attribute that exactly meets your need, you can add more. However, existing attributes (including those added by extension) cannot be modified.

Attributes that have been made part of the schema via extension can be removed as long as they are not currently being used in any object class definition. Attributes that are part of the standard NDS schema cannot be removed from the schema.

The attribute definition in the NDS schema consists of these fields:

- **Attribute Syntax ID**—Identifies the syntax to be used for a particular attribute.
- **ASN1 ID**—The ASN1 ID serves the same purpose as in the class definition, uniquely identifying the attribute definition.
- **Used In**—Contains a list of the classes that use this attribute.
- **Constraint Flags**—Quite a few constraints can be placed on an NDS attribute including whether it is multi-valued, hidden, read-only, or has range or size limitations. Synchronization settings for the attribute can also be assigned, determining whether the attribute synchronizes immediately, on a normal schedule, or not at all.

Attribute Syntax Definition

As described in the X.500 chapter, the syntax definition specifies the data format acceptable for the value of an attribute. The syntax defines how a value is constrained by data type and syntax limits. The NDS syntax definition contains the following:

- **Syntax Name**—Descriptive name of the syntax.
- **Syntax ID**—The syntax ID is a 32-bit integer that uniquely identifies the syntax type. This is the value designated in the Attribute Syntax ID field of the attribute definition.
- **API data structure**—This field specifies a C structure supported by the NDS API.
- **Syntax Flags**—Contains matching rules to be used when comparing values using this syntax, such as ordering, equality, and sub string matches.
- **Used In**—The used in field contains a list of the attributes that use this syntax.

Extensibility Methods

NDS provides support for extending the schema, enabling administrators and developers to create needed objects and attributes. The NDS schema is extensible via a number of methods:

- **Schema Manager**—The NDS Schema Manager provides Windows clients with a graphical means of browsing and manipulating the NDS schema. Schema Manager allows full schema administration and includes wizards that walk through extending the schema in half a dozen steps. Slightly different versions of Schema Manager are included with NDS Manager and ConsoleOne.

- **NDSSCH.EXE** is a DOS command-line tool that ships with NDS 8 and is used to import schema modifications from a text file. Novell provides many of the schema extensions for add-on NetWare services in the form of text (SCH) files.

- **MAPUTIL**—MAPUTIL is used to manage the NDS-LDAP class and attribute mapping. It imports and exports mappings from an LDAP group object, allowing backup, restoration and customization of NDS/LDAP relationships. MAPUTIL is available on Novell's Developer Web site.

- **SCHMAP**—SCHMAP reads in an LDIF file, performs the NDS schema extensions, and then configures the LDAP-NDS mapping in a single step. This DOS command-line tool is available from the Novell Developer site.

- **SCHMIG**—This DOS command-line utility converts a Netscape directory server schema file into an LDIF file for import into NDS.

It is worth noting that changes to the schema always imply compatibility issues with other NDS servers. To deal with this, schema information for the directory is held in a schema partition, a replica of which is held by each NDS server. Schema changes are synchronized to all other NDS servers to maintain schematic integrity throughout the tree.

You can find additional information on the NDS schema at: `http://developer.novell.com/nds/schema.htm`

Schema Registry

Novell has a registry for developers who will be extending the NDS schema. The registry contains the base NDS schema, along with additional schemas from independent developers. By maintaining the schema registry, Novell aims to promote the development of standard schemas and reduce problems due to schema incompatibilities.

Developers can be assigned an OID (like an X.500 OID) and a name prefix, which is used at the start of the new class or attribute name (for example, MyCompany:MyClass) to uniquely identify the schema addition. Novell-assigned name prefixes are designed to map to OIDs in much the same way that DNS host names map to IP addresses.

Novell's Developer Web Site

Novell has a number of excellent resources concerning the NDS schema and schema extensions available at: `http://developer.novell.com`

The NDS Tree

One result of designing NDS around the X.500 standards has been NDS trees that often look and function a lot like X.500 trees. Because partition design and management is generally the final determinant in upper-level tree design, geographic divisions are often represented at the top of the tree. Network administration is often the more important factor lower in the tree, so the business organization is likely to be reflected in the tree design, building a framework for directory management and security.

Novell's approach to network administration includes a design that builds the business logic into the tree, streamlining network management. Any NDS object (container or leaf) can have permissions granted to it. In the case of container objects, those permissions are also automatically granted to all objects within it via *inheritance*.

Inheritance supplies a powerful mechanism for managing NDS security, because much of the NDS access control information can be attached to the tree structure and applied based on an object's location. In this way, NDS container objects function as a sort of "structural group"—a group built into the tree structure. When an object is created, it is a "member" of its parent container and gets "membership rights." NDS uses container objects for almost all the functionality that would otherwise be provided by groups.

Inheritance is an iterative process; an object can inherit rights from each node between it and the root of the tree. By designing your tree to take advantage of inheritance and carefully integrating your network and business requirements, you can substantially reduce the time spent on network administration.

DIB Capabilities and Tree Design

NDS partition requirements have had a lot of influence on NDS tree design. Because each partition requires its own node in the tree to function as the partition root, large enterprises have necessarily had some OU structure that was only there for partition management.

Suppose, for example, that there are 2,500 users with largely the same permissions and configuration—from a management perspective, these users could all reside in the same OU. If you are using NDS 7 or earlier, however, a single partition would normally hold only around a thousand objects. Accordingly, those users would have to be divided between multiple OUs strictly for scalability.

With the introduction of NDS 8, the capacity of a single partition has increased dramatically. The greatly reduced need to partition the directory solely for scalability could impact NDS tree design, flattening some of the structure that has historically been used to support partitioning.

Naming in NDS

Although NDS uses the general X.500 model for names, there are (of course) some differences in exactly how naming is implemented and discussed. By using an X.500-style naming convention, Novell makes it easy for NDS to exchange information with other X.500 and LDAP directories.

Individual objects are named as in X.500, with a designated naming attribute and associated value (for instance, cn=tabitha). Both typed (or *typeful*) and typeless naming are supported, although typeless names are more commonly used due to their relative simplicity. As far as NDS is concerned, the following names are equivalent:

```
cn=tabitha

tabitha
```

NDS Names

Like X.500, NDS naming uses a concatenated series of object names to form distinguished names that are unique across the tree. However, individual object names are combined to form a distinguished name (DN) starting at the *leaf-most* object, like LDAP. Object names are combined using the period (.) as a separator between name components.

In accordance with its X.500 foundations, NDS has several distinct types of names that refer to different styles of referencing objects:

- **Distinguished name (DN)**—Just as with X.500, an NDS DN is the name of the object combined with all objects in the path to the tree root—starting at the *leaf-most* object. For example:
  ```
  ian.dev.netmages
  ```

- **Fully distinguished name (FDN)**—A FDN (also called fully qualified distinguished name) is a DN preceded by a period (.) to indicate to NDS that the name should be treated as complete and resolved from the root.
  ```
  .ian.dev.netmages
  ```

- **Relative distinguished name (RDN)**—Although they use the same name, an NDS RDN is *not* like an X.500 RDN. Instead of giving the FDN, the object name is given in relative reference to the user's current location in the tree structure (or context). A NDS RDN is *a DN relative to the location of the object referencing it.*

> **Typeless Naming Is Cool**
>
> Typeless names require far fewer characters, they are visually analogous to DNS and are cognitively easier to remember and use. However, typeless names can lead to ambiguity. For example
> .tabitha.dev.netmages.us could be .cn=tabitha.ou=dev.ou=netmages.o=us or
> .cn=tabitha.ou=dev.o=netmages.c=us.

A number of constraints apply to NDS names:

- Duplicate object names are allowed within the directory tree, but not within a single container.
- The length of any individual object name cannot exceed 64 characters, and a DN string cannot exceed 255 characters.
- NDS names are not case sensitive (that is, dev is processed the same as DEV).
- The following characters should be avoided because they require special handling or may conflict with internal directory uses of the same character:
  , . ; : + = \ / ? *
- Spaces and underscores (_) are considered equivalent by NDS. Underscores can be used as normal text in name strings, however, names containing spaces require quotation marks, making them more awkward to use.

All RDNs Are Not the Same

In some references, the usual X.500 definition of RDN is applied to NDS. According to these sources, the RDN is just the object name, represented in either typed or typeless format as shown:

cn=ian (typed)

ian (typeless)

However, Novell currently defines an RDN as previously described here.

SAP Naming Constraints

When NetWare uses IPX as its communication protocol, it uses the *Service Advertising Protocol* (SAP) to advertise the network services it is providing, bringing some additional name constraints into play. File servers and printers that connect directly to the network (such as the HP JetDirect series) must follow the SAP guidelines. SAP requires the following:

- Name must be unique across the entire network.
- Names cannot be longer than 47 characters.
- Spaces are not allowed in names.

Context

NDS defines an object's place in the directory tree as its *context*. An object's context is referenced by the string of object names between it and the tree root. Another way to look at it—a DOS analogy would be the current directory as denoted by the path.

Each network client is assigned a default name context, which is the DN of the OU containing the user object. In the case of `chloe.dev.netmages`, Chloe's context is `dev.netmages`. This information is stored in a local configuration file. At login, the username is concatenated with the name context and resolved to the specific user object for authentication. Because of the NDS tree design, a person's name context generally represents a logical group sharing resources or security settings.

You change your current context in one of two ways:

- As you navigate in any of the NDS client or administration tools, your context changes.

- By using the `CX` (*change context*) command (executed at a command line). `CX` is similar to the DOS `CD` (change directory) command, except that it applies to the directory service tree rather than the file system tree. You can use `CX` to change your context in several ways:

  - You can change your context to another container by specifying that container's FDN. As an example, "`CX .corp.netmages`" would change your context to the `corp.netmages` container, regardless of your current context.

  - If you specify the RDN rather than the FDN, your context will change relative to your current position in the tree. If your current context is `netmages`, for example, you can move to the `corp` context by typing "`CX corp`". This will move you down a level of the tree into the `corp` container, much like the way that typing "`CD dos`" from the root of `C:` moves you into the `dos` directory.

  - You can move up the DIT by using periods (.) to indicate the desired number of levels up the tree. If your context is `corp.netmages` and you need to change it to `netmages`, for example, you can just type "`CX .`" to move up one level in the tree. "`CX [root]`" will change your context to the tree [root].

NDS objects can also be easily located relative to your current context. When accessing an object in your current context, for example, you are required only to use the object's RDN. When you request an object using its RDN, NDS uses your current context to locate it in the tree.

Context-Less Logins

NetWare 5 introduced *context-less logins*, which enable a user to log in to the network without needing to know their context. A user just enters their first name and selects the appropriate user object from the presented list, which is created from the NDS catalog. This is especially useful with roaming users who may not always be at an appropriately configured computer.

Periods in NDS Names

In addition to using the period (.) as a separator, Novell uses them in NDS names to identify how a particular name should be treated.

- A leading period indicates that the NDS server should consider the name to be an FDN and assumes the name ends immediately below [root].

- No leading period designates the object name as an RDN, telling NDS to resolve it from the current context.

- Trailing periods are used to identify an object *relative to the user's current context.* This can be used either in the CX command (as described earlier) or in an object name. This can be a bit complicated, so let's look at how it actually works.

Figure 8.1 shows two user objects, Ian and Jody. If Ian needs to locate Jody's user object, he has two choices: He can use the FDN of .jody.net.services.netmages; or he can shortcut it by using periods to indicate the object location relative to his name context. In this case, that would be

jody.net.

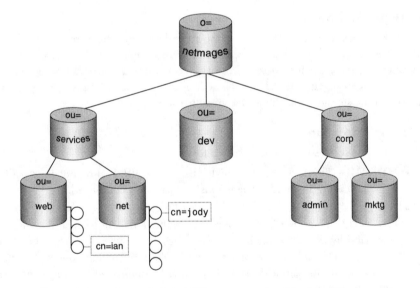

Figure 8.1 Using periods in NDS names can simplify object location.

The single trailing period indicates to NDS that it should first move up one level in the tree (to the services OU) and then move down the tree to resolve the name.

If Ian wanted to access the dev OU, he could enter the following:

dev..

NDS will read the two trailing periods, move up two levels to the netmages OU, and then resolve the name to the dev OU immediately beneath netmages.

NDS Directory Information Base

The information managed by NDS is partitioned and distributed to multiple servers. The collection of servers holding replicas of a single partition is called a replica ring.

A single master replica is designated, although the replication model used by NDS is multi-master in most aspects. NDS replica placement is flexible—servers can hold more than one replica and may also have varying types (master versus read/write) of replicas for different partitions.

NDS is said to be a loosely consistent directory service, meaning that although, by and large, all replicas contain the same information, they will not necessarily match exactly in every detail at any given time.

Storage Method

The method that a directory service uses to store directory information to disk can vary between version as well as between vendors. Although NDS has historically used a multiple file structure for storing directory information, the specifics of the file structure have changed with NDS 8. These changes have brought about a significant increase in the storage capabilities of a single partition.

NDS 8 File Structure

NDS 8 uses these files to store directory information:

- **NDS.DB**—This is the control file for the NDS DIB. It also contains a *roll-back log*, which is used to undo transactions that have not completed.
- **NDS.01**—All the records and indexes on a NDS server are contained in the NDS.01 file. There is a 2GB limit on the NDS.01 file. Additional files are automatically created as the limit is exceeded; these files are named NDS.02 and so on. Attribute indexes contained in the NDS.0x file include the Object Class, dc, Unique ID, and CN fields, as well as strings beginning with Given Name and with the Surname.
- **NDS*.LOG**—The NDS*.LOG file is used for DIB update transaction tracking. Incomplete transactions are logged in this file, which is used as a *roll-forward log*, allowing completion of interrupted transactions.
- **Stream files**—Stream files hold attribute information that is of variable length, like login scripts and print-job configurations. Stream files have an .NDS extension and are named with hexadecimal characters (0–9, A–F).

NDS File Structure (Pre-NDS 8)

In NDS 7 and prior versions, the file structure used to store directory information consisted of the following:

- **PARTITIO.NDS**—PARTITIO.NDS holds a list of all the partitions on the NDS server including system, schema, external reference, and bindery.

- **ENTRY.NDS**—The ENTRY.NDS file contains an entry for each object in any replica on the server.

- **VALUE.NDS**—The VALUE.NDS file contains the values for each object in the ENTRY.NDS file.

- **BLOCK.NDS**—This file is used for overflow data from the VALUE.NDS file.

- **Stream files**—Stream files are much like those in NDS 8, holding the same data and using the same names.

Versions of NDS prior to NDS 8 used Novell's *Transaction Tracking System* (TTS) to guarantee integrity of the DIB by providing a means to roll back changes in the event of incomplete transactions. NDS 8 now uses the rollback log contained in NDS.DB instead of TTS.

Partitioning

NDS provides flexible partition design—any container object can function as a partition root (and names the partition). This flexibility is perhaps far more significant than it may at first appear. The capability to partition at *any* OU enables an administrator to subdivide the directory as needed for performance or operational reasons—and not all directory services allow that.

The number of partition level operations that NDS is capable of indicates its overall flexibility:

- **Create a new partition**—This is probably the most common partition level operation. To create a new partition, you select the container that you want to be the new partition root. NDS will place replicas of the new partition in a configuration that mirrors the replica placement of the parent partition—the server holding the master replica of the parent will be given the master replica of the child, and so on.

- **Merging partitions**—This operation merges a child partition into its parent. First, each NDS server with a replica of the parent is sent a replica of the child, and vice versa, and then the partitions are joined. This is likely to generate a substantial quantity of network traffic while copying replicas, so manually placing replicas on all the appropriate servers before starting may be a good idea.

- **Move container**—Moving a container (such as an OU), requires that two conditions be met; the container must be a partition root, and it must not have any child partitions. When you move any NDS object, you are offered the option to create an alias to replace it. This is particularly a good idea for a container because anyone looking for the old object will be transparently redirected to the new location.

- **Changing replica types**—NDS enables you to change the type of a replica between master, read/write, and read-only. Because any partition must always have a master replica, you cannot directly change the master replica to a read/write or read-only. To change the status of the master replica, you promote another replica to master status, which automatically makes the old master a read/write replica. Other replicas can just be changed between read/write and read-only types.

- **Removing a replica**—Removing a replica is simple, unless it is a master you just delete it. If you want to remove the master replica, you must first designate a new master, and then remove the original master replica afterward.

In addition to being flexible, NDS partitioning is independent of directory functionality that is not related to DIB management. Partitioning the DIB has no inherent impact on security or administration of the directory information.

Prior to version 8, NDS trees required partitioning for scalability. Partitions could only contain a few thousand objects, while an NDS tree was likely to hold many more. NDS 8 increases the capabilities of an individual partition dramatically—theoretically to millions of objects. This is a substantial improvement in the scalability of NDS. Although partitioning will still be required for managing replication traffic and may be desired for administrative reasons, it will no longer be *required* for scalability quite so often.

How Big Is a Million?
According to Novell, the DIB for an NDS 8 tree with one million objects occupies about 1GB of hard drive space.

Replication

NDS uses a multi-master method of directory replication, even though it uses a single master replica to do so. Most operations can take place on any writeable replica, although a few are restricted to the single replica designated as the master.

NDS uses three replica types for storing directory information:

- **Master**—There is a single master of any partition. The master replica is required for partition and replica creation and deletion operations.

- **Read/write**—Read/write replicas can perform most of the functions of the master replica. Read/write replicas are used for redundancy, information distribution, and load balancing.

- **Read-only**—Used for lookups only, read-only replicas cannot support updates, user authentication, or bindery services.

Given the differential level of functionality provided by the various replicas, careful consideration should be taken when determining type and placement of NDS replicas. Read-only replicas are less often used due to their limited functionality.

By default, NDS creates three replicas of a partition, one master and two read/write replicas. The first server installed into an NDS tree (that is, the server that creates the tree) receives a master replica of the entire tree and the next two servers installed into the tree each receive a read/write replica by default. If the DIB is partitioned, this distribution is applied on a per-partition basis.

As previously mentioned, the collection of NDS servers holding replicas of a particular partition is considered a *replica ring*. NDS synchronization is generally performed directly within the replica ring. NDS keeps track of the members of a replica ring with a replica pointer table.

The replica pointer table contains a list of all the servers holding a replica of a given partition, the replica type held by each server, and the current status of the replica. Every server in a replica ring must have a matching copy of the replica pointer table for synchronization operations to work properly.

Replica pointer tables contain the following:

- **Server name**—The DN of the server holding the replica.

- **Replica type**—Master, read/write, or other designation.

- **Replica state**—This indicates the operational status of the replica, and is usually on. Other states include new, join, and split, each of which indicates that a particular partition operation is underway.

- **Replica number**—A unique number is assigned to each replica upon creation.

- **Partition root object ID**—The object ID of the object that serves as the partition root is unique to each server holding a replica.

- **Address**—Network addresses for the server are listed in this field. Multiple addresses may be listed if the server supports multiple protocols.

Figure 8.2 shows the partitioning scheme for the `netmages` tree. The four servers that participate in the `services` replica ring are shown. The partitions held by each server are listed immediately below the server. Three of the servers have only replicas of the `services` partition, but Merlin has two others as well.

Table 8.2 shows the replica pointer table for the `services` partition. There are four replicas of the partition: one master, two read/write, and one *subordinate reference* (SR) (as discussed in the following section).

Table 8.2   **The Replica Pointer Table for the Services Partition**

Server Name	Replica Type	Replica State	Replica Number	Partition Root Object ID	Address
Gandalf	Master (M)	On	1	02972405	192.168.200.42
Zifnab	Read/write (RW)	On	3	93755822	192.168.200.75
Haplo	Read/write	On	2	03947289	192.168.200.18
Merlin	Subordinate reference (SR)	On	4	15005920	192.168.200.145

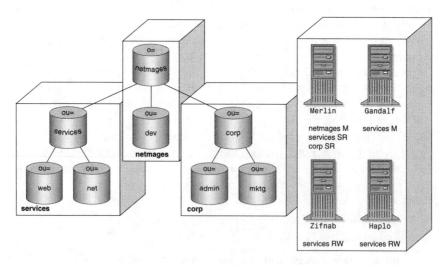

Figure 8.2   The *netmages* tree and NDS servers
holding replicas of the *services* partition.

Subordinate Reference

NDS creates subordinate reference replicas to glue together portions of the directory contained in multiple partitions. Subordinate references function like X.500 knowledge references in providing linkage between distributed portions of the DIT. A subordinate reference is placed on a server that contains a partition that has a child, but does not hold a replica of the child partition. In Figure 8.2, Merlin has a replica of the `netmages` partition, but not `services`; therefore, a subordinate reference is placed on Merlin to provide linkage to the service partition. Note that Merlin is also referenced in the replica pointer table.

A subordinate reference is a very small replica, containing a single object—the partition root of the child partition. The object that serves as the partition root contains information identifying all the servers in the partition's replica ring. By using this information, NDS can locate a server holding a complete replica of the child when it needs to walk down the tree.

However, this also means that all subordinate references are members of the replica ring and must participate in synchronization and partition level operations. The impact of subordinate references on NDS operations is something that should be kept in mind when partitioning NDS.

External Reference

The *external reference* partition contains temporary pointers to objects in the NDS tree that are not part of a partition held on that NDS server. NDS automatically creates external references when it needs to reference information about an object that is not part of a local replica. NDS servers create external references for a number of reasons:

- **Complete a DN**—The entire path from any given object to the root of the NDS tree must be represented for every object referenced by any NDS server. Accordingly, every object between the partition root of any local replica and the root of the tree must have a local reference—if the object is not local, NDS creates an external reference. When an external reference is created, additional external references to complete the tree framework between the initial object and the root of the tree may also be created.

- **Authentication and access control**—External references are created to support user authentication to a server not containing a replica of the user's context.

- **Objects that are also values**—NDS must track information about objects referenced as a value of another object. If a group has members who are not referenced in a partition held by its server, an external reference is created to maintain the linkage between them.

External references contain the object name and an object ID, assigned by the NDS server creating the external reference. They may contain additional information depending on why they were created. For instance, an external reference to a user used for authentication caches the user's public key to improve performance.

Distributed Reference Links

Every object has an attribute that corresponds to the external reference, called a *distributed reference link* (DRL). A DRL maintains a list of all the external references created for an object. NDS periodically verifies DRLs, and if the associated external reference no longer exists, the DRL is deleted.

This functionality was provided by a *backlink* prior to NetWare 5. Although they are highly similar, there is one significant difference between DRLs and backlinks:

- Backlinks use the server DN to locate servers holding replicas containing the external reference for maintenance. This requires that every NDS server be able to communicate directly with every other NDS server, something no longer guaranteed with NetWare 5.

- DRLs reference the DN of the *partition* rather than the server, allowing the use of transitive synchronization, which was also added to NetWare 5.

Synchronization Method

Synchronization is the term used in NDS to describe the replication of directory updates to other NDS servers. Directory synchronization in NDS uses time stamps to ensure that data is correctly synchronized across the network.

Whenever an object is updated, the change is also marked with a time stamp (this is done on a per-property basis). That time stamp is used by NDS to determine which information should be sent when synchronizing replicas. The time stamp can also be used to resolve data collision issues that occur in a multi-master environment.

Each NDS server stores the time of last update performed on every other server in the replica ring in a SynchUpTo vector. During the synchronization process, the supplier checks the time stamp indicating the most recent update to that consumer. Only changes that occurred after that time are sent to the server. At the end of the process, the SynchUpTo vector is updated for use in the next replica synchronization process.

NetWare 5 Changed NDS

The change to native TCP/IP with NetWare 5 required several changes in NDS. NDS is a protocol-independent network service, running on IPX or pure IP equally well. However, some specific internal methods and supportive services needed adjustments. A few particularly significant changes to NDS are as follows:

- Backlinks were replaced with distributed reference links due to changed interserver communication processes.

- Transitive synchronization capabilities were added to support mixed-protocol replica rings.

- The *Service Location Protocol* (SLP) was introduced as a method of locating IP services.

Because each object has a time stamp indicating when it was last updated, that time can be compared against the updated value for that property. If the update about to be applied contains information that was written to NDS prior to the existing data, it can be discarded. This method of synchronization guarantees that the last write to any individual property is written to the DIB.

Unlike many other directory services currently on the market, NDS propagates changes on a prioritized basis. This means that important changes will promptly be sent to all other NDS servers, less-important changes will be sent out on a lower priority. NDS supports two different synchronization speeds:

- **Fast synchronization**—Most updated directory information is synchronized every 10 seconds.

- **Slow synchronization**—Information associated with user login, such as login time and network address, is synchronized every five minutes.

Transitive Synchronization

With NetWare 5, Novell introduced native TCP/IP and dropped the requirement for IPX. This brought with it some changes in NDS. Communications issues arose—for example, how can a server running *only* IPX and a server running *only* TCP/IP synchronize NDS data?

To support the switch to native TCP/IP with NetWare 5, Novell had to modify the synchronization process somewhat. Prior to NetWare 5, every server in a replica ring had to be able to directly contact every other server in the replica ring.

NDS now supports *transitive synchronization*, allowing indirect replication within a replica ring. Transitive synchronization is where NDS server using different protocols synchronize replicas through an intermediary NDS server that supports both protocols.

Each NDS 8 server uses a transitive vector, which stores information pertaining to its replica update status (that is, synchronization). When a synchronization operation is triggered, the source of the update checks the target server's transitive vector to determine whether an update is needed.

Synchronization in a Mixed IPX and TCP/IP Environment

Prior to NetWare 5, TCP/IP was supported only as an additional service. Beginning in NetWare 5, however, TCP/IP is native. NDS servers can now support both IPX and TCP/IP, or only one of the two—a situation that presents replication issues.

For a replica ring with "IPX only" and "TCP/IP only," NDS servers to complete the synchronization process, one member of the replica ring must support both protocols. This server acts as an intermediary during synchronization. Updates that need to pass between servers with different protocols can do so through the one NDS server supporting both.

Time Services

The directory synchronization scheme used by NDS requires time synchronization across the network—all servers must be using the same *network time* to avoid corruption of the directory information. To accomplish this, NDS servers also function as time providers and all client system clocks are synchronized with the network time when the user logs on (which can be disabled if required).

To provide consistent time among the time servers, a polling process occurs periodically. A time server compares its time to the other time servers on the network and adjusts its clock according to a weighted priority. There are several types of time servers, each of which participates in the time synchronization process differently:

- **Single reference**—A single reference time server acts as controller, setting the time for *all* other computers on the network. This type of time server never adjusts its clock based on the polling process. Single reference servers poll other time servers, although only to detect incorrect configurations—because the single reference should be the only *supplier* in the polling process, if another server responds, something is wrong and an error condition is generated. Secondary time servers are the only other time servers allowed with a single reference server.

- **Reference**—Similar to a single reference, but will exist with additional time servers (that is, primaries). Like the single reference, a reference server never adjusts its clock based on the polling process. Reference servers have a polling weight of 16, meaning that primary servers will always adjust their clocks to match that provided by a reference server.

- **Primary**—When a primary time server is used, at least one additional primary must be present. Any additional time servers required, other than a single reference, can be present with the primary server. Primaries have a weight of 1 in the polling process and participate equally in the adjustment process. When a primary polls other time servers, it collects the available times from primaries and averages them—the result is the new time.

- **Secondary**—Secondary time servers are considered *consumers* of time services in that they rely on other time servers to provide the accurate time. A secondary will change its time to exactly match the time it is given by a provider. Secondary time servers provide less-capable, redundant local time servers to provide more robust time services to local clients and servers.

The default configuration for NDS is for the first server to be designated as a single reference and all others as secondaries. Although this is a simple configuration, it is generally used only on smaller networks (20–30 servers), due to inherent limitations with a single time source.

Larger networks commonly use a cascaded configuration where there is one reference server, a few primaries, and a number of secondaries. This configuration provides adequate availability of time services without the overhead involved with a large number of servers participating in the polling process.

NDS Operations

Although NDS operations are far more complex than fits within the scope of this book, this section does describe the NDS client login and name resolution operations, as well as the bindery services.

Server Location

Initial server location in NDS is performed via one of two methods, depending on NDS version and the communications protocols in use (IPX or TCP/IP):

- **Service Location Protocol**—SLP is designed for advertising and location of services for distributed IP networks. SLP is specified in RFC 2165, and provides functionality similar to SAP. SLP does discovery of servers (NDS, DNS, DHCP) and can take advantage of IP multicasting (but doesn't require it). SLP also encapsulates SAP when running in IPX compatibility mode, and allows IPX clients to find IP servers and vice versa.

- **Service Advertising Protocol**—When an IPX-based workstation boots up, the NetWare client locates an NDS server by broadcasting a SAP service request with the desired tree name. Servers holding a replica of a partition in that tree respond to the service request, performing user authentication and providing access to resources.

Name Resolution

To begin the lookup process, an NDS client passes the DN of the object it wants to locate to its local NDS server. The NDS server examines the DN to see if the object is held within a local replica. The client request specifies the required type of replica (master, read/write), so the replica must also be the right kind.

If the sought object is held locally, the server returns its own network address to the client. The client then reconnects to the server with the complete query (for example, a request to read an object).

If the object is not held locally, NDS uses a process called *tree-walking* to locate it. NDS does a partial match on the object DN to determine whether it needs to walk up or down the tree. To do this, each portion of the DN is examined starting at the [root]. By comparing the DN of the requested object with the replicas held locally, NDS determines whether the object is up or down the tree.

If the object is located down the NDS tree from the current server, the server uses the subordinate reference replica to locate a partition and continues the tree-walking process. Each time that a partition boundary is encountered, NDS uses subordinate references (if needed) until the desired object is located.

If the object is located up the tree, the root-most partition on the server is examined. The replica pointer table of this partition will contain information concerning a subordinate reference held by another NDS server. NDS contacts that server and continues walking the tree in the same fashion until it finds the object.

After an appropriate replica containing the object is located, the server returns the network address of the NDS server holding it, to the client. The client then connects to the new server to complete the query.

Bindery Compatibility

NDS provides backward compatibility with NetWare 3.x bindery clients via the bindery service, and supplies NDS management of NetWare 3.x binderies via NetSync.

Bindery Services

NDS provides support for NetWare 3.x clients through *bindery services*. The bindery service designates a container (by default, the container the NDS server is in) to serve as the *bindery context*. When bindery clients access NDS, they are presented with a subset of the contents of the bindery context.

Bindery services can logically combine up to 16 separate contexts (that is, the contents of up to 16 NDS container objects) on a single server. This allows a single NDS server to present tens of thousands of objects to bindery clients. Down-level clients see the complete contents of the bindery context as a single flat namespace, equivalent to a single server under NetWare 3.x.

When NDS is installed on a server, the server's bindery context is automatically set to the container the server is in. This server must hold a writeable replica of the partition of which it is a member (that is, the partition containing the server object).

When a client accesses NDS via bindery services, the client sees only the objects that existed in earlier versions of NetWare. This means that only the user, group, print queue, print server, and profile objects are visible. (The profile object is not actually a bindery object, rather it is provided for compatibility with NetWare Name Services.)

NetSync

NetSync was designed as a temporary solution for administering a mixed NetWare 3.x–4.x environment during the transition to NDS. Many years later, however, it is still being used on many networks that use both versions of NetWare. The primary advantages to NetSync are that it allows management of bindery objects via the standard NDS administration tools and provides a cluster of up to 12 NetWare 3 servers with a more comprehensive, shared database of users, somewhat like NetWare Name Services.

NetSync operates via a pair of agents:

- **NETSYNC4**—The NDS server loads NETSYNC4.NLM.
- **NETSYNC3**—NetWare 3.x servers load NETSYNC3.NLM.

Installing NetSync is a fairly simple process requiring a few actions on each involved server. The NDS server requires a list of the 3.x servers that will be in the NetSync cluster. Each of the NetWare 3 servers must also have an NDS server specified. After configuration is complete, the users and groups from the bindery of each NetWare 3 server in the NetSync group are imported into NDS as NDS objects.

The *complete* contents of the NDS server's bindery context is then copied to the NetWare 3 server. The bindery context contents will consist of the binderies of all the servers in the NetSync cluster as well as any bindery-compatible NDS objects that exist in that OU (users, printers, and so on).

After NetSync is installed, all management on the down-level servers should be performed via NDS tools (NWAdmin or ConsoleOne). This ensures that NDS changes the contents of the bindery context rather than the bindery itself. Changes made by down-level administration tools, such as SYSCON, are *not* made in NDS, but rather in the actual bindery. Changes made to the bindery are not transmitted to the NDS server, so any changes made in this way will remain only on the single server.

Security in NDS

NDS provides a substantial degree of administrative flexibility in its security management. NDS uses a distributed security architecture, employing the directory to contain and provide the information, and the (C-2 level) security services for authentication.

Like X.500, the NDS namespace is structured around a hierarchical directory tree, providing a logical mechanism for security subdivisions. In this hierarchy, each container can be assigned inheritable rights. Filters can be used to determine which of those rights are inherited to subcontainers.

Because every object in the NDS tree is considered a security principal, NDS provides a substantial degree of control over all directory objects and information. As a consequence, NDS provides a powerful mechanism to manage the security of your network, and your information.

Novell uses a proprietary set of security mechanisms for authentication and access control based on the *Public Key Infrastructure* (PKI), and it also supports related Internet security protocols.

PKI technologies supply data integrity and confidential communications across nonsecure networks (such as the Internet). PKI employs digital certificates and asymmetric (public-key) cryptography. NDS provides support for X.509-compliant certificates, and certificate authorities.

NDS also provides support for the *Secure Sockets Layer* (SSL) 3.0. SSL is used to encrypt LDAP passwords and provide a secure communications channel between an NDS client and a server.

Authentication Methods

NDS leverages both proprietary and standards-based technology in the provision of user authentication services. NDS uses shared secret authentication methods as well as PKI certificates for establishing user identity. Both private and public key technologies are used for NDS authentication. NDS uses RSA public key technology security to provide for a single login and encrypted authentication.

During the login process, NDS establishes the user's identity by walking the tree to find a writeable partition containing the user object. After the user has been authenticated to NDS, the user's private keys are retrieved and NDS provides background authentication to other services and servers as needed.

NDS provides support for authentication via the following:

- Encrypted passwords over SSL
- X.509 certificates
- SmartCards

Access Control

Every NDS object has, as one of its properties, an *access control list* (ACL), which is used to determine NDS access permissions. An ACL consists of the security assignments for the object or its properties. NDS ACLs support a high degree of granularity, because access rights can be established at the property level on *individual* objects. Other directory services may allow access control decisions to be made for groups of objects, but not for a single one.

Objects are protected by ACLs with the following entries:

- **Trustee**—Contains the object ID for the trustee. (A *trustee* is an object that has been granted rights to another object.)
- **Type of rights**—Designates whether the ACL is for object or property rights.
- **Type of access**—Lists the rights being granted.

The default ACL template determines the rights for a new instance of a class of objects. For example, a user object is created with the right to modify certain properties of itself, such as the password.

NDS Rights

NDS defines a range of object and property rights that can be set on any directory object.

Object Rights

Object rights apply to an object as a whole rather than to the individual properties of the object.

- **Supervisor**—Grants all object rights.
- **Browse**—Grants the right to see the object.
- **Create**—Grants the right to create a new object.
- **Delete**—Grants the right to delete the object.
- **Rename**—Grants the right to rename the object.
- **Inheritable**—This option is new to NetWare 5 and determines whether permissions granted at the *container* level flow down the tree. Inheritable is on by default for compatibility with previous versions of NDS.

Property Rights

Property rights apply to the individual properties of an NDS object. Access rights can be set for *all* object properties as a group or for one (or more) individual properties.

- **Supervisor**—Grants all property rights.
- **Compare**—Grants the right to compare contents of two properties.
- **Read**—Grants the right to read the property.
- **Write**—Grants the right to write (change) the property.
- **Add self**—Grants the right to write the to the object's ACL.
- **Inheritable**—Functionally equivalent to same setting on object.

Permissions

NDS uses a system of directly assigned and inherited security assignments to determine the access permissions for any object in the tree.

Access rights under NDS are determined using a combination of several settings:

- Trustee assignment
- Security equivalence
- Inheritance
- Inherited rights filter (IRF)

The *effective rights* of a particular object are determined by the combined assessment of these factors.

We need to look at each piece of the NDS security picture in a little more depth to understand how it all works together to control access to directory information.

Trustee Assignment

With NDS every object in the directory is a security principal. This means that any object in the directory can be made a *trustee* of another directory object, or granted rights to that object. For example, a user who has rights to access a server is a trustee of the server and is in its trustee list.

After a trustee assignment is made, permissions can be associated with that object. Default permissions are sometimes associated with an object during an initial trustee assignment. NDS also grants a number of objects default trustee assignments when they are created. The admin object is granted supervisor rights at the [root] of the tree, for example, providing full access to all NDS objects.

Security Equivalence

One of the important concepts of security in NDS is that of *security equivalence*. NDS relies heavily on the use of security equivalence as a means of assigning rights within the directory. Security equivalence can be created in a number of ways:

- **Public**—Every user is considered the security equivalent of the Public object. It is important to note that this security equivalence applies *before* the user is logged in to the tree, to allow tree browsing before being authenticated. Because unauthenticated users have the same rights as Public, you should be very careful which rights are assigned to the Public object. For this reason, only NDS object rights, and *not* file system rights, can be assigned to the Public trustee.

- **[root]**—Any person who is logged in to an NDS server is security equivalent to the [root] object. You should grant [root] the permissions that apply to everyone on the network.

- **Containers**—This is the primary use of security equivalence in NDS. By default, any object is considered to be the security equivalent of every container above it, all the way to the root of the tree. The fastest way to determine which containers a specific object is considered to be a security equivalent of is to look at the object DN. An object is the security equivalent of every container used as a name component in its DN. You should assign those rights that you want all users in a particular container to have to the container they reside in.

- **Groups**—When you create a group in NDS and assign a set of access rights to that group, all people who are added to the group are considered to be a security equivalent of the group object. Any permissions granted to the group are given to the individual objects in its members list. Groups are used to control permissions at a finer level than a container.

- **Security equals property**—There is also an attribute in each NDS object that allows a direct assignment of security equivalence. This is particularly useful if, for example, you need to temporarily assign someone administrator rights. By adding admin (or other appropriate object) to the security equals property of a user object, that user will be granted the administrators rights. The object administrator can be removed from the security equals property when this is no longer needed. Although this is a very powerful method of quickly assigning rights within NDS, you should also carefully keep track of what rights have been granted via this method.

Rights granted via security equivalence cannot be masked by an IRF on the object that has been *granted* the security equivalence.

Inheritance

Security permissions flow down an NDS tree via *inheritance*. Inheritance is a process that allows the rights granted to an object higher in the tree to flow downward, applying to objects below it. Inheritance in NDS is based on the tree hierarchy, allowing the tree structure to control much of the general security for the network with only exceptions needing to be assigned individually.

If the admin object is given the [Supervisor] permission at [root], for example, the admin object has that permission throughout the entire NDS structure. Rights granted via this method are known as *inherited rights*.

Inherited rights can include object rights and rights assigned to all properties, but not individual properties of an object. This means that although you can grant the right to read all properties of an object to a container and have all users in that container be able to do so, you cannot grant the right to read just the email address and have that right flow down the tree.

Inherited ACL

Each partition root has a property called an *inherited ACL*, which contains the *effective* rights for that partition. The effective rights are the combination of all the trustee assignments made minus all the IRFs applied in higher levels of the tree. If no IRFs are applied at the partition root, the rights contained in the inherited ACL will be inherited by all the objects in the partition. By using the inherited ACL, NDS can calculate effective rights without having to actually walk the entire tree.

Runtime Inheritance

In NDS, an object's ACL contains only the permissions granted directly on the object. When access to the object is requested, the directory dynamically determines the access rights by gathering ACLs from the object and the other objects that contain relevant security information (such as parents). NDS assesses the collection of ACLs to determine the effective permissions on the requested object. Runtime inheritance guarantees that the access control decision will be based on absolutely current data, although there may be a nominal trade-off in access time.

Inherited Rights Filters

In the context of a hierarchical directory tree that allows for inheritance of access rights, it is also convenient to have a means to *stop* the inheritance of rights. NDS provides this mechanism via an *Inherited Rights Filter* (IRF), which blocks the inheritance of access rights from higher in the tree.

An IRF can be used on a container level to determine which rights the objects within a container inherit. IRFs can filter inheritance of rights that were granted to the entire object, for all properties, or for only selected properties. This is particularly useful for network administrators—blocking the hierarchical flow of access rights to an entire subtree in one configuration setting.

Note that an IRF cannot grant any permissions; it can only block the inheritance of those that were granted higher in the tree.

Effective Rights

An object's *effective rights* are the set of access rights that result when all the security factors are combined and assessed. Effective rights denote which operations the object can *actually* perform. Effective rights are determined using the object's ACL, explicit assignments, and security equivalents.

To calculate effective rights, NDS does the following:

- Determines the explicit trustee assignments between the object and the partition root.
- Factors in the applicable IRFs.
- Obtains inherited ACL from partition root.
- Adds in the ACL of any object this object is security equivalent to.

This process is done for the two objects in question—the object being accessed and the object doing the accessing. The collection of these security settings determines the effective rights for any given object.

NDS Administration

As noted elsewhere in this book, we are describing directory services from a networking perspective, encompassing architectural and theoretical dimensions. Likewise, we're describing NDS administration from the architectural perspective, describing the range of administrative tools and functionality provided.

Administration Tools

Two core administrative tools are used to manage NDS:

- **NetWare Administrator** (which runs on Windows) has been the main NDS tool since its inception in 1993.

- **ConsoleOne** is a Java-based administrative console for Windows and Web browsers, supplied with NDS 8.

Although the future direction of NDS management is clearly ConsoleOne, some operations can be performed on only one of the two tools. Because of this, you should expect to use both tools in managing your network for the foreseeable future.

NetWare Administrator

NDS management has traditionally been performed using the *NetWare Administrator* (commonly called *NWAdmin*). NWAdmin is an extensible administrative tool, natively providing NDS management functionality, although also furnishing the framework for additional management capabilities.

An application that modifies the directory schema to include application specific objects, for example, must also provide a means to manage those objects. This is provided via a *snap-in*, which is essentially an extension to NWAdmin. By installing a snap-in, a vendor can provide access to the objects and properties that were added to the schema.

A few features of the NetWare Administrator are as follows:

- Individual property pages can be sorted and hidden for any directory object, enabling customized console configurations.

- Multiple objects may be selected and property values for the entire group edited at the same time. The ability to change values one time for multiple containers, templates, groups, or users is a benefit to network administrators who must cope with constantly changing needs of their organization.

- Multiple NDS trees can be managed simultaneously, just by opening additional NDS browse windows.

- Catalog queries can be performed from within NWAdmin.

- NWAdmin provides a centralized point to launch additional management tools, for services such as DNS/DHCP and remote console access to the NetWare server.

- NWAdmin provides easy methods of performing searches quickly. Searches can also be saved as a means of building a library of standard queries.

Delegating Administration

You can use the tree in NDS to delegate administrative authority for discrete parts of the directory, granting specific administrative rights for designated containers and subtrees. OUs are most commonly used for such delegation, to subdivide the administration for business or operational purposes.

ConsoleOne

ConsoleOne is staged to become the primary network management tool used with NetWare. It is an extensible Java console that provides a centralized point of network management. ConsoleOne provides an administrative interface not only to NDS but also to the file system. ConsoleOne was introduced with NetWare 5 and has had two rather different incarnations as a network management tool.

ConsoleOne 1.1, which shipped with NetWare 5, was a server-based console rather than the client-side ConsoleOne provided with NDS 8. The original ConsoleOne tool was highly limited, rather slow, and not very well accepted. To their credit, Novell publicly acknowledged this was perhaps *not* the best approach to dealing with a portable administration tool and thoroughly redesigned ConsoleOne prior to releasing it with NDS 8.

ConsoleOne 1.2 provides support for all the functionality in the preceding administration tool, NetWare Administrator; supports enhanced operations; and, because it is a Java-based utility, is platform independent. ConsoleOne enables you to deal with large trees by paging search results and providing virtual list views. Future versions of ConsoleOne will operate via Web browsers instead of requiring any standalone interface.

Other NDS tools

In addition to the network management afforded by NWAdmin and ConsoleOne, NDS provides a range of other directory tools to manage internal NDS operations, including the following:

- **NDS Manager**—NDS Manager supports partitioning and replication of the NDS database. NDS Manager can also verify synchronization status and trigger synchronization as needed. NDS Manager can initiate database repair by spawning DSREPAIR on the server holding the replica in need of repair, and upgrade the NDS version supported by the NDS server. NDS Manager replaces the DOS-based Partition Manager, which provided this functionality in earlier versions.

- **LDIF Bulkload**—NDS 8 includes the LDIF Bulkload utility, enabling administrators to easily add, delete, or modify large numbers of directory objects. As mentioned earlier, LDIF is the LDAP data interchange format, a text representation of directory objects used as an implementation-independent method of exchanging data between directories.

- **SCANTREE**—This is a DOS-based, read-only NDS utility that produces a basic inventory of the NDS tree. SCANTREE is available from Novell's Web site as DSSCAN.EXE.

- **DSREPAIR**—DSREPAIR is a server console tool that examines, repairs, and compacts the NDS database. Recent versions of DSREPAIR work on a single partition, allowing most operations to be performed without locking the entire DIB.

- **DSMERGE**—DSMERGE supports merging the roots of two NDS trees—combining the two into a single tree. DSMERGE also enables renaming of a directory tree—this is especially useful when attempting to merge two directory trees with the same name.
- **NDS Trace**—You can observe NDS operations in real time by using the NDS Trace options of the Set command. Numerous options enable you to view processes such as synchronization.
- **DSMAINT**—DSMAINT is designed to support replacing NDS servers. Using DSMAINT, an administrator can back up NDS, replace the server hardware, and then restore NDS to the new server with all object IDs intact.
- **SBACK**—SBACK is a basic backup utility that provides a method of backing up the NDS database to tape and restoring it. Although it does afford a simple backup method for NDS, that is about all it does. Because most network backup software also includes a mechanism for backing up NDS, however, it is not widely employed in large network environments.

Login Script Processing

NDS provides comprehensive support for multiple levels of login scripts, assessed according to a predetermined hierarchy. NDS login scripts are processed in the following order:

- **OU login script**—The OU login script is used first.
- **Profile login script**—If a profiles is assigned, the profile login script is used next.
- **User login script**—A login script assigned to the specific user is next.
- **Default login script**—The default script is run unless one of the two following conditions occur: Either there *is* a user login script, or the default script is told not to run using the appropriate variable in one of the other login scripts.

Profile Objects

Each user can have only one profile object assigned. The profile object affords an additional method of attaching a login script to a user. There is no security equivalence conferred via profile objects.

Groups in NDS

Groups are used to collect a set of users, generally for assignment of common access permissions. Like other NDS objects, groups are security principals, so you can assign group permissions and all members will be granted those permissions. A group object does not have login scripts associated with it, although groups may be referenced within a login script.

When group memberships are enumerated, member names are returned one at a time. This means that if the group is not held in a local replica, the process to enumerate members of a group may generate some additional network traffic, and be somewhat slower than if performed locally. Therefore, you may want to keep in mind relative location of groups and their members when designing your network.

Integrated Novell Management Technologies

Novell has integrated a number of management technologies with NDS. These technologies assist network management in common administrative and infrastructure tasks. The following are just two examples of this:

- **ZENworks**—ZENworks is a desktop management system, allowing desktop management and troubleshooting from a remote location. ZENworks integrates policy-based management of workstations with NDS to deliver network-wide support for roaming users and centralized administration of clients. ZENworks stores desktop, application, printer configurations, and help desk information. This information is stored in the directory and pulled by clients upon login. Administrators can perform tasks such as remotely gathering computer inventories, installing software on client machines, and securely accessing workstations from remote locations.

- **BorderManager**—BorderManager provides security at the network boundaries to provide secure Internet and intranet management. BorderManager lets you define security and service rules for devices and services. You can use BorderManager to manage *Virtual Private Networks* (VPNs), firewalls, proxy services, and caching.

The Future of NDS

As mentioned at the beginning of this chapter, NDS has been around for a number of years. As a product, it has expanded considerably over the years, both within the core NDS product as well as in ancillary offerings. That growth is continuing, extending onto the Internet and integrating an ever-increasing number of new technologies.

Before moving on to Active Directory, let's take a brief look at just a few of the things that Novell has up its sleeve for NDS in the near future.

DirXML

As mentioned in Chapter 7, "Evaluating Directory Services," the eXtensible Markup Language is being used in accessing and representing directory service content. Novell is part of the alliance led by Bowstreet Software that seeks to develop a standardized directory markup language based on XML.

Novell is also developing its own version of an XML-based language, called DirXML. DirXML runs on top of NDS 8 to provide directory integration and management. DirXML uses *connectors* to create an application specific view of the information stored in a directory service. Connectors are initially slated to include NDS, Active Directory, Lotus Notes, and Netscape among others.

The information contained in that application view can then be replicated via XML and an XSL processor. XSL is the *eXtensible Stylesheet Language* and consists of a language used to transform XML documents and a vocabulary used to describe formatting semantics. The XSL processor in DirXML can customize the data to the needs of any application.

Single Sign-on

Single Sign-on is another interesting new technology from Novell. It provides a method for securely storing and retrieving passwords used by applications other than NDS. Among the first applications supported are Lotus Notes and PeopleSoft.

Single Sign-on stores passwords to multiple systems within NDS and uses those passwords to authenticate the user to the other applications and services as needed. When an application needs to authenticate a user, it first checks to see whether the user is currently authenticated to NDS. If the user is authenticated, the application just loads. If not, a password is requested.

Provisions are made so that stored passwords cannot be easily compromised. Single Sign-on can be configured so that if a user's NDS password is changed by an administrator, Single Sign-on will request the *old* NDS password at the next use of the stored application credentials. This helps ensure that someone impersonating an administrator cannot easily access and alter stored secret information.

digitalme™

Novell has recently announced what they are calling **digitalme**, a new kind of personal information management system. **digitalme** extends NDS secure information management capabilities across the Internet and enables individuals to use NDS as a means of managing their online identity. Novell envisions **digitalme** using NDS as a relationship manager to "integrate the digital world around the person."

digitalme uses an *identity server*, which is run on a Web server, making it accessible on the Internet. The identity server stores **digitalme** information securely, while making it available according to user-configured policies. Because it is based on standard NDS technology, the identity server can offer capabilities such as Single Sign-on.

Each person who registers with **digitalme** creates one or more *profiles*. Profiles are specific "views" of a person, based on context such as business, family, or a special interest. These profiles are called *mecards*. Each mecard can have its own set of attributes and information, making it possible to have customized personas for various aspects of your Internet identity.

Users can form *relationships* to the mecards, which grant another entity (such as a Web site or another digitalme user) access to the information in that mecard. After a relationship is established with a Web site, **digitalme** can perform actions such as automatically log the user in to the site, fill in forms, and otherwise off load repetitive tasks.

Novell is planning on expanding **digitalme** to store things such as bookmarks, configuration and preference settings, and even files. AOL and Novell have recently announced a partnership allowing Novell to offer a form of instant messaging based on AOL Instant Messenger technology.

For further information regarding **digitalme**, visit `www.digitalme.com`.

...all domains shall be as one,
and speak in tongues of LDAP...

9

Active Directory

THIS CHAPTER EXAMINES THE ARCHITECTURE AND OPERATIONS OF Active Directory, Microsoft's new directory services in Windows 2000. Although the scope of the technical information on Active Directory can fill many books, this material is a concise summary of key factors describing Microsoft's new entry into the networking directory service market.

Within this chapter, you will need to use much that you have learned in previous chapters as AD incorporates directory technologies discussed throughout this book. AD is designed to integrate core Internet technologies with the Windows 2000 networking and security services, leveraging the global DNS namespace and location services, and using LDAP as the core directory protocol.

Introduction to Active Directory

Active Directory (AD) is one of the more technologically inventive networking directory service implementations in the industry. In looking at Active Directory, you can see Microsoft's comprehensive integration of key directory service technologies with their Windows 2000 networking platform.

In observing how Microsoft networks have evolved, some of the more interesting aspects of Active Directory emerge:

- Microsoft has historically provided support for the NT flat NetBIOS namespace, with a physical naming model structured into domains, managing a very limited set of objects, using broadcasts for location services, and storing the *Directory Information Base* (DIB) information in a centralized but replicated database.

- More recent NT versions have included support for *Windows Internet Naming Service* (WINS) providing point-to-point, dynamic NetBIOS name registration and resolution to IP addresses, as well as the DNS domain name resolution.

In Active Directory, Microsoft has blended the support for NetBIOS, DNS, and LDAP namespaces, and integrated Windows 2000 domain security. AD provides for hierarchical structuring of the namespace, stores the DIB in distributed and replicated database, and uses DNS for location services.

Active Directory Design Overview

The architecture of Active Directory integrates Windows 2000 networking and domain security with a native LDAP directory, framed in the DNS domain namespace and using DNS location services. Because Active Directory natively uses LDAP, it incorporates significant aspects of the X.500 models and general methodologies. However, the need to integrate support for NT domains and Microsoft's decision to leverage DNS as the fundamental namespace have led to some divergences from "classic X.500"—and an interesting finished product.

Yet before we get into detailed descriptions, let's take a look at an analogy between terms used in Active Directory and X.500. Table 9.1 shows the correlation between terminology. (Although the correlations may be useful, they are not necessarily accurate in all respects.)

Table 9.1 **Vocabulary Correlations**

Functionality	AD Term	Anagolous X.500 Term
Directory entries	Objects	Objects
Object subentries	Properties	Attributes
Definition of directory contents	Schema	Schema
Logical representation of directory	Forest Domain tree Directory	Directory Information Tree (DIT)
Data Storage	Store	Directory Information Base (DIB)

Functionality	AD Term	Anagolous X.500 Term
Subdivision of directory	Domain, partition, or naming context	Naming context
Data updates	Site replication	Replication
Server agent	Domain controller	Directory System Agent (DSA)
Client agent	AD client	Directory User Agent (DUA)
Query resolution	Recursive & Iterative Chaining & Referral Global catalog lookups	Chaining & Referral
Security boundary	Domain	ACSA

Active Directory is a networking-focused directory service, designed to manage distributed Windows 2000 networks. Active Directory runs as a discrete service within the Windows 2000 security subsystem, supplying a client/server set of directory services via a structured information model, and providing access to network resources in a logically unified namespace.

AD uses *domain controllers* (DCs) to provide DSA-like capability—handle client logon, queries, return results, and referrals to other DCs. The client-side software for AD is built in to Windows 2000 and available as an extension for Windows 95/98 clients.

AD leverages the X.500/LDAP data model with directory *objects* comprised of a series of *properties*. The AD *schema*, however, goes well beyond the base X.521 object set with its wide range of classes, attributes, and syntax.

The *AD namespace* uses DNS to define one or more *Domain Trees*—a tree of domains that comprise a contiguous DNS namespace. AD uses a *forest* to contain multiple disjoint (noncontiguous) domain trees.

A domain in AD is also a functional subdivision of the AD database with each *partition* stored on the DCs for each domain. AD abstracts replication management to *sites*, which automatically performs local replication and allows configurable replication for local and remote DSAs. AD uses multi-master replication with flexible single-master operations for schema (and other) updates.

LDAP and Active Directory

Microsoft implements LDAP (version 3) as Active Directory's core directory protocol. Active Directory is constructed as a native LDAP directory, handling LDAP queries directly and without translation. LDAP provides a rich query capability for directory information access, supplying access to all directory functionality, including managing the schema and query scoping. Active Directory includes an LDAP-based change history interface, which can be used to link to and synchronize with other LDAP directories.

In their strategy white paper, "Comparing Microsoft Active Directory to Novell's NDS," Microsoft describes Active Directory as an inherently scalable LDAP server product that can contain over a million objects in a single partition. (In other documentation, Microsoft describes testing the AD storage subsystem with 1.5 million objects.)

DNS and Active Directory

Active Directory integrates DNS at its core, using DNS for naming and location services. The use of the DNS structure for domain names is a significant change from the NetBIOS name structure used in previous versions of NT.

Domains in AD are structured as DNS domain names while retaining their NT domain security properties. The top of the domain tree can be (and commonly is) the internal or external organization name in the DNS namespace (for instance, mythical.org). Alternatively, for businesses without an assigned DNS name and who are not connected to the Internet, an arbitrary DNS name can be selected.

The integration of DNS allows Active Directory to merge with DNS-based networking environments. Active Directory is integrated with an RFC 2136–compliant version of *Dynamic DNS* (DDNS) to provide dynamic updating of DNS zone entries. Active Directory does not require that you run Windows 2000 DNS, although it is highly recommended. Using DDNS, Active Directory servers can do the following:

- Dynamically publish SRV records containing information about their services, ports, and IP addresses.
- Periodically check their DNS registrations to ensure correct IP address assignment.
- Update the DNS records as servers and services become available or unavailable.

Active Directory adds multiple SRV records to the base DNS configuration, denoting various servers, services, protocols, and ports used in Active Directory operations. The SRV records are used by Active Directory clients to locate the Global Catalog and DCs for network logon and authentication.

DNS provides the core location services, and therefore, correct DNS configuration is essential to effective Active Directory network operations. DNS has the critical role of locating domain controllers and key services in the Active Directory namespace. Clients use DNS as the location service that connects them to the DC containing the needed directory information.

Core Information Source

The information in this chapter is primarily based upon the pre-release Windows 2000 product (RC2) and other information provided by Microsoft. As we are documenting the core directory service architecture, technologies, and operations, any changes in the release version that affect this chapter should be minor. Technical feedback is invited and can be submitted to uds@src.nu.

Client/Server Agents

Active Directory uses a client/server implementation, where its DSA receives directory requests from clients, and interacts with the storage engine layer to access the requested object data. The operations of the DSA effectively isolate Active Directory clients from physical storage management issues for directory objects.

The DSA Component

A core component in any directory is the DSA, which handles access to the DIB, performing all directory read/write operations and management tasks. The *domain controller* (DC) is the DSA of the Active Directory architecture, providing access to its portion of the Active Directory DIB (called the *store*), and supplying updates to remote DSAs and the Global Catalog upon changes to its DIB partition. The Active Directory DCs each contain a discrete portion of the directory information. The DCs supply the DSA interface to which clients and applications can bind for access to directory information held in that partition. Throughout this chapter, when the term *DSA* is used, it refers to a domain controller.

In addition to these base domain controller operations, a DC may be used in a variety of roles:

- **Global Catalog (GC) servers**—A GC server contains an index to all directory objects, providing a efficient means for applications and users to query the directory for objects based on one or more known attributes.

- **Operations masters**—Active Directory uses flexible single-master operations in replication processes. Active Directory defines five *operations master* roles: the Domain Naming Master and Schema Master (required once in each forest), as well as the Relative ID Master, Infrastructure Master, and the PDC Emulator (required for each domain).

The various roles performed by DCs are discussed in more detail in the "Active Directory Operations" section later in this chapter.

The DUA Component

An Active Directory client accesses directory information by using one of the specified interfaces to connect to the DSA and request the needed operation on the selected directory objects.

In Active Directory, the DUA client's connection methods vary, as follows:

- AD clients use LDAP v.3 to connect to the DC.
- Clients using MAPI use the MAPI RPC interface.
- Down-level clients use the SAM interface.

Active Directory APIs

The primary API for Active Directory is called the *Active Directory Service Interfaces* (ADSI). ADSI is an object-oriented interface to Active Directory objects and methods, masking the details of the underlying LDAP communications. The ADSI design abstracts the functionality of multiple types of directory services and integrates directory access and management into a set of unified interfaces.

An Active Directory *provider* supports a namespace-specific implementation of AD objects. Active Directory includes an ADSI namespace provider for NT 4, NDS, NetWare 3.x, as well as LDAP (versions 2 and 3). Applications written for ADSI have the capability of performing directory operations across disparate namespaces.

In addition to ADSI, Active Directory can be accessed via the following:

- **LDAP C API**—The LDAP C API can be used to access Active Directory services and objects.

- **MAPI**—Active Directory supports the MAPI interface for compatibility with applications based on MAPI; however Microsoft does recommend that new applications use ADSI.

- **SAM API**—The *Security Accounts Manager* (SAM) interface is a protected subsystem used by Active Directory to administer user and group security account information maintained within the registry. In NT 4, security principals (either local or domain) are stored in the SAM database; therefore, when AD operates in mixed mode (with mixed AD DCs and NT 4 BDCs on the network), down-level NT clients use the SAM APIs to communicate with the SAM server for authentication. The SAM APIs are also used in mixed mode for replicating the SAM database to down-level domain controllers. Security account information for workstations is stored in a registry (of the local computer); however, the DC security account information is stored within Active Directory.

The ADSI interfaces are also accessible to scripts, easing the automation of administrative tasks. ADSI provides application development support for multiple scripting languages including Visual Basic, Java, Perl, as well as the Windows Scripting Host environment.

Directory Initiatives

The *Directory Enabled Networks* (DEN) initiative is advanced by Microsoft and Cisco and is designed to integrate network hardware management into directory services including Active Directory. Integrating the network infrastructure devices (such as switches and routers) can supply the capability needed to control the network via policies enforced by the directory.

Additionally, Microsoft and other vendors have allied with Bowstreet Software to develop the *Directory Services Markup Language* (DSML) for accessing directory services via a common markup language. DSML will support vendor efforts in developing directory-centric applications.

Active Directory Models

In their white paper called the "Active Directory Technical Summary," Microsoft defines the architecture of Active Directory as subdivided into a number of primary components and several models. Although these models do not have the depth or focus of the X.500 models, they can nevertheless be useful in assessing Microsoft's design intent for Active Directory.

The Active Directory models are as follows:

- **Data model**—Microsoft describes the Active Directory data model as deriving its origins from the data model referenced in the X.500 specifications. In Active Directory, the directory is an information datastore containing objects that represent network resources and users (and a wide range of information). Each of the objects in the Active Directory datastore is defined by the schema that specifies each object class, and the optional and mandatory attributes for that object class, its container class, and as well as permissible attribute syntax.

- **Security model**—The Active Directory security model fully participates in the Windows 2000 security infrastructure and utilizes *access control lists* (ACLs) to protect directory objects, where user permissions to access objects are validated against the object's *access control entries* (ACEs) by the Windows 2000 access validation routines. Active Directory employs multiple security technologies and protocols, using Kerberos for authentication and transitive trusts, SSL/PCT for encryption, and SAM for authentication with down-level systems.

- **Administration model**—The administration model implemented in Active Directory supports finely detailed delegation of administrative tasks. Active Directory allows the authorization of selected people to perform specific sets of actions on designated sets of objects or attributes within a specified subtree or organizational unit. The capability to specify ranges of actions that can be performed and to set the scope of the subtree in which the operation can be performed provides for delegation of appropriate network authority over the specified tasks.

- **Replication model**—In their Windows 2000 SDK, Microsoft also defines a replication model. They define this model as "*multi-master loose consistency with convergence*," where a directory will be comprised of a system of replicas, and changes made at any replica will be propagated to all others. The directory content will only be loosely consistent because the replicas will not necessarily be the same at any given point in time. Convergence occurs after all changes are propagated to all replicas, and the directory information is consistent between all replicas.

Active Directory Objects and Schema

This section briefly describes the objects and schema used in Active Directory, primarily noting the distinctions and differences presented.

Active Directory Objects

At a basic level, the Active Directory objects and properties are fairly consistent with X.500, but the approach is also somewhat different. Only two types of container objects are available in the primary management tool, for example—a container is either a domain (with all the related contingencies) or an OU.

Unlike X.500, Active Directory defines a substantial number of objects—more than 125 *structural* objects in the base schema alone. Although the range of objects may seem extensive, you are actually only presented with a handful of context-appropriate classes to select from when you create an object.

Container Object Classes

As just mentioned, AD supports only two administrator-created classes of container objects in the AD tree: domain and OU. The X.521 base container object classes Country, Locality, and Organization are not supported in the tree by Active Directory, which uses the domain component objects instead. There are many similarities between the domain object and the OU. They both provide containers for directory structure, administrative rights can be delegated at either level, and a group policy can be attached to either object. They differ significantly, however, in their structure and usage:

- **Domain**—The domain object is one of the most critical in Active Directory, providing the basic tree structure, as well as security and partitioning boundaries. A domain object is created (from the domainDNS class) automatically when DCPromo is used to create a new domain. To guarantee the continuity of the DNS namespace, domain objects can only be created subordinate to other domain objects. Attributes for this class primarily consist of SAM information in addition to the basic properties assigned to all classes. In fact, the only attribute not from Top or one of the SAM classes is the dc attribute, which is used as the naming attribute of the class. The definitions of the two auxiliary SAM classes, SAMDomain and SAMDomainBase supply the properties necessary to support NT domain functionality.

- **OU**—The Active Directory OU is similar to an X.500 OU in that it provides a container for objects without any inherent security or partitioning boundaries. OUs are used to subdivide the contents of a domain into smaller units for administrative purposes. An OU can be contained by either a domain or another OU.

Leaf Object Classes

Active Directory uses a substantial number of object types to represent the resources and entities on the network. AD leaf objects correspond to a wide range of individual network elements (printers, servers, users), as well as to logical subdivisions of resources, properties, and processes.

These objects are presented in subsets depending on the management task being performed (that is, which tool is being used and what the context is). Quite a few AD objects are created automatically by the system as part of an installation or configuration process and cannot be created manually through normal administrative tools.

The list of leaf objects is far too long to include here. It is possible, however, to look at a few general categories as an example of what AD provides:

- **Network management objects**—Objects providing basic network management such as users, computer, printers. These objects are available via AD Users and Computers console.

- **Replication management objects**—Objects such as sites, site links, and site link bridges are used in DIB management. Replication-related objects can be accessed via AD Sites and Services console.

- **Service management objects**—A set of objects for managing services is also provided, including DHCP and PKI services. Service objects are also available via the AD Sites and Services console, although they are hidden by default. To view service objects, you must select the option to view the Services node in the Sites and Services management tool.

Clearly, many other objects are available in AD. Some of these objects will become apparent when you encounter them in a management tool; however, others you will never see unless you dig into the "hidden" portions of the directory (via the Active Directory Schema snap-in).

Active Directory Schema

From an overview perspective, the AD schema is similar to the schema defined in X.500. Although the class and attribute definition details vary, the underlying model is the same.

AD stores its schema as objects in a schema container subordinate to the configuration node. There is one schema, and therefore one schema container, per forest. The configuration partition (and, therefore, the AD schema) is replicated to every DC in the forest. The default DN of the schema container is as follows:

```
cn=schema,cn=configuration,dc=mythical,dc=org
```

By storing the schema in the directory, Active Directory allows applications and developers to easily access and modify schema information. This access to schema information provides necessary support for directory-enabled applications, and allows application to verify and extend the schema. AD also supports dynamic schema updates, allowing applications to use their schema extensions immediately.

Class Definitions

Class definitions in Active Directory specify valid objects, the information used to create the object, and valid object relationships. Class definitions define the structure rules, as well as mandatory and optional attributes. Each class is derived from its parent object class (and, therefore, all objects are ultimately derived from top). Every object is created as an instance of its specified class.

Active Directory uses the following fields in the class definitions:

- **Class Type**—The class type defines the type of object (structural, abstract, or auxiliary) and the designation as a container or not.
- **X.500 OID**—This is the object identifier (assigned by industry organizations such as ANSI).
- **Category**—This field specifies the LDAP name for the object class. AD LDAP agents and AD clients use the LDAP name to read or write the class.
- **Parent Class**—Identifies the parent class definition from which this class inherits portions of its definition (like an X.500 superclass).
- **Auxiliary Class**—Lists additional classes from which this class derives some portion of its definition.
- **Possible Superior**—Lists the types of objects this object class can reside within.
- **Common Name**—Identifies the attributes that will be used to name instances of this object class.
- **Mandatory Attributes**—Contains a list of properties for which the object instance must have values.
- **Optional Attributes**—Additional properties for which an instance of the object class may or may not have values.

It should be noted that the preceding list is what is viewable from the Active Directory Schema snap-in. The system uses other fields, but these are not visible in the schema browser. Other schema options control whether instances of a particular class are displayed for browsing. A default security template (ACL) can also be associated with each class.

Attribute Definitions

Attribute definitions describe the properties of objects. Each attribute defines the specific sort of information it contains and can be single-valued or multi-valued.

Attributes can be added to the AD schema, but once added, they cannot be modified. Attributes that have been made part of the schema via extension can be removed so long as they are not currently being used in any object class definition. Attributes that are part of the standard AD schema cannot be removed from the schema.

The attribute definition in the AD schema consists of these fields:

- **Description**—The descriptive text that explains the purpose of the attribute.
- **Common Name**—The LDAP CN is the name by which the attribute is referenced in the class definition.
- **X.500 OID**—The object identifier assigned to the attribute.
- **Syntax and Range**—Identifies the syntax to be used for a particular attribute, and allows for entry of minimum/maximum range values.

Within the attribute definition, you can select whether the attribute is shown while browsing, indexed, and replicated to the GC. You can also determine whether to copy the attribute value when duplicating a user.

Syntax Definitions

The syntax definitions specify the format of the data to be used within the attribute and matching rules.

- **Syntax ID**—Uniquely identifies the syntax type—the value designated in the attribute Syntax field of the attribute definition.
- **Syntax Name**—Descriptive name of the syntax.
- **Syntax Flags**—Contains matching rules to be used when comparing values using this syntax.

Extending the Schema

The schema is managed through the AD schema objects. Extending the schema creates new objects representing class or attribute definitions. Extensions to the Active Directory schema can be implemented in a variety of ways:

- The Active Directory Schema MMC snap-in enables administrators to directly alter the schema.
- The schema can be extended programmatically using ADSI interfaces, MAPI, or the LDAP C API.
- Schema extensions can also be performed via LDIF files.

Active Directory doesn't currently allow deletions from the schema, but objects can be disabled. The following conditions apply when disabling components of the AD schema definitions:

- Classes and attributes with certain access categories' values cannot be disabled. The access category indicates the type of rights required to access AD information.

- Disabling an attribute definition requires that no class definitions are using the attribute. If a class definition includes the attribute, the class must be removed or disabled, before the attribute can be disabled.

- Disabling a class definition prevents new instances of the object from being created, but it has no effect on current instances of the class.

The Active Directory DIT

The *Directory Information Tree* (DIT) in Active Directory differs significantly from the namespace used in NT 4, and it has interesting differences from the DIT defined in X.500. The Active Directory tree contains a unique blend of aspects of DNS, LDAP, and NT domains.

The AD namespace can be viewed as stratified into three aspects:

- The *forest* is a collection of discontiguous AD trees.

- A *domain tree* is a tree of contiguous DNS domains representing the upper nodes of the AD tree.

- The *directory tree* is a single complete tree of DCs and OUs, from the root of the tree to the leaf objects.

The Forest

Active Directory uses a construct called a *forest* to support combining multiple AD trees into a common (shared) logical namespace. This is useful for companies that need to accommodate more than one DNS name or want to maintain different namespaces on each side of a firewall.

Forests are not used *only* when multiple AD trees are present in the directory service—rather, a forest is an inherent part of AD. A forest is created when a new domain tree is created, unless the domain tree is installed to an existing forest. Just as partitions and trees have a root node, so do forests. The first domain of the first tree in the forest defines the *forest root*. Note that the forest root cannot be changed without destroying the forest and completely re-creating it.

As shown in Figure 9.1, a forest is a collection of discontiguous DNS namespaces, each of which is an independent AD tree. In this example, the triangle symbol represents a single domain tree in the forest. This figure shows three AD trees, `mythical.org`, `netmages.org`, and `src.nu`, each comprising its own domain root within the shared forest. The figure also shows the LDAP name that corresponds to the DNS domain name. Domain controllers are located using DNS, and objects within the directory are then accessed using LDAP.

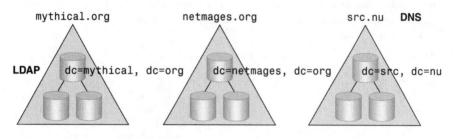

Figure 9.1   The Active Directory forest of disjoint/discontiguous AD trees.

Characteristics of a forest include the following:

- Contains one or more AD trees
- Common schema, configuration, and GC
- Automatic trusts between trees in forest

From a technical perspective, forests exist as a set of Kerberos trust relationships and cross-references between the member trees. However, there are limitations on forests. LDAP searches do not cross trees in a forest, for example, because LDAP does not natively represent the forest construct.

Forest-Level Design Considerations

In creating a forest in Active Directory, consider how you want to use the "logical grouping of domain trees." Do you want

- A single DNS namespace and therefore a single AD tree?

- Discontiguous AD trees to provide for different internal and external DNS trees?

- Discontiguous AD trees in a forest with enterprise partners?

The Domain Tree

One of the more significant Windows 2000 features for NT administrators is the ability to arrange domains into a hierarchical structure with automatic trusts established between domains. When looking at the namespace in this fashion (that is, consisting of a tree of domains), Microsoft defines it as a *domain tree*. A domain tree is a tree of contiguous DNS domains contained within an Active Directory forest.

As shown in Figure 9.2, the domain tree represents the top-level container objects of the directory tree. The three DNS domains shown are each a single node in the domain tree. Note that the portion of the LDAP directory tree contained *within* each domain is ignored from this angle—only the objects representing domains are relevant.

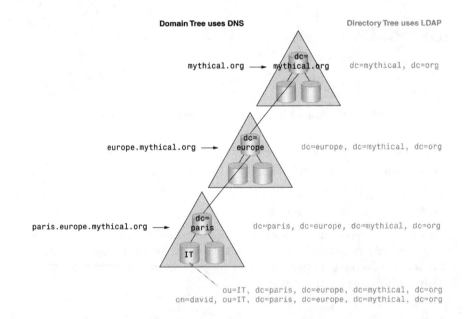

Figure 9.2 A domain tree describes the domain structure of the directory.

Active Directory enforces security boundaries at the each domain and administrative permissions assigned higher in the tree do not flow downward across domain boundaries. In this arrangement, each domain is effectively its own domain subtree, an automatic trust relationship between all domains in the tree.

All the domains in a single domain tree share the following common characteristics:

- A contiguous namespace
- Hierarchical transitive trusts between domains
- Common schema, configuration, and GC (common to forest)

Domains in Active Directory

AD domains are a security, administrative, and storage partition of the directory requiring one or more dedicated DCs. A single AD domain can theoretically contain millions of objects, representing network users or resources that can be located and managed. For larger enterprises where more complex networks are employed containing a large number objects, multiple distinct domains can be linked into one Active Directory domain tree.

Key benefits of AD domains include the following:

- Segregates domain object information and administration
- Centralizes security management by domain policy

Domain Hierarchy and Transitive Trusts

Nodes in the domain tree are arranged in a hierarchy, establishing logical parent-child relationships between domains. By default, AD parent domains automatically have a two-way trust relationship with all child domains. The creation of a child domain establishes a two-way parent-child trust between the parent domain and the new child domain.

AD supports transitive trusts, allowing all domains within a forest or a domain tree to automatically trust each other. A transitive trust is where a trust relationship with a specific domain. is automatically extended to any other domain trusted by the trusted domain. (If C trusts B, and B trusts A, then C trusts A.) Referring back to the `mythical.org` tree, for example: If `paris.europe.mythical.org` trusts `europe.mythical.org`, and `europe.mythical.org` trusts `mythical.org`, then `paris.europe.mythical.org` trusts `mythical.org`, and vice versa. (This example also helps illustrate the issues that arise with long names.)

Domain Tree–Level Design Considerations

When creating an Active Directory domain tree, think about how you want to use the hierarchical grouping of domains. Consider these aspects of your domain tree design:

- Assess constraints, such as the effects of domain subdivision on security and partition boundaries.
- Carefully examine domain boundaries, considering replication load on your network bandwidth in your domain design.
- Determine the number and placement of DCs that are required in each role to adequately support each domain given your expected usage levels. Be sure to factor in the required operations master roles for each domain.

Four different types of domain trusts exist:

- **Tree root**—Trust between domains and the tree root
- **Parent Child**—Trust between parent and child domains
- **Shortcut**—A cross-link trust to a peer domain
- **External**—A trust to an external domain

A *trust path* is the set of trust links between domains used for passing authentication requests. A trust path is the route between the DC for a server receiving a request and the DC in the domain of the requesting user.

You can also still explicitly create a nontransitive trust where needed. Trusts between NT 4 domains and AD domains are always nontransitive.

The Directory Tree

The DIT represents the logical organization of the *entire* directory. Active Directory is an LDAP-based directory, and the AD tree can be looked at like an LDAP tree.

It may be helpful to examine how AD structures its LDAP tree:

- There are two kinds of container objects: domain and OU.
- A single domain must exist immediately below the root node, and additional domains can be contained only by other domains.
- OUs can only exist under a domain or another OU, not in the root.

Figure 9.3 shows the entire LDAP tree for the `mythical.org` AD tree. Notice that both domain objects and other OUs form the structure of the directory tree.

The directory tree can be viewed from two perspectives:

- As a complete LDAP tree comprised of all objects from root to leaf objects
- As a domain subtree consisting of the portion of the LDAP namespace that exists *within* a single domain

A domain subtree (consisting of OUs) can be used within the domain to model your organization or operational requirements. This provides you with:

- **Logical organization within a domain**—Domains can be further subdivided into OUs to facilitate delegation of administration tasks.
- **Finer ability to delegate authority**—Administrative rights over object and attribute access in OUs can be delegated.

Within a domain, users can inherit administrative permissions from parent objects. You can also choose to filter those permissions that can be inherited by child objects.

Directory Tree uses LDAP

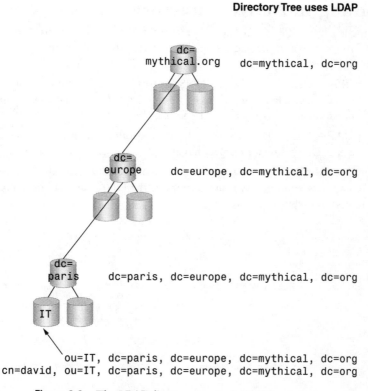

dc=mythical, dc=org

dc=europe, dc=mythical, dc=org

dc=paris, dc=europe, dc=mythical, dc=org

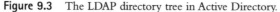

ou=IT, dc=paris, dc=europe, dc=mythical, dc=org
cn=david, ou=IT, dc=paris, dc=europe, dc=mythical, dc=org

Figure 9.3   The LDAP directory tree in Active Directory.

Directory Tree–Level Design Considerations

When structuring your directory tree, consider how you want to use the hierarchy of OUs. From an NT 4 perspective, the hierarchy provided in AD is a valuable administrative addition. The hierarchy can be used to group business efforts, systems, and people, while supplying access control and the ability to delegate authority over organizational subdivisions. Instead of being limited to domain or local administrative options, AD administration can be delegated for each OU. The hierarchy supplies the mechanism to enable you to more effectively structure your network directory to model your business operations.

Directory tree factors to keep in mind include the following:

- Examine your reasons and needs for directory subdivision (usually business, organizational, or operational).

- Use OUs to assign hierarchy of management and operational subdivisions.

- Use subsequent OUs to delegate business units within a larger division.

- Policies can also be applied at the OU level.

- Keep your tree shallow—don't make unnecessary OUs in the hierarchy because deep hierarchies make long and complicated DNs.

Naming in Active Directory

Naming is a little different in Active Directory from many other directory services. Instead of natively representing a single namespace, AD uses multiple namespaces as shown in Figure 9.4:

- **DNS**—Active Directory uses DNS for naming and location of domains and DCs. Domains, hosts, and services are represented in the DNS namespace, but only domains are part of the AD domain tree.

- **LDAP**—Active Directory uses LDAP for naming and accessing directory objects. Every directory object has an LDAP name.

- **UNC/NetBIOS**—AD supports the use of NetBIOS names (for users, computers, and domains), and it supports the UNC naming convention for access to network resources.

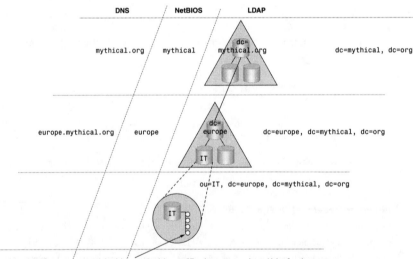

Figure 9.4   Active Directory naming uses DNS, NetBIOS, and LDAP.

Windows 2000 security principals must be represented in each of these namespaces. This requires Active Directory to support multiple forms of naming for each computer, user, and domain. These naming forms are compliant with the namespace they support, either NetBIOS, DNS, or LDAP.

NetBIOS Naming

Windows 2000 uses NetBIOS names and UNCs for backward compatibility with NT 4 and the Windows 95/98 client operating systems. NetBIOS namespace support provides compatibility with NT domains and for communications with down-level clients and applications.

NetBIOS names and UNC naming conventions are familiar to many people from their use in Windows networking. In Active Directory, NetBIOS names are comprised of (up to) the first 15 characters of the DNS name assigned to the user, computer, or domain. NetBIOS user and computer names must be unique within the domain, and they are concatenated with domain names to form full computer or user names.

DNS Naming

Active Directory integrates DNS domain naming and resolution, and it follows the DNS naming convention. Active Directory uses DNS names in these ways:

- **User principal names (UPNs)**—To ease user access to the directory, Active Directory specifies users and groups with *user principal names* (UPNs). A UPN is an attribute of the user object, and it must be unique across the tree. UPNs are comprised of two parts: the UPN prefix, which is the user logon name; and the UPN suffix, which is the DNS name of the domain containing the user object. The two parts are combined with the "@" symbol to form the familiar email-style name. For example, the UPN for Debra within the `mythical.org` domain would be constructed as `debra@mythical.org`. The UPNs are substantially shorter than DNs, and they are easier for people to remember and use.

- **DNS host name**—Windows 2000 uses the DNS host name to identify the security account for the computer at the local DC. The domain name is appended to the host name, to form a full computer name.

- **DNS domain names**—The DNS domains used in Active Directory are named in accordance with the DNS naming convention, using a dot-delimited domain hierarchy.

LDAP Naming

LDAP naming is used to provided access to objects within the directory tree. Active Directory uses LDAP attributed naming with LDAP URLs, and it follows LDAP naming conventions as described in Chapter 5, "Lightweight Directory Access Protocol." For the three security principals reviewed here, the user and computer both use `CN` as their naming attribute, and domains use the LDAP standard of `dc`.

Unique to the Domain

Active Directory guarantees LDAP DN uniqueness by the usual method of not allowing two objects with the same RDN to exist under the same parent object. Windows 2000 domains have a requirement that each username (UPN) and computer name (DNS host name) be unique within a domain.

The Globally Unique IDentifier

To implement the location of directory objects via a query on object attributes, the Active Directory schema specifies a *Globally Unique IDentifier* (GUID) for every object in the directory. The GUID is a unique 128-bit number generated for each directory object at the point that it is created.

The GUID is never changed or altered, even when a directory object is moved or renamed, providing a consistent internal identifier unique to every object. The use of the GUID allows directory-aware applications to store an object's unique identifier and reliably retrieve that specific object from the directory irrespective of the object's current DN.

Active Directory's Global Catalog utilizes the GUID as its primary index reference to objects within the directory. The algorithm generating the 128-bit value controls the uniqueness of a GUID.

The Active Directory DIB

Directory information storage in Active Directory has been substantially enhanced beyond the capabilities of its NT 4 predecessor. The Active Directory information *store* (Microsoft's term for the DIB) is based on the Exchange directory data structure and storage engine, supplying fast indexed access to directory information.

Storage Method

Active Directory employs a unified storage mechanism for all the directory information. As shown in Figure 9.5, Active Directory abstracts new layers of directory information storage, providing database and tree support to the DC with indexed, transaction-based storage. These new layers are as follows:

- **Database layer**—The database layer operates as an abstraction layer between the data store and applications, including the AD DSA. Directory clients access the database layer either indirectly (via the DSA layer) or directly via (MAPI). This layer also structures the entries in the DIB into the DIT for the DSA, and forms DNs from RDNs for name resolution. The database layer constructs the directory hierarchy from the parent-child relationships of objects contained within the directory.

- **Extensible Storage Engine**—Active Directory uses a proprietary database engine called the *Extensible Storage Engine* (ESE) as its data storage layer. The ESE is an enhanced version of Jet, an *Indexed Sequential Access Method* (ISAM) table manager, which is used by Exchange and other Microsoft applications. The ESE employs a transaction-based storage system, using log files for transaction verification. The ESE uses the NTFS subsystem for storage to disk.

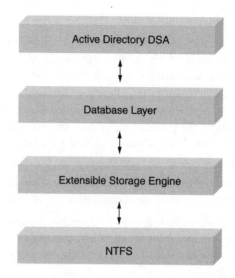

Figure 9.5   Storing the Active Directory information.

Active Directory information is written to the NTDS.DIT file on an NTFS partition on the DC. Private directory information is protected from access. Public directory information is stored on the system volume where it can be shared with other DCs.

Microsoft recommends storing the AD DIB on mirrored file system partitions and, for performance, dividing the Windows 2000 operating system files, the AD DIB file, and the AD log file among separate drives on the server.

Theoretically, an AD database can reach 16 terabytes in size and hold millions of objects per domain. According to Microsoft, the ESE has been tested with 1.5 million objects per domain.

Defragmenting the DIB

Active Directory supports online defragmentation of the AD database (via the ESE), which rearranges content without releasing the allocated file system space. To defragment the DIB and free allocated space, the DC must be taken offline, booted into Directory Service Repair mode, and defragmented with a command line tool (NTDSUTIL.EXE), which creates a new deframented copy of NTDS.DIT in another directory.

Partitioning the DIB

Like most other directory services, linkage between partitions is maintained automatically. AD takes a different approach to partitioning the DIB, however, as AD's partition management is largely done in an indirect fashion:

- AD partitions the DIB at every domain boundary, meaning each domain is *required* to be its own partition of the DIB (as shown in Figure 9.6). Because Microsoft has linked DIB partitioning to domain boundaries, normally unrelated factors (such as security boundaries) come into play.

- A DC can hold only one replica and therefore only a single partition.

- Replication traffic routing and management is handled via sites (that is, areas of good connectivity) and configured connections between them.

Although this may mean that administrators will not have to spend as much time manipulating DIB partitioning as they might with other products, it also means that there is less flexibility in partitioning, as well as a requirement for an individual directory server for *each* replica.

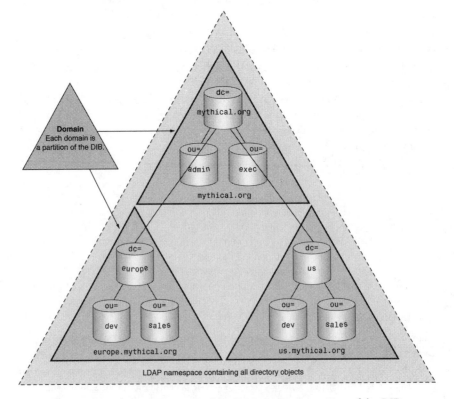

Figure 9.6 An Active Directory domain constitutes a partition of the DIB.

Each Active Directory DC holds three partitions:

- The *schema* partition contains the schema data and is replicated to every DC in a forest.

- The *configuration* partition contains the replication topology and related metadata (references to domains, trees, and forests, as well as the locations of GCs and DCs), and it is also replicated to every DC in a forest.

- The *domain directory* partition contains the all objects within the domain, and it is only replicated to DCs for that specific domain. A domain directory partition can be considered a *domain subtree* because it contains the subtree belonging to a single domain.

Partition handling is mostly automatic as Active Directory is designed to perform most partition and replication management without administrator intervention. There are few partition operations in Active Directory, and administration of partitions is rather indirect:

- Because a partition is a domain, you create and delete partitions as you create and delete domains.

- Because a DC must hold a replica of its domain, a replica is created for a DC when it is promoted (to a domain controller) and destroyed when the DC is demoted.

Replication of the DIB

Microsoft describes the AD replication model as using *multi-master loose consistency with convergence* approach with *non-deterministic latency* (an unknown degree of update latency).

Multi-master replication in this context means that each Active Directory server can function as a master (writeable) replica of the partition and can propagate changes to other DCs within the domain. Multiple DCs with replicas of a domain partition can be established to distribute the client-access load and increase fault tolerance of the directory service.

Active Directory information is updated on a per-property basis, minimizing the amount of information that must be transmitted across the network to synchronize partition replicas.

Knowledge References

In Active Directory, knowledge references to other partitions are contained in cross-reference objects, and they are used by DCs to refer requests that exceed the local partition. Cross-references can be also used to point to other domains within a forest or external LDAP directories. Referrals are generated when contacting a non-authoritative DC, or when searching the domain tree.

Directory Replication Service

AD replication is performed via the *Directory Replication Service* (DRS) APIs, and operates differently when replicating within or between sites. A site in AD is a collection of local subnets with fast connections. DRS operates using one of two methods:

- Intra-site replication is always RPC, automatic, and doesn't use compression.
- Inter-site replication notifies DCs of updates using one of three methods: *Remote Procedure Calls* (RPCs), SMTP, or IP, and can be compressed and scheduled.

Updates to the directory replicas may occur rapidly via point-to-point links (RPC), or a delayed basis using store-and-forward links (SMTP).

Replication Roles

Active Directory uses more than one type of DSA role in replication. AD divides replication roles into intra-site (DCs) and inter-site (bridgehead servers) operations management.

- **Domain Controllers**—DCs automatically handle replication between all DCs within the local site.
- **Bridgehead server**—A bridgehead server is used to manage replication between sites, and across slower communications links (commonly WAN connections). Inter-site updates to the AD DIB are managed by the local and remote bridgehead servers, which are responsible for updating the intra-site domain controllers. Each site can have one bridgehead server.

Inter-DSA communications for replication use a variety of different types of connections and transport protocols. Replication in Active Directory uses three types of connections:

- High speed, uniform (via RPC)
- Low speed, point-to-point, synchronous (via RPC)
- Low speed, store-and-forward, asynchronous (via SMTP)

Active Directory defines the configuration, schema, and domain directory partitions as individual units of replication. These are replicated as follows:

- The schema and configuration partitions are replicated to all DCs in the forest.
- The domain directory partition containing all objects and properties within a given domain are replicated to each DC in that domain.
- All objects (with a small subset of properties) are replicated to the GC. GCs are updated in tandem with the replication cycles, ensuring that catalogs remain current.

Replication Depends on Mode

Pure Active Directory networks update all DCs using multi-master replication, but mixed NT 4 and Active Directory networks still perform replication in compliance with NT 4 methods using the SAM interface.

Sites

Microsoft uses the term *site* to designate a set of TCP/IP subnets with good connectivity (currently, 10Mbps or more). A site commonly houses multiple DCs. DCs for a domain may be distributed across sites—for example, a DC for a remote domain may be placed within the local site topology for administrative purposes.

Active Directory uses the topology information stored in the site objects to determine directory replication. The specific site topology should reflect the physical topology of your connected LANs. Sites can be used to manage replication bandwidth allocation, isolate logon traffic, and locate proximate resources.

Site links represent the connections between networks and tell Active Directory how to use the network connection for replication of the DIB. Replication frequency, cost, and availability can be configured for each site link. Site links that overlap can be combined into *site link bridges*.

Connections within a site are automatically configured by AD, but site links usually are not (unless the site is already a site link and has a DC). DCs use site links to communicate with remote DCs and, therefore, cross-domain updates depend on these site links. Active Directory supplies flexible inter-site replication using variable scheduling and multiple protocols to support WAN-linked communications.

Synchronization

As described in Microsoft's white paper, "Active Directory Technical Summary," Active Directory implements a replication model that allows updates to occur at any of multiple replicas, but replicas must then be synchronized to ensure directory consistency. Although some other directory services rely solely on time stamps to control replica synchronization, the method employed in Active Directory relies on unique 64-bit *update sequence numbers* (USN). Active Directory uses the USN synchronization system to track directory changes, and it uses time stamps only as a tiebreaker in cases of collision of replicated data.

When changes are replicated, only objects with a higher USN are sent to the receiving replica. As an object is written to the receiving DC, it is assigned a new USN and a version number incremented at every change to the object (as well as a digital signature of the supplier DC), and it is stored with the object. As part of the replication process, each replica requests all changes with any USN later than the last USN received and is provided all relevant changes.

Defining Your Sites

To determine the subnets that will comprise each site, review your network infrastructure, determining numbers and locations of subnets, bandwidth of each subnet, speed of remote links, amount of replication data crossing remote links, as well as the overall capacity and utilization of your networks.

USNs are organized using a table of USNs maintained at each DC. A DC receives its table entries (USNs) from its replication partners, tracking the highest USN received from each replication partner. During replication, a DC requests all directory changes with USNs higher than the USN stored in its table for the replication partner. The incrementing and storage of the USN, as well as the write operation on the designated object or property, succeeds or fails together. The USN tables on DCs simplify recovery upon directory failure—to re-initialize a DC, the DC requests changes from all replication partners with USN numbers greater than what is stored in its USN table. An interrupted replication cycle can be restarted without duplication or loss.

A replication collision can happen if additional changes to a property occur in multiple replicas before the first replica change had been supplied to all other DCs. Active Directory manages collision detection with version numbers on properties, and by tracking the original updates. AD uses propagation dampening to prevent redundant updates.

- **Property version numbers (PVNs)**—AD's replication model uses PVNs to enable management of replication collisions. PVNs are property-based replication values (in contrast with the server-based USNs) directly associated with an object property. A PVN is instanced the first time an AD object property is written to.

- **Originating writes**—PVNs are incremented by *originating writes* on the associated property (a successful write updating a property on the DC initiating the change). Updates via replication are not considered originating writes and will not increment the PVN. If a DC receives an update PVN higher than the stored PVN, the update is valid and applied (if lower, the update is rejected).

- **Replication collision**—A *replication collision* happens when a replicated PVN is received that is the same as the stored PVN, and the property's values are not the same. If a replication collision occurs, the update time stamp is evaluated, and the receiving replica will apply the changes with the latest time stamp.

- **Propagation dampening**—AD implements *propagation dampening* to prevent redundant transmission of changes. AD's replication process uses *up-to-date vectors* for propagation dampening. An up-to-date vector is a set of server-USN pairs maintained by every replica server. The up-to-date vector for a replica lists all other replicas for that site, and contains the highest USN received from each replica server. During replication, a server receives an update and sends its up-to-date vector to the initiating server, which uses it to filter propagated changes.

Active Directory Operations

Although there is far more detail to the operations in Active Directory than fits within the scope of this material, this section very briefly discusses the key server roles and operations. For more detailed information, refer to the Windows 2000 online help or Resource Kit books.

DSA Operational Roles

The DC is the Active Directory DSA, managing access to the information stored in its partition and providing updates to other DCs and the GC. The following points highlight some aspects of what the DCs contribute to Active Directory operations:

- **DCs play an active role in site management.** From the perspective of the domain controller, a site is a system of domain controllers on a high-connectivity set of subnets. The site information for the entire forest is stored in the Configuration container on the DC. DCs use site information to compare client IP addresses to known subnets, thus determining the appropriate site and DC for client logon and authentication.

- **DCs publish their services.** DCs publish their name and addresses upon startup, where each DC server registers its name with DNS and WINS. Each DC dynamically updates DNS with a host address (A) record to register the IP address of the DC for the specified domain. The host address record allows down-level clients (without support for SRV records) to find a DC via DNS. In addition to DNS, a DC advertises its NetBIOS name via broadcast or directly to a specified WINS server, allowing down-level Windows clients to also locate the DC.

- **DCs help manage DNS records.** The NetLogon service is responsible for creating the initial DNS records during installation of Active Directory. Each DC dynamically manages SRV records locating and identifying servers by service type or protocol. SRV records are used to locate LDAP and Kerberos services and to indicate the site at which the DC is located. DNS in Active Directory searches for site-specific records prior to searching the general records.

A DC may perform a variety of roles, such as a GC or other operations master roles.

Global Catalog Servers

To facilitate faster directory lookups, Active Directory implements a forest-wide index called the Global Catalog (GC). A GC server is a DC containing a partial replica of each domain in the forest, and a complete replica of one domain. The first DC installed into a forest is a GC by default.

The GC server must be a domain controller, and it can be located at any point within the directory hierarchy. Although you are required to have one GC in each forest, you should put one GC server at every site.

The GC is used within Active Directory to help network users locate resources and information represented by directory objects. The GC enables network clients to quickly locate directory objects without knowledge of the domain the objects are contained in, and to find directory objects across discontiguous namespaces. Each AD object has an entry (with summary object information) within the GC, which allows a very fast multi-attribute search for directory objects.

In addition to a partial read-only replica of every domain directory partition in the forest, the GC contains structural information about Active Directory, including the schema and configuration partitions. All partitions on a GC server are written to one database (NTDS.DIT), which also contains the GC attributes stored as additional data. Object and attribute security is enforced at the GC; therefore, lookup of Active Directory information is constrained by the domain security services.

The replication process implemented by Active Directory automatically builds the GC (as changes are propagated, the GC is updated). Although Microsoft has defined a set of properties that are replicated to the GC by default, AD administrators can specify additional properties as needed by modifying the schema. Attributes to be included in the GC can be selected in the Active Directory Schema administration tool.

Operations Masters

Although Active Directory does implement multi-master replication, some directory *operations* require a single master. Microsoft terms this type of operation a *flexible single-master operation* (FSMO). Active Directory defines five operations master roles used in managing Windows 2000. Some of these operations master roles are required for each forest; others are required for each domain. Active Directory requires the following operations master roles:

- **Domain Naming Master**—The Domain Naming Master controls the additions and deletions of domains within the forest and ensures the uniqueness of the domain names. The Domain Naming Master operates on a forest-wide basis, so there must be only one within the forest.

- **Schema Master**—The Schema Master is responsible for controlling all changes to the schema. There can be only one Schema Master as it also must be unique within the forest.

- **Relative IDentifier (RID) Master**—The RID Master supplies the RID sequences to all DCs within the forest. A RID is an identifier used with a domain identifier to construct the SIDs for security principals within the domain. To enforce forest-wide uniqueness, RIDs are assigned by a single DC in the forest.

- **Infrastructure Master**—The Infrastructure Master role enforces object consistency for operations that span domains and is performed by one server per domain. An Infrastructure Master is used to synchronize the group-to-user references in the directory when group memberships are altered or updated.
- **PDC Emulator Master**—The PDC Emulator Master supplies compatibility with down-level clients and NT 4 backup domain controllers (BDCs), handling NT 4 client authentication and replication. Only one DC in each domain can be used to perform the PDC Emulator role.

Client Logon

As Active Directory supports down-level clients, there are two forms of user logon to an AD domain. When a user logs on to a domain, one of the two name forms is used:

- **DNS**—If the logon uses a DNS domain name (AD client), NetLogon uses DNS to find a DC for authentication.
- **NetBIOS**—If the logon uses a NetBIOS domain name (down-level client), NetLogon sends a mailslot message to find a DC performing the PDC emulator role for the domain.

On client startup, the client Locator initiates an RPC to the local NetLogon service and passes the information (domain name, GUID, site, and flags) needed to select a DC. Again, this process varies depending on logon name:

- A client using DNS names locates a DC by querying a DNS name server. DNS returns the list of IP addresses indicated in the SRV records, and the client sends an LDAP query to each IP address. The first DC that responds to the query is returned to the client for logon.
- A client using NetBIOS names locates a DC via WINS (or other NT 4 transport-specific discovery method). When an NT 4 (NetBIOS) domain name is sought, discovery begins upon the NetBIOS name query from the client NetLogon service and uses the DC providing the domain's PDC emulation.

Name Resolution

As Active Directory is designed as an LDAP directory, it uses LDAP queries for access to directory objects. The Active Directory name resolution process uses DNS to locate the DCs and LDAP to locate objects within the directory. Active Directory object names must be specified in accordance to LDAP RFC 2247, and they are located in the directory by the object's DN.

Active Directory uses DNS name resolution for location of domain controllers and network service providers. DCs operate as the Active Directory name server, performing name resolution for all directory operations. Using its knowledge of the DIB, a DC determines whether the query can be fulfilled locally, or whether it must be referred to another DC.

Because DNS domains and LDAP domains differ, Active Directory also provides a DNS-to-LDAP mapping of domain components, via the standard LDAP method that maps an LDAP domain component for each DNS domain name component. For example:

- **DNS**—mythical.org
- **LDAP**—dc=mythical, dc=org

With Active Directory's integration of LDAP, when an LDAP string contains domain components, resolution depends on the following:

- If the contacted DC is a member of the sought domain, the DC can process the operation.

- If the contacted DC is not a member of the domain, the DC returns a referral to another DC, or supplies an error message denoting operation failure.

Active Directory resolves a submitted LDAP URL by performing the following sequence of steps:

1. Using DNS, Active Directory locates a GC server.

2. Using server IP, AD submits an LDAP query to the GC server.

3. With the reply IP information supplied by the GC, AD submits an LDAP query to a DC with a replica containing the object(s).

Active Directory also provides backward-compatible support for UNC naming conventions and NetBIOS names. NetBIOS names are provided to DCs for name resolution by WINS or another transport-specific mechanism. Down-level clients use NetBIOS names in logon and authentication.

Native versus Non–Native Mode

The Active Directory "mode" references aspects of the domain controller's behavior in the AD authentication and replication infrastructure:

- **Mixed mode**—Mixed mode is the default mode, and provides the maximum compatibility with down-level servers and clients. Mixed mode supports NT 4 replication methods as well as AD domain replication and will use either depending on whether the client is a down-level BDC or is an AD domain controller. With down-level domain controllers, AD replication works like single-master replication, where the DC functions like a PDC (via the PDC Emulator), which does all updates.

- **Native mode**—Native mode uses multi-master replication between DCs and, thus, removes the backward-compatible support for NT 4 BDCs. However, native mode provides other enhancements. New types of groups (Universal, Domain Local) and nested groups are supported. Native mode must be specifically selected and, once implemented, cannot be undone.

Extensibility

Active Directory is a native LDAP directory service, and LDAP operations can be easily extended. AD currently supports LDAP extensions or controls that provide enhanced search capabilities such as server-side sorting and paged results. Microsoft has also proposed an extension to LDAP they call DirSynch to serve as a synchronization mechanism between AD and NDS. Synchronization performed via DirSynch is one-way only—from NDS to AD—although Microsoft plans to release a bi-directional version soon.

Security in Active Directory

Active Directory is designed with a distributed security architecture, which uses the directory to manage the information and enhanced Windows 2000 security services for authentication. A new set of distributed security services are tightly integrated with Active Directory, allowing more flexible management of user accounts and much finer control over network objects and properties than was possible in NT 4.

A Mixed Environment Is Not Mixed Mode

A *mixed environment* refers to having AD in native mode (where all DCs are running Windows 2000) but still having servers and clients on the network that are not AD aware. In contrast, *mixed mode* applies to a mix of Windows 2000 and NT 4 *domain controllers.*

Previous NT Security

Security operations in previous versions of NT are rooted in a domain model that provides domain-wide security with user access to domain resources. Security accounts for each domain are maintained in a flat namespace by the Security Accounts Manager (SAM), and the user and group account information is stored in a secure section of the PDC's registry.

For NT domains to allow users from foreign domains to access resources, a trust relationship between domain controllers would have to be established. NT inter-domain trusts are connected via an *explicit* one- or two-way trust relationship that is specified at each participating domain controller.

Although the NT 4 domain trust and pass-through-authentication features provided some degree of flexibility in security account and resource management, the degree of scalability was inadequate for use in enterprise-wide security. (As the number of domains increase, the domain trust relationships become increasingly complex.

New Security Capability

Active Directory runs as a service in the Windows 2000 security subsystem. The *Security Reference Monitor* (SRM) is the enforcing authority in the security subsystem, and the Active Directory DSA is part of the *Local Security Authority* (LSA).

One significant enhancement to security in Windows 2000 is that Active Directory uses Kerberos to supply an automatic trust relationship for all domains within a domain tree. This vastly reduces the amount of administrative effort required to allow users to access resources between domains. Additional security enhancements supported by Active Directory include the following:

- **Directory stores security data**—Active Directory contains the security policy and account information for the network—all user and group account data, as well as domain, OU, and local access policies. As the policies are stored in a group policy object, Active Directory distributes the security information by replication operations to other domain controllers within the domain.

- **Security and directory interdependence**—In Active Directory, the directory services and security services are interdependent subsystems relying on each other for basic operations. Directory operations obtain authentication and access from the security services, and the objects that the security services act on are accessed via the directory services.

- **A security hierarchy**—Another substantial enhancement is the new security functionality in the hierarchical structure of the Active Directory namespace. This hierarchy provides the structure for security delegation and permissions filtering (within domain boundaries).

- **New security policy management**—The new integrated Group Policy Editor allows centralized administration of domain-wide security policies, as well as policy application on specific OUs. The domain policy can even be linked to IP security policies to provide control over the encryption of IP network traffic.

Other Security Features in W2K

Other security additions in Windows 2000 include its use of IP Security (IPSec) for encrypted networking, as well as the Encrypted File Systems (EFS) for file system security.

Security Is Based in Domains

An Active Directory domain uses a DNS name, yet the Windows domain-level security boundaries apply. Security is implemented within the context of the domain—all security principals are defined within a domain and are "owned by" that domain.

You can envision domains in Active Directory as comprised of the following:

- **Windows 2000 domain**—Controls security, authentication, access control
- **DNS domain**—Provides naming and location service
- **DIB partition**—Stores domain directory information

In Active Directory, user authentication can extend beyond the domain boundary via automatic inter-domain trusts. Administration permissions granted within a domain are blocked at the domain boundary, however, as shown in Figure 9.7.

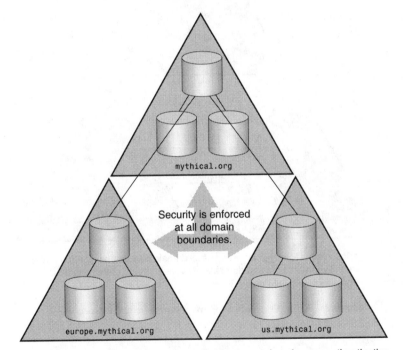

Domains act as a security boundary, allowing cross-domain user authentication with automatic two-way trusts, and blocking administrative permissions.

Figure 9.7 Security in Active Directory is based in domains.

Inter-Domain Trusts

Windows 2000 implements a new security model where the domains in a tree (and a forest) are automatically interconnected via (Kerberos-based) *implicit* trust relationships. Domain trust relationships have been built in to the AD tree, allowing tree-wide transitive trusts, as shown in Figure 9.8. A transitive trust is effectively authentication by referral from an implicitly trusted source—in Active Directory, a domain trusts any other domain that shares a common ancestor (parent, grandparent).

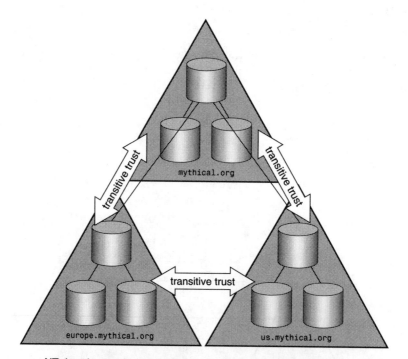

NT domain security is enforced at all domain boundaries, yet automatic transitive trusts between domains allow users to be authenticated in all domains within the domain tree.

Figure 9.8 Active Directory supports transitive trusts between domains.

Hierarchy Within Domains

Active Directory objects are linked to their parent domain and controlled by its domain policy, but security policy and administration can also be assigned at the OU level. Within a domain, rights are controlled by the hierarchy of the policies assigned at the domain and OU levels, as well as by the permissions inherited from parent OUs.

By using the hierarchy of the AD tree, administration can be subdivided by OU, delegating administration where needed by network or business subdivisions, as shown in Figure 9.9. Within a domain, AD provides the ability to assign security values at nodes high in the directory tree and to have these values inherited by all child nodes lower in the tree. Users can inherit permissions to entire directory objects or only specific attributes.

Security Within the Directory

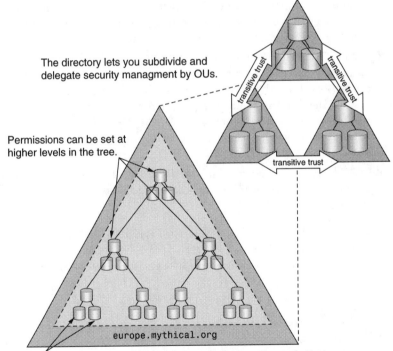

The directory lets you subdivide and delegate security managment by OUs.

Permissions can be set at higher levels in the tree.

transitive trust

transitive trust

transitive trust

europe.mythical.org

Users in child nodes can inherit directory object and attribute permissions.

Figure 9.9   Active Directory allows hierarchical security delegation within domains.

Security Standards and Protocols

With corporate networks being connected with the Internet, additional security concerns are being addressed via the development and use of Public Key encryption and Certificate Authorities.

Windows 2000 supplies flexibility in its supported security protocols, which includes the integration of Kerberos, support for PK and X.509 certificates, extensions of Kerberos for PK, as well as Secure Sockets Layer (SSL), and Private Communications Technology (PCT) security protocols for authentication. Active Directory integrates the key security protocols via the *Security Support Provider Interface* (SSPI).

- **Kerberos**—Active Directory uses Kerberos, an Internet security protocol based on RFC 1510. Kerberos implements a *Key Distribution Center* (KDC), which is comprised of two components: an *authentication server* (AS), which provides the user authentication services; and the *ticket-granting server* (TGS), which supplies the tickets used in subsequent authentication processes. Kerberos is implemented as an Active Directory security provider that utilizes the SSPI.

- **X.509 certificates**—Certificates are used in Active Directory to grant access for Internet users, remote users, and systems not supporting Kerberos version 5. Certificate-based security in Active Directory is integrated with other services such as Internet Information Server (IIS). In Active Directory, X.509 certificates are a security token derived from the CryptoAPI Version 2 certificate library APIs, but applications that handle public key certificates can use any standard format.

- **SSL/PCT**—Active Directory also provides support for the Secure Sockets Layer (SSL) 3.0 and Private Communications Technology (PCT) channel security protocols.

Certificate Services

A network administrator needs to select which certificate authorities are trusted on the network and to control which certificates can be used for authentication and access. In Active Directory, a certificate authority (CA) is used to create and validate certificates for network servers and users. The user certificate authenticates the user to all network servers, services, and other users.

Windows 2000 includes the Microsoft Certificate Server for creation, management, and revocation of X.509-compliant certificates. The Microsoft Certificate Server enables you to establish the CA for your network, and to create a hierarchy of certificate authority. For external networks or Web sites, a commercial CA (such as VeriSign) can be used to provide industry recognized validation and credentials. You can implement MCS as an enterprise CA (or subordinate) and a standalone root CA (or subordinate).

Authentication

Windows 2000 includes security protocols that provide strong authentication based on Kerberos and NTLM Challenge/Response. Active Directory also supplies strong client authentication by mapping public key certificates to user accounts. The authentication protocol used is determined by the client and server capabilities; Windows 2000 clients and servers use Kerberos, and down-level clients and servers use NTLM.

Kerberos is the default authentication protocol for Windows 2000. Kerberos is used when the user is logging on with a Windows 2000 computer, and the computer and user accounts are in a Windows 2000 domain. A Kerberos ticket-granting server (TGS) supplies the *ticket-granting tickets* (TGTs) used by clients to obtain session tickets that provide access to the specific servers and applications.

When an AD client authenticates via Kerberos, the client's SID, as well as those of any groups the user is a member of, are sent to the KDC. If there is more than one domain, the KDC queries the GC and collects SIDs from universal group memberships. The collection of SIDs is listed in the authorization data field of the TGT.

When the client requests a session ticket, the KDC puts the SIDs listed in the TGT into the authorization data field of the session ticket. If the session ticket is to be used in another domain, the KDC also queries AD for group memberships in that domain and adds those SIDs to the session ticket. When a user connects to a server, the server can directly validate session tickets obtained by the client from the TGS.

One extension of the security in AD is mutual authentication, where the client authenticates to the DC, and the DC also authenticates to the client. To supply this capability, a *service principal name* (SPN) is used to identify and register a specific instance of a service in AD. The SPN is registered in the directory upon installation of the service and must be a unique name. When mutual authentication is performed, the client retrieves the service SPN from directory and then uses the SPN in the authentication of the service.

Access Control

Active Directory access control determines which users can see what objects and attributes, and which operations they are allowed to perform. Active Directory leverages the Windows 2000 security infrastructure, using ACLs to protect all objects in the directory. An ACL consists of a set of access control entries for the directory object.

An *access control entry* (ACE) is a single security-related directory entry linked to a specific object. An ACE can grant or deny a particular user (or group) a specific set of access rights to a directory object. (One key element of an ACE is the SID of the security principal the ACE applies to.) The set of available access rights directly corresponds to related operations on the directory object.

Down-Level Authentication

The NTLM Challenge/Response authentication protocol is supported for down-level clients. When a down-level NTLM client connects to a server, that server contacts the domain PDC Emulator DC to provide the authentication service to verify the client.

Active Directory uses the Windows 2000 security subsystem to control access to objects by validating the user permissions against the list of ACEs in the object's ACL. Access requires authentication and validation of the permissions of the security principal. Access control is operationally controlled by the SRM and the security subsystem. The *security context* for access control is comprised of the user account data (including SID, groups, and privileges), and it is implemented when a user attempts to access a protected object.

An ACL is stored in a binary form called a *security descriptor*. A directory object is available only when its security descriptor grants access rights to the requesting security principal.

If an ACL changes, and those changes are to be inherited by subordinate objects, the ACL is marked. When the ACL change is replicated to other DSAs, the inherited changes are propagated locally. This uses much less bandwidth than the alternative—applying the inherited change locally and then replicating every object that is changed.

Directory Permissions

In Active Directory, you can grant or deny permissions and determine how the permissions are applied and propagated. Active Directory supports the following types of permissions:

- **General permissions**—Five general object permissions are provided, including `Full Control`, `Read`, `Write`, `Create/Delete All Child Objects`, and `Apply Group Policy`.

- **Advanced permissions**—Advanced permissions include all general permissions, as well as `List Contents`, `Delete`, `Delete Subtree`, `Read` and `Modify Permissions`, `Modify Owner`, `All Validated Writes`, and `All Extended Rights`.

- **Permission to create and delete specific objects**—You can grant or deny permissions to create or delete `User`, `Computer`, `Contact`, `Group`, `Printer`, `Shared Folder`, `Trusted Domain`, and other specific objects.

- **Permission to read or write properties**—Property read/write permissions in Active Directory include the permissions on all properties or a subset of selected properties.

- **Application of permissions**—You can determine how permissions are applied. Permissions may be applied to `this object`, `this object and all child objects`, `child objects only`, or specific classes of objects (by name). You can determine whether these permissions propagate or apply only to objects within the local container.

Schema Objects

The schema objects defining object classes and attributes are also controlled via ACLs, allowing only authenticated and authorized users to modify the directory schema.

Inheritance of Administrative Rights

Active Directory enables you to assign administrative permissions at any node of the domain subtree that are subsequently inherited by objects in child nodes. Inheritance can be combined with administrative delegation to easily grant rights to manage designated directory subtrees.

Inheritance is a property of the container object that allows the values of an ACE to propagate to all child objects. Inheritance is controlled via Security Descriptor Inheritance, where a new object inherits the combined security descriptors of the process creating the object, the parent container, and the class definition.

When inherited permissions are determined varies among directory service vendors. Active Directory uses create-time inheritance rather than the runtime inheritance used by NDS. When an object is created or its ACL modified, for example, the change is calculated and written to the object's ACL. When the permissions granted to an object need to be determined, the directory just reads the ACL. This provides a fast response in security decisions, but does not guarantee the results are exactly current as, depending on synchronization latency, the ACL may be slightly out of date.

Group Policy

A *group policy* is a set of policies enforced on a group of computers or users within the directory. Domain-based security is set by policy and assessed via a hierarchy of policy settings.

Active Directory uses group policies to enable administrators to configure security, desktop, application, and Start menu selections for users and computers within an OU or a domain. Policies only apply to AD computer and user objects. Computers receive an additional *local group policy object* (LGPO) by default. An LGPO only supplies security-specific policies.

Policies can be Registry based, or can contain a range of policy data from domain security, IP security, scripts, to file or application deployment.

Policies overwrite previous policies by default when settings differ and are applied in the following order: NT 4 policy file (NTCONFIG.POL), local, site, domain, and OU. Multiple policy settings are collectively assessed to create the effective policy (except where settings conflict).

A *group policy object* (GPO) is a uniquely named set of policies that can be applied to a domain, OU, or site. GPOs are either stored in the group policy container that contains version, status and other policy information (application objects), or in the group policy template (found in the domain controller's System volume) that contains deployment, software policy, script, and file-based data.

Administration of Active Directory

As the range of administration in Active Directory far exceeds the scope of this material, this section only briefly discusses key management tools, delegation of administration, and groups in Active Directory.

Delegation of Administrative Authority

Active Directory enables you to delegate administrative authority to users, granting specific administrative rights for designated OUs and subtrees. In general, use OUs (rather than domains) for administrative delegation of business or management subdivisions.

OUs are the nodes in the tree commonly used to do the following:

- Delegate total administrative control
- Delegate administrative control over certain object types or properties
- Delegate administrative rights to create and delete objects or certain types of objects

Using the new Delegation of Control Wizard, you can delegate one of these tasks or any combination. You can delegate administrative rights to the following:

- **User management**—Read all user information, create, delete, and manage users accounts, and reset passwords on user accounts
- **Printer management**—Create, delete, and manage printers
- **Group management**—Create, delete, modify the members of a group, and manage group policy links

Alternatively, you can create a custom task to delegate control (at the OU level) of the current folder, existing objects, and/or in creating new objects; or you can delegate control on specified objects only (determined by class membership).

You can selectively delegate general permissions, the permission to create and delete specific object(s) (as described previously under "Directory Permissions"), and property-specific permissions.

You can also delegate the property-specific permissions that provide read and write access control on individual object properties, including Managed By, countryCode, street, postalAddress, postalCode, and others.

The Delegation of Control Wizard simplifies the assignment of administrative responsibility for specific tasks or for an entire directory subtree.

Administrative Tools

Administrative tools for Active Directory are mostly provided through a common interface—the *Microsoft Management Console* (MMC). Active Directory supports the delegation of administrative tasks via customizable tool sets and flexible directory permissions.

The MMC is a Windows 2000 console interface that integrates the Active Directory administration tools. The MMC is *only* a console in that it provides no management capability but only hosts programs constructed as snap-ins. The MMC provides the mechanism to add, remove, and manipulate snap-ins. The MMC enables you to customize which administration tools will be contained within the console, and to store the configuration into portable files.

The administration tools for Active Directory are provided in the form of MMC snap-ins. Snap-ins are modular software agents that supply a limited functionality, and which are designed to handle a specific set of operations. Snap-ins are constructed as either *standalone* or *extension* snap-ins; standalone snap-ins provide independent management functionality and operate without dependence on any other snap-in. Extension snap-ins extend (and depend on) another snap-in type. For instance, the Group Policy snap-in is an extension snap-in of the AD Users and Computers snap-in.

The MMC enables you to create custom sets of snap-in tools, and to save them into .msc files. MSC files are portable, enabling a network administrator to design custom tools for delegated tasks and easily distribute copies. By default, AD administration tools can be invoked from different menu selections; but they can also be organized into a single MMC console. You can use MMC to create a new console and add all snap-ins needed for your directory administration.

Four primary directory tool snap-ins enable you to manage domains, users, computers, sites and services, as well as the directory schema.

- **Active Directory Domains and Trusts**—The Domains and Trusts snap-in enables you to manage domain trusts between domains. This MMC tool supports managing inter-domain relationships and allows a multiple domain view of AD (you can see and work with domain trees). The Domains and Trusts snap-in operates on the domain tree, enabling you to view, create, edit, or remove any specific trust relationships established between domains.

- **Active Directory Users and Computers**—This snap-in enables you to manage the users, computers, and related properties within a domain. The Users and Computers snap-in provides management access to domain subtree contents, the OU structure, users, groups, and network resources. Each domain represented in Active Directory Users and Computers includes the `Built-in`, `Computers`, `Domain Controllers`, `ForeignSecurityPrincipals`, `LostAndFound`, `System`, and `Users` nodes that contain corresponding directory objects. Using the Active Directory Users and Computers snap-in, you can create a new computer, contact, group, OU, printer, user, or shared folder, delegate control, assign operations masters, or locate objects within the directory.

- **Active Directory Sites and Services**—The Sites and Services snap-in is used to manage site configuration for replication management, and supports service management functionality. The Sites node supplies access to inter-site replication parameters, enabling you to create and delete sites, as well as to delegate administrative control. Windows 2000 publishes service information via Active Directory, providing greater availability and easier management of the service. The Services node is not displayed, however, unless you select Show Services Node from the View menu. The Services node contains the information on Public Key, RRAS, and Windows services.

- **Active Directory Schema**—The Active Directory Schema snap-in is used to manage the contents of the directory schema, and it supplies the means to view and modify the objects and attributes within the schema. The Active Directory Schema snap-in lets you set schema permissions, reload the schema, determine which attributes are replicated to the GC, and whether the permissions are inherited.

In addition to the four primary AD snap-ins just described, some other tools are used to manage Active Directory, including the following:

- **DCPromo**—The DCPROMO.EXE program is used to promote a server to an Active Directory domain controller. When a server becomes a domain controller, you can choose to install it into a new forest or to an existing forest, and you can select to create a new domain tree or to create a new child domain within an existing domain tree. To remove DC status from a server, run DCPromo again, and demote the DC to a member server.

- **Group Policy Editor**—Active Directory includes a new Group Policy Editor to simplify the creation and editing of security policies. The Group Policy Editor can be launched from the Properties, Group Policy tab of an OU or domain. The Group Policy snap-in enables you to import, review, configure, and apply a group policy object.

- **DNS**—The DNS administration tool is another MMC-based console. The AD DNS snap-in differs substantially from the DNS tool in NT 4, but provides similar functionality. The DNS Wizard is a nice enhancement, simplifying the creation of DNS domains and zones. The representation of the DNS information is more complex in Windows 2000, displaying an unusual arrangement of zone entries arranged in an extended tree. (Some DNS records even use an Active Directory object GUID in place of a host name, obscuring some DNS configuration details.)

Groups in Active Directory

Active Directory uses groups both for security as well as for providing distribution lists. In Active Directory, security groups are the method of implementing security for directory and network resources. In the Active Directory security model (like NT), users should be assigned to groups, and groups should be assigned permissions to access resources.

In general, groups may contain users, groups, and shared resources existing on the local server, in the local domain tree, or in remote domain trees in the forest.

Active Directory contains both the NT-compatible groups called Built-in groups, as well as new Security groups.

The Built-in groups correspond to the default NT 4 built-in local groups, and provide the same functionality. The Built-in groups on an AD server are Account Operators, Administrators, Backup Operators, Guests, Print Operators, Replicator, Server Operators, and Users.

The Security groups incorporate the NT 4 domain groups and provide additional Security groups specific to Active Directory. The security groups include the following:

- **Administration**—Enterprise Admins, Domain Admins, DnsAdmins, Schema Admins, Group Policy Creator Owners, and DHCP Administrators

- **Computers**—Domain Computers, Domain Controllers, RAS and IAS Servers, Cert Publishers, and DnsUpdateProxy

- **Users**—Domain Guests, Domain Users, WINS Users, DHCP Users

Security Groups and Distribution Lists

If the AD-integrated version of Exchange is installed on the DC, security groups can also be used for distribution lists. AD security groups have features supporting distribution lists such as allowing non-security members to exist in a group, and allowing the disabling of security for a group.

OUs for Admin, Groups for Security

Active Directory groups should be used differently from OUs:

- Use OUs for administrative hierarchy within a domain.

- Use groups to control user access to resources throughout the domain tree and forest.

In Active Directory, permissions cannot be assigned or granted to objects other than the security principals, (user, computer, and groups) and are specific to the domain in which the object exists. This fundamentally affects how you organize and manage people and resources within your directory tree.

As explained in the preceding chapter, with NDS if you grant permissions to an OU, all objects within that OU inherit these rights. AD uses groups rather than the OU structure (as NDS does) to provide permissions to users. Each user is added to one or more (usually more) groups and those groups are granted the permissions. Group membership is also restricted to security principals.

Scope of Security Groups

Active Directory security groups have three distinct ranges, or *scopes,* to which they apply. These ranges are defined as being of Universal, Global, and Domain Local scope. The groups with a Universal scope (that is, Universal groups) provide forest-wide access, whereas Global groups operate between domains, and Domain Local groups are used within a specific domain.

When operating in native AD mode, AD also enables you to *nest* groups within other groups, providing a hierarchy of group security membership. This can be especially beneficial for enterprise network administrators who can use this capability to manage large environments. Nesting a group with another group makes it a member of the other group. Permissions assigned can be inherited by nested (child) groups and all members within the group. This nesting capability substantially extends the functionality of groups for use in security organization and control.

Universal Groups

In brief, groups with Universal scope can provide all selected users within any domain tree in the forest the ability to access resources in all other domain trees. Universal groups can do the following:

- Accept members of all domains, users, Global, or Universal groups in the forest
- Be a member of Domain Local and Universal groups
- Grant permissions on all domains in the forest
- Be used in an ACL on any object in the forest

When updating Universal groups, the entire membership list is replicated to all GCs in the forest. To avoid undue replication traffic related to Universal groups, keep membership as static as possible, and keep the total number of objects as small as possible.

GC Required at Logon for Universal Groups

Universal groups are only stored on GCs; therefore, if Universal groups are used, the GC must be available on logon. If the GC is not available, the logon process uses locally cached data.

Global Groups

Groups with a Global scope are equivalent to the NT 4 global groups and can be used throughout the forest. Global groups can do the following:

- Accept as members only Global groups and users within the parent domain of the group
- Be a member of all groups in the forest
- Grant permissions on all domains in the forest
- Be used in an ACL on any object in the forest

Domain Local Groups

Groups with a Domain Local scope are new in AD, and they are used to grant access to resources within the domain. Domain Local groups can do the following:

- Accept members from Global and Universal groups and users from all domains in the forest, as well as Domain Local groups within the parent domain of the group
- Be members of only the Domain Local groups within the parent domain of the group
- Grant permissions on only the parent domain of the group
- Be used only in ACLs on objects within the local domain

The Future of Active Directory

Active Directory is in its first release, establishing the foundation of what it offers as a directory service product. It is not clear at this point exactly how Active Directory will evolve, what features will be added, and which technologies will be incorporated. However, a quick look at what *is* known about plans for AD development and enhancements provides some hints:

- **Cisco Networking Services for AD**—Cisco, in partnership with Microsoft, is developing Cisco Networking Services for Active Directory (CNS/AD), a set of services designed to allow the integration of network device management with information contained in AD. This integration will enable administrators to use Active Directory to manage Cisco network devices. CNS/AD will allow the provisioning of network services according to profiles and AD security information. Cisco will also publish a standard schema, allowing third-party application developers to access the services provided by CNS/AD.

- **Integration of ZOOMIT technologies**—Microsoft is currently working on integrating ZOOMIT Corp's meta-directory technologies into Active Directory. Incorporating ZOOMIT's meta-directory technologies will allow Active Directory to integrate user identity across disparate namespaces in the enterprise network. These additions to Active Directory will provide user access to resources managed by different directories and applications with a single logon. The integration of these meta-directory technologies will provide synchronization of the Active Directory information with these external namespaces.

- **Directory-enabled applications**—There will be many products released that take advantage of the services offered by Active Directory. As of September of 1999, Microsoft reported more than 2,200 vendors building 4,600 Windows 2000–certified applications with 1,000 of these vendors prepared to ship products upon release of Windows 2000.

The business awareness of the need for, and uses of, directory services is rapidly expanding, and Microsoft seems committed to delivering comprehensive directory solutions for enterprise networks. Active Directory is an ambitious undertaking and Microsoft is hitting the ground running with many available directory-enabled applications, business partnerships, technical support alliances, and plans for enhancements.

As the cornerstone of Microsoft's approach to network management, and with wide support from application vendors, Active Directory is clearly a serious contender for the enterprise network. Whatever the future holds for Active Directory, it should be an interesting product to watch.

A

References

X.500

Books

Understanding X.500: The Directory. David Chadwick. (International Thomson Computer Press, 1996). This title is out of print, but portions of the text are available at www.salford.ac.uk/its024/version.web/contents.htm.

X.500 Directory Services. Sara Radicati. (International Thomson Computer Press, 1994). ISBN: 1-850-32879-x.

Standards

X.500 *Information Technology—Open Systems Interconnection—The Directory: Overview of Concepts, Models, and Services*, first published in 1988.

X.501 *Information Technology—Open Systems Interconnection—The Directory: Models*, first published in 1988.

X.509 *Information Technology—Open Systems Interconnection—The Directory: Authentication Framework*, first published in 1988.

X.511 *Information Technology—Open Systems Interconnection—The Directory: Abstract Service Definition*, first published in 1988.

X.518 *Information Technology—Open Systems Interconnection—The Directory: Procedures for Distributed Operation*, first published in 1988.

X.519 *Information Technology—Open Systems Interconnection—The Directory: Protocol Specifications*, first published in 1988.

X.520 *Information Technology—Open Systems Interconnection—The Directory: Selected Attribute Types*, first published in 1988.

X.521 *Information Technology—Open Systems Interconnection—The Directory: Selected Object Classes*, first published in 1988.

X.525 *Information Technology—Open Systems Interconnection—The Directory: Replication*, first published in 1993.

X.530 *Information Technology—Open Systems Interconnection—The Directory: Use of Systems Management for Administration of the Directory*, first published in 1997.

RFCs

1249 "DIXIE Protocol Specification." T. Howes, M. Smith, and B. Beecher, (August 1991, Informational).

1274 "The COSINE and Internet X.500." Schema P. Barker and S. Kille. (November 1991, Proposed standard).

1275 "Replication Requirements to Provide an Internet Directory Using X.500." S. E. Hardcastle-Kille. (November 1991, Informational).

1276 "Replication and Distributed Operations Extensions to Provide an Internet Directory Using X.500." S. E. Hardcastle-Kille. (November 1991, Proposed standard).

1279 "X.500 and Domains." S. E. Hardcastle-Kille. (November 1991, Experimental).

1308 "Executive Introduction to Directory Services Using the X.500 Protocol." C. Weider, J. Reynolds. (March 1992, Informational).

1309 "Technical Overview of Directory Services Using the X.500 Protocol." C. Weider, J. Reynolds, and S. Heker. (March 1992, Informational).

1330 "Recommendations for the Phase I Deployment of OSI Directory Services (X.500) and OSI Message Handling Services (X.400) Within the ESNET Community." ESCC X.500/X.400 Task Force, ESnet Site Coordinating Committee (ESCC). (May 1992, Informational).

1373 "Portable DUAs." T. Tignor. (October 1992, Informational).

1430 "A Strategic Plan for Deploying an Internet X.500 Directory Service." S. Hardcastle-Kille, E. Huizer, V. Cerf, R. Hobby, and S. Kent. (February 1993, Informational).

1431 "DUA Metrics (OSI-DS 33 [v2])." P. Barker. (February 1993, Informational).

LDAP

Books

Understanding and Deploying LDAP Services. Timothy A. Howes, Mark C. Smith, and
Gordon S. Good. (MacMillan Technical Publishing, 1999). ISBN: 1-57870-070-1.

*LDAP: Programming Directory-Enabled Applications with Lightweight Directory Access
Protocol.* Timothy A. Howes and Mark C. Smith. (MacMillan Technical Publishing,
1997). ISBN: 1-57870-000-0.

RFCs

As with DNS, quite a few RFCs concern LDAP. You can search for any RFC by
number or keyword at `www.rfceditor.org/rfcsearch.html`.

In addition to the RFCs listed here, you may want to consult the IETF postings
regarding the current status of working groups at:
`www.ietf.org/html.charters/wg-dir.html`.

The LDAP RFCs are listed below in numeric order:

1778   "The String Representation of Standard Attribute Syntaxes." T. Howes, S. Kille,
W. Yeong, and C. Robbins. (March 1995, [obsoletes 1488, updated by 2559] Draft
standard).

1823   "The LDAP Application Program Interface." T. Howes and M. Smith. (August
1995, Informational).

1959   "An LDAP URL Format." T. Howes and M. Smith. (June 1996, Proposed
standard).

2164   "Use of an X.500/LDAP Directory to Support MIXER Address Mapping."
S. Kille. (January 1998 [obsoletes 1838], Proposed standard).

2247   "Using Domains in LDAP/X.500 Distinguished Names." S. Kille, M. Wahl,
A. Grimstad, R. Huber, and S. Sataluri. (January 1998, Proposed standard).

2251   "Lightweight Directory Access Protocol (v3)." M. Wahl, T. Howes, and S. Kille.
(December 1997, Proposed standard).

2252   "Lightweight Directory Access Protocol (v3)." M. Wahl, A. Coulbeck, T. Howes,
and S. Kille. (December 1997, Proposed standard).

2253   "Lightweight Directory Access Protocol (v3)." M. Wahl, S. Kille, and T. Howes.
(December 1997, Proposed standard).

2254   "The String Representation of LDAP Search Filters." T. Howes. (December
1997 [obsoletes 1960], Proposed standard).

2255   "The LDAP URL Format." T. Howes and M. Smith. (December 1997,
Proposed standard).

2256   "A Summary of the X.500(96) User Schema for Use with LDAPv3." M. Wahl.
(December 1997, Proposed standard).

2307   "An Approach for Using LDAP as a Network Information Service."
L. Howard. (March 1998, Experimental).

2559   "Internet X.509 Public Key Infrastructure Operational Protocols – LDAPv2."
       S. Boeyen, T. Howes, and P. Richard. (April 1999 [updates 1778], Proposed
       standard).

2587   "Internet X.509 Public Key Infrastructure LDAPv2 Schema." S. Boeyen,
       T. Howes, and P. Richard. (June 1999, Proposed standard).

2589   "Lightweight Directory Access Protocol (v3): Extensions for Dynamic
       Directory Services." Y. Yaacovi, M. Wahl, and T. Genovese. (May 1999, Proposed
       standard).

2596   "Use of Language Codes in LDAP." M. Wahl and T. Howes. (May 1999,
       Proposed standard).

2649   "An LDAP Control and Schema for Holding Operation Signatures."
       B. Greenblatt and P. Richard. (August 1999, Experimental).

2657   "LDAPv2 Client versus the Index Mesh." R. Hedberg. (August 1999,
       Experimental).

Online Resources

IETF LDAP Extension working group:

`www.ietf.org/html.charters/ldapext-charter.html`

IETF LDAP Duplication/Replication/Update Protocols working group:

`www.ietf.org/html.charters/ldup-charter.html`

DNS

Books

DNS and BIND (third edition). Paul Albitz and Cricket Liu. (O'Reilly & Associates,
   1998). ISBN: 1-56592-512-2.

Windows NT DNS. Michael Masterson, Herman Knief, Scott Vinick, and Eric Roul.
   (New Riders, 1998). ISBN: 1-56205-943-2.

RFCs

Many RFCs collectively make up the DNS standards. You can search for any RFC by
number or keyword at `www.rfc-editor.org/rfcsearch.html`.

The DNS RFCs are listed here in numeric order:

805   "Computer Mail Meeting Notes." J. Postel. (February 1982).

811   "Hostnames Server." K. Harrenstien, V. White, and E. Feinler. (March 1982).

819   "The Domain Naming Convention for Internet User Applications." Z. Su and
      J. Postel. (August 1982).

881   "The Domain Names Plan and Schedule." J. Postel. (November 1983 [updated
      by 897, 921]).

897 "Domain Name System Implementation Schedule." J. Postel. (February 1984 [updates 881; updated by 921]).

920 "Domain Requirements." J. Postel and J. Reynolds. (October 1984).

921 "Domain Name System Implementation Schedule." Revised by J. Postel. (October 1984 [updates 897, 881]).

974 "Mail Routing and the Domain System." Craig Partridge. (January 1986, Standard).

1032 "Domain Administrator's Guide." M. Stahl. (November 1987).

1033 "Domain Administrators Operations Guide." M. Lottor. (November 1987 [updated by 1912]).

1034 "Domain Names—Concepts and Facilities." P. Mockapetris. (November 1987 [obsoletes 882, 883, 973; updated by 1101, 1122, 1183, 1706, 1876, 1982, 2181, 2308 2535], Standard).

1035 "Domain Names—Implementation and Specification." P. Mockapetris. (November 1987 [obsoletes 882, 883, 973; updated by 1101, 1122, 1183, 1706, 1876, 1982, 1995, 1996, 2052, 2136, 2137, 2181, 2308, 2535], Standard).

1101 "DNS Encoding of Network Names and Other Types." P. Mockapetris. (April 1989 [updates 1034, 1035], Proposed standard).

1122 "Requirements for Internet Hosts—Communication Layers." Edited by R. Braden. (October 1989 [updates 1034, 1035], Standard).

1123 "Requirements for Internet Hosts—Application and Support." Edited by R. Braden. (October 1989 [updated by 2181], Standard).

1178 "Choosing a Name for Your Computer." D. Libes. (August 1990, Informational).

1183 "New DNS RR Definitions." C. Everhart, L. Mamakos, and R. Ullmann, and edited by P. Mockapetris. (October 1990 [updates 1034, 1035; updated by 2052], Experimental).

1464 "Using the Domain Name System to Store Arbitrary String Attributes." R. Rosenbaum. (May 1993, Experimental).

1480 "The US Domain." A. Cooper and J. Postel. (June 1993 [obsoletes 1386], Informational).

1535 "A Security Problem and Proposed Correction with Widely Deployed DNS Software." E. Gavron. (October 1993, Informational).

1536 "Common DNS Implementation Errors and Suggested Fixes." A. Kumar, J. Postel, C. Neuman, P. Danzig, and S. Miller. (October 1993, Informational).

1591 "Domain Name System Structure and Delegation." J. Postel. (March 1994, Informational).

1611 "DNS Server MIB Extensions." R. Austein and J. Saperia. (May 1994, Proposed standard).

1612 "DNS Resolver MIB Extensions." R. Austein and J. Saperia. (May 1994, Proposed standard).

1706 "DNS NSAP Resource Records." B. Manning and R. Colella. (October 1994 [obsoletes 1348, 1637; updates 1034, 1035], Informational).

1713 "Tools for DNS Debugging." A. Romao. (November 1994, Informational).

1794 "DNS Support for Load Balancing." T. Brisco. (April 1995, Informational).

1876 "A Means for Expressing Location Information in the Domain Name System." C. Davis, P. Vixie, T. Goodwin, and I. Dickinson. (January 1996 [obsoletes 1712; updates 1034, 1035], Experimental).

1884 "IP Version 6 Addressing Architecture." Edited by R. Hinden and S. Deering. (December 1995, Proposed standard).

1886 "DNS Extensions to Support IP Version 6." S. Thomson and C. Huitema. (December 1995, Proposed standard).

1912 "Common DNS Operational and Configuration Errors." D. Barr. (February 1996 [obsoletes 1537], Informational).

1956 "Registration in the MIL Domain." D. Engebretson and R. Plzak. (June 1996, Informational).

1982 "Serial Number Arithmetic." R. Elz and R. Bush. (August 1996 [updates 1034, 1035], Proposed standard).

1995 "Incremental Zone Transfer in DNS." M. Ohta. (August 1996 [updates 1035], Proposed standard).

1996 "Notify: A Mechanism for Prompt Notification of Authority Zone Changes." P. Vixie. (August 1996 [updates 1035], Proposed standard).

2010 "Operational Criteria for Root Name Servers." B. Manning and P. Vixie. (October 1996, Informational).

2052 "A DNS RR for Specifying the Location of Services (DNS SRV)." A. Gulbrandsen and P. Vixie. (October 1996 [updates 1035 1183], Experimental).

2053 "The AM (Armenia) Domain." E. Der-Danieliantz. (October 1996, Informational).

2136 "Dynamic Updates in the Domain Name System (DNS UPDATE)." P. Vixie (editor), S. Thomson, Y. Rekhter, and J. Bound. (April 1997 [updates 1035], Proposed standard).

2137 "Secure Domain Name System Dynamic Update." D. Eastlake III (April 1997 [updates 1035], Proposed standard).

2146 "U.S. Government Internet Domain Names." Federal Networking Council. (May 1997 [obsoletes 1816], Informational).

2163 "Using the Internet DNS to Distribute MIXER Conformant Global Address Mapping (MCGAM)." C. Allocchio. (January 1998 [obsoletes 1664], Proposed standard).

2168 "Resolution of Uniform Resource Identifiers Using the Domain Name System." R. Daniel and M. Mealling. (June 1997, Experimental).

2181 "Clarifications to the DNS Specification." R. Elz and R. Bush. (July 1997 [updates 1034, 1035 1123; updated by 2535], Proposed standard).

2182 "Selection and Operation of Secondary DNS Servers." R. Elz, R. Bush, S. Bradner, and M. Patton. (July 1997).

2219 "Use of DNS Aliases for Network Services." M. Hamilton and R. Wright. (October 1997).

2230 "Key Exchange Delegation Record for the DNS." R. Atkinson. (November 1997, Informational).

2240 "A Legal Basis for Domain Name Allocation." O. Vaughan. (November 1997, Informational).

2247 "Using Domains in LDAP/X.500 Distinguished Names." S. Kille, M. Wahl, A. Grimstad, R. Huber, and S. Sataluri. (January 1998, Proposed standard).

2307 "An Approach for Using LDAP as a Network Information Service." L. Howard. (March 1998, Experimental).

2308 "Negative Caching of DNS Queries (DNS NCACHE)." M. Andrews. (March 1998 [updates 1034, 1035]).

2317 "Classless IN-ADDR.ARPA Delegation." H. Eidnes, G. de Groot, and P. Vixie. (March 1998).

2345 "Domain Names and Company Name Retrieval." J. Klensin, T. Wolf, and G. Oglesby. (May 1998, Experimental).

2377 "Naming Plan for Internet Directory-Enabled Applications." A. Grimstad, R. Huber, S. Sataluri, and M. Wahl. (September 1998, Informational).

2517 "Building Directories from DNS: Experiences from WWWSeeker." R. Moats and R. Huber. (February 1999, Informational).

2535 "Domain Name System Security Extensions." D. Eastlake. (March 1999 [obsoletes 2065; updates 2181, 1035, 1034], Proposed standard).

2536 "DSA KEYs and SIGs in the Domain Name System (DNS)." D. Eastlake. (March 1999, Proposed standard).

2537 "RSA/MD5 KEYs and SIGs in the Domain Name System (DNS)." D. Eastlake. (March 1999, Proposed standard).

2538 "Storing Certificates in the Domain Name System (DNS)." D. Eastlake and O. Gudmundsson. (March 1999, Proposed standard).

2539 "Storage of Diffie-Hellman Keys in the Domain Name System (DNS)." D. Eastlake. (March 1999, Proposed standard).

2540 "Detached Domain Name System (DNS) Information." D. Eastlake. (March 1999, Experimental).

2541 "DNS Security Operational Considerations." D. Eastlake. (March 1999, Informational).

Online Resources

```
www.dns.net/dnsrd/
www.ietf.org/rfc/
www.rfc-editor.org/rfcsearch.html
ftpeng.cisco.com/fred/rfc-index/rfc.html
www.pmg.lcs.mit.edu/rfc.html
www.acmebw.com/askmr.htm
```

Novell Directory Services

Books

The Complete Guide to Novell Directory Services. David Kearns and Brian Iverson.
  (Sybex Network Press, 1998). ISBN: 0-7821-1823-2.
Novell's Guide to NetWare 5 Networks. Jeffrey F. Hughes and Blair W. Thomas.
  (IDG Books Worldwide, 1999). ISBN: 0-7645-4544-2.
NDS for NT. Jeffrey F. Hughes and Blair W. Thomas. (IDG Books Worldwide, 1998).
  ISBN: 0-7645-4551-5.
Novell's Guide to IntranetWare Networks. Jeffrey F. Hughes and Blair W. Thomas.
  (IDG Books Worldwide, 1996). ISBN: 0-7645-4516-7.
Novell's Four Principles of NDS Design. Jeffrey F. Hughes and Blair W. Thomas.
  (IDG Books Worldwide, 1996). ISBN: 0-7645-4522-1.
Novell's Guide to Integrating IntraNetware and NT. J. D. Marymee and Sandy Stephens.
  (IDG Books Worldwide, 1998). ISBN: 0-7645-4523-x.
NDS Troubleshooting. Peter Kuo and Jim Henderson. (New Riders, 1995). ISBN:
  1-56205-443-0.

RFCs

2165   "Service Location Protocol." J. Veizades, E. Guttman, C. Perkins, and S. Kaplan.
  (June 1997, Standards track).

Online Resources

NDS:
```
www.novell.com/nds
```
Online NDS 8 documentation:
```
www.novell.com/documentation/lg/nds8/docui/index.html
```
NDS glossary:
```
www.developer.novell.com/research/devnotes/1999/septembe/a2frame.htm
```
digitalme:
```
www.digitalme.com
```

Single Sign-on:
> www.novell.com/products/sso/

ZENworks:
> www.novell.com/products/nds/zenworks/

NDS for Solaris:
> www.novell.com/products/nds/nds4solaris/

NDS for NT:
> www.novell.com/products/nds/nds4nt/

NDS development:
> www.developer.novell.com/nds/

NDS schema:
> www.developer.novell.com/nds/schema.htm

Schema Registry
> www.developer.novell.com/engsup/schreg2c.htm

NetWare Connection:
> www.nwconnection.com

Active Directory

Books

Planning for Windows 2000. Eric K. Cone, Jon Boggs, and Sergio Perez. (New Riders, 1999). ISBN: 0-7357-0048-6.

Windows NT DNS. Michael Masterson, Herman Knief, Scott Vinick, and Eric Roul. (New Riders, 1998). ISBN: 1-56205-943-2.

Microsoft Windows NT Administrator's Bible, Option Pack Edition. Doug Sheresh, Beth Sheresh, Kenneth Gregg, and Robert Cowart. (IDG Books Worldwide, 1999). ISBN: 0-7645-3213-8.

Online Resources

Exploring AD:
> www.microsoft.com/Windows/server/Overview/exploring/directory.asp

AD technical walkthroughs:
> www.msdn.microsoft.com/developer/windows2000/adsi/adsiwalk.asp

AD technical documentation:
> www.microsoft.com/windows/server/Technical/directory/default.asp

Deploying AD:
> www.microsoft.com/Windows/server/Deploy/directory/default.asp

ADSI:
> www.microsoft.com/windows/server/Technical/directory/adsilinks.asp

AD Programmer's Guide:
> www.msdn.microsoft.com/developer/windows2000/adsi/actdirguide.asp

AD glossary:
```
www.microsoft.com/Windows/server/Overview/features/glossary.asp
```
Windows 2000:
```
www.microsoft.com/windows/server/default.asp
```

Other Resources

Standards

ISO 3166   *Codes for the representation of Countries.* The International Organization for Standardization, 1988 (third edition).

RFCs

1760   "The S/Key One-Time Password System." N. Haller. (February 1995, Informational).

2078   "Generic Security Service Application Program Interface, Version 2." J. Linn. (January 1997 [obsoletes 1508], Proposed standard).

2222   "Simple Authentication and Security Layer (SASL)." J. Myers. (October 1997, Standards track).

2289   "A One-Time Password System." N. Haller, C. Metz, and P. Nesser. (February 1998 [obsoletes 1938], Standards track).

Online Resources

Directory Interoperability Forum:
```
www.directoryforum.org
```
Directory-Enabled networking:
```
www.cisco.com/warp/public/cc/cisco/mkt/enm/diren/index.shtml
```

Articles

"Active Directory Interoperability." Luke Howard. Copyright© 1999, PADL Software Pty. Ltd. (`www.padl.com`).

"The Business Case for Directory-Guided IT." Aberdeen Group, March 1999 (`www.aberdeen.com`).

Glossary

[root] [root] is the traditional NDS reference for the root of the directory tree.

abstract classes Abstract classes are used as templates to define other classes.

Abstract Syntax Notation One (ASN.1) ASN.1 defines the syntax used for storing information that will be exchanged between different systems, and specifies the storing of data in a series of type-value pairs.

access control Access control mechanisms provide differential levels of access to directory objects. The specifics of access control mechanisms vary between directory service implementations.

Access Control Decision Function (ACDF) The ACDF is an algorithm defined in the X.500 standards to determine access control permissions by examining the contents of the ACI items of both the object and DUA.

Access Control Entry (ACE) An ACE is a single security-related directory entry linked to a specific object. An ACE can grant or deny a particular user (or group) a specific set of access rights to directory object.

Access Control Information (ACI) ACI is stored with each protected item in the directory and is used to determine which users are granted access, and what kind of access is granted.

Access Control Inner Administrative Area (ACIA) An ACIA is a permeable security boundary used by X.500 to allow delegation of access control administration.

Access Control Lists (ACL) An ACL contains security information concerning a directory object, such as who can access the object and what operations they can perform.

Access Control Service Element (ACSE) X.500 uses ACSE to create and tear down associations between directory agents, essentially managing the bind (connection) and unbind (disconnect) processes.

Access Control Specific Administrative Area (ACSA) An ACSA defines an autonomous area of security in X.500.

Access Control Specific Point (ACSP) An ACSP is the administrative point of an ACSA.

ACI items Access Control Information (ACI) items are the operational attributes that control access to protected items in the directory.

Active Directory (AD) AD is Microsoft's network directory service, first released as part of Windows 2000.

Active Directory Services Interface (ADSI) ADSI is Microsoft's proprietary API, which is used for Active Directory, as well as to support accessing directory objects residing in multiple namespaces.

Address (A) record An Address resource record is used in DNS zone files to specify the linkage between a host (computer) name and its corresponding IP address (also commonly called a host record).

Administrative and Operational Information Model This X.500 model describes the directory from the perspective of the network administrator, viewing all the directory information in a unified DIT.

administrative point The administrative point is the root node of an X.500 administrative area. There are two major categories of administrative

points—Specific (SAP) and Inner (IAP), which correspond to the root nodes of SAAs and IAAs.

alias An alias is a secondary logical representation of an existing object that functions as a pointer to the original object.

ASN1 ID An ASN1 ID is a globally unique number assigned by Novell when schema extensions are registered with them (like the X.500 OID).

asymmetric cryptography Asymmetric cryptography uses pairs of keys (public/private) to encrypt information (also called public key).

asynchronous Asynchronous communications allow multiple client requests to be sent to a DSA without requiring prior return of results from earlier requests.

attribute access Attribute access refers to when a user or application attempts to access information held within an object (such as a telephone number), as opposed to the object itself (browsing the directory tree).

attribute access permissions The sets of permissions that can be set on attribute access. These permissions commonly include actions such as read, compare, add, and remove.

attribute definition The schema definition of an attribute, which includes the attribute syntax and any constraints placed on the attribute.

attribute syntax The attribute syntax defines the acceptable data structure of an attribute.

attributes An individual value of a directory object, such as name. Attributes hold the information associated with directory objects.

authentication Authentication is the mechanism that verifies that the individual user is who they claim to be, usually by association with a shared-secret password or public key.

Authentication Server (AS) An Authentication Server provides the user authentication portion of Kerberos security.

authoritative name server An authoritative name server (as defined in DNS) contains current resource records for a specified zone and is designated via an SOA record.

Autonomous Administrative Areas (AAA) In the X.500 model, an AAA denotes a directory subtree managed by an independent organization. Each organization is completely responsible for their portion of the global DIT.

auxiliary class An auxiliary class is like an abstract class because it defines a set of attributes and object characteristics. Auxiliary classes are used to support an additional derivation of an existing object.

backlink NDS uses backlinks to keep track of external references to an object.

Berkeley Internet Name Domain (BIND) BIND is a UNIX-based vendor-specific version of DNS that (among other distinctions) notably specifies the use of a boot file for startup functionality.

bindery A bindery is a single server directory used by NetWare 2.x–3.x. The bindery is a flat namespace with entries corresponding to users and physical network resources.

bindery services NDS's bindery service supports down-level clients and provides them with a bindery-style view of a subset of the directory contents.

boot file A text file used by DNS to specify configuration commands to be executed at startup of the DNS service.

bridgehead server A bridgehead server is used to manage AD replication between sites and across slower communications links such as WAN connections.

cache file A DNS file containing host address resource records for the root DNS name servers.

caching-only name server A DNS name server that is not linked to any specific zone and does not contain its own zone files.

catalog Catalogs contain a subset or an index of the directory contents to provide a fast method of locating network resources.

centralized directory A centralized directory holds the entire directory namespace on a single server. Copies of the directory information may be stored on additional servers.

certificate An X.509 certificate is a collection of data that associates the public keys of a network user with their DN in the directory. The certificate is stored within the directory as user object attributes.

Certificate Authority (CA) A Certificate Authority creates and manages X.509 certificates for users, servers, and other CAs.

chaining Chaining is defined by X.500 as a process where a DSA passes a query to other DSAs, collects results, and compiles them before they are returned to the client.

changelog A changelog contains a record of all the changes that have been made to the directory. Using this method, when a replication process is initiated, the supplier "replays" the changelog to the consumer.

class definition   An object class definition specifies the information required
to create an instance of a particular type
of object. Class definitions also determine how objects work in relationship
to other objects in the directory.

classes   A class is a schematic definition of a type of object allowed within
the directory. A class is a possible object,
not an *actual* object—that is, the User
object for Brynna is an *instance* of the
User *class*.

CNAME record   A Canonical
NAME (CNAME) resource record is
used within a DNS zone file to specify
an alias for a host name (similar to an
X.500 alias).

complete replication   Complete
replication sends a copy of the entire
directory database to each server with
every directory update.

Connectionless LDAP (CLDAP)
CLDAP provides the functionality of
LDAP over a connectionless protocol
(UDP).

ConsoleOne   ConsoleOne is a Java-
based administrative console for NDS; it
is available in both Windows and Web
versions.

consumer reference   An X.500 DSA
uses a consumer reference to identify a
replication consumer (that is, a shadow).
This information is the reciprocal of
that in the supplier reference.

container object   Container objects
are used to provide structure and organization for the directory tree and hold
other objects.

content rules   Content rules define
what attributes each object class
contains.

context   An object's place in the
directory tree is its context, which is
referenced by the string of object names
between it and the tree root. Also called
context prefix.

convergence   Convergence is when
all replicas of a partition contain the
same data.

create-time inheritance   With
create-time inheritance (used by AD),
effective permissions are determined and
written to the object's ACL at the point
of creation or change.

cross references   Cross references are
used to point to a naming context that
is neither superior nor subordinate to
the current naming context.

database layer   The database layer in
AD abstracts the DIB management
operations, isolating the DSA from the
storage subsystem (the ESE).

delegation   In directory services, delegation is the assignment of administrative control over directory subtrees or
objects.

dereferencing   Dereferencing is the
process by which the directory determines the underlying object an alias is
referring to.

DIB Fragment   A DIB fragment is
the portion of the DIB that is held by a
single DSA.

digital signature   A digital signature
is a summary of the data that is signed,
produced by a one-way hash function
encrypted with the sender's public key.

digitalme™   digitalme is an NDS-
based technology that acts as a personal
information management system for
individuals to use in managing their
online identity.

Directory Access Control Domain (DACD)   A DACD is an X.500-defined access control area subdivided by sets of directory entries.

Directory Access Protocol (DAP)   DAP is the X.500 protocol that provides client access to the directory.

Directory Administrative Authority Model   This X.500 model assumes different people or organizations will administer different parts of the DIT and provides a way for the DIT to be divided into subtrees, which can be delegated as needed.

Directory Distribution Model   The X.500 Directory Distribution Model defines how directory information is shared by multiple DSAs.

Directory Enabled Networking (DEN)   DEN is a collaboration between network infrastructure device vendors and directory service vendors seeking to enable directory-based control over infrastructure devices (such as routers and switches).

Directory Functional Model   The X.500 Directory Functional Model defines the directory as one or more DSAs that collectively provide DUAs with access to directory information.

Directory Information Base (DIB)   The DIB (an X.500 term) contains all the information in the directory, and is commonly distributed, partitioned, and replicated to enhance availability and responsiveness.

Directory Information Shadowing Protocol (DISP)   The X.500 DISP is used by a DSA to replicate a partition to another DSA and to transmit information during replica update operations.

Directory Information Tree (DIT)   A directory information tree is a hierarchical arrangement of container objects within a contiguous namespace. The DIT is used to represent a logical hierarchy, as well as to visually display the arrangement of objects within the tree.

Directory Interoperability Forum (DIF)   DIF is a group of vendors who have joined efforts to support the development of directory enabled application development and open directory standards.

Directory Management Domain (DMD)   An X.500 DMD consists of a set of DSAs and DUAs administered by a specific organization. DMD policies apply to DSA operations and can be used to limit the services provided by one or more DSAs.

directory object   A directory object is an instance of an underlying class definition, representing a network entry or set of information.

directory operational attributes   Directory operational attributes are used for operational parameters that apply to every DSA, such as access control.

Directory Operational Protocol (DOP)   DOP is an X.500 protocol used by a pair of DSAs to establish a binding agreement for use in distributed operations.

directory service   In its most general definition, a directory service provides the means to hierarchically organize and manage information and to retrieve the information by name association.

Directory System Agent (DSA)   DSA is the X.500 term for the server component of a directory service. Each DSA handles a portion of the DIT and multiple DSAs interoperate as a system to provide transparent access to the distributed directory.

Directory System Protocol (DSP)
DSP is an X.500 protocol that supports the interaction between DSAs necessary for distributed directory operations.

Directory User Agent (DUA)
A DUA is the client application of an X.500 defined directory service.

DirXML DirXML is Novell's implementation of an XML-based language, used as a means of providing directory integration and management.

Distinguished Name (DN) A DN is a fully qualified X.500 object name that unambiguously identifies and positions an object within the directory tree.

distributed directory A distributed directory subdivides the directory namespace. Multiple copies of the *subsets* of directory information are spread throughout the network, but are logically linked into one directory. X.500 directory services are designed to extend this distribution to the entire world.

Distributed Reference Link (DRL)
A DRL contains a list of all the external references created for an NDS object.

DIT Domain In X.500, a DIT Domain is the section of the global DIT managed by a specific Domain Management Organization (DMO). A DIT Domain consists of one or more Autonomous Administrative Area (AAAs), which may be disjoint (that is, unconnected).

DNS domain namespace The DNS domain namespace defines a hierarchical tree of domains.

Domain A DNS domain is a logical organizing structure for naming and location services.
Windows NT 4 organizes resources into NT domains that enforce security boundaries and that usually represent a subdivision of the company.

Active Directory domains combine DNS domains with NT 4 domains and provide DNS naming and location services with NT security boundaries and controls.

domain component (dc) LDAP domain components map to DNS domains, providing an integration of the DNS and LDAP namespaces.

Domain Controller (DC) A Domain Controller (DC) is the Active Directory DSA.

domain directory partition In AD, a domain directory partition contains all objects within the domain and is only replicated to DCs within a specific domain.

Domain Local groups Domain Local groups are used in AD to grant access to resources within a single domain to any user or group in the forest.

Domain Management Organization (DMO) A DMO is the administrative authority for a section of the global X.500 DIT (a DIT Domain).

Domain Name System (DNS)
DNS performs name–to–IP address resolution for domain names.

Domain Naming Master The Domain Naming Master controls the additions and deletions of domains within an AD forest, ensuring the uniqueness of the domain names.

domain subtree A domain subtree is the contiguous directory subtree contained with a single AD domain.

domain tree AD uses a tree of domains that collectively comprise a contiguous DNS namespace.

domain trusts Domain trusts are a process where a relationship is formed between domains to support an exchange of security credentials, allowing users in one domain to gain access to resources in the trusting domain. AD uses automatic two-way transitive trusts between domains.

DSA Information Model   The information contained in this X.500 model locates a DSA in relationship to other DSAs and describes how various DSAs interact to control shared directory information.

DSA Information Tree   A DSA Information Tree is comprised of the complete set of names (and associated DSEs) known by a specific DSA.

DSA Specific Entry (DSE)   A DSE is an entry in the DIT as held by a specific DSA.

DSAPI   DSAPI is the traditional method of programming NDS, providing all the functionally of the XDS APIs from X.500.

DSA–shared operational attributes The information used between DSAs to perform replication, containing information that applies to a single DSA, such as the time of the last replica update.

dynamic directory entries   Nonpersistent directory objects that disappear from the directory after a designated length of time if not refreshed.

Dynamic DNS (DDNS)   DDNS provides a mechanism for DNS resource records to be dynamically updated to reflect changing server and client availability and IP addresses.

Dynamic Host Configuration Protocol (DHCP)   DHCP is used to manage a pool of IP addresses and dynamically supply
those addresses to network clients.

effective rights   The set of access rights that result when all security factors are combined and assessed; effective rights denote which operations can actually be performed.

entry   An entry is another term for directory object.

entry access   Entry access is when a user accesses an object as a named entity in the directory (browsing the directory tree) rather than information held within an object (such as a telephone number).

entry access permissions   Entry access permissions are the set of permissions that can be granted or denied when accessing named objects. These permissions typically include read, browse, add, remove, modify, and rename.

Extensible Storage Engine (ESE) AD uses the ESE as its data storage layer. ESE works with the database layer to provide the DIB functionality for AD. The ESE is an enhanced version of Jet, an indexed database engine used by Exchange.

extensions   Extensions allow the use of arguments to support new directory operations and enhanced functionality. Extensions rely on a pre-arranged agreement between the communicating directory components on the set of new operations, along with the methods used to invoke the functionality.

external reference   An external reference is a temporary pointer to an object created by NDS when a server needs to reference an object that it is not contained in a local replica.

federated naming   Federated naming (also called federation) is the capability to perform name resolution across different namespaces, a process that is at the core of interoperability between directories.

filter A filter is a constraint applied to a directory query that restricts the information returned.

flat namespaces A flat namespace is one in which all objects are held below a single superior object, as if in a common container.

floating master A floating master is a server that has been temporarily assigned the role of a master for a particular directory operation, such as replication or schema modifications.

Floating Single Master Operation (FSMO) An operation that requires the election of a single master. Microsoft calls this a *flexible* single master operation.

forest A forest is an AD namespace containing one or more disjoint (non-contiguous) domain trees.

forest root In Active Directory, the first domain of the first tree in the forest defines the forest root.

Fully Distinguished Name A FDN is an NDS name treated as complete and resolved from the tree root. A FDN is a DN preceded by a period (.) (for example, .meggan.mythical.org).

Fully Qualified Domain Name (FQDN) An FQDN is a DNS domain name specified with the complete set of required values and with the terminating root delimiter (.) as the rightmost value (for example, host.domain.tld.).

Generic Security Service API (GSSAPI) GSSAPI defines an interoperable security system for use on the Internet. GSSAPI provides a protocol and mechanism-independent interface to underlying security methods.

Global Catalog (GC) A Global Catalog (GC) server contains an index to all AD objects in a forest, providing a efficient means for applications and users to query the directory for objects based on one or more known attributes.

Global groups AD Global groups are equivalent to NT 4 Global groups, and can be used to grant access to any resources in the forest to members of its domain and other Global groups.

Globally Unique Identifier (GUID) The GUID is a unique 128-bit number generated for each AD directory object at the point that it is created.

granularity Granularity refers to the ability to control operations such as replication and access control to a fine degree, usually meaning down to the attribute level. This provides extremely flexible security and minimizes replication traffic.

group policy A group policy is a set of policies enforced on a group of computers or users within the AD directory.

in.addr.arpa in.addr.arpa is a reserved domain name suffix used in DNS for reverse lookups.

incremental replication Incremental replication sends only a subset of the DIB, containing only the data that has been changed.

incremental zone transfers An incremental zone transfer (used in DNS) allows the master name server to send only the resource record information that has changed since the last zone transfer with that secondary server.

Infrastructure Master In AD, an Infrastructure Master enforces object consistency for operations that span domains and synchronizes group-to-user references.

inheritance Inheritance is the mechanism by which permissions granted to objects high in the tree flow to objects below them.

inherited ACL Each NDS partition root has an inherited ACL, which contains the effective rights at the root of that partition.

Inherited Rights Filter (IRF) An IRF blocks the inheritance of access rights from higher in the tree.

Inner Administrative Areas (IAA) X.500 defines an IAA as a type of administrative division within a directory, designating an area with delegated administrative tasks or collective attributes.

Inner Administrative Point (IAP) An administrative point for the IAA. See *administrative point*.

instance An instance of a directory object is a specific occurence of an object based on a class definition.

Internet Corporation for Assigned Names and Numbers (ICANN) ICANN is a non-profit corporation formed to manage critical Internet infrastructure administration functions formerly performed by the IETF.

Internet Engineering Task Force (IETF) An organization of internetworking engineers, vendors, researchers, and others who form *working groups* to work on an area of Internet development. IETF has two LDAP-related working groups LDUP (LDAP Duplication/Replication/Update Protocols) and LDAPExt (LDAP Extension).

iterative name resolution Iterative name resolution is a DNS process (similar to the X.500 referral process) where the name server receiving the name query either answers the query authoritatively or refers the client to another name server.

JNDI SunSoft's proprietary API that provides access to LDAP, NIS+, NDS, and other directory services.

Kerberos The Kerberos protocol is essentially a shared secret authentication methodology where both the user and the security services share the user's secret password. Kerberos security uses a security token called a ticket to authenticate users to network resources.

Key Distribution Center (KDC) A KDC is the collective reference to an Authentication Server (AS) and a Ticket Granting Server (TGS), used by Kerberos security.

knowledge references References to remote DIB partitions maintained by DSAs as a means of piecing together the DIT for searches and replication.

lame delegation Lame delelagion occurs when a DNS name server is delegated as authoritative for a specific DNS zone, but does not respond to name queries with authoritative results.

LDAP C API The LDAP C API is a low-level programming interface supporting all DAP operations, and is used in the development of directory applications written in C.

LDAP Data Interchange Format (LDIF) LDIF has been defined as a means of describing LDAP entries in a standardized text format to facilitate the exchange of directory information.

LDAP Uniform Resource Locator (URL) An LDAP URL provides a means of locating directory servers using DNS and then completing the query via LDAP.

leaf object A leaf object in a directory represents a manageable object—in network directories, leaf objects commonly represent network entities (users, servers, and so on) applications, and services.

Lightweight Directory Access Protocol (LDAP) LDAP defines a standard method for a client to access and modify directory information.

location services A network service providing name-to-address resolution for clients. Also called lookup services.

Location independence Location independence means that the name of a network object is not dependent on its location in the network.

logical naming model A logical naming model uses symbolic names transparently mapped to physical device names.

loosely consistent With loosely consistent replication, the data on all directory servers does not have to be exactly the same at any given time. Changes to the DIB are replicated more slowly and network servers gradually "catch up" to the changes made on other directory servers.

mandatory attributes Mandatory attributes are those directory attributes that must have values at all times during an object's lifetime.

master DSA In X.500, a master DSA is the DSA that holds the master copy of each directory entry—the copy of the object that is writeable.

master name server A master name server is the source of the DNS zone resource records during a zone transfer.

master replicas Master replicas are fully functional, allowing all directory operations. Everything in the directory, objects, tree design, the schema, and so on is updateable via a master replica. At least one master replica must exist per partition.

meta-directory A meta-directory does some form of integration or integrated management of multiple directory services. This may take the form of a top-layer directory, synchronization tools, or a transitional management tool used during a long migration process.

Microsoft Management Console (MMC) The MMC is a console interface that provides the framework for the AD administration tools, hosting programs constructed as snap-ins. The MMC provides the mechanism to add, remove, and manipulate modular snap-in programs.

mixed environment In AD, a mixed environment refers to having AD in native mode (that is, all DCs are running Windows 2000) yet still having network servers and clients that are not AD compliant.

mixed mode Mixed mode is the AD default operating mode and provides the maximum compatibility with down-level servers and clients. Mixed mode supports NT 4 replication methods as well as AD domain replication.

multi-casting Multi-casting occurs when a DUA sends a request to multiple DSAs simultaneously.

multi-master replication Multi-master replication is where more than one replica of a partition can accept changes. Use of multi-master replication ensures that non-availability of a given replica will not impede the use or administration of the network.

multi-valued RDNs A multi-valued RDN is where an object has more than one naming attribute designated.

name queries   A name query is when a client sends a DNS name to a name server requesting the IP address.

name resolution   The process by which name queries are resolved. (It varies between directory service implementations.)

name servers   In DNS, name servers resolve host and domain names to corresponding IP addresses.

namespace   A namespace is a collection of objects that reside within a common logical container and follow the same naming convention.

naming attribute   A naming attribute is the attribute designated within a class definition to name instances of that class.

naming context   In X.500 a naming context is a subdivision of the directory information stored on a specific DSA and managed by a common Administrative Authority. It is analogous to a partition.

naming model   The naming model is the structure that determines how objects within a directory are named. It is also called naming format or naming convention.

native mode   Native mode provides operational enhancements to AD, including new types of groups, nested groups, and multi-master replication between DCs. Native mode also thus removes support for NT 4 BDCs.

NetSync   NetSync is used with NDS to administer a mixed NetWare 3.x–4.x environment.

NetWare Administrator   NetWare Administrator is one of the primary NDS management tools.

NetWare Name Services (NNS)   NNS was designed as an add-on to NetWare 3 to synchronize the binderies of a group of NetWare servers.

Non-Specific Subordinate References (NSSRs)   NSSRs are a special type of subordinate reference containing the name of a DSA holding a child-naming context but not the RDN of that context.

Novell Directory Services (NDS)   NDS is Novell's directory service implementation, originally designed to control the NetWare environment. In recent years, NDS has been shed its dependence on NetWare and now operates on Windows NT, Sun Solaris, and Linux, widening the scope of networks that NDS can manage.

object   An object is a data structure with a specified set of attributes and syntax, and represents a network entitiy or other information set. Also referred to as a directory object.

Object Identifier (OID)   The OID uniquely identifies each schema element and is assigned by ANSI, IETF, or similar organizations.

operational attributes   Operational attributes contain information used internally by the directory to keep track of directory modifications and subtree properties.

operations masters   An operations master is an AD domain controller that has been assigned a flexible single master operations role (Domain Naming, Schema, Relative ID, Infrastructure, or PDC Emulator).

optional attributes   Optional attributes do not require values for object creation.

originating writes   A successful write updating a property on the DC performing the update is called an originating write. Replication updates are not considered originating writes.

partition root   The partition root is the container object at the root of the partition and usually names the partition.

partition   A subdivision of the DIB or directory information.

PDC Emulator   In AD, the PDC Emulator supplies compatibility with down-level clients and NT 4 BDCs, handling NT 4 client authentication and replication. Only one DC in each domain can be used to perform the PDC Emulator role.

permutability   Permutability is a property of some asymmetric encryption methods, where either key in the pair can be used to encrypt the message contents, and the other key can be used to decrypt the contents.

physical naming model   A physical naming model uses actual network device names to locate attached resources.

primary name server   In DNS, the primary name server for a given zone, holds the master copy of the DNS data.

primary shadowing   In X.500, primary shadowing is where the shadow consumer gets data directly from the Master DSA.

propagation   Propagation is a process where by a server sends directory updates to other servers containing partition replicas.

Property Version Numbers (PVN)   PVNs are property-based replication values directly associated with an object property. AD uses PVNs to manage replication collisions.

Public Key Infrastructure (PKI)   PKI refers to the security infrastructure using public-key cryptographic technologies.

Relative Distinguished Name (RDN)   The term RDN is used to refer to two different names:
In X.500, a RDN is the name of an object paired with the appropriate name type attribute, such as cn=brynna.
In NDS, a RDN is a DN relative to the location of the object that is referencing it.

recursive query   A recursive query in DNS is similar to the X.500 chaining process, in which query resolution is pursued on the server-side and only complete results are returned to the client.

referral   A referral is the process by which a DSA sends a DUA the names of other DSAs to contact to fulfill a submitted query.

relative domain names   DNS domain names not ending in a trailing (.) are referred to as relative domain names such as www.mythical.org.

Relative Identifier (RID)   A RID is an identifier used with an AD domain identifier to construct the SIDs for security principals within domains. A RID is assigned by a single DC in the forest, the RID Master.

Relative ID (RID) Master   In AD, a RID Master is responsible for supplying the RID sequences to all DCs within the forest.

Remote Operation Service Element (ROSE) ROSE provides support (on an application sublayer of the OSI model) for the request/reply style of interaction between X.500 protocols.

replica ring The collection of NDS servers holding replicas of a particular partition.

replication Replication is the process of copying the contents of a DIB partition to another DSA.

replication agreement A replication agreement specifies the parameters that will govern the replication process. This includes factors such as the role of each server, dataset to be replicated, and scheduling.

replication consumer A replication consumer is the DSA that is receiving updates to the directory.

replication supplier A replication supplier is the DSA sending the directory updates.

Request For Comments (RFC) A RFC is a technical document published as a proposed standard at the end of the public review process managed by the IETF.

resolver Analogous to a X.500 DUA, the client-side software component in DNS is referred to as a DNS resolver.

resource record (RR) A resource record (RR) is a single entry in the DNS database, roughly analogous to a directory object. A RR consists of a series of fields identifying the RR type and information associated with the record.

reverse lookup files A special zone file referenced when a DNS name server is searching the `in-addr.arpa` domain to perform a reverse lookup.

reverse lookup A reverse lookup is the DNS process of finding a host name based on the IP address.

root context The root context is a logical construct referring to the entries immediately subordinate to the root of the directory tree.

root domain The theoretical root of the DNS namespace, delimited by the terminating ".".

root name server The root name servers in DNS are the authoritative servers for top-level domains.

run-time inheritance When using run-time inheritance, the directory dynamically gathers the relevant ACLs and calculates permissions at the time of access. NDS uses run-time inheritance.

S/KEY The S/KEY One-Time Password system was designed to prevent intruders from obtaining user passwords (via packet sniffers and such), and is designed to counter a replay attack.

schema The directory schema is the core information structure that defines the directory objects and their properties.

Schema Master The Schema Master is used by AD to control all changes to the schema for the entire forest.

secondary name server A secondary name server is a backup server for a DNS zone providing redundancy for load balancing and fault tolerance.

secondary shadowing In X.500 replication, secondary shadowing occurs when a shadow consumer becomes a shadow supplier for other shadow consumers.

second-level domain In DNS, a second-level domain is a domain immediately subordinate to the top-level domains, which is assigned to a specific organization or person.

Secure Sockets Layer (SSL)   The authentication process of Secure Sockets Layer (SSL) uses certificates to provide a secure connection.

Security Authority   X.500 defines a Security Authority as the administrative authority for a specific ACSA.

security context   In AD, a security context for access control is comprised of the user account data (including SID, groups, and privileges), and is assessed when a user attempts to access a protected object.

security descriptor   In AD, an ACL is stored in a binary form called a security descriptor.

Security IDentifier (SID)   SIDs are defined by the NT security subsystem, and are used to identify security principles.

security policy   A security policy is a group of ACI items implemented as a set.

security pricipal   A security principal is a network entity (such as a user or a group) which has assigned access control permissions to directory objects and network resources.

Service Advertising Protocol (SAP)   SAP is used by NDS to support advertising and discovery of directory servers on IPX networks.

service control   Service controls can be used to specify preferred modes of functionality or restrictions on how the DSA handles a particular request and provides a method of specifying constraining information for a single query.

Service Location Protocol (SLP)   SLP is used for advertising and location services by NDS running on TCP/IP networks.

Service Principle Name (SPN)   A SPN is a unique name used to identify and register a specific instance of a service in AD.

shadow   In X.500, any non-master replica of a partition is described as a shadow.

shadow DSA   An X.500 DSA holding a shadow copy of an object is considered the shadow DSA for that object.

Simple Authentication and Security Layer (SASL)   SASL allows for the use of different security providers by supplying a way for connection-oriented protocols to specify an authentication method and optional security layer.

single master replication   In single master replication, data can only be modified on one server—although there are usually copies of the DIB on other servers. The directory server holding the master replica is responsible for updating all other replicas whenever there is a change to the directory.

Single Sign-On   A Novell technology providing a method for securely storing and retrieving passwords used by applications other than NDS.

site link bridges   Site link bridges are combined sets of overlapping site links.

site links   Site links represent the connections between networks. Site links contain the information AD uses to manage the network connections for replication, defining frequency, cost, and availability for each site link.

sites   A site is an AD term denoting a set of TCP/IP subnets with good connectivity—subnets that are interconnected at 10mbps or more.

Specific Administrative Areas (SAA) An SAA is defined by X.500 as a subtree of autonomous administration in which entries are viewed from a specific administrative perspective.

SRV record The Service resource record (SRV) is a DNS record used to specify the location of named services. The SRV record maps the name of a network service to the IP address of the server providing the service (such as LDAP).

Start Of Authority (SOA) The SOA record is the first entry within a DNS zone file, and refers to the DNS name server that is authoritative for the specified DNS domain.

store AD defines the physical storage of the directory replica as the directory store.

strong authentication Strong authentication uses public key cryptography to produce security credentials, providing controlled access to the directory.

structural class Structural (or effective) classes are those used to form the directory tree.

structure rules In a directory schema, structure rules define the logical tree structure of the directory and determine where objects can reside and how they are named.

subdomains Subdomains are used within DNS to specify organizational subdivisions and are prepended to the second-level domain name.

subentries Subentries are used to select a subportion of the directory and then define specific properties that should be applied to that portion of the DIT.

subordinate knowledge references Subordinate knowledge references indicate a DIB partition directly below the current partition and are used to walk down the tree.

subtree A directory subtree starts at a container object and extends downward until another subtree definition is encountered. The subtree description can also be filtered by object type so that, for example, a subtree could consist of only the user objects within a directory subtree.

super classes Those classes from which a class definition inherits some attributes and characteristics.

superior knowledge reference Superior knowledge reference is information used by a DSA holding a naming context to locate the naming context immediately above it.

superior rules Superior rules are used in an object class definition to delimit which container objects can hold a particular object class.

supplier reference A supplier reference contains information used in replication to identify the DSA that will be providing the update.

symmetric cryptography With symmetric (also called shared-secret or private key) cryptography, the sender and receiver share the same user-provided key.

synchronization Directory synchronization is the process by which changes made to one replica of a partition are propagated to other replicas of that partition.

syntax The attribute syntax determines syntactical constraints of the attribute and matching rules, defining the range of acceptable content. Also referred to as attribute syntax.

target object   The object that an alias points to—that is, the aliased object.

ticket   A ticket is a Kerberos security token.

Ticket Granting Server (TGS)   A TGS is part of the Key Distribution Center functionality provided by Kerberos, and supplies the tickets used in authentication processes.

time servers   Time servers (used by NDS) provide standardized network time to directory servers and clients that rely on time stamps for data integrity.

top-level domain (tld)   In DNS, a top-level domain is one of the reserved domain names (.com, .org, .net, and more) used to group domains by type of organization.

Transitive synchronization   Transitive synchronization is used by NDS to synchronize replicas on servers using different protocols, by employing an intermediary NDS server that supports both protocols.

transitive trust   AD defines a transitive trust as one where a trust relationship with one domain is extended automatically to any other domain trusted by the trusted domain. (If C trusts B, and B trusts A, then C trusts A.)

Transport Layer Security (TLS)   TLS is a secure authentication process that uses password authentication over a secure connection. TLS requires that both the client and server have public key certificates.

tree-walking   Tree-walking is the process of following a series of knowledge references from partition to partition to locate a directory object.

trust link   In AD, a trust link is a relationship established between domain controllers to pass authentication information between domains.

trust path   A trust path is defined in AD as the set of trust links between domains, used for passing authentication requests—essentially the route between the DC for a server receiving a request and the DC in the domain of the requesting user.

typed names   If the abbreviation corresponding to the object's naming attribute is used when forming its name, it is considered typed (for example, cn=jody). This style of naming is also known as attributed.

typeless naming   Typeless naming does not use the naming attribute abbreviation in the object name (for example, jody).

unit of replication   The information set that is sent with a directory update.

Universal groups   In AD, Universal groups can be used to provide users within the forest access to any resources in the forest.

Update Sequence Numbers (USNs)   A USN is a unique 64-bit value used by Active Directory synchronization. When an object (or property) is updated, the version number is incremented and stored in the object with a new USN. USNs are compared during replication to ensure data consistency.

useful attribute sets   In X.500, useful attribute sets provide a way of quickly adding a logical collection of attributes to support a specific functionality.

user attributes   X.500 defines user attributes as those that represent the information a directory client would normally see: names, telephone numbers, and so on. User attributes do not include administrative data.

User Information Model The X.500 User Information Model describes the directory as a typical directory user would see it. The entire directory appears as one large tree with no boundaries and contains only user attributes.

User Principal Names (UPNs) A UPN is an attribute of the AD user object, and it must be unique across the tree. UPNs have two parts: the UPN prefix, which is the user logon name; and the UPN suffix, which is commonly the DNS name of the domain containing the user object.

X.500 X.500 is a set of ISO/ITU specifications defining a distributed directory service.

XDS XDS (open Directory Service) was initially developed by X/Open (now the Open Software Foundation) and the XAPI Association as a programmatic interface to X.500 DSAs, providing access to DAP functionality.

zone file A zone file contains the data regarding a specific portion of the DNS directory—the specific set of resource records defining hosts, services, and so on within that zone.

zone transfer A zone transfer transmits a copy of the resource records of a specific zone to the receiving (secondary) server.

Index

D

E

J-K

L

Q-R

T

Windows 2000 Answers

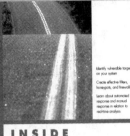

Updated edition of New Riders' best-selling *Inside Windows NT 4 Server*. Taking the author-driven, no-nonsense approach we pioneered with our Windows NT *Landmark* books, New Riders proudly offers something unique for Windows 2000 administrators—an interesting and discriminating book on Windows 2000 Server, written by someone in the trenches who can anticipate your situation and provide answers you can trust.

INSIDE Windows 2000 Server

ISBN: 1-56205-929-2

Windows 2000 ESSENTIAL REFERENCE

Architected to be the most navigable, useful, and value-packed reference for Windows 2000, this book uses a creative "telescoping" design that you can adapt to your style of learning. Written by Steven Tate, key Windows 2000 partner and developer of Microsoft's W2K Training Program, it's a concise, focused quick reference for Windows 2000.

ISBN: 0-7357-0869-X

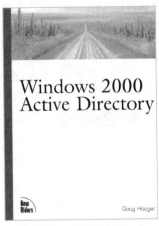

Windows 2000 Active Directory

Windows 2000 Active Directory is just one of several new Windows 2000 titles from New Riders' acclaimed *Landmark* series. Focused advice on planning, implementing, and managing the Active Directory in your business.

ISBN: 0-7357-0870-3

Advanced Information on Networking Technologies

New Riders Books Offer Advice and Experience

LANDMARK

Rethinking Computer Books

We know how important it is to have access to detailed, solutions-oriented information on core technologies. *Landmark* books contain the essential information you need to solve technical problems. Written by experts and subjected to rigorous peer and technical reviews, our *Landmark* books are hard-core resources for practitioners like you.

ESSENTIAL REFERENCE

Smart, Like You

The *Essential Reference* series from New Riders provides answers when you know what you want to do but need to know how to do it. Each title skips extraneous material and assumes a strong base of knowledge. These are indispensable books for the practitioner who wants to find specific features of a technology quickly and efficiently. Avoiding fluff and basic material, these books present solutions in an innovative, clean format—and at a great value.

MCSE CERTIFICATION

Engineered for Test Success

New Riders offers a complete line of test preparation materials to help you achieve your certification. With books like the *MCSE Training Guide*, *TestPrep*, and *Fast Track*, and software like the acclaimed *MCSE Complete* and the revolutionary *ExamGear*, New Riders offers comprehensive products built by experienced professionals who have passed the exams and instructed hundreds of candidates.

New Riders

Books for Networking Professionals

Windows NT Titles

Windows NT TCP/IP

By Karanjit Siyan
1st Edition
480 pages, $29.99
ISBN: 1-56205-887-8

If you're still looking for good documentation on Microsoft TCP/IP, then look no further—this is your book. Windows NT TCP/IP cuts through the complexities and provides the most informative and complete reference book on Windows-based TCP/IP. Concepts essential to TCP/IP administration are explained thoroughly and then are related to the practical use of Microsoft TCP/IP in a real-world networking environment. The book begins by covering TCP/IP architecture and advanced installation and configuration issues, then moves on to routing with TCP/IP, DHCP Management, and WINS/DNS Name Resolution.

Windows NT DNS

By Michael Masterson, Herman L. Knief, Scott Vinick, and Eric Roul
1st Edition
340 pages, $29.99
ISBN: 1-56205-943-2

Have you ever opened a Windows NT book looking for detailed information about DNS only to discover that it doesn't even begin to scratch the surface? DNS is probably one of the most complicated subjects for NT administrators, and there are few books on the market that address it in detail. This book answers your most complex DNS questions, focusing on the implementation of the Domain Name Service within Windows NT, treating it thoroughly from the viewpoint of an experienced Windows NT professional. Many detailed, real-world examples illustrate further the understanding of the material throughout. The book covers the details of how DNS functions within NT, then explores specific interactions with critical network components. Finally, proven procedures to design and set up DNS are demonstrated. You'll also find coverage of related topics, such as maintenance, security, and troubleshooting.

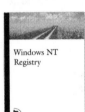

Windows NT Registry

By Sandra Osborne
1st Edition
550 pages, $29.99
ISBN: 1-56205-941-6

The NT Registry can be a very powerful tool for those capable of using it wisely. Unfortunately, there is little information regarding the NT Registry due to Microsoft's insistence that their source code be kept secret. If you're looking to optimize your use of the Registry, you're usually forced to search the Web for bits of information. This book is your resource. It covers critical issues and settings used for configuring network protocols, including NWLink, PTP, TCP/IP, and DHCP. This book approaches the material from a unique point of view, discussing the problems related to a particular component and then discussing settings, which are the actual changes necessary for implementing robust solutions.

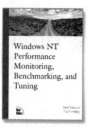

Windows NT Performance
Monitoring Benchmarking and Tuning
By Mark Edmead
and Paul Hinsberg
1st Edition
288 pages, $29.99
ISBN: 1-56205-942-4

Performance monitoring is a little like preventive medicine for the administrator: No one enjoys a checkup, but it's a good thing to do on a regular basis. This book helps you focus on the critical aspects of improving the performance of your NT system, showing you how to monitor the system, implement benchmarking, and tune your network. The book is organized by resource components, which makes it easy to use as a reference tool.

Windows NT Terminal Server and Citrix MetaFrame
By Ted Harwood
1st Edition
416 pages, $29.99
ISBN: 1-56205-944-0

It's no surprise that most administration headaches revolve around integration with other networks and clients. This book addresses these types of real-world issues on a case-by-case basis, giving tools and advice on solving each problem. The author also offers the real nuts and bolts of thin client administration on multiple systems, covering relevant issues such as installation, configuration, network connection, management, and application distribution.

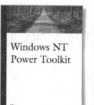

Windows NT Power Toolkit
By Stu Sjouwerman and
Ed Tittel
1st Edition
900 pages, $49.99
ISBN: 0-7357-0922-X

This book covers the analysis, tuning, optimization, automation, enhancement, maintenance, and troubleshooting of Windows NT Server 4.0 and Windows NT Workstation 4.0. In most cases, the two operating systems overlap completely and will be discussed together; in other cases, where the two systems diverge, each platform will be covered separately. This advanced title comprises a task-oriented treatment of the Windows NT 4 environment, including both Windows NT Server 4.0 and Windows NT Workstation 4.0. Thus, this book is aimed squarely at power users, to guide them to painless, effective use of Windows NT both inside and outside the workplace. By concentrating on the use of operating system tools and utilities, Resource Kit elements, and selected third-party tuning, analysis, optimization, and productivity tools, this book will show its readers how to carry out everyday and advanced tasks.

Windows NT Network Management: Reducing Total Cost of Ownership
By Anil Desai
1st Edition
400 pages, $34.99
ISBN: 1-56205-946-7

Administering a Windows NT network is kind of like trying to herd cats—an impossible task characterized by constant motion, exhausting labor, and lots of hairballs. Author Anil Desai knows all about it; he's a consulting engineer for Sprint Paranet who specializes in

Windows NT implementation, integration, and management. So we asked him to put together a concise manual of the best practices, a book of tools and ideas that other administrators can turn to again and again in managing their own NT networks.

Planning for Windows 2000

By Eric K. Cone, Jon Boggs, and Sergio Perez
1st Edition
400 pages, $29.99
ISBN: 0-73570-048-6

Windows 2000 is poised to be one of the largest and most important software releases of the next decade, and you are charged with planning, testing, and deploying it in your enterprise. Are you ready? With this book, you will be. *Planning for Windows 2000* lets you know what the upgrade hurdles will be, informs you how to clear them, guides you through effective Active Directory design, and presents you with detailed rollout procedures. Eric K. Cone, Jon Boggs, and Sergio Perez give you the benefit of their extensive experiences as Windows 2000 Rapid Deployment Program members, sharing problems and solutions they've encountered on the job.

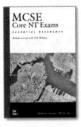

MCSE Core NT Exams Essential Reference

By Matthew Shepker
1st Edition
256 pages, $19.99
ISBN: 0-7357-0006-0

You're sitting in the first session of your Networking Essentials class, the instructor starts talking about RAS, and you have no idea what that means. You think about raising your hand to ask, but you reconsid-

er—you'd feel foolish asking a question in front of all these people. You turn to your handy *MCSE Core NT Exams Essential Reference* and find a quick summary on Remote Access Services. Question answered. It's a couple months later, and you're taking your Networking Essentials exam the next day. You're reviewing practice tests and keep forgetting the maximum lengths for the various commonly used cable types. Once again, you turn to the *MCSE Core NT Exams Essential Reference* and find a table on cables, including all the characteristics you need to memorize in order to pass the test.

BackOffice Titles

Implementing Exchange Server

By Doug Hauger, Marywynne Leon, and William C. Wade III
1st Edition
400 pages, $29.99
ISBN: 1-56205-931-9

If you're interested in connectivity and maintenance issues for Exchange Server, this book is for you. Exchange's power lies in its capability to be connected to multiple email subsystems to create a "universal email backbone." It's not unusual to have several different and complex systems all connected via email gateways, including Lotus Notes or cc:Mail, Microsoft Mail, legacy mainframe systems, and Internet mail. This book covers all of the problems and issues associated with getting an integrated system running smoothly and addresses troubleshooting and diagnosis of email problems with an eye toward prevention and best practices.

Exchange
System
Administration

Exchange System Administration

By Janice K. Howd

1st Edition

400 pages, $34.99

ISBN: 0-7357-0081-8

Okay, you've got your Exchange Server installed and connected; now what? Email administration is one of the most critical networking jobs, and Exchange can be particularly troublesome in large, heterogeneous environments. Janice Howd, a noted consultant and teacher with over a decade of email administration experience, has put together this advanced, concise handbook for daily, periodic, and emergency administration. With in-depth coverage of topics like managing disk resources, replication, and disaster recovery, this is the one reference book every Exchange administrator needs.

SQL Server
System
Administration

SQL Server System Administration

By Sean Baird, Chris Miller, et al.

1st Edition

352 pages, $29.99

ISBN: 1-56205-955-6

How often does your SQL Server go down during the day when everyone wants to access the data? Do you spend most of your time being a "report monkey" for your coworkers and bosses? *SQL Server System Administration* helps you keep data consistently available to your users. This book omits introductory information. The authors don't spend time explaining queries and how they work. Instead, they focus on the information you can't get anywhere else, like how to choose the correct replication topology and achieve high availability of information.

Internet
Information Services
Administration

Internet Information Services Administration

By Kelli Adam, et. al.

1st Edition Winter 2000

300 pages, $29.99

ISBN: 0-7357-0022-2

Are the new Internet technologies in Internet Information Server giving you headaches? Does protecting security on the Web take up all of your time? Then this is the book for you. With hands-on configuration training, advanced study of the new protocols in IIS, and detailed instructions on authenticating users with the new Certificate Server and implementing and managing the new e-commerce features, *Internet Information Server Administration* gives you the real-life solutions you need. This definitive resource also prepares you for the release of Windows 2000 by giving you detailed advice on working with Microsoft Management Console, which was first used by IIS.

SMS 2.0
Administration

SMS 2.0 Administration

By Darshan Doshi and Michael Lubanski

1st Edition Winter 2000

350 pages, $39.99

ISBN: 0-7357-0082-6

Microsoft's new version of its Systems Management Server (SMS) is starting to turn heads. Although complex, it allows administrators to lower their total cost of ownership and more efficiently manage clients, applications, and support operations. So if your organization is using or implementing SMS, you'll need some expert advice. Darshan Doshi and Michael Lubanski can help you get the most bang for your buck, with insight, expert tips, and real-world examples. Darshan and

Michael are consultants specializing in SMS, having worked with Microsoft on one of the most complex SMS rollouts in the world, involving 32 countries, 15 languages, and thousands of clients.

UNIX/Linux Titles

Solaris Essential Reference
By John Mulligan
1st Edition Spring 1999
350 pages, $19.99
ISBN: 0-7357-0023-0

Looking for the fastest, easiest way to find the Solaris command you need? Need a few pointers on shell scripting? How about advanced administration tips and sound, practical expertise on security issues? Are you looking for trustworthy information about available third-party software packages that will enhance your operating system? Author John Mulligan—creator of the popular Unofficial Guide to Solaris Web site (sun.icsnet.com)—delivers all that and more in one attractive, easy-to-use reference book. With clear and concise instructions on how to perform important administration and management tasks and key information on powerful commands and advanced topics, *Solaris Essential Reference* is the book you need when you know what you want to do and only need to know how.

Linux System Administration
By M Carling, et. al.
1st Edition Summer 1999
450 pages, $29.99
ISBN: 1-56205-934-3

As an administrator, you probably feel that most of your time and energy is spent in endless firefighting. If your network has become a fragile quilt of temporary patches and work-arounds, this book is for you. For example, have you had trouble sending or receiving email lately? Are you looking for a way to keep your network running smoothly with enhanced performance? Are your users always hankering for more storage, more services, and more speed? *Linux System Administration* advises you on the many intricacies of maintaining a secure, stable system. In this definitive work, the author addresses all the issues related to system administration, from adding users and managing file permissions, to Internet services and Web hosting, to recovery planning and security. This book fulfills the need for expert advice that will ensure a trouble-free Linux environment.

GTK+/Gnome Application Development
By Havoc Pennington
1st Edition
492 pages, $39.99
ISBN: 0-7357-0078-8

This title is for the reader who is conversant with the C programming language and UNIX/Linux development. It provides detailed and solution-oriented information designed to meet the needs of programmers and application developers using the GTK+/Gnome libraries. Coverage complements existing GTK+/Gnome documentation, going into more depth on pivotal issues such as uncovering the GTK+ object system, working with the event loop, managing the Gdk substrate, writing custom widgets, and mastering GnomeCanvas.

Developing Linux Applications with GTK+ and GDK
By Eric Harlow
1st Edition
400 pages, $34.99
ISBN: 0-7357-0214-7

We all know that Linux is one of the most powerful and solid operating systems in existence. And as the success of Linux grows, there is an increasing interest in developing applications with graphical user interfaces that take advantage of the power of Linux. In this book, software developer Eric Harlow gives you an indispensable development handbook focusing on the GTK+ toolkit. More than an overview of the elements of application or GUI design, this is a hands-on book that delves deeply into the technology. With in-depth material on the various GUI programming tools and loads of examples, this book's unique focus will give you the information you need to design and launch professional-quality applications.

Linux Essential Reference
By Ed Petron
1st Edition Winter 2000
400 pages, $24.95
ISBN: 0-7357-0852-5

This book is all about getting things done as quickly and efficiently as possible by providing a structured organization to the plethora of available Linux information. We can sum it up in one word—value. This book has it all: concise instructions on how to perform key administration tasks, advanced information on configuration, shell scripting; hardware management, systems management, data tasks, automation, and tons of other useful information. All of this coupled with an unique navigational structure and a great price. This book truly provides groundbreaking information for the growing community of advanced Linux professionals.

Lotus Notes and Domino Titles

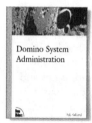

Domino System Administration
By Rob Kirkland
1st Edition
850 pages, $49.99
ISBN: 1-56205-948-3

Your boss has just announced that you will be upgrading to the newest version of Notes and Domino when it ships. As a Premium Lotus Business Partner, Lotus has offered a substantial price break to keep your company away from Microsoft's Exchange Server. How are you supposed to get this new system installed, configured, and rolled out to all your end users? You understand how Lotus Notes works—you've been administering it for years. What you need is a concise, practical explanation of the new features and how to make some of the advanced stuff work smoothly. You need answers and solutions from someone like you, who has worked with the product for years and understands what you need to know. *Domino System Administration* is the answer—the first book on Domino that attacks the technology at the professional level, with practical, hands-on assistance to get Domino running in your organization.

Lotus Notes and Domino Essential Reference
By Dave Hatter
and Tim Bankes
1st Edition
500 pages, $49.99
ISBN: 0-7357-0007-9

You're in a bind because you've been asked to design and program a new database in Notes for an important client that will keep track of and itemize a myriad of inventory and shipping data. The client wants a user-friendly interface without sacrificing speed or functionality. You are experienced (and could develop this application in your sleep) but feel that you need to take your talents to the next level. You need something to facilitate your creative and technical abilities, something to perfect your programming skills. The answer is waiting for you: *Lotus Notes and Domino Essential Reference.* It's compact and simply designed. It's loaded with information. All of the objects, classes, functions, and methods are listed. It shows you the object hierarchy and the relationship between each one. It's perfect for you. Problem solved.

Networking Titles

Cisco Router Configuration & Troubleshooting
By Mark Tripod
1st Edition
300 pages, $34.99
ISBN: 0-7357-0024-9

Want the real story on making your Cisco routers run like a dream? Why not pick up a copy of *Cisco Router Configuration & Troubleshooting* and see what Pablo Espinosa and Mark Tripod have to say? They're the folks responsible for making some of the largest sites on the Net scream, like Amazon.com, Hotmail, USAToday, Geocities, and Sony. In this book, they provide advanced configuration issues, sprinkled with advice and preferred practices. You won't see a general overview on TCP/IP. They talk about more meaty issues, like security, monitoring, traffic management, and more. In the troubleshooting section, the authors provide a unique methodology and lots of sample problems to illustrate. By providing real-world insight and examples instead of rehashing Cisco's documentation, Pablo and Mark give network administrators information they can start using today.

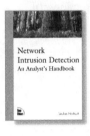

Network Intrusion Detection: An Analyst's Handbook
By Stephen Northcutt
$39.99 US / $59.95 CAN
Available Now
0-7357-0868-1

Get answers and solutions from someone who has been in the trenches. Author Stephen Northcutt, original developer of the Shadow intrusion detection system and former Director of the United States Navy's Information System Security Office at the Naval Security Warfare Center, gives his expertise to intrusion detection specialists, security analysts, and consultants responsible for setting up and maintaining an effective defense against network security attacks.

Understanding Data Communications, Sixth Edition
By Gilbert Held
6th Edition Summer 1999
500 pages, $39.99
ISBN: 0-7357-0036-2

Updated from the highly successful
Fifth Edition, this book explains how
data communications systems and their
various hardware and software components work. Not an entry-level book,
it approaches the material in textbook
format, addressing the complex issues
involved in internetworking today.
A great reference book for the
experienced networking professional,
this offering was written by the noted
networking authority Gilbert Held.

Other Books By New Riders

Windows Technologies

Planning for Windows
2000 0-7357-0048-6
Windows NT Network Management:
Reducing Total Cost of Ownership
1-56205-946-7
Windows NT DNS
1-56205-943-2
Windows NT Performance Moni-
toring, Benchmarking, and Tuning
1-56205-942-4
Windows NT Power Toolkit
0-7357-0922-X
Windows NT Registry: A Settings
Reference
1-56205-941-6
Windows NT TCP/IP
1-56205-887-8
Windows NT Terminal Server and
Citrix MetaFrame
1-56205-944-0
Implementing Exchange Server
1-56205-931-9
Exchange Server Admnistration
0-7357-0081-8
SQL Server System Administration
1-56205-955-6

Networking

Cisco Router Configuration and
Troubleshooting
0-7357-0024-9
Understanding Data Communications, Sixth Edition
0-7357-0036-2

Certification

A+ Certification TestPrep
1-56205-892-4
A+ Certification Top Score Software
0-7357-0017-6
A+ Certification Training Guide, 2E
0-7357-0907-6
A+ Complete v1.1
0-7357-0045-1
A+ Fast Track
0-7357-0028-1
MCSE Essential Reference: Core
NT Exams
0-7357-0006-0
MCSD Fast Track: Visual Basic 6,
Exam 70-176
0-7357-0019-2
MCSE Fast Track: 6-in-1 Bundle
1-56205-909-2
MCSE Fast Track: Internet
Information Server 4
1-56205-936-X

MCSE Fast Track: Networking
Essentials
1-56205-939-4
MCSE Fast Track: TCP/IP
1-56205-937-8
MCSD Fast Track: Visual Basic 6,
Exam 70-175
0-7357-0018-4
MCSE Fast Track: Windows 98
0-7357-0016-8
MCSE Fast Track: Windows NT
Server 4
1-56205-935-1
MCSE Fast Track: Windows NT
Server 4 Enterprise
1-56205-940-8
MCSE Fast Track: Windows NT
Workstation 4
1-56205-938-6
MCSE Simulation Guide: Windows
NT Server 4 Enterprise
1-56205-914-9
MCSE Simulation Guide: Windows
NT Workstation 4
1-56205-925-4
MCSE TestPrep: Core Exam Bundle,
Second Edition
0-7357-0030-3
MCSE TestPrep: Networking
Essentials, Second Edition
0-7357-0010-9
MCSE TestPrep: TCP/IP, Second
Edition
0-7357-0025-7
MCSE TestPrep: Windows 95,
Second Edition
0-7357-0011-7
MCSE TestPrep: Windows 98
1-56205-922-X
MCSE TestPrep: Windows NT
Server 4 Enterprise, Second Edition
0-7357-0009-5
MCSE TestPrep: Windows NT
Server 4, Second Edition
0-7357-0012-5
MCSE TestPrep: Windows NT
Workstation 4, Second Edition
0-7357-0008-7
MCSD TestPrep: Visual Basic 6
Exams
0-7357-0032-X
MCSE Training Guide: Core Exams
Bundle, Second Edition
1-56205-926-2
MCSE Training Guide: Networking
Essentials, Second Edition
1-56205-919-X
MCSE Training Guide: TCP/IP,
Second Edition
1-56205-920-3

MCSE Training Guide: Windows 98
1-56205-890-8
MCSE Training Guide: Windows
NT Server 4, Second Edition
1-56205-916-5
MCSE Training Guide: Windows
NT Server Enterprise, Second
Edition
1-56205-917-3
MCSE Training Guide: Windows
NT Workstation 4, Second Edition
1-56205-918-1
MCSD Training Guide: Visual Basic
6 Exams
0-7357-0002-8
MCSE Top Score Software: Core
Exams
0-7357-0033-8
MCSE + Complete, v1.1
0-7897-1564-3
MCSE + Internet Complete, v1.2
0-7357-0072-9

Graphics

Inside 3D Studio MAX 2, Volume I
1-56205-857-6
Inside 3D Studio MAX 2, Volume
II: Modeling and Materials
1-56205-864-9
Inside 3D Studio MAX 2, Volume
III: Animation
1-56205-865-7
Inside 3D Studio MAX 2 Resource
Kit
1-56205-953-X
Inside AutoCAD 14, Limited
Edition
1-56205-898-3
Inside Softimage 3D
1-56205-885-1
HTML Web Magic, Second Edition
1-56830-475-7
Dynamic HTML Web Magic
1-56830-421-8
Designing Web Graphics.3
1-56205-949-1
Illustrator 8 Magic
1-56205-952-1
Inside trueSpace 4
1-56205-957-2
Inside Adobe Photoshop 5
1-56205-884-3
Inside Adobe Photoshop 5, Limited
Edition
1-56205-951-3
Photoshop 5 Artistry
1-56205-895-9
Photoshop 5 Type Magic
1-56830-465-X
Photoshop 5 Web Magic
1-56205-913-0

New Riders

We Want to Know What You Think

To better serve you, we would like your opinion on the content and quality of this book. Please complete this card and mail it to us or fax it to 317-581-4663.

Name _____

Address _____

City_____State_____Zip _____

Phone _____

Email Address _____

Occupation _____

Operating system(s) that you use _____

What influenced your purchase of this book?

❑ Recommendation   ❑ Cover Design
❑ Table of Contents   ❑ Index
❑ Magazine Review   ❑ Advertisement
❑ New Riders' Reputation   ❑ Author Name

How would you rate the contents of this book?

❑ Excellent   ❑ Very Good
❑ Good   ❑ Fair
❑ Below Average   ❑ Poor

How do you plan to use this book?

❑ Quick Reference   ❑ Self-Training
❑ Classroom   ❑ Other

What do you like most about this book?
Check all that apply.

❑ Content   ❑ Writing Style
❑ Accuracy   ❑ Examples
❑ Listings   ❑ Design
❑ Index   ❑ Page Count
❑ Price   ❑ Illustrations

What do you like least about this book?
Check all that apply.

❑ Content   ❑ Writing Style
❑ Accuracy   ❑ Examples
❑ Listings   ❑ Design
❑ Index   ❑ Page Count
❑ Price   ❑ Illustrations

What would be a useful follow-up book to this one for you?_____

Where did you purchase this book? _____

Can you name a similar book that you like better than this one, or one that is as good? Why?

_____

How many New Riders books do you own? _____

What are your favorite computer books?_____

What other titles would you like to see us develop? _____

Any comments for us? _____

_____

_____

_____

Understanding Directory Services 0-7357-0910-6

www.newriders.com   •   Fax 317-581-4663

Fold here and tape to mail

- -

New Riders Publishing
201 W. 103rd St.
Indianapolis, IN 46290

New Riders How to Contact Us

Visit Our Web Site

www.newriders.com

On our Web site you'll find information about our other books, authors, tables of contents, indexes, and book errata.

Email Us

Contact us at this address:

newriders@mcp.com

- If you have comments or questions about this book
- To report errors that you have found in this book
- If you have a book proposal to submit or are interested in writing for New Riders
- If you would like to have an author kit sent to you
- If you are an expert in a computer topic or technology and are interested in being a technical editor who reviews manuscripts for technical accuracy

newriders@mcp.com

- To find a distributor in your area, please contact our international department at this address.

nrmedia@mcp.com

- For instructors from educational institutions who wish to preview New Riders books for classroom use. Email should include your name, title, school, department, address, phone number, office days/hours, text in use, and enrollment in the body of your text, along with your request for desk/examination copies and/or additional information.

Write to Us

New Riders Publishing

201 W. 103rd St.

Indianapolis, IN 46290-1097

Call Us

Toll-free (800) 571-5840 + 9 +4511

If outside U.S. (317) 581-3500. Ask for New Riders.

Fax Us

(317) 581-4663

Colophon

The Madrona tree pictured on the cover is on the west edge of Camano Island in Puget Sound, across the street from the authors' former residence.

Madrona trees are said to have saved some of the indigenous northwest tribes from the great flood by giving them a safe place to tie up their canoes. This particular tree serves as a hunting perch for great heron and bald eagles.

In keeping with the authors' philosophy of using inexpensive open source/freeware products, the photo was taken with a disposable camera, scanned in on a $49 scanner, and manipulated with freeware.

Photo credit goes to Beth Sheresh.